HOME ECONOMICS
AQA CHILD DEVELOPMENT FOR GCSE

Heather Brennand & Valerie Hall

3RD EDITION

HODDER EDUCATION

AN HACHETTE UK COMPANY

Orders: please contact Bookpoint Ltd, 130 Milton Park, Abingdon, Oxon OX14 4SB. Telephone: (44) 01235 827720. Fax: (44) 01235 400454. Lines are open from 9.00–6.00, Monday to Saturday, with a 24-hour message answering service. You can also order through our website: www.hoddereducation.co.uk

If you have any comments to make about this, or any of our other titles, please send them to educationenquiries@hodder.co.uk

British Library Cataloguing in Publication Data
A catalogue record for this title is available from the British Library

ISBN: 978 0340 975 077

First Edition Published 2001
Second Edition Published 2006
This Edition Published 2009
Impression number 1
Year 2009

Hachette UK's policy is to use papers that are natural, renewable and recyclable products, and made from wood grown in sustainable forests.
The logging and manufacturing processes are expected to conform to the environmental regulations of the country of origin.

Cover photo © Blend Images/Photolibrary
Illustrations by Kate Nardoni/Cactus Design
Typeset by Fakenham Photosetting Limited, Fakenham, Norfolk
Printed in Italy for Hodder Education, an Hachette UK Company, 338 Euston Road, London NW1 3BH

CONTENTS

INTRODUCTION

As with the first and second edition this book has been written primarily to support the new AQA specification for GCSE Home Economics: Child Development, although it continues to cover the specification requirements of other GCSE Examining Boards as well as the requirements of aspects of Health and Social Care courses, BTEC related courses at a variety of levels and National Vocational Qualifications (NVQs).

The new edition has provided the opportunity to review and update the text to reflect changes in related child care issues and to implement some of the suggestions made by teachers using the book in the classroom.

The book is concerned with the growth and development of children from birth up to the age of five. It is divided into five main sections for ease of reference:

Part One 'Parenthood' recognises the changing structures and wide variety of families today and focuses on the importance of the family unit in ensuring the healthy growth and development of children. Additionally, it investigates planning and preparing for a family in today's society. This section also examines all aspects of safety, accident prevention and first aid.

Part Two 'Pregnancy' begins with reproduction and investigates planning for a family as well as the stages of pregnancy from conception to birth. Additionally, it includes the post-natal care of the new baby and mother.

Part Three 'Diet, Health and Care of the Child' includes the importance of nutrition, healthy eating and food choices for the newborn baby, toddler and young child. This section also recognises the wider aspects of care in relation to the child's health and wellbeing, as well as the importance of immunisation and care for a sick child.

Part Four 'Development of the Child' examines how children develop and learn physically, intellectually, emotionally and socially. It shows the importance of toys, books and play among other factors that may influence development and learning. This section also looks at important issues related to technology and play, play for special children and play malnourishment.

Part Five 'Support for the Parent and Child' looks sympathetically at the needs of all children, examining causes of disability and the support required by both children and their families. This section also includes childcare provision and current information about The Early Years Foundation Stage.

At the end of each part, suggested relevant web links are given that will enhance students' knowledge and understanding.

Throughout the book up-to-date information is presented in a user-friendly and accessible way with clear cross-referencing. Colour coding is used both to identify each of the five sections of the book and to highlight the four areas of development (PIES), making it easier for students to navigate through the book and access information.

Keywords are highlighted at appropriate points within the text to enhance students' understanding and use of specialist terminology. Questions and investigations at the end of each chapter enable students to develop, extend and test their knowledge and understanding. Activities are included to encourage discussion and sharing of ideas and opinions and to develop observation, research and investigative skills needed for the written examination and controlled assessments. An extensive Glossary and advice on exam preparation is included in the final section.

Acknowledgements

We would like to thank the many colleagues and friends, and especially Ken and Dave, who have encouraged and supported us throughout the revision of this book.

We would particularly like to acknowledge the huge debt of gratitude we owe to Judith Fairclough, Eileen Nicholson and Enid Rees for the magnificent contribution to the first edition of this book.

We would also like to thank all the students of Child Development we have worked with – both past and present – whose interest and enthusiasm have been a continued source of inspiration for us.

Finally we would like to dedicate this revised edition to Eve, Alex, James and Rachael, to our families – with love and never ending thanks for their patience and understanding.

PICTURE CREDITS

The author and publishers would like to thank the following for permission to reproduce material in this book:

page 3 top © FutureDigitalDesign – Fotolia.com; page 3 bottom © Digital Vision / Alamy; page 8 © Rob – Fotolia.com; page 13 © iofoto – Fotolia.com; page 14 © Pavel Losevsky – Fotolia.com; page 16 © Monkey Business – Fotolia.com; page 21 © Tatyana Gladskih – Fotolia.com; page 24 © Thomas Wagner – Fotolia.com; page 31 © Emma Lee, Life File Photographic Library Ltd; page 33 top © Westend61 GmbH / Alamy; page 33 bottom © Bob Johns/ expresspictures.co.uk / Alamy; page 37 © Wimbledon – Fotolia.com; page 41 © Joe Gough – Fotolia.com; page 42 © Artyom Yefimov – Fotolia.com; page 43 © Purepix / Alamy; page 44 © nyul – Fotolia.com; page 45 top © PictureArt – Fotolia.com; page 45 bottom © soupstock – Fotolia.com; page 46 Valerie Hall page 51 Valerie Hall page 68 left © DR YORGOS NIKAS / SCIENCE PHOTO LIBRARY; page 68 right © JUERGEN BERGER / SCIENCE PHOTO LIBRARY; page 69 © PROFESSOR P.M. MOTTA ET AL / SCIENCE PHOTO, LIBRARY; page 70 top © Science Photo Library/Dr Yorgos Nikas; page 70 bottom © Bubbles/Loisjoy Thurston; page 75 top © EDELMANN / SCIENCE PHOTO LIBRARY; page 75 bottom © SCIENCE PICTURES LTD/SCIENCE PHOTO LIBRARY; page 76 top © EDELMANN / SCIENCE PHOTO LIBRARY; page 76 bottom © BIOPHOTO ASSOCIATES / SCIENCE PHOTO LIBRARY; page 77 © NEIL BROMHALL / SCIENCE PHOTO LIBRARY; page 78 © IAN HOOTON/SCIENCE PHOTO LIBRARY; page 83 left © Stockbyte/Getty Images; page 83 right © Stockbyte/Getty Images; page 84 © anshuca – Fotolia.com; page 85 left © OlgaLIS – Fotolia.com; page 85 right © Ingram Publishing Limited; page 86 © CORDELIA MOLLOY / SCIENCE PHOTO LIBRARY; page 103 © Monkey Business – Fotolia.com; page 111 © SHOUT / Alamy; page 113 © Monkey Business – Fotolia.com; page 116 © Sally & Richard Greenhill; page 132 © Rebecca Peters; page 136 © Inga Spence/Index Stock Imagery/Photolibrary.com; page 137 © Bubbles Photo Library /Pauline Cutler; page 138 © PETIT FORMAT / SCIENCE PHOTO LIBRARY LIBRARY; page 143 © Picture Partners/age fotostock/Photolibrary.com; page 147© Sally & Richard Greenhill; page 148 © Anthea Sieveking/ Wellcome Photo Library; page 149 © Sally & Richard Greenhill; page 151 © Anthea Sieveking/ Wellcome Photo Library; page 156 © BRUCE MIREYLESS / SCIENCE PHOTO LIBRARY; page 157 © D. Hurst / Alamy; page 159 © Anthea Sieveking/ Wellcome Photo Library; page 161 © Anthea Sieveking/ Wellcome Photo Library; page 167 © Photofusion /Paula Glassman; page 168 1) © PUBLIPHOTO DIFFUSION / SCIENCE PHOTO LIBRARY; page 168 2) © Photofusion/Sacha Lehrfreund; page 168 3) © GARRY WATSON / SCIENCE PHOTO LIBRARY; page 168 4) © Anthea Sieveking/ Wellcome Photo Library; page 169 © Photofusion /Paula Glassman; page 170 © Adam Przezak – Fotolia.com; page 171 © Dron – Fotolia.com; page 172 © David Hernandez – Fotolia.com; page 175 © sonya etchison – Fotolia.com; page 188 © Shaun Finch www.Coyote-Photography.co.uk; page 189 © 2002 PA / Topham; page 191 © Vladislav Gansovsky – Fotolia.com; page 193 © Gyssels/BSIP Medical/Photolibrary.com; page 195 © microimages – Fotolia.com; page 197 © Sally & Richard Greenhill; page 198 top © Emma Lee, Life File Photographic Library Ltd; page 198 bottom © Mother and Baby Picture Library; page 201 © Adam Borkowski – Fotolia.com; page 207 © The Eatwell Plate, Food Standards Agency © Crown copyright

PART 1

PARENTHOOD

This part of the book will look at the importance of the family.

In society there are many types and sizes of family – all unique, none perfect.

The family is one of the most important influences on the health, growth and development of the child. Having a child is a huge responsibility and should begin with planning and preparation to ensure the child has the best possible start in life.

This section includes information on:

- the family
- planning for a family
- preparing for the baby
- providing a safe environment.

 REMEMBER!

Children deserve good parenting. Stability and love are key factors.

1 The Importance of the Family

The family is a central part of British society today. It is a group of people living together, and related by blood, marriage or adoption, consisting of a parent or parents, with their child or children. The nature of the family has changed in Britain, becoming more complex, and there are now many different types of family to be found. Whatever the type, however, the family continues to perform many functions and one central role is to ensure the healthy growth and development of children.

Children have many needs and the cohesive family unit, whatever its type, must ensure a sound, stable environment is provided to enable children to flourish. Children have basic requirements to survive. These are:

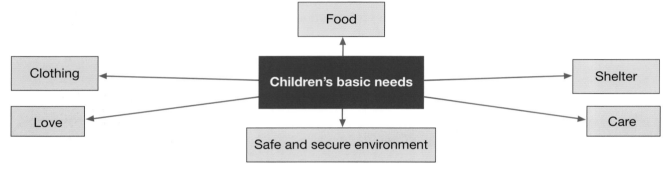

In addition to these basic needs, children require many other parenting skills that are essential to their overall development. The 'tree of life' illustrated in the diagram below identifies many of the needs that children have.

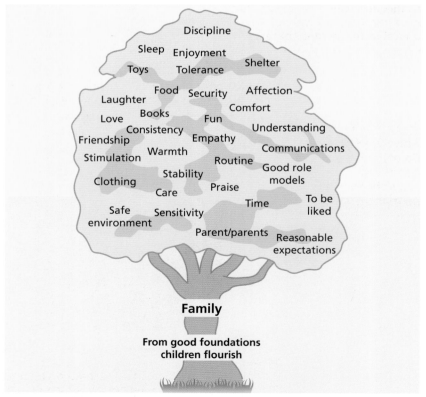

Children need many things to grow and develop, and this starts and continues within the family

Children will learn what is expected behaviour, as well as customs and values, from the group of people closest to them. Children learn this social behaviour from family and friends. This is called primary socialisation.

Children will also learn other social rules from other people or sources – teachers, school, TV, radio, newspapers, and so on. This is called secondary socialisation.

Types of family

There are many different types of family; some are described below.

Extended family
A large group – may include grandparents, parents, brothers, sisters, aunts, uncles, cousins – who all live locally and support one another.

Nuclear family
Parents and their children live away from the rest of their family. There is no support or help from the family as they live too far away. More effort is required to keep contact with the family members if parents work.

Step-(reconstituted) family
When a marriage occurs, one or both partners may bring children from a previous marriage or relationship.

One-parent family
Where one parent lives with a child or children. The other parent may share responsibility for the children but this can vary. Some parents look after the child without any contact from the other parent.

Same-sex (homosexual) family
Adults may also choose to live together as a couple with someone of the same sex. This contemporary family may also include children.

Looked-after children

Looked-after children are children who for some reason do not live with their family (see pages 7–11). They are usually in the care of the local authority and may be placed in one of the following:

Adoptive family
Parent/parents legally adopt the child/children. It is permanent.

Residential care homes
These homes are there to ensure that the needs of children are met when they cannot live with their own family. They may go from here to a foster family.

Foster family
Parents look after a child or children on a temporary basis. Children who may or may not have their own families live in other people's houses for a long or short period of time. They may return home at some stage.

Extended family

The extended family is one where other close members of the family – very often grandparents, aunts, uncles, cousins, etc. – live with the family, or close by. There is evidence to suggest that extended families are not the norm. However, Pakistani and Bangladeshi families contain the highest number of dependent children and usually have grandparents living with them. They also represent the smallest proportion of the group of people living on their own. It is much more common for this ethnic group to have three generations living within the home. They also take greater responsibility for looking after grandparents and elderly relatives.

Some of the advantages and disadvantages of being part of an extended family are outlined in the table below.

Advantages	Disadvantages
✓ Family members can help out and look after each other. ✓ There is always someone available to look after the children when an emergency arises. ✓ Advice is close at hand. ✓ There is close family bonding. ✓ The family members can enjoy each other's company. ✓ The children can easily see if their parents are sick or in need of assistance. ✓ Grandparents see their grandchildren growing up. ✓ Children have cousins to play with.	✗ The family knows all your business. ✗ Advice from interfering grandparents or parents may be given when not requested ('This is how you should do it …'). ✗ There may be too many visitors in the home. ✗ Lack of privacy and personal space. ✗ There may be disagreements about how to bring up a child.

The nuclear family

The nuclear family is the most common in British society. It is a smaller unit than the extended family, consisting of parents and their children. This family may live a long distance from other relatives; however, improved transportation and technology in the form of mobile phones and e-mail make it easier to keep in touch.

Some of the advantages and disadvantages of being part of a nuclear family are outlined in the table below.

Advantages	Disadvantages
✓ There is no interference from other family members. ✓ The parents can make their own childcare provision. ✓ The family can visit relatives when they choose to. ✓ Smaller family units/houses are more affordable.	✗ Being away from parents and close family. ✗ May miss family and close geographical location. ✗ Parents, grandparents and children will miss out on a close relationship (it will require more effort). ✗ Family members can't look after the children or help the family in times of crisis. ✗ Childcare will have to be paid for (i.e. childminder/nursery). ✗ May be difficult to get to the family in times of crisis.

There are many reasons for the increase in the number of nuclear families.

The role of women has changed

Dual incomes, enabling people to buy their own homes

Geographical location of jobs

Increase in the number of nuclear families

Family planning has allowed people to limit the number of children within the family

Higher education has meant that people often set up home away from their roots

The old concept of large family houses in built-up areas has changed. Smaller, family-sized houses are now available at an affordable price in most areas

Improved transport has enabled families who live apart to meet regularly

Step- (reconstituted) families

A step- (or reconstituted) family is a family consisting of a couple who may be married or cohabiting, with one or more children who are the natural children of one of them but not both. The parent who is not the natural parent is the step-parent, and the family may include stepbrothers and -sisters and/or half-brothers and -sisters.

Step-families bring with them very different issues for children from previous relationships. This will largely depend on the age of the children, how many of them there are, the size of the family home and many other factors.

The table below lists some of the advantages and disadvantages that can occur with step-families.

Advantages	Disadvantages
✓ The family may have a better quality of life. ✓ There may be more money coming into the home if both partners are working. ✓ Parents have an adult relationship. ✓ There may be a new house and a new start.	✗ Older children may find it difficult to adapt to living with another family. ✗ Jealousy may be evident among the children, particularly if they are of a similar age. ✗ There may be confusion with roles (e.g. who is the disciplinarian – the birth parent or step-parent?). ✗ There may be animosity towards the step-parent.

 REMEMBER!

It is estimated that lone mothers will remarry within five years. One in ten children lives with step-parents.

One-parent families

One of the most significant changes in the family structure is that of the single-parent household. The evidence is clear that the number of one-parent families has more than trebled since 1961. Most single parents are mothers.

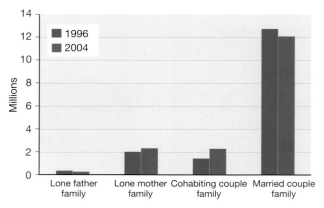

All families by family type, 1996 and 2004, UK
Source: Social Trends 2008

The above graph shows the percentage of family types (2004). It also shows that there are very few men living alone with children compared to women. In addition, while there are a lot of people living together there is still a large number of married couples. The reason for this may be accounted for by the number of people who divorce and then remarry, creating a step-family (see above).

There are a number of reasons why people become lone parents. Some of these are noted in the diagram below.

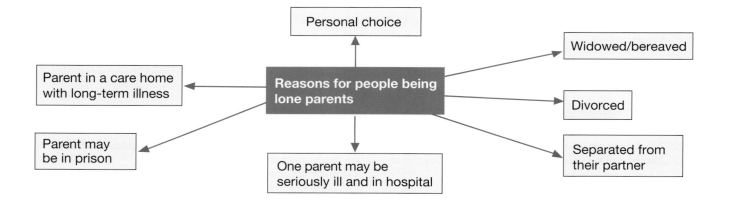

The table below lists some of the advantages and disadvantages of being a lone parent.

Advantages	Disadvantages
✓ It may be better to be out of an unhappy relationship. ✓ The children may be less traumatised. ✓ The parent may be happier and more relaxed on their own. ✓ The parent may find a new partner. ✓ The parent may be in a good position financially. ✓ The atmosphere at home may be happier. ✓ The parent remains independent.	✗ The child may be lacking a father/mother figure. ✗ The children may grow up with problems associated with having one parent. ✗ One parent may find it considerably harder to support the family financially, emotionally and physically. ✗ The other parent is not readily available to share worries (although they may be contacted by telephone). ✗ The child misses contact with the other parent.

Same-sex (homosexual) family

Same-sex families occur when two people form a partnership and both are either male or female. They can have a civil ceremony (like a wedding) to make this relationship legal, or can live together without the ceremony.

It is legal for couples of the same sex to look after children either by fostering or legally adopting. It is also possible for female couples to have their own biological child by using sperm donation. A male couple could use surrogacy as a method of becoming a parent. Surrogacy is where a female carries the baby for the couple (which could also be a male/female couple).

The table below lists some of the advantages and disadvantages of same-sex (homosexual) families.

Advantages	Disadvantages
✓ The family provides a loving, caring environment. ✓ There may be more money coming into the household.	✗ The child has either no male or no female role model. ✗ Children may find it difficult to accept that their parents are different, and may experience unpleasant comments about their parents because they are both the same sex.

Looked-after children

Looked-after children are those children who are housed or cared for by their local authority. Children who are looked after are some of the most vulnerable groups in society. It is always the intention of the local authority to work alongside the parents and keep links with the children and families. Some children may eventually return home to the family.

Fostering and adoption provide homes for children whose parents can't bring them up

Who looks after these children?

Young people can be looked after by a number of people, such as foster and adoptive carers, carers from residential homes or members of the extended family (e.g. grandparents).

All looked-after children will have a social worker who is responsible for their future, to make plans with them and be responsible for their day-to-day care.

People who look after these children try to think about how they might be feeling – a child may feel lonely, scared and sad at not being able to see their parents regularly.

There are many reasons why children are looked after. Some are subject to a care order, which means that the courts are satisfied that the child may come to harm if they are left with the family and they are removed from the home for their own protection. Listed below are some of the reasons why children are looked after:

Adoption

Adoption is a legal procedure where all the responsibilities of the child's 'birth parents' are transferred to the adopters. It provides a permanent new family for children whose own parents can't bring them up.

Once a child is adopted, all legal ties with the birth parents are broken. The child usually takes the name of the new family.

Adoption can be changed back only in rare or exceptional circumstances.

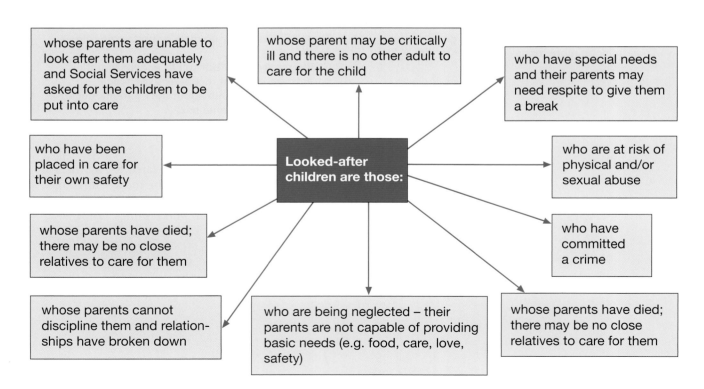

whose parents are unable to look after them adequately and Social Services have asked for the children to be put into care

whose parent may be critically ill and there is no other adult to care for the child

who have special needs and their parents may need respite to give them a break

who have been placed in care for their own safety

Looked-after children are those:

who are at risk of physical and/or sexual abuse

whose parents have died; there may be no close relatives to care for them

who have committed a crime

whose parents cannot discipline them and relation-ships have broken down

who are being neglected – their parents are not capable of providing basic needs (e.g. food, care, love, safety)

whose parents have died; there may be no close relatives to care for them

Adopters

People who wish to adopt may do so for a variety of reasons. They may:

- be unable to have a child naturally for medical or health reasons
- have had numerous failed attempts at IVF treatment
- have one or more children of their own but feel their family is incomplete
- be unable to have another child naturally
- wish to give a home to a child who has no parents
- wish to adopt children from a previous marriage (this is not as simple as it seems because it severs the child's legal links with their other birth parent and the wider family)
- be foster carers who wish to adopt the child or children they have been fostering.

Advantages of adoption

- It gives the adopters a sense of fulfilment.
- It gives children who have little stability and no family a chance to enjoy a good home life.
- It ensures that children are not sent from one children's home or foster carer to another.
- It gives the children a real sense of belonging.
- There is less of a burden on state resources.

Fostering

Fostering involves the care of a child or children within another home, when the birth parent or parents are unable to look after them. Fostering is not permanent and that is how it is different from adoption.

When a child is fostered the birth parents keep their responsibilities for their children, and will help to make decisions for them while they are in foster care.

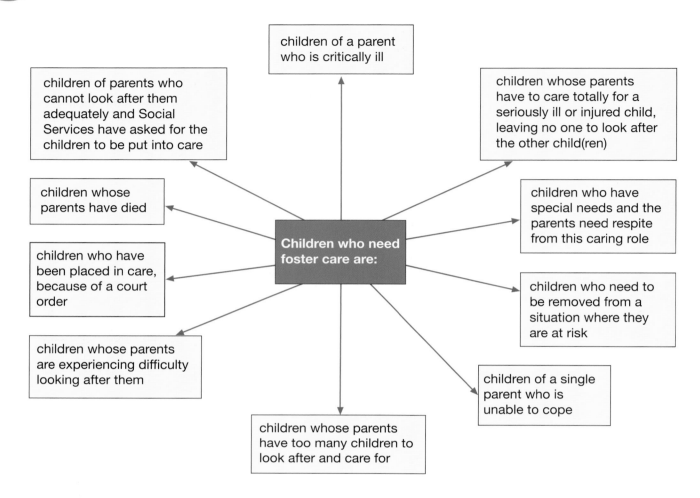

children of a parent who is critically ill

children of parents who cannot look after them adequately and Social Services have asked for the children to be put into care

children whose parents have to care totally for a seriously ill or injured child, leaving no one to look after the other child(ren)

children whose parents have died

Children who need foster care are:

children who have special needs and the parents need respite from this caring role

children who have been placed in care, because of a court order

children who need to be removed from a situation where they are at risk

children whose parents are experiencing difficulty looking after them

children of a single parent who is unable to cope

children whose parents have too many children to look after and care for

Types of fostering

Fostering can be long or short term depending on the individual family circumstances:

- short term is usually about three months
- long term could be for weeks, months or years.

Short-term fostering

Short-term fostering is used when the parent/parents are unable to cope with their children for only a few weeks. An example would be if the mother has had a serious operation from which she will make a good recovery, but has no family or friends who can help out.

The table below lists some of the advantages and disadvantages of short-term fostering.

Advantages	Disadvantages
✓ Children can visit their parent/parents. ✓ Children know it is only a temporary measure. ✓ It enables the family to remain together in the long term, but gives parents time to get over illness, breakdown or exhaustion from, say, caring for a child with special needs. ✓ The birth parents know that their children are in safe hands.	✗ Children are suddenly put into a situation with strangers and may have difficulty settling. ✗ Children may be moved to several different short-term homes. ✗ It may make the child feel insecure and homesick. ✗ Children may become disruptive and attention-seeking.

Long-term fostering

Long-term fostering may be an option with children whose birth parents do not wish them to be adopted but who are unable to cope with them on a regular basis Sometimes the children may not be allowed to return to their parents if the parents are unfit to look after them.

The table below lists some of the advantages and disadvantages of long-term fostering.

Advantages	Disadvantages
✓ The child has stability with one family and is not being placed in several different homes. ✓ There may be contact with the birth parent/parents, which eliminates the curiosity that can surround adoption (e.g. children wanting to know where they have come from and who their parents are). ✓ A good, stable home can provide the child with the chance of success. ✓ Financial assistance may be given to support the foster parents.	✗ Children may be very unhappy away from their parents even though the situation at home may not have been good. ✗ If the foster home does not work out for the child or the parent they may be moved on to another home. ✗ Other children from the foster home may be difficult with the new children; and foster children coming into the home could influence a previously sheltered child. ✗ There may be deep attachment between the foster parents and foster children. However, children often choose to return to their blood parents, which could be hurtful to the foster parents.

Residential care homes

Residential care homes are usually run by Social Services and are situated all over the country. The purpose of these homes is to look after children who are unable to remain with their birth family.

Who might need residential care?

Care homes can vary in their delivery of care, although there have been recent government recommendations to regulate and control the care given in these homes. Such homes may care for children:

- who have been orphaned (their parents have died)
- who have problems such as drug or alcohol dependency, whose parents are unable to cope with them
- whose parents cannot control them and may volunteer them to go into the home
- whose parents have been compelled to hand over the child to the local authority
- who are neglected by their parents
- who are at risk from abuse in the family home (e.g. physical, sexual or emotional abuse).

The table below lists some of the advantages and disadvantages of residential care.

Advantages	Disadvantages
✓ Children are looked after by professionals. ✓ It provides a comfortable home, with food and basic essentials. ✓ It may allow a cooling-off period for a child from a difficult home environment. ✓ It provides immediate care for a child who may have been removed from his/her family due to a court order.	✗ Children may be very unhappy away from the family. ✗ The children do not have a 'normal' home environment. ✗ There are many shared facilities. ✗ It may lack the privacy of the child's home. ✗ There are strict regulations. ✗ Children may miss the physical bonding with their parents.

KEY WORD

Family a group of people living together, and related by blood, marriage.

QUESTIONS

Question 1

a What is a family?

b Define the following family types:

   (i)   extended

   (ii) one-parent

   (iii) nuclear

   (iv) step.

c Design a chart to list two of the advantages and two of the disadvantages of different types of family.

d Discuss why families are important.

Question 2

a Suggest two events that could result in a child being brought up by one parent.

b Identify two ways in which the family life of children in a single-parent family may differ from that of children with two parents.

c What effect may it have on the children of two families who join together and form a step-family?

Question 3

a What is meant by the term 'looked-after children'?

b Suggest five reasons why some children may need to be 'looked after'.

c Explain the difference between adoption and fostering.

d Explain why there are few babies available for adoption today.

e Give four important facts about the people who would be able to adopt.

f What is the main aim of fostering?

g Suggest three situations where a child may need to be fostered.

h Explain the difference between long- and short-term fostering.

i List four advantages and disadvantages of fostering.

Question 4

a What is a residential care home?

b Which children may be placed in a residential care home?

c Give two advantages and two disadvantages of a child being placed in a residential care home.

 DISCUSSION TOPIC

In small groups, discuss which family type you belong to. Do you think that the type of family you belong to has affected your own development?

 CHILD STUDY ACTIVITY

• For your child study, investigate what type of family the child you are studying belongs to. Comment on the effect this might have had on the child. For example, it may be a step-family and this may have affected the behaviour of the child you are studying.

• Find out if the grandparents or other family members look after/care for the child. What relationship does the child have with these people? How might this affect their development?

2 Modern-day Families

Within the family people take on different roles. These will vary depending on the culture and society that people live in. The role of the family has changed considerably in the last century, and the speed at which British society is changing and evolving means that family roles are constantly being challenged and updated.

A century ago the roles of men, women and children were clearly defined no matter which class of society they belonged to. Men dominated the family and were the main 'breadwinners', or income providers, in all classes. Women were subservient to men and their role was to stay at home, look after the children and care for the family.

Modern family life

Modern family life has been influenced and changed by many factors – for example, the changing role of women in society, greater equality for all, and the fact that both parents are often working. Other factors include:

- Both men and women have greater education opportunities and careers.
- Legal rights have ensured that all family members are treated equally and without discrimination.
- Men and women have a right to maternity or paternity leave, together with career breaks. This enables both parents to spend valuable time at home with their families.
- Parents are able to work with some degree of flexibility as a result of improved childcare provision – for example, nurseries with free vouchers.
- There is greater acceptance within society of role reversal – for example, a man wishing to stay at home and look after the family as a house husband.
- Increased technology, particularly ICT (information and communication technologies), has enabled family members to work from home, which has ensured that there is a parent at home who could, for example, take children to and from school.
- Industry and commerce recognise the valuable contribution both sexes can make to the workforce.
- There is often more money coming into the household if two parents are working, which may enable families to travel abroad, enjoy a comfortable lifestyle and pursue leisure activities.
- In some instances, the fact that both parents may be working long hours could be putting pressure on family life, and some parents may be struggling with the work/life balance. The government is attempting to address this issue with the first ever Children's Plan (2008), whose aim is to support families and attempt to address the balance between work and home life (see page 374).

Parents who share responsibility for childcare, work and household tasks demonstrate positive role models to their children.

The changing roles and responsibilities of modern family life include grandparents as carers for their grandchildren. Grandparents are often living longer due to improved diet and medical care. The impact of this is that they will need to be cared for in their later years. The shared responsibilities of childcare demonstrate positive role models to the children from both parents.

Sharing roles is part of modern family life

Many grandparents today take on the role of carer for their grandchildren

Children within the family are encouraged to share views and ideas. They are encouraged to be educated and go on to higher education. They enjoy a social life with the family as a whole, and are expected to help with looking after younger siblings. Help is also required within the home, which helps children to learn more about the values of running a home and teaches them to become independent.

What is marriage?

Marriage is a legally binding commitment between a man and woman who wish to live together in a permanent relationship. It can take the form of a religious or civil service.

Despite the number of people living together today, marriage remains the usual partnership between men and women. However, the relatively high number of marriages reflects the fact that a higher proportion of people these days divorce and then remarry, sometimes more than once.

Living together (cohabitation)

Cohabitation means living together. Today there are many more people living together before marriage, or instead of marrying. This can bring complications as far as legal rights are concerned, particularly if the relationship breaks down.

Divorce

The term 'divorce' describes what happens when the legal marriage between a man and a woman ends. This is carried out in a court of law and is much easier to obtain than it was before 1971.

Over the past 20 years there has been much evidence to suggest that children are living in many different types of home environment. A high percentage of children are living with a couple but one or both of the adults may be divorced.

Effects of the breakdown of the traditional family

All children will be affected by the break-up of a family. Some will be able to deal with it better than others. This will depend on the age of the child (younger children seem to be more adaptable than teenagers), how the child has been treated and the reasons for the break-up.

- For some families it might be a relief to live apart, free from arguments and conflict.
- Single parents may not get support from another adult.
- The parent who remains with the children becomes exhausted, sometimes 'hitting out' at a child when they are at 'breaking point'.
- Children may accept this family type as the norm and then choose a single-parent option for themselves (e.g. 'My mum had a baby at 16, got a flat, and managed on state benefits and help from her own mum').
- There may be a lack of discipline within the household, with too much to do and not enough time to spend with the children.
- It may be more difficult, or not financially viable, to work as a single parent.
- There is no one to look after the elderly, who are living longer, and more private nursing homes are emerging.

- Children may never sit down together to eat a healthy meal around a table. The art of conversation and socialising is an important part of development.
- With one wage coming into a house, as opposed to two, there could be financial problems, and perhaps a burden on the state.
- Step-families may create their own problems, requiring large accommodation when two sets of children join together. If they are of a similar age, much rivalry could take place between the children, creating a lack of harmony within the household.
- Children may feel insecure and miss the parent that has left the family home.
- Children may get involved in custody battles, which may cause them emotional stress.

Cultural variations

The family in Britain today is not as straightforward as it was during the first half of the twentieth century. After the Second World War the British government actively encouraged a cheap labour force to come over to this country from places such as India, Pakistan and the West Indies. There was a shortage of people required to work in industry and a surge in the number of immigrants (people who moved from another country to live in Britain) who came to this country. This trend continues today.

These people sometimes came from different cultural backgrounds and have brought different dimensions to family life in Britain.

What is a culture?

A culture is a set of norms, beliefs and values that belong to a group, which make them different from other groups. It is also acceptable within a given culture to follow certain traditions.

The diagram below notes some of the factors that may differ between cultures.

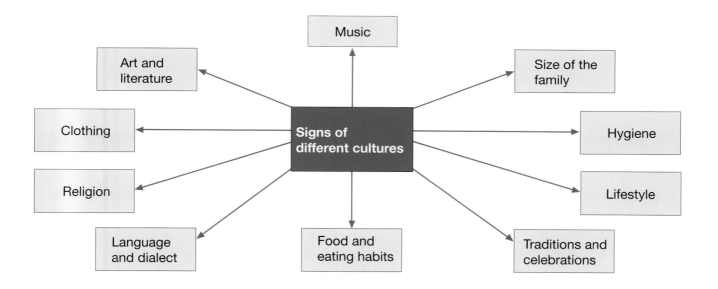

Different ethnic groups help to make Britain a multicultural society

Traditions are certain patterns of behaviour that you carry out within the family because your family has always 'done it that way'.

For example, in your household a turkey may be roasted and eaten on Christmas Day as a celebration of the Christian religion and the birth of Jesus. For some families who are not Christian – for example, Muslims – celebrating Christmas will have little meaning since they do not celebrate the birth of Jesus.

Multicultural society

Britain is a multicultural society. A multicultural society is one that is made up of many different ethnic groups, whose countries of origin may have very different cultures.

While it may appear within some cities that there are large numbers of minority ethnic groups living in Britain, in fact they are just that – a minority (that is, a very small percentage of the total population in Britain).

What often distinguishes these groups of people is the colour of their skin. However, there are many groups, such as the Italians who have settled in this country, that are not as obviously 'different'.

Sociologists refer to these minority groups of people whose culture is different from the culture of the people living in the dominant society as ethnic groups or minority ethnic groups.

When people from ethnic groups join another culture they have to adapt to the accepted behaviour in the culture of that country (e.g. go to school). This can very often lead to a situation where children are 'between two cultures'. For example, being westernised during the day at school and returning home to a different language and culture after school.

Discrimination

To discriminate is to make a difference between things. For example, to choose not to give a person a job simply because of their skin colour, sex, age, etc. There are laws to protect people living in British society from this sort of discrimination.

? QUESTIONS

Question 1

a Suggest five factors that have influenced and changed modern families.

b Explain how changing roles of men and women have affected family life.

c What roles might grandparents carry out today?

Question 2

a What is marriage?

b What is divorce?

c What does the term cohabitation mean?

Question 3

Describe six negative effects of the breakdown of the traditional family.

Question 4

a Define the term culture.

b What is meant by discrimination?

c What is meant by multicultural society?

d List four possible cultural differences in a multicultural society.

RESEARCH ACTIVITY

Interview parents, grandparents and family about their family life, roles within the family and how these have changed since their childhood.

Try to talk to people from a range of age groups and find out what opportunities they had (e.g. to go to school, university, get a job, pursue a career, etc.). Write a short report and present your findings to the group. Discuss some of the following points.

- Make a list and see which activities are carried out by the male/female members of the household.

- Who carries out household chores in your family?

Research different ethnic groups in more detail.

- Find out about the different celebrations/festivals/customs that different ethnic groups are involved in and why.

- Write a leaflet for a health visitor to inform them about one chosen ethnic group.

 CHILD STUDY ACTIVITY

Observe any cultural differences in the home that the child you are studying comes from. What do you notice about their:

- food and eating habits?
- style of dress?

- language?
- music, songs and play?

How might some of these customs affect and influence the child's development?

3 *Planning a Family*

Couples who are considering parenthood are usually at a stage in their relationship where they feel stable, secure and confident that they will be able to provide for a baby and be responsible enough to cope with all of the changes this will bring to their lifestyle.

The birth of a baby can be one of life's most wonderful and rewarding experiences. A child also demands much of the parents' time and this can be exhausting when the baby is young. This overwhelming sense of responsibility can be quite terrifying, yet most parents take it in their stride.

Factors to be considered when planning a family

When planning to bring a new life into the world it is important that the baby is 'wanted'. It is also important to recognise that many children who are not planned become wanted and loved as much as those that are planned.

Becoming a parent

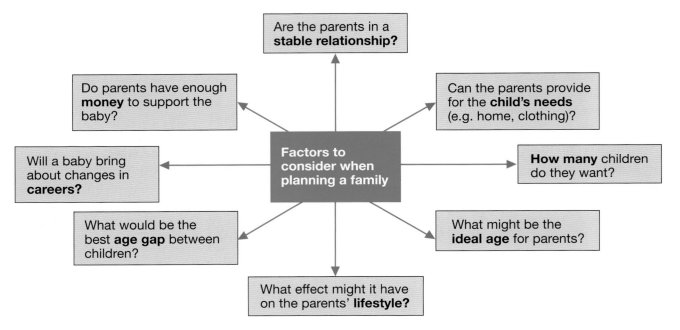

Are the parents in a **stable relationship?**

Do parents have enough **money** to support the baby?

Can the parents provide for the **child's needs** (e.g. home, clothing)?

Will a baby bring about changes in **careers?**

Factors to consider when planning a family

How many children do they want?

What would be the best **age gap** between children?

What might be the **ideal age** for parents?

What effect might it have on the parents' **lifestyle?**

A stable relationship

A stable relationship between the partners is an important factor when bringing a child into the world. The word stable suggests that the relationship is steady, secure and happy. It is a relationship based on love, trust, caring for and sharing with one another. The relationship allows the couple to talk openly about any worries, concerns and thoughts while preparing for the role of parenthood.

In a loving, caring relationship, it is important that each partner considers what the other would like, and that they respect each other's feelings. If one partner desperately wants children and the other doesn't, it could lead to a difficult time and the partners may end up resenting one another.

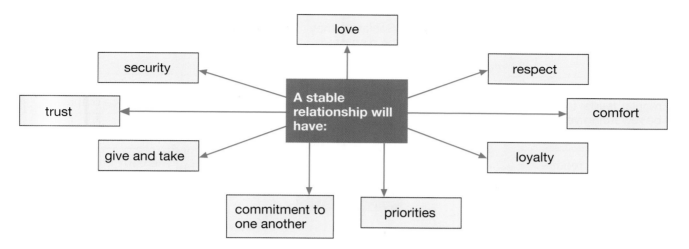

People consider bringing a child into the world for different reasons:

- to improve a faltering relationship
- because the mother may feel her 'body clock' ticking
- grandparents hinting they are waiting for the big day
- to escape a difficult situation at work
- pressure from friends to have a baby
- romantic notions about 'cute' babies.

Children's needs

There are many factors to consider as a new parent and these should include discussion about whether or not the parents can provide for the child's needs. Parents should also consider whether they have sufficient money to be able to support the child and provide a suitable home.

Prospective parents may also look at the type of home environment they can provide and think about how they will encourage the child to grow, develop, and be happy and healthy.

Parents may wish to provide a home for the child that is:

- loving and caring
- warm and secure
- clean and safe
- stimulating, with books, suitable toys, etc.
- able to provide food and clothing
- encouraging and provides opportunity for play with other children
- able to provide opportunities for conversation and the chance to meet other people.

REMEMBER!

Becoming a parent is for **life**.

Changes in lifestyle

Some parents insist that a baby will not change their lifestyle, although many parents will suggest that it does. The diagram below lists some of the changes that may occur for parents once a baby has become part of the family.

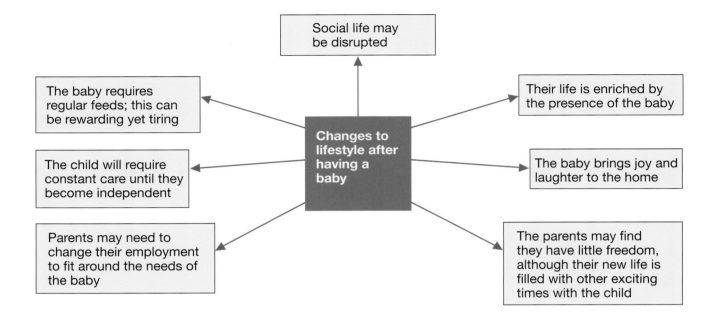

Parental age

The age at which a mother has her first child, or indeed any other children, has been greatly influenced by availability of free contraception (see Chapter 11). Contraception (which prevents pregnancy) has given women and men a greater choice of when to have children.

The mother

The mother's age is of concern when planning a child because the quality of women's eggs depletes as they get older, as does their ability to conceive.

Once a woman has passed through the menopause (when her reproductive cycle stops) she is unable to have any more children.

It is a personal choice at what age a mother chooses to conceive a child with her partner. It will also depend on their personal circumstances.

There is a trend today for women to have their babies older – between 35 and 45 years of age.

Possible reasons for this trend for women to have their first children in their thirties may be:

- they get married later
- they have attended further education courses
- they have pursued a career
- they have been achieving financial security.

The father

The father can continue to produce sperm until he dies and, provided he is capable of sexual intercourse, can father a child into old age.

Being a younger parent

Being a younger parent brings many advantages but also some disadvantages, as outlined in the table below.

Advantages	Disadvantages
✓ The parents may be fitter and healthier. ✓ The life expectation may be greater. ✓ The mother's body may recover more quickly. ✓ The parents will have more energy. ✓ The young mother will be young enough to pursue qualifications and career after having a family. ✓ The grandparents may be young enough to look after and enjoy the grandchildren, to help with care, etc. ✓ There is less risk of having a Down's syndrome baby if the mother is under 35.	✗ The parents may be less secure financially. ✗ The parents may not have the confidence to look after a young family. ✗ They may resent not having a career that brings financial security. ✗ It will affect their social life. ✗ They may not feel ready for the responsibility of a young family. ✗ They may not feel secure and settled in the relationship. ✗ They may not have had time to get their home organised and secure.

Being an older parent

Being an older parent brings many advantages but also some disadvantages, as outlined in the table below.

Advantages	Disadvantages
✓ The parents may be relaxed and may enjoy the children more. ✓ The parents are likely to be more secure financially. ✓ The parents may be more mature and more patient. ✓ The parents may not be particularly worried about missing out on a social life. ✓ The parents may have been able to have a career, travel, etc., before the baby is born. ✓ The parents may have experienced more of life.	✗ The mother is at greater risk of having a Down's syndrome baby over the age of 35. ✗ Older parents may get more tired and don't have the same energy levels as they did when they were younger. ✗ The mother's body may take longer to get back into shape after the birth. ✗ Children may be embarrassed because their parents look older than those of other children.

Size of the family

Once a child has been born into a family the parents may feel strong urges to produce a sibling (a brother or sister) for the child, or they may have quite the opposite feelings.

The size of families varies

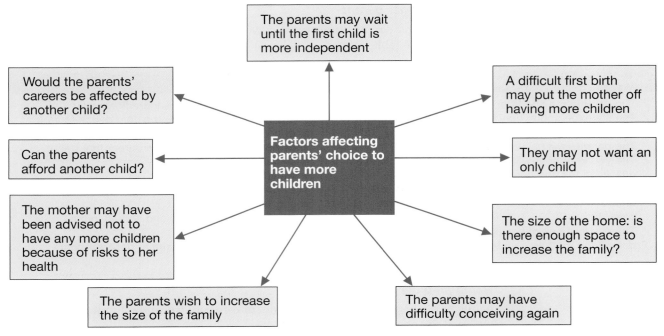

Position in the family

The age gap between sisters and brothers

It is not always possible to choose when to have a baby as the exact time of ovulation can be difficult to pinpoint. However, some couples are able to conceive at the first attempt.

It is physically possible for a woman to become pregnant as soon as her periods return, which means that she could conceive two children within a year.

The current average age gap between children is three years.

As mentioned previously, some parents remarry, creating step-families. If they then choose to have a family together there may be a larger gap between children's ages.

What is the best age gap?

There is no correct answer to this question. It will depend on many factors. Here is a list of some of the advantages and disadvantages.

Small age gap (one to two years)

Advantages	Disadvantages
✓ Some baby equipment and clothing can be used with the second child. ✓ Having children close together means that a career break is less disruptive. ✓ Having the children close together means less time away from a career in the long run. ✓ Children will probably have common interests, and more choice of toys they wish to play with. ✓ Children will tend to be closer and play together.	✗ If there are complications with the pregnancy it may be difficult to cope with two very young children. ✗ If the gap is around two years the toddler may have temper tantrums. ✗ Children over two may feel their world has fallen apart because they are no longer getting the attention they had before the baby was born. ✗ The older child may get jealous and regress in their behaviour. They may start wetting the bed. ✗ Could be very expensive with two childcare places to pay for.

Age gap of three years and over

Advantages	Disadvantages
✓ The toddler may be old enough to go to a pre-school group or school, allowing the mother time with the newborn baby. ✓ An older child will understand what is happening and enjoy the prospect of having a sister or brother. ✓ Mother will be able to give the same attention to the newborn as the older child received. ✓ The older child will become more independent. ✓ Parents may be financially more secure. Mother may have returned to work and saved money in anticipation of the pregnancy.	✗ Younger children may pester and spoil the older child's games. ✗ Small pieces from games (e.g. K'NEX, LEGO) may be around for the baby to pick up and choke on. ✗ Children may have different interests. ✗ The older child is often expected to act more responsibly and set a good example, although they are still very young themselves.

The only child

Some couples have just one child, either as a matter of choice or for other reasons. Some of the reasons for this are as follows.

- The parents do not have enough money to provide for other children.
- There is not enough space for more children.
- A partner may have left the home.
- The mother may have suffered severe post-natal depression after having the first child.
- The child may have been conceived with IVF treatment and there is no money left for further attempts.
- The parents may want to devote attention to one child only.
- The mother may not be able to conceive a second time.

The table below highlights some of the advantages and disadvantages of having an only child.

Advantages	Disadvantages
✓ It is easier to look after one child. ✓ Parents are able to give the child a lot of attention. ✓ It is less costly. ✓ There is no sibling rivalry.	✗ The child may have difficulty sharing and mixing with other children. This would have to be encouraged by the parents. ✗ The child may be lonely. ✗ The child may be spoilt. ✗ The child may be demanding and seek attention.

Health issues

A couple planning a family may need to consider particular health issues affecting one or both parents. Health issues to consider for pre-pregnancy planning are listed below.

- Hypertension: if a woman has high blood pressure (hypertension) and it is not controlled, this can cause pre-eclampsia and foetal death due to problems with the placenta.
- Diabetes: women with severe diabetes may cause the unborn child to have heart and spinal canal defects, and possibly lead to foetal death. These women will require very careful monitoring and control of their diet.
- Fertility problems: for example, a male who may have had testicular cancer or

a female with ovarian cancer may have been offered the option of freezing their sperm or eggs to enable them to have IVF treatment at a later stage. Various treatments are available, such as drugs and surgery, to assist with the problem.

- Diseases of the heart: women with heart conditions – for example, a hole in the heart – will need to be assessed by a doctor to determine whether it is safe to have a baby as complications could arise.
- Other diseases: women who have thyroid problems, kidney problems and cancer will also need to undergo check-ups to ensure it is safe for them to try to get pregnant.
- Genetic disorders: certain genetic disorders can be passed from the male only, and others from the female; where previous pregnancies have resulted in a genetic disorder, couples will be offered genetic counselling (see Chapter 17); examples are cystic fibrosis, haemophilia and Huntington's disease.
- Urinary infections and sexually transmitted diseases: these would require treatment before pregnancy is planned.

Career and work issues

The effect of women working alongside men, with equal career opportunities and salaries, has changed the traditional family lifestyle. Both men and women go out to work in many situations and provide for the family. Biologically the mother must take time off work to give birth, and to recover and spend time with the baby. The mother can choose the length of time she will take from work; this is called maternity leave. The father may take paternity leave.

The role of the house husband is becoming increasingly popular. According to recent figures from the Office for National Statistics, a number of men are giving up their careers to stay at home and raise their children. According to the statistics, around 200,000 fathers in the UK are choosing this option.

There is no right or wrong choice for parents – it is simply a matter of what best suits the family circumstances at the time. However, it is still usually the mother who stays at home or works part-time and looks after the family.

To raise a child costs a considerable amount of money; figures released in 2008 show that, on average, the cost of raising a child from birth to adulthood is (including university years) £165,668. One of the most expensive outlays is from the age of two to five years with a cost of £12,129 per year. Other expenses include after-school care and holiday clubs, school uniforms, trips, extra-curricular activities, holidays, food, clothing, hobbies and toys, and university fees. These figures demonstrate that family life can be a long-term expense and a very important consideration for parents who are choosing their career path.

More men are choosing to become house husbands

Full-time work

The table below highlights some of the advantages and disadvantages of the mother returning to full-time work.

Advantages	Disadvantages
✓ She can continue with her career. ✓ She can enjoy the companionship of other colleagues and adults. ✓ She gets out of the house and away from mundane household chores ✓ She may have felt depressed, lonely and unhappy at home. ✓ She may bring a significant wage/salary into the home. ✓ The family may be able to afford extra luxuries (e.g. holidays) because of the extra salary. ✓ She will be financially independent.	✗ She is not in control of the care of the children. ✗ She has little time to see the children if they are dropped early at a nursery and picked up late. ✗ She may feel too tired to give the children attention after work and pursue leisure activities. ✗ She may feel she is missing out on milestones that the children achieve. ✗ The children may have a greater attachment to the childminder/grandparent, or whoever is caring for them. ✗ She misses the children. ✗ She may worry about the pressures of work and find it difficult to relax.

Part-time work

(This could range from a few hours to days.)

Advantages	Disadvantages
✓ Keeping up to date with their job. ✓ The employer may be flexible about the hours of work. ✓ The parent can have precious time with the child. ✓ The parent remains in control of some of the children's day, routine and stimulation. ✓ This enables a parent to attend toddler groups and social mornings, and make friends with other parents and small children. ✓ It gives the parent time to pursue leisure activities. ✓ The parent has the best of both worlds, keeps their confidence, mixes with adults at work and the parents of other children. ✓ The parent has time on days off to catch up with chores, etc. ✓ The parent may be able to keep some financial independence (e.g. to run a car).	✗ The expectations of work and the family are demanding and sometimes it is hard to get the balance right (e.g. working on days off to catch up). ✗ The parent does not belong fully to either lifestyle – the full-time working parent or the one who stays at home. ✗ There may not be sufficient income to allow for luxuries. ✗ The wage may only just cover childcare costs.

Staying at home to look after the children

Advantages	Disadvantages
✓ The parent is in total control of children's routine and who they mix with. ✓ The parent can enjoy and build a close and special bond with the children every day. ✓ The parent has time to visit and socialise with other parents who have children of a similar age. ✓ This enables friendships to develop between parents as well as between the children. ✓ The parent may have time to help out with other parents and their children who in turn will help them out (this saves money). ✓ The parent may receive some financial assistance from the government. ✓ There is time to keep the home and family happy and organised.	✗ There is less income coming into the house. ✗ The parent may feel lonely and depressed away from work colleagues, and may miss adult conversation. ✗ They may live far away from their family, which makes loneliness worse. ✗ They may feel isolated if there is no money to run a car. ✗ There may be little money to socialise or pursue hobbies. ✗ The parent may lose confidence and feel it is hard to return to work. ✗ The parent may have spent a long time training for a career and feels it has been wasted.

QUESTIONS

Question 1

What factors should be considered when planning a family?

Question 2

a What do you understand by a stable relationship?

b A stable relationship is based on trust. List four other factors that would contribute to a stable relationship.

Question 3

Give four ways parents can provide for a child's needs.

Question 4

Many women are choosing to have a first baby at a slightly older age.

a Give three possible reasons for this.

b Suggest one possible advantage of being an 'older' mother.

Question 5

a What advice would you give to a mother who is considering the age gap between her first child and having another baby?

b List four advantages and four disadvantages of having an only child.

Question 6

Many women choose to return to work after having a baby.

a Give three advantages of going back to work part-time.

b Give three disadvantages of going back to work full-time.

Question 7

Describe four health issues a couple might have to consider when planning to have a baby.

 DISCUSSION TOPIC

Discuss in small groups what factors you would consider to be the most important when choosing to bring a child into the world. Report your findings to the class.

 RESEARCH ACTIVITY

Interview parents, both male and female, and find out what they chose to do in respect of work after having children. Why did they make these choices? It may be of interest to ask grandparents, who may have experienced different attitudes from society than those of today.

Record your results and present them in the form of a written report.

 CHILD STUDY ACTIVITY

Carry out an interview with the parents of your chosen child about the thoughts and feelings they had before planning to have a family.

Observe how the parent(s) provide for the needs of the child that you are studying.

4 Preparation for the Baby

Planning and preparing for the arrival of a new baby can be an exciting time, especially for those expecting their first baby. Although it is possible for the parents to find out the sex of their baby before it is born, some choose not to be told whether the baby is a boy or a girl. They may, therefore, choose equipment, furnishings and decor that are unisex (suitable for a boy or a girl). If parents are preparing for their second or subsequent baby, there is a good chance that some of the equipment and furnishings they already have could be used again.

Shops have a wide variety of attractive and often expensive ideas for equipment and clothing for new babies, while parenting magazines are full of articles and ideas of what should be bought. It is very easy (and costly) to 'impulse buy' and while this is not a serious problem for small items such as clothes or toys, larger items need to be thought about very carefully.

Parents need to think realistically about what they *need* for the baby and then consider whether what they have decided is actually essential or simply desirable!

What might a baby need?

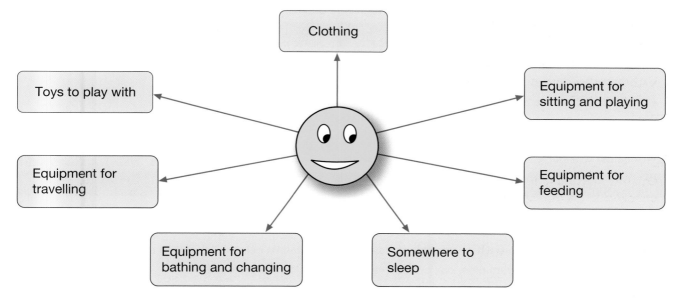

Choosing items in preparation for the baby

There are many choices available for the baby, and it can be quite difficult to decide which piece of equipment will be best. It is important to look around to compare different makes and prices from different shops, and to talk to other parents who have recently had babies.

Very often, grandparents or other relatives may offer to help and support financially with larger items.

Sometimes, second-hand items can be passed on or bought, and it is important that these are checked thoroughly to ensure they are safe. Many friends and relatives may purchase gifts for the new baby.

There are four main factors parents could consider when buying larger items of equipment for a new baby. These are discussed in the table below.

Cost

- Consider the cost of large items and buy something that is within budget.
- Look for value for money.
- Compare prices – either using the internet or consumer magazines, or simply by looking in different shops.
- Consider buying second-hand.

Hygiene

- Fabric items need to be machine washable.
- Surfaces need to be easy to clean.

Safety

- Look for safety labels such as the Kitemark.
- Buy items that are suitable for the age and weight of the baby.
- If flat-pack items are bought, make sure they are easy to assemble.
- Make sure large items are secure and stable.
- Items such as prams and pushchairs should have secure brakes.

Suitability

- Look for items that have multiple uses (e.g. pram/buggy/cot).
- Consider how long the item will be of use.
- Think about the size and space available in the room/house.
- Consider whether an item will store easily when not in use.
- Think about whether it can be assembled easily.
- Consider whether it will fit in with the style/decor of the nursery.

Environmental issues

- Consider using reusable nappies instead of disposable nappies.
- Choose clothing and bedding made from natural fibres (e.g. cotton and wool).
- Use second-hand furniture where possible to save on new materials being used, and to save money.
- Choose furniture made from pine, oak or beech as these trees can be replaced.

Baby clothes

The most important thing to remember is that babies need to be kept warm and comfortable, and that they need their nappies changed often! They also don't really like to be dressed and undressed or moved around a lot.

When choosing baby clothes look for items that are:

- machine washable
- easy to put on and take off (e.g. with 'popper' fastenings) and 'envelope' neck openings
- loose and comfortable
- soft
- warm
- flame resistant (will not catch fire easily)
- non-irritant (will not itch or irritate the skin).

Baby clothes

> ## ⚠ REMEMBER!
>
> Several layers of lightweight clothing will be warmer than one thick layer.
>
> The amount of clothing needed will depend on the weather and temperature.
>
> All clothing bought for babies up to three months must have a low flammability label (see page 39).

What is needed?

Vests	Babies are not very good at keeping themselves warm and will need vests in both summer and winter. These need to be soft and should have a stretch neck.
Stretch sleep suits	These make dressing and changing nappies easier because they have popper fastenings. They also keep babies warm, but it's important to remember that babies grow quickly. Wearing a stretch suit that is too small can damage the feet.
Knitted clothes	Cardigans and shawls can be useful when extra warmth is needed. Open lacy patterns should be avoided as toes and fingers can get caught in them.
Socks, mittens and hats	All of these will be needed during colder weather, while a summer baby will need sunhats for protection. New babies often need 'scratch mittens'. These are made from soft, thin fabric and prevent babies from scratching their faces.
Other clothes	An all-in-one suit that is fleecy or padded can be useful for a winter baby especially if using a buggy instead of a pram.

Equipment for sleeping

Moses basket

Moses baskets, cribs and carrycots	Young babies will be comfortable sleeping in these for the first few months. Carry cots can be bought separately or as part of a 'travel system'.
Cots	By about four or five months babies may need to be moved into a cot. When buying both new and second-hand cots the following safety checks should be carried out: • bars should be 45–67 cm apart to prevent baby's head from getting trapped • mattresses should carry British Standard labels (see page 39) • mattresses should fit snugly, with no gaps of more than 4 cm so that arms, legs and head cannot be trapped • catches on drop-down sides must be secure and too difficult to be undone by a baby or child • paint must be non-toxic • pillows should not be used until after two years old.
Travel cot	These are useful for holidays or when visiting. They usually fold away and can double as a playpen.

Equipment for travelling

(a) Baby seat

(b) Carrycot with chassis

Prams and buggies	These are usually one of the most expensive items needed and will often be used for more than one child.
	It is important to choose something that will fit in with your lifestyle. If travelling with the baby involves using mainly a car or public transport a pram is probably not a good choice.
	Modern travel systems, although quite expensive, are very versatile and can double as buggies, cots, pushchairs and so on.
	Whatever is chosen it should:
	• carry British Standard labels • have good brakes • be easy to handle and steer • be very stable, especially when carrying shopping • have anchor points for a safety harness • be comfortable and have good suspension as babies will spend a lot of time in it • be easy to clean • have swivel wheels to make it easier to move in tight places • be easy to store in the available space.
Car seats	These must always be used when travelling by car, including taxis. Rear-facing seats can easily be attached to existing seat belts (see page 45).
	When choosing and using child safety restraints in cars the following points must be remembered:
	• all restraints should conform to the United Nations standard, ECE Regulation 44.03 or 44.04, or have a British Standard Kitemark • for babies that cannot sit up and who weigh less than 10 kg (22 lb), rear-facing restraints are the best option • once a baby can sit up a child safety seat can be used; these are usually front-facing and adjustable, and suitable for children weighing between 9 and 18 kg (20–40 lb) • once a child weighs more than 18 kg (40 lb) or is four years old, a safety harness can be used; these should be adjustable, have a quick-release button and should be used with a special booster.

Equipment for feeding

Various feeding bottles

Bottles	Bottles come in a variety of shapes and sizes – most hold 225 ml (8 fl oz) of milk. Most bottles are made from plastic (see below) as glass breaks and splinters easily.
	No one bottle has any great advantages over the others; it is just a matter of personal choice. But it would be sensible to choose a bottle that: • is made from a clear material • has clear, easy-to-read measurements on the side • has a wide neck for easier filling • includes a cap to protect the teat.
Teats	Teats are made from either latex or silicone.
	Latex feels more like a real nipple, while silicone lasts longer.
	How fast the milk goes into baby's mouth is known as the 'flow rate', and depends on the number and type of holes in the tip of the teat. Newborn, slow, medium, fast-flow and variable-flow teats can be bought, but choice is not really related to age.
	A slower-flow teat is needed if the baby is spluttering or seems to be choking on the milk; a faster one if the baby is sucking hard but seems to be getting frustrated.
Sterilisers	Whether breast- or bottle-feeding, a steriliser is essential (see pages 197–198). The main types of commercial steriliser are: • electric steam sterilisers • microwave steam sterilisers • cold-water sterilisers.
	An alternative and cheaper way to sterilise bottles is to use a pan of boiling water.

Plastic feeding bottles

Most feeding bottles are made from plastic. Recent research has suggested that a chemical known as BPA, often used in reusable plastic bottles to stop them shattering, *could* cause changes in children's behaviour and affect the age at which females reach puberty. Although the Food Standards Agency says that the amounts used are well below levels that could be harmful, some manufacturers are now producing ranges of BPA-free bottles.

Equipment for bathing

Bath	The first time new parents bath their baby is probably one of their scariest moments as the baby seems so small and the bath so big! For this reason many choose to buy and use a rectangular washing-up bowl for the first weeks until they become more confident.
	A bath is needed for a relatively short time so it is best not to spend too much on it, but choosing one with a non-slip bottom can help to stop baby sliding about as much.
	Once a baby can sit up – usually about six months – a bath seat can be bought and used in the big bath.
Plastic bowl	Until a baby is six months old, the eyes, ears, mouth and face should be washed with cool boiled water. A small plastic dish or bowl should be kept and used only for this.
Top-and-tail dish	This has two sections – one for washing the face and one for the bottom.

And, finally, a word about . . .

Nappies

Nappies are probably one of the biggest ongoing expenses. They are available in a variety of materials, shapes and sizes, but they can be divided into two main groups: disposable and washable. In recent years many parents have been using disposable nappies but as people become more aware of environmental issues a move back to the classic terry towelling squares is gathering pace.

Some nappy facts

- Each baby is estimated to have around 5000 nappy changes before becoming toilet trained.
- In the UK, approximately 3 billion disposable nappies are thrown away each year.
- Disposable nappies create approximately 700,000 tonnes of waste, which is 4 per cent of all household waste.
- Disposable nappies can take up to 500 years to degrade.

When choosing the type of nappy suitable for the baby, parents will need to think carefully and decide which is best and most convenient for them. Some of the factors that may affect their choice are noted in the following diagram.

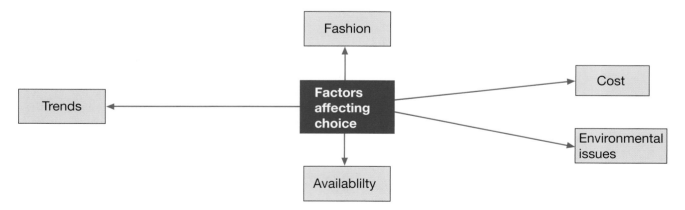

There is a very wide and confusing range of disposable nappies available. The major manufacturers are constantly trying to improve their products.

Disposable nappies

Disposable nappies are simple to use. There is no folding, no pinning and no plastic pants are needed. They are completely discarded when they are wet or dirty. Disposable nappies might appear expensive but remember there are no costs for water, detergents, sterilising solutions, etc.

Disposable nappies come in a range of sizes to suit different ages and weights, and can be for boys or girls. Their advantages and disadvantages are listed in the table below.

Disposable nappies

Advantages	Disadvantages
✓ Very absorbent – the absorbent granules in the nappy attract urine away from the baby's skin, preventing a sore bottom. ✓ Very convenient – the soiled nappy is put in a nappy bag and thrown away. ✓ No folding, no pinning, no liners, no plastic pants. ✓ They are quick and easy to use. ✓ They fit different-sized babies.	✗ They are expensive. ✗ They are bulky to store. ✗ There are environmental issues because the nappies are not biodegradable (the materials will not break down).

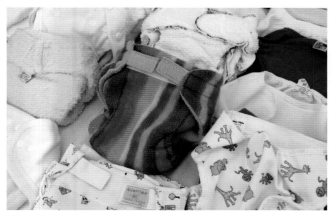
Washable nappies are becoming more popular because of environmental concerns

Washable nappies

These nappies involve more work but they are kinder to the environment. It is wise to buy the best you can afford as these usually last longer and are more absorbent, and are therefore more comfortable for the baby.

Traditionally washable nappies were white, cotton, terry towelling squares; they needed to be folded before use and were generally used with nappy liners; they had to be pinned with nappy pins, and plastic pants were needed to prevent leakages.

Modern washable nappies are more user-friendly – they can be bought in bright colours and designs, are shaped and filled with an absorbent inner material on a waterproof backing, and use poppers or Velcro instead of nappy pins.

There are two basic types of reusable nappy.

1. Two-part nappies: these consist of a nappy part and a 'wrap' part. The nappy may be a traditional terry or a folded nappy (called a pre-fold), or a shaped nappy. Around it goes the wrap – this is waterproof and could be pull-up or wraparound. These can be used from birth to potty training.
2. All-in-one nappies: with these the inner nappy and the outer waterproof are combined. They look like disposables and are usually fastened with Velcro or poppers.

There are a number of advantages and disadvantages to this type of nappy but one of the most appealing benefits is that they can reduce the number of disposable nappies that are disposed of in waste sites, and are therefore environmentally friendly. One of the biggest disadvantages is that they do cost more to buy in the first place, although some people would say that, in the long run, they work out cheaper.

These nappies need to be sterilised and washed, so nappy buckets, sterilising powders or liquids, washing machines and drying facilities are all essential.

Advantages	Disadvantages
✓ Cheaper in the long term than disposable. ✓ Kinder to the environment. ✓ No folding of nappies. ✓ Modern designs are colourful and attractive. ✓ New designs are quick to wash and dry. ✓ Two-part nappies can last from birth to potty training.	✗ Cost more at the beginning, whereas disposable nappies are paid for week by week. ✗ Have to be sterilised and laundered. ✗ Need to buy extras (e.g. nappy liners, bucket for sterilising). ✗ Not as easy to use if out shopping or on holiday.

Pull-up nappies

These are sometimes known as 'trainer nappies' and are very similar to disposable nappies. They have elasticated waists and can be pulled on and off by the child. The idea is that children who are potty training may use them instead of underwear. The child has the independence to go to the potty or toilet and be able to pull the nappy up and down by themselves. Two-part reusable nappies can be used as pull-up nappies.

Other items

As the baby gets older and becomes more mobile she or he will need other pieces of equipment – for example:

- high chair
- play pen
- baby walker
- safety gates and fireguards.

RESEARCH ACTIVITY

1. Visit a retail outlet that sells baby equipment. Research how much it would cost to buy the basic equipment needed for a new baby.

2. Present your findings, using ICT if possible.

3. Carry out some research into the cost of and advantages and disadvantages of using both disposable and washable nappies.

4. Include a survey or questionnaire. Use your information to produce a fact sheet that would help parents make an appropriate choice.

QUESTIONS

Question 1

When preparing for the arrival of a new baby what items might parents need?

Question 2

Name four factors you might consider when buying larger items of equipment for a new baby.

Question 3

a What factors should be considered when choosing baby clothes?

b What items of clothing would a new baby need?

Question 4

One of the most common pieces of equipment bought for the new baby is a cot. List six considerations when buying new and second-hand cots.

Question 5

What should a parent think about when choosing a pram or buggy?

5 Safety

An accident can be 'an incident or event that happens by chance and causes damage or injury', yet in many cases accidents can be predicted and can, therefore, be prevented.

We tend to think that a home should be the safest place for children to be. Yet statistics show that the main causes of death and accidents to children under the age of five occur in or around the home.

> **Some accident statistics**
>
> In the UK:
>
> - 500,000 children under the age of four are injured in the home every year
> - three children die each week as a result of accidents in the home
> - the largest number of accidents happen in the lounge/living area
> - the most serious accidents happen in the kitchen
> - 35,000 children under the age of four fall down stairs each year
> - every year, eight children under the age of five drown in garden ponds
> - every year 25,000 under-fives are rushed to hospital because they have swallowed something harmful.

Why do children have accidents?

The risk, frequency and place of accidents, as well as the type of accident, depend on the child's age and stage of development.

Babies and young children have more accidents at home as this is where they spend most of their time. As they develop new skills and become more mobile the risk of accidents increases and, as they become older, they become more adventurous and curious, so the type of accident likely to happen changes. Because they lack experience they have no real understanding of danger, so for them something like water is fun because they play with it in the bath.

Preventing accidents

To prevent accidents, parents need to have some understanding of development so that they can be one step ahead and spot potential hazards before they become dangerous for the child.

Although very young babies tend not to be very mobile and therefore have fewer accidents, they can wriggle and kick, and quickly learn to roll over. They should not be left alone on high surfaces or even in baby bouncers as this could result in bumps and falls.

By six months babies have begun to pick up and hold objects; everything they pick up they explore with their mouth (mouthing). This means that there is a greater risk of choking and suffocation, so parents have to make sure that all small and dangerous items are out of reach.

By seven to eight months they are becoming much more mobile and can often pull themselves up onto their feet. By nine to 12 months many will be crawling, 'cruising' and beginning to walk. At this age they can often move quite quickly but are not very well balanced or steady and so will often bump into things. They can see lots more interesting things that they want to touch and explore but because they are small they cannot always see or understand danger. At this age they could be involved in a range of different accidents. Identifying possible hazards as well as supervision can prevent lots of accidents at this stage.

By the time children are two years old they are much more stable and very mobile but are becoming more independent, wanting to explore more and try to do things for themselves. Their language skills and memory are improving and they begin to understand cause and effect: that touching a hot radiator will hurt.

Three-year-olds are much more independent and want to try things out for themselves. At this stage parents can explain about dangers and the children will understand more but will often forget if they see something new or exciting.

Four-year-olds are very mobile, well balanced and can often walk and run very steadily. At this age they may be riding bicycles or tricycles, will play outdoors, visit play areas and are more likely to be near busy roads. For this reason this age group tends to be involved in more accidents outdoors than in the home. They are still likely to have falls, but there is also the danger of being involved in traffic accidents. They are still small, cannot see over parked cars and cannot judge speed and distance.

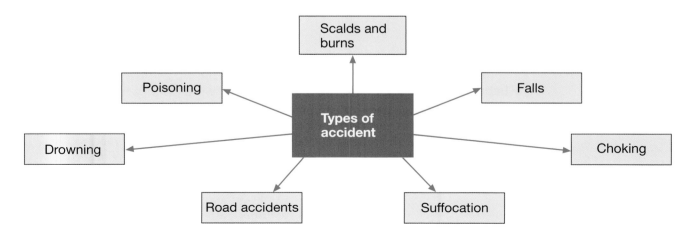

As children become more adventurous they can be more accident-prone

Statistically, boys are more likely to have accidents than girls. This could be because girls might be overprotected or because boys are by nature more active, adventurous or aggressive. Also, where children live and play could increase their chance of having an accident: living in high-rise flats and playing in streets where cars are parked, because they don't have gardens or parks to play in, can increase the chance of accidents happening.

When might accidents happen?

Most accidents happen when children are unsupervised. This may be because parents are busy, working or stressed.

Scalds and burns

Poisoning

Falls

Types of accident

Drowning

Choking

Road accidents

Suffocation

More accidents tend to happen in the late afternoon or evening, in summer, on Sundays and at weekends. This is often when children – especially older children – have more opportunities to play with friends or outdoors.

Parents who are stressed for various reasons or not feeling well, or simply feeling tired, are more likely to be careless when watching children.

Drinking alcohol and taking medicines and drugs can make people careless and can affect their judgement, making accidents more likely.

Many of these accidents can be avoided simply by being aware of the possible risks and using appropriate safety equipment.

Parents should also make sure that they check labels when buying household cleaners and chemicals and that, when buying toys and equipment for babies and young children, they look for labels that show they have been approved for safety.

Labels on household substances

Many everyday cleaning powders and liquids, such as bathroom and kitchen cleaners, washing powders and liquids, may sometimes contain substances that might be harmful to both adults and children, and need to be handled carefully. To be on the safe side, all cleaning materials should be stored out of reach of children and preferably in a high, locked cupboard.

	This shows that the content is **harmful** or an **irritant**, although it does not usually pose a serious health risk.
	Anything with this symbol will contain something that is **toxic** or **very toxic**. It would cause a serious health risk if swallowed, inhaled or spilt on the skin.
	Anything with this label is **corrosive**. It may cause painful burns and destroy living tissue.

Labels on furniture and equipment

When buying large items of equipment and furniture for babies, such as prams and cots, as well as electrical equipment, such as sterilisers and bottle warmers, it is best to look for the following labels, which will show that they meet safety standards. Parents should also check that any furniture, either new or second-hand, has an appropriate fire safety label.

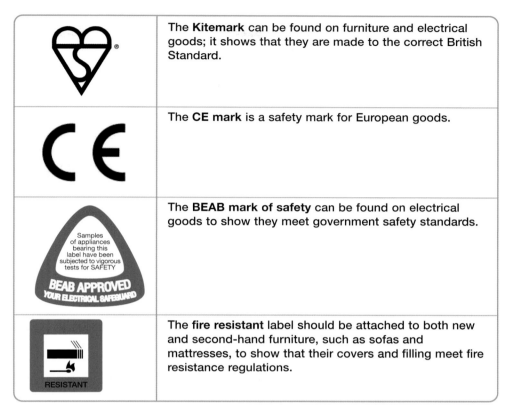

	The **Kitemark** can be found on furniture and electrical goods; it shows that they are made to the correct British Standard.
	The **CE mark** is a safety mark for European goods.
	The **BEAB mark of safety** can be found on electrical goods to show they meet government safety standards.
	The **fire resistant** label should be attached to both new and second-hand furniture, such as sofas and mattresses, to show that their covers and filling meet fire resistance regulations.

Labels on clothing

The law requires that all nightdresses and dressing gowns should be made from material that does not flare up or burn easily. Labels on these garments must be permanent and sewn in.

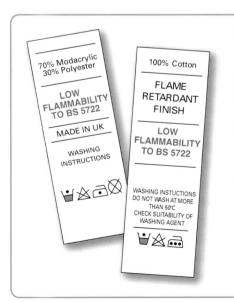

Pyjamas, baby clothes and cotton terry towelling bathrobes that claim to meet flammability regulations *must* include a label with one of the following:

- 'LOW FLAMMABILITY TO BS 5722', in black lettering
- 'LOW FLAMMABILITY TO BS 5722', in black lettering, plus 'KEEP AWAY FROM FIRE', in red lettering
- Pyjamas, baby clothes and cotton terry towelling bathrobes that are not flame resistant must include the wording 'KEEP AWAY FROM FIRE', in red lettering.

These labels do not mean that a garment is totally flameproof. All clothing should be kept away from fire.

? QUESTIONS

Question 1

a What is an accident?

b Give four reasons why children have accidents.

Question 2

Explain how and why children of the following ages might have accidents:

a six months

b nine to 12 months

c three years

d four years.

Question 3

a List four occasions when accidents might happen. Give reasons.

b List the main types of accident.

Question 4

a Draw and label the safety labels you might find on the following:

(i) a cleaning fluid that is harmful or an irritant

(ii) a cot that has been designed and made to the British Standard

(iii) a chair that is fire resistant

(iv) a baby monitor approved to British safety standards

(v) a nightdress that is flame resistant.

6 Preventing Accidents

The most effective way to prevent accidents is to make sure that children are supervised, but it is not always possible to do this every minute of the day.

All parents need to encourage their children to become independent and to learn how to handle everyday risks, and bumps and bruises are all part of growing up. However, no child should be put at risk.

By taking sensible precautions and using appropriate safety equipment, parents can help to create a safer environment that will make it easier to supervise their children, prevent accidents, and still give some freedom and independence.

Preventing falls

Falls are one of the main causes of injury to young children under the age of five. They can happen both inside and outside the home and result in minor bumps, cuts and bruises as well as more serious injuries.

The risk of falls can be reduced by:

- fitting safety gates and barriers at the top and bottom of stairs, or to prevent children from getting into kitchens or out into the garden if doors are open
- using window latches, which prevent windows from opening more than 10 cm, especially to upstairs windows
- using safety harnesses when a baby is in a high chair, pushchair or pram
- making sure rugs are non-slip, especially when used on laminate, wood and vinyl flooring
- picking up toys, shoes and any other item that might cause children to trip up.

Fire safety

Fires are dangerous because they can spread very, very quickly and often result in thick smoke that can also be dangerous. Accidents involving cigarettes are one of the most common causes of house fires.

Fires can be prevented by:

- making sure smoke alarms are fitted and working
- using fire and heater guards
- making sure that matches and cigarette lighters are not left where children might reach them
- not using candles where there are young children
- emptying ashtrays, especially at bedtime
- not leaving a chip pan unattended, or using a thermostatically controlled one
- keeping a small fire extinguisher handy
- fitting socket guards
- checking labels on furniture cushions when buying
- not leaving children unsupervised at barbecues or bonfires
- making sure children's nightwear is flame resistant.

Water safety

Children can drown in just one inch of water, so great care must be taken at bathtime and when children are playing around water. However, it must be remembered that water and hot liquids can also cause scalds and burns, and hot drinks are the main cause of scalds among the under-fives.

To reduce the risk of drowning:

- always collect everything needed before bathing children so that they are not left alone
- use only about 7 cm (2–3 in) of water for bathing babies and toddlers
- use a non-slip bath mat
- supervise children in swimming pools or when playing in paddling pools
- use arm bands when near the sea or in a swimming pool
- cover garden ponds and empty paddling pools when not being used
- teach children to swim at an early age.

To reduce the risk of scalds and burns:

- put cold water into the bath before hot water, and test the temperature before putting the child in
- cover bath taps with a cloth
- don't drink hot drinks when holding a child
- keep kettles and irons out of reach
- where possible, buy electrical equipment with curly flexes
- use cooker guards and turn pan handles inwards.

Preventing suffocation and choking

Babies are most at risk from choking and suffocation, because whatever they pick up they tend to put into their mouths.

To help prevent choking and suffocation:

- keep small items, such as buttons, coins and pieces of LEGO, out of reach
- pillows should not be used for babies under one year old
- when putting young babies to bed, put them in the 'feet to foot' position (see page 172 in Chapter 31)
- never leave a baby alone with a propped-up bottle
- don't give large, hard sweets to children and never give peanuts to children under four years
- keep plastic bags out of reach
- purée food for babies or chop into a size that is easy for them to swallow.

Preventing poisoning

Children aged between one and three are the most likely to have accidents with poisonous substances, and most homes contain hazardous substances that could be very harmful to children (e.g. bleach, aftershave, toilet cleaners, perfume, alcohol). Medicines and pills look no different to young children than drinks and sweets.

To help prevent poisoning:

- keep all household chemicals out of reach, preferably in a high or locked cupboard
- always keep hazardous substances in their original containers – never in water or lemonade bottles, for instance
- keep all medicines and pills in childproof containers out of reach of children
- try not to take medicines or pills in front of children as they tend to copy.

 QUESTIONS

Question 1

a What is the most effective way for parents to prevent accidents?

b Suggest four possible ways of preventing each of the following accidents:

(i) falls

(ii) fire

(iii) scalds and burns

(iv) suffocation

(v) poisoning.

 RESEARCH ACTIVITY

1. Investigate how much it would cost to make a home safer for young children. Use a range of different resources to find out about the safety equipment available for different areas of the home. Evaluate how useful and effective you think each one would be. Present your results as a report, identifying what you would recommend as 'best buys'.

2. Carry out a risk assessment of the main areas of the home where the child plays. Identify possible dangers and suggest ways of reducing the risk of accidents.

7 Safety Outdoors

Care must be taken when children play in public play areas

Giving children the opportunity to play outdoors is very important for many reasons (see pages 263–265). The most popular places for children to play are in gardens or at playgrounds, which give children the opportunity to run around, explore and be adventurous.

Both of these places can result in accidents of various kinds if care is not taken and children are left unsupervised for any length of time.

When children play in the garden make sure that:

- all large toys, such as swings and climbing frames, are stable and secure
- care is taken with positioning trampolines
- all garden tools, equipment and chemicals are stored away in a locked area
- garden ponds are covered
- paddling pools are emptied when not in use
- sandpits are cleaned out regularly and covered to prevent cats using them as a toilet
- dog faeces are cleared up
- any poisonous plants are removed (e.g. laburnum)
- you try to avoid having plants with thorns.

When taking a child to a playground:

- check that equipment is suitable for the age of the child
- check that equipment is stable, safe and in good condition
- try to choose a playground that is fenced in to keep dogs out
- check that the surfaces under the equipment are rubberised or covered with bark or woodchips that will absorb some of the shock of falls
- check that the area is free from broken glass, etc.

Sun safety

Sunshine is important because it makes us feel happy and it also provides us with our main source of vitamin D, which helps to absorb calcium and strengthen bones.

Too much sun can be bad, however. Many doctors and specialists believe there is a direct link between childhood sunburn and malignant melanoma – the most serious form of skin cancer.

Children must be protected from the sun

How to reduce the risk of sunburn:

* babies under six months should be kept out of the sun
* keep children out of the sun between 11 am and 3 pm
* take extra care with children with fair skin and red hair
* use a parasol on prams and pushchairs
* dress young children in loose, cool clothing such as long-sleeved T-shirts
* make sure children wear hats that protect their neck and ears
* use sun block on very young children and re-apply regularly
* always use suntan lotion with an SPF (sun protection factor) of no less than 15 on older children.

Car safety

The law on using child safety restraints in cars was changed in September 2006. The current seat belt laws are as follows.

Age	Front seat	Back seat
Children under three years of age	The correct child restraint *must* be used. Rear-facing baby seats *must not* be used in the front if a front passenger air bag is fitted.	An appropriate child restraint *must* be used.
Children aged three to their 12th birthday or less than 1.35 m tall	The child *must* use an appropriate child restraint.	An appropriate child restraint *must* be used. In exceptional circumstances if a child seat is not available an adult seat belt *must* be used.

Using a suitable safety restraint or seat belt can reduce the seriousness of injuries if involved in an accident – without them a child thrown forwards in a car travelling at just 5 mph could be killed.

As well as obeying the seat belt laws outlined above parents and drivers should:

- choose a seat suitable for the child's age and weight
- make sure the seat is fitted correctly
- make sure child locks are fitted to the rear doors and switched on
- never leave a child of any age alone in a car
- have cars serviced regularly
- drive within speed limits
- never allow children to stand on the back seat or between the front and back seats
- never allow children to put their arms or hands out of a window or to lean out of the windows.

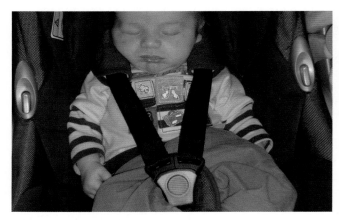

When choosing and using child safety restraints in cars the following must be remembered.

- All restraints should conform to the United Nations standard, ECE Regulation 44.03 or 44.04, or bear a British Standard Kitemark.
- For babies who cannot sit up and who weigh less than 10 kg (22 lb) rear-facing restraints are the best option.
- Once a baby can sit up a child safety seat can be used . These are usually front-facing and adjustable, and are suitable for children weighing between 9 and 18 kg (20 and 40 lb).
- Once a child weighs more than 18 kg (40 lb) or is four years old, a safety harness can be used. This should be adjustable, have a quick-release button and should be used with a special booster.

Road safety

Many thousands of children are killed each year on the roads and many more are injured in road accidents.

Children under five years old will need constant supervision near roads, and cannot really judge speed and distance until they are about 11 or 12 years old.

Parents should:

- hold a young child's hand or use reins near busy roads
- talk to children about the dangers of traffic when out walking
- teach children the Green Cross Code
- keep reminding children what to do when crossing roads
- set a good example, as children will copy adults
- not allow children to play in the streets.

KEY WORDS

Accident an incident or event that happens by chance and causes damage or injury

Hazard anything that might cause an accident

Melanoma a cancerous (malignant) tumour

Toxic poisonous

QUESTIONS

Question 1

Suggest four possible ways of preventing accidents:

a in the garden

b in the playground.

Question 2

a What are the benefits of sunshine for children?

b Why can too much sun be dangerous for children?

c List six precautions parents should take to protect children from the sun.

Question 3

a What does seat belt law say about:

(i) a child under the age of three years old travelling in the front of a car?

(ii) a child over three years old travelling in the back of a car?

b Give five other precautions to take when travelling with children in a car.

c Why do children under the age of four years old need to be supervised near roads?

CHILD STUDY ACTIVITY

1. Carry out a risk assessment of any outdoor play areas and equipment used by the child. Identify possible dangers and suggest ways of reducing the risk of accidents.

2. Plan and carry out a role-play activity or some small-world play to encourage awareness of safety.

RESEARCH ACTIVITY

1. Working as part of a small group use a range of different sources (e.g. textbooks, the internet, CD-ROMs, interviewing family and friends) to find out about the number and type of accidents involving children under five years old.

   Plan and carry out a survey about accidents and accident prevention for the under-fives. Record your results and compare them with your research information.

2. Most children like to play in parks and play areas.

   Investigate how these areas should be made safe for young children.

   Visit different parks and play areas in your local area.

   If possible, use a digital camera to help to carry out a risk assessment of each area – but don't take any photos of children.

   Produce your results as a fact sheet for parents of young children.

3. Find out more about the benefits and dangers of children playing in the sun.

8 Toys and Pet Safety

Toys and safety

Over 35,000 children under 15 go to hospital each year in the UK as a result of an accident with a toy. The majority of these are toddlers between one and three years old.

It is very important that parents and other carers make sure that the toys they buy children, and the ways in which they are used, do not put children in danger.

Some facts: accidents and toys

- Toys that children ride on, such as cars and rocking horses, can cause cuts, bruises or fractures if the children fall from them. Each year, over 5500 injuries are caused by this type of toy.

- Toy boxes cause nearly 4000 accidental injuries each year. Over 70 per cent of these accidents involve children between one and four years old.

- Model cars, planes and trains are also responsible for nearly 4000 visits to A & E each year. Many of these accidents involve children under three and are caused by small parts in these toys.

- Soft toys, such as teddies, dolls or action figures, cause more than 1500 accidents each year. As with other toys, it is children under three that are most at risk, and it is small parts such as eyes, buttons or pieces of stuffing that cause many of these accidents.

- Toys that fire objects, such as toy guns or bows and arrows, water pistols or catapults, cause over 1000 accidents each year.

 REMEMBER!

- Children under two are likely to put things in their mouths.

- Young children will play with older children's toys.

Some safety pointers

It is very important to look at the labelling on both the toy and its box, as this will offer essential information and guidance. Some of the most common labels and symbols you might come across on toys and their packaging are discussed below.

Look for a label that gives an age recommendation on toys – and be guided by it!

A toy that is labelled as not suitable for a child under 36 months is likely to have small parts a younger child could choke on.

The Lion Mark was developed in 1988 by the British Toy and Hobbies Association (BTHA). It means consumers can be certain that a toy bearing the Lion Mark is safe and conforms with all relevant safety information.

In 1991 the British Association of Toy Retailers (BATR) joined with the BTHA in launching the Approved Lion Mark Retailer Scheme. Shops showing this sign will sell only products conforming to BS EN 71. This does not mean that all products in the shop carry the Lion Mark, but that all products meet the Toy Safety Standard.

Every manufacturer of toys in the European Union wanting to sell toys in other countries in the EU must place a CE mark on the toys to show that they have been made to conform with the essential safety requirements agreed by the EU.

Although this is not a sign of quality or safety, it does show that the toy has been made to conform with essential safety requirements.

The following points should also be considered.

All toys need to meet British Standards BS 5665 and European Standard EN 71.
Check age guidance instructions on the package.
Age labelling is the manufacturer's guide to the consumer as to the suitability of the product for a particular age group.
Follow manufacturers' instructions for the use and care of toys.
If buying toys second-hand – from car boot sales or market stalls – check carefully.
Check toys regularly for wear and tear, and throw out broken or damaged toys.
Toys regularly handled and put into children's mouths should be washed regularly.
Follow manufacturers' instructions for the use and care of toys.
Keep toys for young children in their reach – this will stop children from climbing up to reach them and perhaps falling and injuring themselves.

Pet safety

A pet is often an important part of many families, whether it's a goldfish, a hamster, a dog or a budgerigar. Having a pet in the family is often a good way of giving children some responsibility and for them to learn about caring for others. Children with special needs, and especially children with autism, can benefit greatly from having a pet to love and care for.

However, care must always be taken when children are around pets, especially dogs and cats.

Dogs and cats

Dogs and cats come in all shapes and sizes, but no matter how gentle and well behaved they might seem, and how well trained, they are descended from wild animals and children should *never* at any time be left alone with them.

Dogs

Statistics show that the most serious dog bites involve children under the age of five years, and that the dogs are actually known to them.

- To a dog, a small baby might seem like just another toy to play with, so they may try to pick it up in their mouth and shake it – with very serious consequences.
- Both dogs and cats can become jealous of a new baby, especially when the baby is being given all the attention and they are being pushed aside.
- Toddlers often think of dogs and cats as just another toy or plaything, and can unintentionally torment them until they lose patience. This might only result in a growl, which might frighten the child and result in tears – however, it could result in a serious attack on the child, which could be fatal.

- Never leave children on their own with dogs.
- Teach children to be gentle with dogs, and show them how to stroke a dog gently.
- Teach children to leave dogs alone if they are sleeping or feeding.
- Clean up all animal faeces from the garden.
- Keep dogs' feeding dishes out of reach of children.

Cats

Cats are soft and furry and very cuddly – but they have very sharp teeth and claws. They are not usually aggressive unless their tail is pulled, but can get jealous.

They also like to curl up and cuddle in warm, soft places – such as a cot or a pram, which could lead to suffocation of the baby.

- Use cat nets on prams and cots.
- As with dogs, clear up any faeces in the garden and change cat litter regularly.

QUESTIONS

Question 1

How many children are injured each year by:

a toys such as ride-on cars and rocking horses

b toy boxes

c model cars and trains

d teddies and soft toys

e toy guns?

Question 2

a Draw and describe three safety labels you might find on toys.

b List five points to consider when buying and using toys.

Question 3

a Give three reasons why a young child should never be left alone with a dog.

b Suggest four ways parents could make sure their child is safe if they own a dog.

c Why can a cat be dangerous around a young baby?

RESEARCH ACTIVITY

1. Carry out an inventory on both the outdoor and indoor toys of a young child. You could look at:
   (i)   safety features/symbols
   (ii) hygiene
   (iii) manufacturers' instructions
   (iv) overall condition of the toy
   (v)   suitability for child's age.

2. Interview the parents of a young child about toy safety and what they look for when buying toys.

9 First Aid

First aid is a means of giving help to a person who has had an accident or injury – usually until medical help arrives. The accident or injury may range from minor to life-threatening. It is hoped that any assistance from a trained first aider will help to reduce the symptoms of a minor complaint or, in a serious situation, keep the person alive until professional medical help arrives. The assistance will be simple or basic because it is the first help that is given, hence the words 'first aid'.

In a serious situation a first aider will check the following:

- the airway
- if the patient is breathing
- circulation.

First aid at home

First aid at home is usually more about dealing with minor cuts and bruises, scratches and stings that are part of everyday life – especially for young children.

It is a good idea for anyone, not just parents, to keep a first aid box in the home and in the car. There will be situations where parents may have to deal with minor situations such as a cut, bee sting, nosebleed, etc. It is useful, therefore, to have the following equipment accessible in a box clearly marked with the words 'First Aid'.

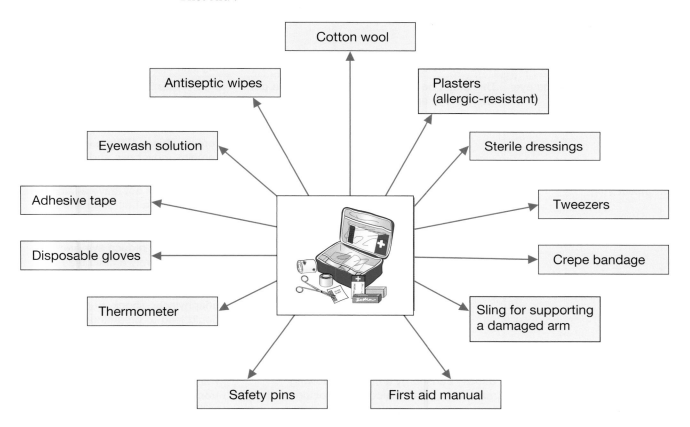

First aid situations

The table below describes some of the first aid situations a child or adult could experience. The possible causes and first aid suggestions are also stated.

Accident or situation	Cause	Treatment
Bleeding nose	Many children have nose bleeds; these can start for no reason.	Pinch the soft part of the nose for 10 minutes to apply pressure. Repeat this for the next 20 minutes.
Bruise	This is often caused by children tripping over in the playground or falling off skateboards, etc. A bruise is caused by bleeding under the skin.	A cold compress may help to reduce the bruising.
Burns and scalds	These can be caused by heat, cold, chemicals, hot liquids or the sun.	Run cold water over the burn for 10 minutes, only remove clothing if it is not stuck to the burn. Cover with cling film or a non-fluffy material. Do not put on any creams or ointments.
Choking	Choking in a child can happen because they don't chew food properly or they put objects in their mouth.	Lay a baby down or bend an older child over your knee, slap five times between the shoulder blades.
Convulsion	A convulsion can happen in a pre-school child when they have a high temperature. If there is no fever it could be epilepsy.	Stay with the child; if child is feverish, cool them down, loosen clothing and place in the recovery position, if possible.
Cuts and grazes	Children can often fall off their bikes, trip when running, etc., and graze their skin.	Clean the area with soapy water, dry and apply a dressing or plaster.
Foreign object in the eye	This could be dust, grit or flies that have got into the eye and irritated it.	Pour water into the eye to wash out the particle. Pull the upper lid over the lower one, getting the child to blink. This may remove the foreign object. If the particle remains, cover eye and take child to the GP.
Insect sting	A bee or wasp, for example, may sting a child and they will feel a sharp pain. It is not usually serious.	A wasp does not leave a sting in the skin but a bee sting needs to be removed with tweezers if possible. Rinse area and use a cold compress to reduce swelling and pain. Very rarely a child may be stung in the mouth or have an allergic reaction to a sting (see anaphylactic shock, page 216). This could lead to breathing difficulties resulting in loss of consciousness, which could be fatal. Medical help must be given as soon as possible.
Poisoning	Usually caused by a child swallowing medicines, plants, alcohol or poisonous berries.	Remove any visible material from the mouth. Rinse mouth with milk or water. Call GP.
Sunburn	Sunburn is caused by too much sun and not enough high-factor sun cream applied to the skin.	Take child out of the sun. Give a cool drink. Cool the red area with cold water. Apply calamine lotion. If the skin blisters seek advice from GP.

If the child becomes unconscious, experiences severe bleeding or difficulty breathing this would be a situation that would require an ambulance to be called or for the child to be taken immediately to the accident and emergency department of the nearest hospital.

 QUESTIONS

Question 1

a What is first aid?

b In a serious situation the first aider will check three things. What are they?

Question 2

a Make a list of items that it would be useful to keep in a first aid box.

b Describe why each item is important and what it might be used for.

Question 3

Most children have minor injuries from time to time. Copy the table below and, in the right-hand column, describe how the following injuries should be treated.

Injury	Treatment
Nose bleed	
Grazed knee	
Insect bite	

 DISCUSSION TOPIC

Choose one of the following scenarios below and note down the course of action you would take.

Scenario 1: James is a toddler who is ready to transfer from a cot to a bed. He was put into his cot on a warm evening with the bed clothes laid over the end of the cot. The parents heard a thud and ran upstairs to find James on the floor. He was crying but there was no apparent injury. He had a restless night and on awakening next morning could not use his right arm to eat his breakfast.

Scenario 2: Emily is six months old and has fallen out of her pram and onto the concrete pavement in a busy town centre. Emily is not crying but looks dazed. She also appears to have some grazes to her face.

 CHILD STUDY ACTIVITY

Find out what first aid equipment the parents of the child you are studying have at home. Ask the parents when they have had to administer first aid to the child.

Web Links	
www.bounty.com	Information and features on planning for pregnancy, pregnancy, babies and toddlers.
www.capt.org.uk	Child Accident Prevention Trust. Useful leaflets and information on safety products and child safety.
www.gingerbread.org.uk	Self-help association for one-parent families. Support, friendship, information and advice.
www.changeanappy.co.uk	Information on using 'real' nappies and local laundry services.
www.safekids.co.uk	Lots of information on health and safety, including indoor and outdoor safety, food allergies, internet and technology, and pets and play.
www.oneparentfamilies.org.uk	Lots of information on issues affecting one-parent families and where help is available.
www.rospa.com	Royal Society for the Prevention of Accidents. Advice on accident prevention and safety.
www.wen.org.uk	The Real Nappy Project at the Women's Environmental Network. Information about modern cloth nappies.

PART 2

PREGNANCY

This part of the book looks at everything about pregnancy, labour and the birth of the new baby. It includes information about:

- reproduction
- pre-conceptual care
- pregnancy
- preparation for the birth
- labour and birth
- the newborn baby
- post-natal care.

REMEMBER!

Pre-conceptual and antenatal care are essential to the health and well-being of the mother and baby.

10 Reproduction

Human reproduction can occur when a male and female have matured to adulthood, their reproductive organs have fully developed and the couple have sexual intercourse. A baby is created from a male sperm and a female egg.

The female reproductive system

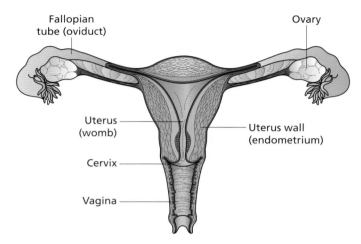

The female reproductive system: front view

Ovaries	A female usually has two **ovaries.** These control the female hormones **oestrogen** and **progesterone**, and contain hundreds of undeveloped female sex cells, eggs or **ova** (a single egg is called an **ovum**). Once a month, a mature egg, or ovum, is released from the ovary. This process is known as **ovulation.**
Fallopian tube	Fertilisation takes place here. Each ovary is connected to the uterus by a **Fallopian tube (oviduct).** Each tube is lined with tiny hairs. Every month an egg is released from an ovary. The tiny hairs in the tube help the egg to travel down this tube. If sexual intercourse has taken place, sperm may swim up the Fallopian tubes and may fertilise an egg if one has been released.
Uterus (womb)	This is a pear-shaped muscular bag with a soft lining called the **endometrium.** It is the space where the baby will develop and grow.
Cervix	A strong ring of muscle between the uterus and the **vagina**. It keeps the baby in place while the mother is pregnant. Normally the cervix is closed, with only a small opening to allow **menstrual** flow to leave the body and semen to enter.
Vagina	This is a muscular tube about 10–12 cm long that leads from the cervix to the outside of the body. During intercourse sperm are deposited here.

The menstrual cycle

The purpose of the menstrual cycle is to produce an egg and prepare the uterus (womb) to receive the egg if it is fertilised.

The average menstrual cycle for women occurs every 28 days although it is possible for some women to have longer or shorter menstrual cycles.

The chart below shows an average 28-day cycle (starting with menstruation on day one).

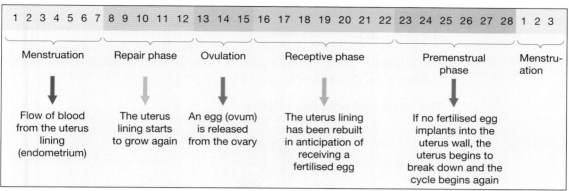

Menstrual cycle chart

During the menstrual cycle, the lining of the uterus (endometrium) goes through five different stages, as follows.

Stage 1 – menstruation

This is often known as a period. It is when the lining of the uterus leaves the body as a flow of blood, and will happen only if the egg is not fertilised.

Stage 2 – repair phase

During this stage a new lining for the uterus starts to build up.

Stage 3 – ovulation

Every month an egg is released from one of the ovaries. This usually happens halfway through the menstrual cycle, around the 14th day.

Stage 4 – receptive phase

By this stage the lining of the uterus has become much thicker and is ready to receive a fertilised egg, which will be travelling along the Fallopian tube. When it reaches the uterus the fertilised egg will implant into the lining of the uterus (endometrium) and the menstrual cycle will stop.

Stage 5 – premenstrual phase

If the egg is not fertilised, the lining of the uterus begins to break down again. (The cycle moves back to stage 1.)

The male reproductive system

The main hormone stimulating physical sexual development of the male is testosterone. In addition to the physical changes, it affects emotional development, bringing about great periods of uncertainty and extremes of feelings from depression to great excitement.

The male reproductive organs

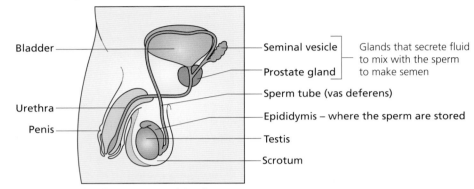

The male reproductive system: side view

Testes	There are two testes; these are the male equivalent of the ovaries. They have two functions: to produce millions of male sex cells, called **sperm**, and to make the male hormone **testosterone**.
Scrotum	A bag of skin containing the testes, which hangs outside the body. This enables the sperm to be stored outside the body at a temperature of 35°C. Sperm may not survive at body temperature or above.
Prostrate and seminal vesicle glands	These secrete a fluid to mix with the sperm to produce **semen**. Sperm are transported to the female sex organs in this fluid.
Sperm tube	This as also known as vas deferens. Sperm travel along the **sperm tube** and pass the **seminal vesicle**, which stores and produces seminal fluid. This fluid mixes with the sperm, producing semen.
Penis	This has two functions: to pass urine out of a man's body, and during intercourse when sexually aroused and erect to pass semen into the vagina of a woman.
Urethera	This is the tube inside the penis that can carry urine or semen. A ring of muscle makes sure that there is no chance of urine and semen getting mixed up.
Epididymis	This is where the mature sperm are stored ready for ejaculation. It is a narrow, coiled tube at the end of the testes.

Hormones

Hormones are chemical messengers produced from endocrine glands. Their job is to signal changes within the body that transform a person from a child to an adult.

The hormone that triggers the male sex organs is testosterone.

The main hormone that triggers the female sex organs is oestrogen. However, once an egg released from the ovary is fertilised, a woman's hormones change considerably.

Progesterone works in conjunction with oestrogen to control the menstrual cycle. It is also the 'pregnancy hormone'.

Female hormones	Main functions
FSH LH	• Stimulate the ovaries to produce oestrogen
Oestrogen	• Development of female sex organs • Stimulates release of eggs • Responsible for thickening of the lining of the womb, so that the fertilised egg can implant
Progesterone	• Needed to be able to prepare for ovulation, conception and pregnancy • Helps to prepare the uterus to receive the fertilised egg • Helps control menstrual cycle
HCG	• Hormone produced by placenta after fertilisation • Stimulates ovaries to produce higher levels of oestrogen and progesterone to sustain the pregnancy
Oxytocin	• Stimulates the uterus to contract during labour and birth
Prolactin	• Controls milk production

 QUESTIONS

Question 1

a Draw and label a diagram of the female reproductive system. Include the following: ovary, cervix, vagina, Fallopian tube, endometrium.

b Describe the functions of the following: Fallopian tube, ovaries, uterus, cervix.

c What is the endometrium and why is it important?

Question 2

Explain what happens during the menstrual cycle from day 1 to day 28.

Question 3

a Draw and label a diagram of the male reproductive system. Include the following terms: sperm tube, testis, scrotum, penis, seminal vesicle.

b Describe the functions of the following: testes, sperm tube.

Question 4

a Where are sperm made and stored?

b At what temperature are sperm stored and why?

Question 5

a What is a hormone?

b What is testosterone?

c Name the female hormones responsible for:
   (i) controlling milk production
   (ii) stimulating the ovaries to produce oestrogen
   (iii) helping to sustain pregnancy
   (iv) controlling the menstrual cycle
   (v) stimulating the release of the eggs (ova).

 KEY WORDS

Hormone a chemical messenger

Menstruation (period) when the uterus lining breaks down and there is a small flow of blood from the vagina

Ovulation the release of an egg from the female's ovary

11 Contraception

Today, planning a family is possible due to the ease of access to free contraception. The word contraception derives from two other words, contra, which means against, and ception, meaning to conceive. Contraception means to prevent the male sperm and female egg joining together to create a baby.

Contraception enables men and women to plan for a baby. This means that every baby is a wanted baby.

When a man and woman have sexual intercourse it could result in a pregnancy. It is quite natural for sexual relationships to occur between adults without them wanting a baby. There is a very high risk of pregnancy for a woman who has unprotected sex.

It is important for people who are sexually active to be aware of the different types of contraception available so that they can make informed choices about which methods would be most suitable for them and why.

Types of contraception

Combined pill

99 per cent effective

How it works

The combined pill contains progesterone and oestrogen. It works by stopping ovulation (eggs being released from the ovary) and the fertilised egg implanting in the uterus wall.

Advantages	Disadvantage
✓ It does not interfere with the sex act. ✓ If side effects occur it can be easily removed and they will stop almost immediately. It can relieve premenstrual tension.	✗ There may be side effects such as headaches, spots, weight gains, depression and breast tenderness. ✗ Forgetting to take the pill will render this method ineffective. ✗ Antibiotics, vomiting and diarrhoea can make it unreliable.

Contraceptive implants and injections

99 per cent effective

How they work

Both implants and injections release the hormone progesterone into the bloodstream. When it reaches the ovaries it prevents them from releasing eggs.

The implant is about the size of a thin matchstick. It is usually inserted under the skin of the woman's left upper arm, not far above the elbow. It can easily be felt, but it's not very visible.

It usually lasts for three years.

Injections are given into a muscle and are usually effective for 12 weeks.

Advantages	Disadvantage
✓ Immediately effective.	✗ There may be side effects such as headaches, spots, weight gain, depression and breast tenderness.
✓ If side effects occur the implant can easily be removed and they will stop almost immediately.	✗ Injections need to be given every 8–12 weeks and if they produce side effects it takes longer for the hormone injected to leave the body.
✓ The woman does not have to remember to take the pill, therefore more reliable.	✗ They have not been available for long, so the long-term effects are not known.
	✗ They do not protect against STIs.

Male condom

98 per cent effective

How it works

This is a barrier method of contraception. A thin rubber sheath is placed over the erect penis and collects the semen that is ejaculated during sexual intercourse. This prevents the sperm and egg meeting.

Advantages	Disadvantage
✓ The man can take responsibility for contraception.	✗ The condom can only be used once and must be discarded after use.
✓ It can protect against sexually transmitted infections (STIs).	✗ It can impair the enjoyment of the sex act.
	✗ The thin rubber can split and sperm can be released, resulting in the possibility of pregnancy.

Intrauterine device (IUD)

(known as 'the coil')

98–99 per cent effective

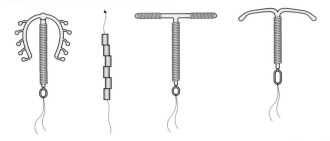

How it works

A small device is placed into the uterus by a doctor or trained expert. This device is made of copper or plastic and can stay in place for up to three to ten years. It prevents pregnancy by stopping a fertilised egg from implanting in the uterus.

Advantages	Disadvantage
✓ It works as soon as it is inserted.	✗ Periods may be heavier, longer or even more painful.
✓ It can stay in the uterus for up to ten years.	✗ The IUD can move and possibly come out.

Intrauterine system – Mirena

More than 99 per cent effective

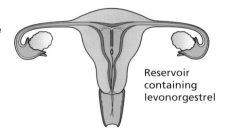

Reservoir containing levonorgestrel

How it works

This device contains levonorgestrel (a synthetic form of progesterone) and, when it is inserted into the uterus, this is released slowly. It stops sperm fertilising the egg.

Advantages	Disadvantage
✓ Very reliable.	✗ It is possible for the device to become dislodged.
✓ It can stay in the uterus for five years.	

Male sterilisation

Over 99.5 per cent effective

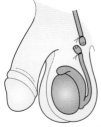

How it works

The sperm tubes (vas deferens) are cut and tied. This stops the sperm mixing with the semen and, when ejaculation takes place, the semen no longer contains sperm.

Advantages	Disadvantage
✓ It does not interfere with sexual intercourse.	✗ It can take a few months for all the sperm to disappear from the semen and therefore it is not instantly reliable.
✓ It is a simple operation.	✗ It is possible that the tubes could rejoin, making the man fertile again.

Female sterilisation

99.5 per cent effective

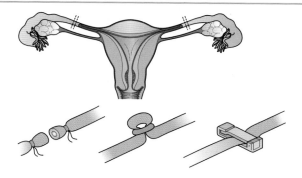

How it works

The Fallopian tubes are blocked, either by cutting or by using rings or clips. This stops the egg released from the ovaries travelling down the tube and meeting the sperm.

Advantages	Disadvantage
✓ The operation is very effective. ✓ It does not interfere with sexual intercourse.	✗ It is possible that the Fallopian tubes could rejoin, making the woman fertile again. ✗ Other forms of contraception will be necessary for a short while after the operation.

Natural family planning (safe period)

Up to 98 per cent effective

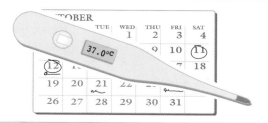

How it works

Natural family planning helps women to recognise the fertile and infertile times of the menstrual cycle to avoid pregnancy. It does this by teaching women to observe and record the different natural signs of fertility such as temperature, cervical secretions and the length of the menstrual cycle.

Advantages	Disadvantage
✓ Most women can use it provided they are properly taught and keep records. ✓ If used correctly it can be very effective. ✓ There are no side effects. ✓ It does not break religious beliefs.	✗ Takes up to six cycles to learn, and daily records need to be kept. ✗ It requires commitment by both partners. ✗ It does not provide protection against sexually transmitted infections. ✗ It is not 'safe' for women who have irregular periods. ✗ Illness and stress can affect its effectiveness.

Withdrawal method

This is a natural method of contraception where the male withdraws the penis from the female vagina prior to ejaculation. It is a very unreliable method of contraception because some men release a little semen prior to ejaculation, which could result in a pregnancy.

Emergency contraception

If sexual intercourse has taken place, and no method of contraception was used at all, or the couple think that the method they are using has failed in some way, then they can use emergency contraception. There are two methods of emergency action that can be taken: emergency pills and copper IUD.

The pills must be taken within three days of unprotected sex as sperm can survive for 72 hours. They work by stopping a fertilised egg settling in the womb or by preventing an egg being released from the ovary.

Help and advice on contraception

You can find help and advice on contraception at the following places:

- there should be lists of GPs in your local library or Post Office, in advice centres, and at health authorities and health boards
- family planning or sexual health clinics
- the Brook Advisory Service
- websites.

Advice on contraception is readily available to people of all ages, both male and female, whatever their personal circumstances.

REMEMBER!

- There are many different types or methods of contraception, and different methods suit different people at different times of their lives.
- Most contraceptives need to be prescribed by a doctor.

- All contraceptives are free, via your health clinic, but you may prefer to purchase them if you do not want the clinic or your doctor to know.
- Only barrier methods protect against sexually transmitted infections (STIs).

There is no doubt that contraception has given people the freedom of choice to:

- limit family size
- choose the age of conception
- plan a career
- gain an education/further education qualification
- provide a good-quality standard of living
- be financially independent
- be in control.

KEY WORD

The word **contraception** is formed from two other words: **contra**, which means against, and **ception**, meaning to conceive.

QUESTIONS

Question 1

What does the word contraception mean?

Question 2

What could happen if a man and woman have sexual intercourse without using contraception?

Question 3

How do the following types of contraception work:

a combined pill

b condom

c IUD

d male sterilisation

e female sterilisation

f contraceptive implants.

Question 4

Choose two different methods of contraception and find out three advantages and three disadvantages of each.

Question 5

a Which method of contraception can help to prevent sexually transmitted infections (STIs)?

b Explain why natural family planning might not be a reliable form of contraception.

c Explain what is meant by 'emergency contraception' and how it works.

 DISCUSSION TOPIC

Discuss each type of contraception described in this chapter. Which methods of contraception would you advise for:

a young people?

b parents who wish to have no more children?

12 Conception: the Start of a New Life

The miraculous moment when a male sperm penetrates and fertilises a female ovum (egg) is known as conception. For conception to occur, the mother and father need to be sexually stimulated, enabling sexual intercourse to take place.

The urge to reproduce is a strong and natural way to continue a species. It can also be a loving and caring way of expressing emotions to a partner.

During sexual intercourse the male's penis will become erect and will be placed inside the female's vagina. At the height of sexual stimulation the penis will ejaculate sperm inside the vagina, usually at the top, near to the cervix. This will enable the sperm to swim (propelled by their tails) towards the uterus and into the Fallopian tubes.

If an egg has been released from the ovary the sperm will meet with a female egg and try to penetrate it, and fertilisation may take place within the Fallopian tube (oviduct).

The ovum can live for 12 to 24 hours after being released from the ovary. Sperm can survive for up to 72 hours inside the woman's body. To increase the chances of conception occurring, intercourse should take place the day before ovulation so that the sperm will be waiting in the Fallopian tube when the egg is released.

The ovum and the sperm

An ovum (egg) is a female sex cell. Once a month a ripe ovum is released from the ovary and travels down the Fallopian tube. A jelly-like coating prevents the egg from sticking to the sides of the Fallopian tube. The ovum is more likely to be fertilised 12 to 24 hours after ovulation.

A sperm is a male sex cell. A sperm is about 1/25th of a millimetre long. Its long tail is able to move from side to side, enabling it to swim up the vagina, through the uterus to the Fallopian tube.

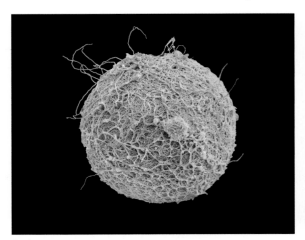

A ripe ovum

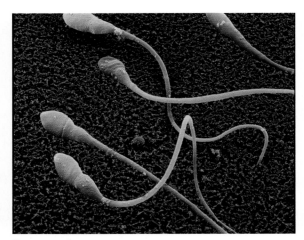

Sperm cells

Sperm live longer than ova (about three days). It takes about an hour for them to swim from the cervix (neck of the womb) through the uterus to meet the egg in the Fallopian tube.

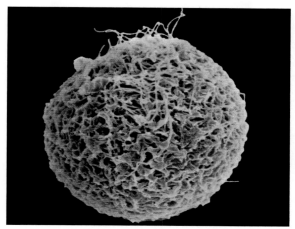

Sperm attempting to penetrate an ovum

When the sperm meet the ovum they will try to penetrate it. Although millions of sperm may be released during intercourse, only one can fertilise an ovum.

Ovulation, conception and implantation

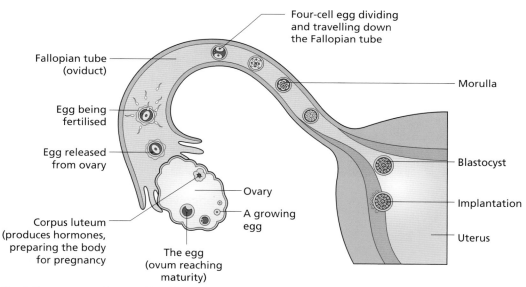

Ovulation, conception and implantation

1. A ripened egg is released from the ovary on about the 14th day of the menstrual cycle. This is called ovulation.
2. The fringe-like projections of the Fallopian tube will encourage the egg to travel down the Fallopian tube.
3. Fertilisation happens when a sperm successfully penetrates the egg. Once this has happened, no other sperm can enter. The sperm no longer requires its tail, which is discarded. The sperm and egg fuse and become one cell.
4. As the egg moves along the Fallopian tube it divides rapidly and begins to look like a blackberry (morulla).
5. Four to five days after conception, the fertilised egg is made up of about 16 cells and this cell mass forms a tiny hollow ball of new tissue called the blastocyst.
6. After approximately seven days the fertilised egg reaches the uterus. It will then embed itself into the endometrium, which is the enriched lining of the

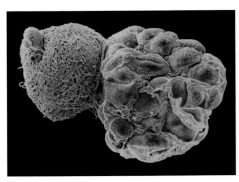

Blastocyst

uterus. This is known as implantation. When the egg is firmly attached to the lining of the womb conception is complete.

The fertilised egg is now called the embryo. The cells continue to divide very rapidly. The outer cells of the embryo settle into the uterus lining and link with the mother's blood supply to form the baby's support system – the placenta, the umbilical cord and the amnion (see page 73). The inner cells will develop into the different parts of the baby's body.

Once conception has taken place, levels of the female hormones oestrogen and progesterone increase, causing the lining of the uterus to have a good blood supply, the breasts to enlarge and the ligaments to relax.

Multiple pregnancies

Normally one egg is fertilised and develops in the uterus. A multiple pregnancy occurs when more than one baby is carried in the womb. The most common multiple pregnancy is twins and this can occur quite naturally.

Quads

Multiple pregnancies were often more likely for couples who had undergone fertility treatment. This was because, as a result of the fertility drugs used to stimulate ovulation, often several eggs were produced that might be fertilised. With IVF (see page 94) several embryos were often placed into the womb to increase the chances of success, sometimes resulting in triplets, quadruplets, quintuplets and sextuplets. Now, for women under 40 years old only one or two embryos can be placed, and for those over 40 years old a maximum of three can be used.

How twins are conceived.

Twins can occur in one of two ways:

1. when one egg fertilises and splits into two cells, forming identical (uniovular) twins
2. when two separate eggs are released and fertilised by two separate sperm to produce non-identical (binovular) twins.

 KEY WORDS

Conception the start of pregnancy; the moment when a male sperm and a female egg join together to form a new cell

Embryo the term for a baby less than seven weeks old

Endometrium the lining of the womb; if conception occurs, the fertilised egg implants in the endometrium

Fertilisation the joining together of the egg and sperm

Ovulation the release of a mature egg from the ovary

Zygote another name for the fertilised egg cell created by the sperm and egg

Identical (uniovular) twins

Uniovular

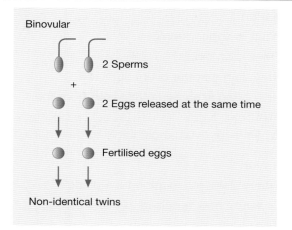

Sperm

+

Egg

Fertilised

Egg splits into two

Identical twins

- One egg produced from ovary.
- One egg is fertilised and divides to produce two babies.
- Both babies share the same placenta and are enclosed by the same outer membrane.
- Each baby has the same genes so they will be the same sex, look exactly alike and have the same blood group.
- If the two cells do not split properly this results in 'Siamese twins', whose bodies are joined at various places.

Non-identical (binovular) twins

Binovular

2 Sperms

+

2 Eggs released at the same time

Fertilised eggs

Non-identical twins

- Two eggs are released from the ovaries at the same time.
- Two eggs are fertilised by two different sperm.
- Babies will not necessarily be of the same sex.
- More likely to be born to a younger mother.
- They will be no more alike than any brother and sister.
- They will have separate placenta and outer membranes.
- The chances of having non-identical twins increases with the mother's age.
- There may be a history of non-identical twins on the mother's side.

 RESEARCH ACTIVITY

Parents who are worried about coping with a multiple birth can seek help from TAMBA (the Twins And Multiple Births Association). Carry out research into this organisation. Find out what support it offers.

? QUESTIONS

Question 1

a What is conception?

b What is an ovum?

c How long can the ovum survive?

d How often is an ovum released from the ovary?

e When is an ovum most likely to be fertilised?

Question 2

a Where does fertilisation take place?

b Describe how fertilisation takes place.

c What happens to the egg after fertilisation?

Question 3

a How long can the sperm survive inside the woman's body?

b To increase the chances of conception, when should intercourse take place?

Question 4

Explain the following terms:

a morulla

b blastocyst

c embryo

d implantation.

Question 6

a What is a multiple pregnancy?

b Why did fertility treatment often result in multiple pregnancies?

c Explain how both identical and non-identical twins are formed.

13 The Baby's Support System

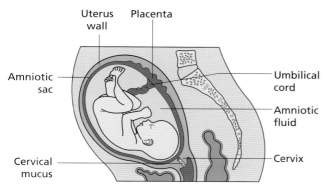

Labels: Uterus wall, Placenta, Amniotic sac, Umbilical cord, Amniotic fluid, Cervical mucus, Cervix

Baby's support system

Once the egg is fertilised, the ball of multiplying cells (the blastocyst) embeds itself into the lining of the uterus. Some cells begin to form the embryo, while others form the placenta, amniotic sac and fluid and umbilical cord. This will be the baby's support system for the whole of the pregnancy.

The placenta

The placenta develops from the chorion during the first 12 weeks of pregnancy. One side of it is attached to the wall of the uterus and the other side to the baby via the umbilical cord. By the end of the 40 weeks of pregnancy the placenta is about 2.5 cm thick and 20 cm wide, and weighs approximately 500 grams; it is deep red in colour. Shortly after the baby is born the placenta (afterbirth) is expelled from the uterus. This is known as the third stage of labour, or the placental stage.

The main functions of the placenta are to:

- produce hormones that maintain the pregnancy
- act as a barrier against some harmful substances
- allow the foetus to breathe, eat and dispose of its waste products
- link the blood supply of the mother to the baby
- pass antibodies from the mother to give the baby some resistance to infections.

The placenta transfers oxygen from the mother's circulation to the foetus's circulation, and removes carbon dioxide and waste products form the foetus's blood to the mother's blood for excretion by her lungs and kidneys. The placenta also conveys nutrients from mother to baby.

The mother's blood and baby's blood never mix. The baby's blood flows via the umbilical cord to the placenta, where it enters tiny blood vessels that are arranged in finger-like projections called chorionic villi. These are surrounded by a pool of the mother's blood and the exchanges take place.

Amniotic sac and fluid

Inside the uterus there is a sac, known as the amniotic sac, which contains the developing embryo and the foetus. The main purpose of the sac is to ensure that the foetus can grow safely. The warm fluid inside the sac is very important and without it the foetus would have difficulty continuing to grow. By the end of pregnancy there will be about 1.2 litres of fluid surrounding the baby – too much or too little fluid can mean that there is a problem with the baby's growth.

The main functions of the amniotic fluid are to:

- enable the foetus to float freely in the early stages, allowing limbs to stretch and flex
- keep the foetus at a constant warm body temperature of approximately 37°C
- support, cushion and protect the foetus from knocks, jolts, falls and bangs, acting like a cushion.

Other factors

- The foetus may drink a little of the amniotic fluid; this is safe and healthy.
- Although most of the waste products are taken out via the umbilical cord, a small amount of urine may pass out of the foetus into the amniotic fluid.

Umbilical cord

This is the baby's lifeline. It connects the baby to the placenta, and it carries blood and nutrients to the baby and removes waste products. Immediately after birth the cord is clamped and cut, leaving a stump. This dries and falls off in about a week.

Cervix and cervical mucus

The cervix is the neck of the womb. During pregnancy the cervix is blocked with a mucus plug. This protects the uterus from infections. During labour the mucus plug comes away and the cervix dilates to allow the baby to pass through the birth canal.

The uterus

This is the baby's home for the nine months of the pregnancy. It is normally about the size and shape of an upside-down pear, but during pregnancy it expands in size. The uterus wall is a strong muscle, which keeps the baby secure and protected. During labour the muscles of the uterus wall contract strongly to push the baby out through the birth canal. The position of the uterus is usually checked at each antenatal visit as this can show how well the baby is growing.

? QUESTIONS

Question 1

What is the baby's support system?

Question 2

a From what does the placenta develop?

b Describe the size of the placenta at 40 weeks of pregnancy.

c Name five functions of the placenta.

d Do the mother's and the baby's blood ever mix?

Question 3

a Name the sac that contains the developing embryo and foetus.

b What is the main purpose of the sac?

c Describe three functions of amniotic fluid.

Question 4

a What is the umbilical cord?

b (i) What does the umbilical cord carry to the baby?

(ii) What does the cord remove from the baby?

Question 5

a Why is the cervix blocked with a mucus plug during pregnancy?

b The uterus wall is a strong muscle. What is the purpose of this muscle during pregnancy and birth?

14 Development of the Foetus During Pregnancy

Once the fertilised egg is implanted in the lining of the womb (endometrium) it will begin to develop rapidly. At this stage it is known as an embryo.

After eight weeks the embryo is called the foetus and, by 12 weeks, the unborn baby is fully formed. From now until the end of the pregnancy the foetus will continue to grow and develop.

Week 6

Embryo facts (four weeks after conception)

- Embryo is 4–6 mm (0.25 in) from crown to rump
- Embryo floats in a fluid-filled sac
- A tiny heart beats, seen as a bulge on the front of the chest
- Eyes and inner ears begin to form
- Four limb buds begin to develop
- Simple brain, spine and cerebral nervous system develop
- Internal organs, blood, bone muscle and blood vessels begin to develop

Pregnant woman

- No visible signs
- Breasts may be uncomfortable
- Areola and nipple begin to darken
- Tiredness and irritability caused by the pregnancy hormone progesterone
- Morning sickness gets worse; some women feel sick all day
- Some have experience of light bleeding or spotting
- May need to urinate more frequently due to increased hormones

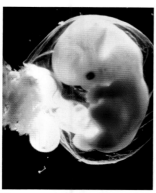

The embryo is the size of a grain of rice

Week 8

Foetus facts (six weeks after conception)

- The embryo is now called a foetus
- Measures 2.2 cm (1 in) from crown to rump
- The foetus has heart valves
- Spine and neural tube are rapidly developing (hence the importance of taking folic acid to prevent spina bifida)
- Foetus moves around
- Arms, legs, shoulders, elbows, hips and knees are detectable
- Fingers and toes are forming, although joined by webs of skin
- Middle part of baby's ear will have developed, responsible for balance and hearing
- Eyes are starting to form
- All the major organs are present in simplistic form

Pregnant woman

- Sickness and nausea. This could be severe
- Weight gain 0.5–1 kg (1–2 lb)
- Breasts are tender, enlarging, and blood vessels form under the skin
- Pain down the back of the legs caused by pressure on the sciatic nerve from the growing uterus
- Slight thickening of the waist
- Increased need to pass urine caused by pressure on the bladder
- Constipation caused by increased levels of progesterone causing the bowel to slow down
- Very tired, caused by a increase in the pregnancy hormone progesterone
- Affects a woman's feelings towards intercourse; some people avoid sex and others feel the need for more
- Mother must continue to take folic acid until week 12 of the pregnancy to prevent spina bifida

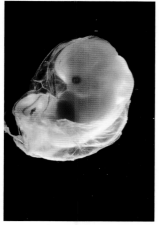

Foetus at eight weeks

Week 12

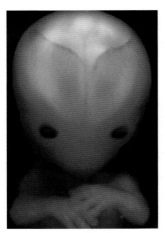

Foetus at 12 weeks

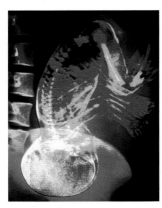

Back of foetus's spinal cord

Foetus facts (ten weeks after conception)

- Foetus is approximately 6 cm (2.5 in) from crown to rump and 9–14 g (0.5 oz); it would fit into the palm of your hand
- Foetus looks like a human; it is fully formed in miniature
- Foetus can swim and make a fist
- Foetus is moving but cannot be felt
- Organs, muscles, limbs, bones and sex organs are well developed
- Heart is beating strongly and fast (twice as fast as that of an adult)
- Foetus can suck thumb
- Foetus is sensitive to heat, touch, light and sound
- Foetus takes sips of the amniotic fluid
- Fingers and toes separate and nails begin to grow
- Eyelids cover the eyes, which will remain closed for three months
- Head becomes more rounded
- Hiccups, and can open and close mouth

Pregnant woman

- At 12 weeks the foetus cannot be felt, although some 'flutters' (foetal movements known as 'quickening') may be felt at 16 weeks
- Breasts will be heavier and tender
- Top of uterus can be felt above the pubic bone
- Thickening of the waist
- Sickness may begin to ease
- Pressure on the bladder is not so great so the desire to pass urine should be less
- Hormonal changes may make the mother emotional
- Constipation
- The lung, heart and kidneys will be working harder due to the increased blood circulation in the mother's body

This foetus is covered in lanugo and vernix at about 20–24 weeks; these often disappear before the birth

Week 24

Foetus facts

- Foetus measures 21 cm (8 in) in length and weighs around 700 g (1.5 lb)
- Substantial weight gain
- The UK recognises 24 weeks as legally **viable** for a baby to survive outside the uterus (termination after this date is illegal unless severe abnormalities are evident)
- Chances of survival would be reasonable in the neonatal intensive care unit (NICU), although the lungs would be inactive and would require ventilation
- Face is fully formed
- Soft nails
- **Vernix** (white greasy substance) forms
- **Lanugo** (downy hair covering the foetus) forms
- Hair grows on head
- Skin is red and wrinkled
- Eyelids are still fused together (open during the 26th week)
- Bones are starting to harden
- Exercises vigorously
- Fingerprints have formed
- Has definite periods of sleep and waking
- May respond to loud noises or music

Pregnant woman

- May have gained 4–4.5 kg (8–10 lb) and is putting on weight at a more rapid rate
- The **fundus** (top of uterus) is about 5–7 cm (2–3 in) above the navel and a definite bulge can be seen
- Can feel the foetus kicking, somersaulting and turning
- May feel the foetus change position
- A clear heartbeat can be heard by the midwife
- Often 'blooms' at this stage, with excellent skin, nails and hair, due to hormones
- Some women notice a change in skin pigmentation (more common in dark-haired mothers)
- Gums may bleed and feel a little swollen
- Water retention and puffy hands can be a problem
- Stretch marks develop
- May experience back ache
- Should wear flat shoes if possible
- Heartburn and shortness of breath; mother needs to sit up straight
- Uterus pressing on the bladder causes discomfort and the need to urinate frequently

A pregnant woman at 36 weeks

Week 36

Foetus facts

- Weighs around 2.5 kg (5 lb), length 33.5 cm (13 in)
- Hair may have grown about two inches
- The foetus has put on weight and has a more rounded appearance
- Skin is pink
- The head may have dropped into the pelvis ready for birth; this is called engaging
- Nails have grown on fingers and toes
- Testicles descend in a boy
- Foetus should gain approximately 28 g (1 oz) per day from now on
- Foetus would have an excellent chance of survival if born early
- Vernix and lanugo disappear

Pregnant woman

- Once the foetus drops into the pelvis and the height of the foetus lowers, the mother may find that her indigestion and breathlessness disappear
- Continued need to pass urine
- Legs may feel swollen and heavy; needs to sit with her legs up
- Skin is stretching and itchy; more stretch marks may develop
- Ribs can feel uncomfortable
- May not feel the foetus move as frequently because of restricted space
- Varicose veins may be a problem
- May be a little anxious prior to the birth
- May have difficulty sleeping

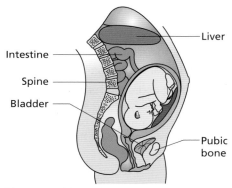

Foetus at 36 weeks, in relation to mother

Liver

Intestine

Spine

Bladder

Pubic bone

🔑 KEY WORDS

Fundus the height of the uterus, measured by feeling the mother's abdomen

Lanugo fine, downy hair that covers the foetus from the fifth month of pregnancy

Vernix a white, greasy substance that covers the baby

Viable legally the age when a baby could realistically be expected to survive if born early – currently 24 weeks

🔍 RESEARCH ACTIVITY

Research and find pictures of the embryo/foetus at the following stages of development:

- 6 weeks
- 12 weeks
- 24 weeks
- 36 weeks.

Label each picture with aspects of development.

QUESTIONS

Question 1

a What is an embryo?

b What is the difference between an embryo and a foetus?

c At how many weeks of development is the foetus fully formed?

Question 2

At six weeks of the pregnancy (four weeks after conception) the mother may start to experience changes to her body.

a Name four changes the mother may experience.

b Describe what the embryo looks like at six weeks of development.

Question 3

Copy and complete the chart below using facts from this chapter.

Question 4

Define the following terms:

(i)   lanugo

(ii) vernix

(iii) fundus.

Number of weeks of development	Three facts about the foetus	Three changes to the pregnant mother
8 weeks	• The foetus measures 2.2 cm (1 in) from crown to rump • Spine and neural tube developing • Eyes start to form	Sickness could be very severe • Breasts are tender and large • Very tired due to the hormone progesterone
12 weeks		
24 weeks		
36 weeks		

15 Pre-conceptual Care

Pre-conceptual care involves preparing for pregnancy and thinking about possible changes to lifestyle that would improve the chances of having a healthy pregnancy and labour. To be effective, pre-conceptual care should involve both partners and, ideally, should start at least three months before trying for a baby. This is especially important if there is a family history of congenital disease or if either partner is on long-term medication for medical problems.

Why is pre-conceptual care important?

Pre-conceptual care is important for a couple planning to have a baby because it can help to produce healthy sperm and ova, and provide a healthy environment for the foetus to grow safely. The first 12 weeks of the baby's life (the first trimester) are the most important. During this time all the main organs, such as the heart, liver, lungs and brain, are being formed and, by three months, most are beginning to work. However, most women will not even know that they are pregnant until they miss a period and many will not have their pregnancy confirmed until about eight or nine weeks. Although the majority of babies are born fit and healthy it makes sense not to take chances, and there are certain environmental and genetic factors that could cause problems during this time.

Environmental factors

By identifying and reducing known risks, such as smoking, poor diet, and so on, it is possible to improve fertility, to increase chances of conceiving and to create the best possible environment for an embryo to grow and develop into a healthy baby. As a rule, healthy parents will produce healthy sperm and ova, and have a better chance of a trouble-free pregnancy.

The environment in which the baby is conceived and in which the embryo and subsequently the foetus grows will have a tremendous impact on its life. The diagram below shows some of the environmental factors that could affect the development of the foetus.

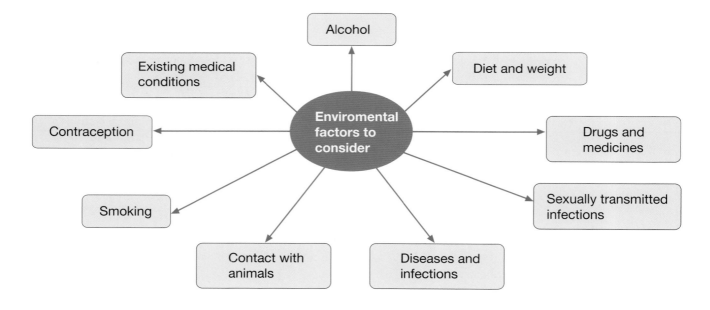

Diet and weight

Healthy eating

The diet of a mother, particularly in the pre-conceptual stage, is important and should be taken seriously. The mother is the only provider of the healthy nutrients needed for her baby to grow and develop and she should, therefore, take full responsibility for ensuring that her baby receives the very best nourishment. Research carried out into mothers' diets during pregnancy has shown that what they eat affects not only the unborn child but also the child after it has been born.

So a healthy balanced diet is especially significant, both before and during pregnancy. It is important to try to eat a variety of foods and the Food Standards Agency recommends that this should include:

- plenty of fruit and vegetables – at least five portions a day
- plenty of starchy foods such as bread, pasta, rice and potatoes
- protein such as lean meat and chicken, fish, eggs and pulses (beans and lentils); these foods also supply iron
- fish at least twice a week, including some oily fish
- dairy foods such as milk, cheese and yoghurt, which contain calcium, in moderation.

Weight

Being overweight or obese is one of today's main health problems, and it can affect fertility and reduce chances of conception because it may cause problems with ovulation (releasing eggs). It can also lead to problems during pregnancy, including high blood pressure, pre-eclampsia and diabetes, making it more difficult to monitor the baby's growth and increasing the chances that a Caesarean will be necessary.

However, being underweight can also affect periods and prevent the pituitary gland from sending the correct messages to the ovaries to stimulate ovulation. So it is not wise to go on a strict weight-loss diet before trying for a baby, unless under medical supervision.

Folic acid

Folic acid (folate) is one of the B vitamins and is very important because it is known to help prevent spina bifida and other neural tube defects (NTDs). Because NTDs occur early in pregnancy it is recommended that supplements are taken before trying for a baby. The Department of Health recommends that a daily dose of 400 micrograms (mcg) should be taken and that folic-rich foods should be included in the diet (see the table below). This should be done for three months before trying for a baby and until at least three months into the pregnancy.

- Folic acid capsules come in 400 mg doses, so one capsule per day should be taken from three months before conception, and throughout the first 12 weeks of the pregnancy.
- A folic acid milk drink is available from chemists for women who dislike taking capsules or tablets. One carton of this milk contains the daily requirement of folic acid.

During pregnancy the need for folic acid is greatly increased, particularly in women who have been taking oral contraceptives (the pill) for a long time.

Folic acid content of food		
Foods with high levels of folic acid	**Foods with medium levels of folic acid**	**Foods that are fortified with folic acid**
Liver Brussels sprouts Kidney Spring greens Beef extract Kale Broccoli Spinach Green beans Yeast extract Leafy green vegetables (these are very good, particularly the darker green ones)	Soya beans Potatoes Lettuce Peas Wholemeal bread Cauliflower Chickpeas Oranges and orange juice Baked beans Parsnips	Some breads Most breakfast cereals

What is spina bifida?

Spina bifida literally means 'split spine'. The backbone usually provides a tube of bones (vertebrae) to protect the nerves (spinal cord) that run down the middle. In spina bifida, the bones do not close round the spinal cord, leaving a split or gap where the nerves can bulge out on the unborn baby's back and become damaged (see the illustration below). It is possible for the condition to occur anywhere along the spinal cord, but it is more usual for it to happen quite low down the back.

This happens very early on in pregnancy – often before the woman even knows she is pregnant.

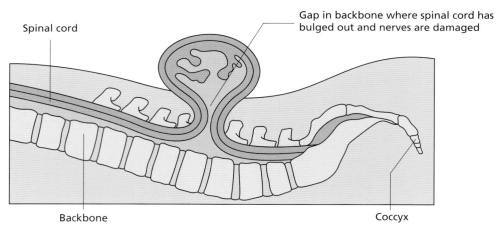

Cross-section of back showing spina bifida

- Whatever the age of the mother, all babies are at risk of developing spina bifida and other neural tube defects, such as hydrocephalus.
- A healthy mother, who has already given birth to healthy children, is as much at risk as a mother experiencing her first pregnancy.
- Women who have had several children are particularly vulnerable because they

have had little time to top up their folic acid levels before getting pregnant again.

- Women who have had one child with spina bifida are far more at risk than women who have given birth to 'normal' children.

Caffeine

Caffeine is a stimulant that occurs naturally in some foods and hot drinks, such as tea, coffee and chocolate, and is added to some other soft drinks, such as cola and 'energy' drinks. It can cause feelings of restlessness, fatigue or increased heart rate in some people. These symptoms may cause harm or discomfort before and during pregnancy, so it is best if the woman reduces the amount of caffeine she takes into her body. Although it is not necessary to cut out caffeine completely, pregnant women should limit the amount they have per day to no more than 200 mg. This is because high levels of caffeine can lead to low birth weight, or even miscarriage. This can be achieved by drinking weaker tea/coffee or by leaving it out altogether and drinking mineral water or fruit drinks instead.

Both of these contain caffeine

Food poisoning

Certain foods contain high levels of harmful bacteria that can cause miscarriage, stillbirth and serious illness in a newborn baby. A woman who is planning to have a baby or who is already pregnant could easily put herself and her growing baby at risk if the food she is eating is contaminated by salmonella, listeria or toxoplasmosis.

Salmonella

This is an infection from the salmonella bacterium and is usually traceable to raw eggs and raw chicken. Although your baby will not be directly harmed, you may be very unwell.

Eggs should be cooked until both the yolk and the white are solid and safe.

It's best to avoid home-made sorbets, meringues, mousses and mayonnaise, as raw eggs are sometimes used to make these foods. However, supermarket mayonnaise in jars is made with pasteurised eggs, so is safe to eat. Salmonella can be avoided if food is cooked thoroughly at a high temperature.

Listeriosis

This is a type of food poisoning. It is caused by bacteria found in foods such as raw fish, unpasteurised milk, soft cheese (such as Brie and Camembert), pâté, undercooked poultry and pre-cooked chilled foods. The symptoms of listeriosis are similar to flu, and could include a high temperature, feeling hot and cold by turns, muscle aches, back pain, nausea, vomiting and diarrhoea.

Listeria can be passed from mother to baby during pregnancy and birth. It can lead to miscarriage or stillbirth, and in newborn babies it can cause breathing problems, hypothermia, meningitis (a serious brain infection) and even death. Babies who seem healthy at birth may develop symptoms later on, such as feeding problems and a high temperature.

Toxoplasmosis

This is a disease caused by a parasite. It can be caught by eating raw or undercooked meat, from cat faeces or from gardening in contaminated soil.

Each year, only about 2000 women in the UK will catch toxoplasmosis during pregnancy and, for them, the symptoms will usually be mild and not serious. For a baby in the womb the effects of toxoplasmosis can be very serious, however. The earlier in pregnancy a baby is infected, the worse the damage may be. It can result in miscarriage or stillbirth, or the baby could be born with hydrocephalus (water on the brain), or damage to the eyes or other organs.

Exercise

The fitter and healthier the mother is both before and during pregnancy, the better she will be able to cope. Being pregnant puts a great deal of strain on the body, and being aware of this, and actually doing something to prepare for it, will undoubtedly help both mother and baby. Nowadays we recognise that exercise is not only beneficial, but necessary too, provided that it:

- is regular (before and during pregnancy)
- does not overtire the mother (during pregnancy) (see page 132)
- is in moderation (before, but particularly during, pregnancy).

Activities such as cycling, horse riding, walking and swimming can all be carried out, as long as they are planned with care and common sense. It is important to emphasise that the mother can continue with her chosen activities until she feels uncomfortable, particularly during pregnancy itself.

Harmful substances

Certain substances that people knowingly take in to their body can affect fertility, damage the developing baby and have long-term effects on the baby after birth. In particular, tobacco smoke, alcohol and drugs.

Smoking

The facts

Smoking before pregnancy can affect a woman's fertility, while men that smoke tend to have a lower sperm count and often produce more abnormal sperm.

Both smoking and passive smoking (inhaling other people's smoke) during pregnancy are among the most damaging factors to the health and development of an unborn child.

When a pregnant woman smokes a cigarette, some of the chemicals in the smoke pass from her lungs into her bloodstream, and then to the placenta. At the placenta, the chemicals pass from the mother's bloodstream to that of her unborn baby. Two of the harmful chemicals in smoke are nicotine, which will make the baby's heart beat much faster, and carbon monoxide (a poisonous gas), which replaces oxygen in the blood. The baby will then receive less oxygen than it needs and will not grow as well as it should.

The risks

During pregnancy smoking increases the risk of:

- premature birth
- miscarriage and stillbirth
- placental damage, where the baby does not receive the nourishment it needs to grow
- low birth weight – the average birth weight of babies born to smokers is approximately 200 g (8 oz) less than the norm
- foetal abnormalities
- poor growth.

After the birth there is a greater risk that babies may suffer:

- poor growth, and learning difficulties (development tests have shown that children of heavy smokers often have these conditions).

Often, children born to mothers who smoke, and live in a home where several people smoke, are more likely to develop asthma, bronchitis, pneumonia and other chest infections, and are twice as likely to die from sudden infant death syndrome (cot death).

Some research shows that this passive smoking can be a contributory factor towards leukaemia and other types of cancer.

Alcohol

The facts

It is well known that men who drink heavily have lower sperm counts and, although nobody knows how much or how little alcohol can harm a developing baby, scientists agree that heavy or binge drinking by the mother on a regular basis is very damaging to the baby, especially during the first three months.

When a pregnant woman drinks alcohol, it very quickly passes into her bloodstream. Once there, it crosses the placenta and enters the baby's bloodstream as well.

The risks

Alcohol increases the risk of:

- miscarriage
- stillbirth
- mental retardation
- retarded growth
- damage to the brain and nervous system
- alcohol addiction (it is a well-known fact that an alcoholic woman's baby can be born addicted)
- foetal alcohol syndrome (FAS) (see below).

Foetal alcohol syndrome (FAS)

Women who drink heavily during pregnancy are more likely to have babies with **foetal alcohol syndrome** (FAS). Babies born with FAS have brain damage, a low birth weight, small heads and facial abnormalities. Many also have a short attention span, language problems, hyperactivity and behavioural problems. Obviously, these conditions do not become apparent until the baby is born.

Current research suggests that there is no safe level of alcohol consumption during pregnancy, and that even a small amount of alcohol makes a baby more likely to suffer abnormal spasms in the womb.

Drugs and medicines

The facts

Technically, all medicines are drugs but not all drugs are medicines. When the word 'drugs' is used, people usually think of heroin and cocaine. Here, we will look at those drugs that are considered to be harmful and those that are not.

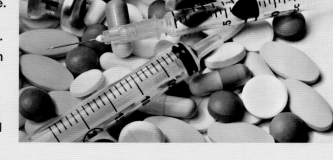

A drug is any substance that has some effect on the workings of the body, so two very simple definitions of drugs are as follows.

1. *Medicines:* given or prescribed by a doctor to treat disease or illness. These may be harmful to the mother before and during pregnancy. Medicines known to be harmful to an unborn baby are travel sickness pills and some antibiotics. Pain relievers, such as aspirin, paracetamol and so on, should be taken with caution.

2. *Drugs:* these are often taken illegally for the effects they have. They are often called social drugs and are habit forming (addictive). Such addictive drugs will cross the placenta and enter the baby's bloodstream, affecting development and possibly making the baby addicted too.

The risks

Whether medicines or so called 'social' drugs, these substances may be harmful to the mother before and during pregnancy. Research into drug-related problems before and during pregnancy shows that:

- marijuana (even though it is known as a 'soft' drug) interferes with the normal production of male sperm, and the effects of using such a drug take between three and nine months to wear off
- the baby of an addicted mother may have a low birth weight
- hard drugs, such as heroin, cocaine, morphine and cannabis, can damage the chromosomes both in the sperm and the ovum, which will ultimately lead to abnormalities in the baby's development
- often the baby will have withdrawal symptoms from the drugs immediately after birth.

REMEMBER!

A woman who is hooked on heroin, cannabis, glue-sniffing or any similar addictive substance, should consult her doctor to get help before trying to conceive.

KEY WORD

Pre-conceptual before conception

QUESTIONS

Question 1

a What does pre-conceptual care involve?

b Give three reasons pre-conceptual care is important.

c When should pre-conceptual care start?

Question 2

List six environmental factors that might affect the development of the foetus.

Question 3

a What is folic acid and why is it important?

b Name four foods rich in folic acid.

Question 4

Salmonella, listeriosis and toxoplasmosis are all types of food poisoning.

Copy and complete the chart below to show:

a main causes

b possible effects on the unborn baby.

Question 5

a Why is smoking harmful before pregnancy?

b List six ways smoking can harm the baby.

Question 6

a What is foetal alcohol syndrome and how might it affect the baby?

b What is the difference between drugs and medicine?

c Why should drugs be avoided both before and during pregnancy?

Name	Causes	Effects
Salmonella		
Listeriosis		
Toxoplasmosis		

RESEARCH ACTIVITY

1. Research the effects of alcohol, smoking and drugs on the mother and her unborn baby. Use this information to design a poster for use in an antenatal clinic, warning of the dangers.

2. Design a quiz sheet for 14–16-year-olds about the dangers of smoking and drugs during pregnancy. Analyse and evaluate the results, and present them as a report.

16 Sexually Transmitted Infections (STIs)

Sexually transmitted infections are passed from one person to another through sexual activity. You cannot tell if a person has an STI simply by looking at them, because many people with STIs have no obvious symptoms. However, they can have very serious effects, including infertility, and the more sexual partners a person has, the greater the risk.

STIs can be caused by both bacteria and viruses. Bacterial infections can be cured by antibiotics. Viral infections are not curable but many can be controlled and risks reduced. If not treated, as the chart below shows, many STIs can affect the unborn baby both during and after pregnancy.

Bacterial STIs

STI	Possible symptoms	Possible effects	Treatment
Chlamydia	Symptoms may include abdominal pain, vaginal discharge, pain when passing urine, and bleeding between periods. Up to 78 per cent of women and 50 per cent of men who have chlamydia have no symptoms.	Can lead to **pelvic inflammatory disease**. This affects the uterus, ovaries and Fallopian tubes, and can result in infertility. There is also a greater risk of ectopic pregnancy, which can be fatal, and possible links with miscarriage and premature births.	Antibiotics
Gonorrhoea	Symptoms often occur 2–10 days after being infected. In young women they include a painful burning sensation when passing urine and a vaginal discharge that is yellow or bloody.	Can result in ectopic pregnancy and also lead to **pelvic inflammatory disease** and possible infertility (see 'Chlamydia'). Bacteria can pass to baby during birth, resulting in eye infections.	Antibiotics
Syphilis	Raised lump on or near the genitals or anus, which may then form a painless sore. This can take 1–12 weeks to develop. Generally followed by feeling unwell, such as headaches, fever and tiredness. Possible white patches on tongue or roof of mouth.	Especially harmful during pregnancy as it can cause miscarriage, stillbirth and foetal abnormalities. The disease can also be passed to the foetus via the placenta.	Antibiotics
Trichomoniasis	Symptoms usually include itching and soreness in and around the vagina and an unusual discharge, which may be yellow, smelly or frothy. Up to one in two people don't have any symptoms.	It can cause damage to the Fallopian tubes, and result in premature birth and low birth weight.	Antibiotics

Viral STIs

STI	Possible symptoms	Possible effects	Treatment
Genital herpes	Similar to a 'cold sore', and found on or around the vagina or penis and anus. There may be pain on passing urine and a general feeling of being unwell.	If a woman has a first outbreak while pregnant, and especially in the first three months, this could result in babies being stillborn or suffering damage to the brain, nerves, eyes or skin.	No cure but can be treated with antiviral drugs.
Hepatitis B	It causes inflammation of the liver and can cause long-term damage to the liver.	Can also be passed from an infected mother to her unborn baby, and if not treated immediately the baby will be a carrier for life.	Rest and possible treatment with anti-viral drugs.
HIV and AIDS	Signs of HIV include: • sore throat • fever • rash on body or face • headaches • ulcers on mouth or genitals • painful muscles and joints. People with HIV usually have no symptoms for a long time as the virus acts slowly to weaken the body's immune system. Once the immune system has broken down, the body becomes vulnerable to serious illnesses and infections, including some cancers. At this stage the person is often diagnosed as having **AIDS**, which can be fatal.	The virus can cross the placenta during pregnancy and infect the baby in the birth canal during delivery. It can also be transferred during breast-feeding.	There is no cure for HIV. Use of anti-HIV medicines can slow down the disease and can mean that a person can have a near-normal life expectancy.

REMEMBER!

Any type of infection requires time to develop. Just because symptoms have not appeared does not mean that an infection has not begun.

When planning to have a baby, both partners should get checked out for STIs.

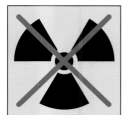

Other environmental factors

X-rays

It is not a good idea for a woman planning to become pregnant to be subjected to X-rays, or any form of radiation, unless it is absolutely necessary (i.e. if the mother's life is at risk). This is because any developing baby (foetus) will be rapidly making new cells and X-rays and radiation rays will destroy new or healthy cells.

Rubella (German measles)

Rubella (German measles) is one of the most common of all childhood diseases and is relatively mild, but if a woman has German measles, especially in the first three months of pregnancy, it can cause serious damage to her baby.

Although all women should have received rubella vaccination at school, those who are thinking about having a baby should find out from their doctor whether or not they are immune to German measles. If they are not, the doctor can vaccinate against it. After being vaccinated, and provided that the vaccination was successful, a woman should wait for about three months before trying to conceive.

A woman who comes into contact with a person infected with, or suspected of having, German measles should tell her doctor immediately. The doctor will then arrange for the woman to have a blood sample taken, which will be tested for antibodies. The result will determine whether or not the woman needs to be treated.

Vaccinations and immunisation

Shortly before conception, and certainly during pregnancy, it is not wise for a woman to be immunised. However, there are exceptions and these are:

- if the mother-to-be has been exposed to infectious diseases
- if she is to travel outside the UK and, therefore, requires typhoid or cholera protection.

In both cases, a woman should consult her GP.

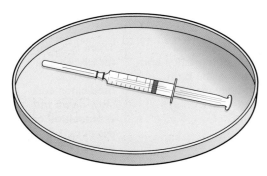

Vaccination can be dangerous during pregnancy

Contraception (family planning)

The majority of methods can be stopped immediately, but there are two that need some thought before this can happen.

The pill

Women who wish to become pregnant are often advised to stop taking the pill for two to three months before they start trying to conceive. This allows time for periods to adjust to their natural cycle. In addition, some experts believe that, as well as the prevention of ovulation, oral contraceptives cause changes in the lining of the uterus. This could make it more difficult for a fertilised egg to implant.

Occasionally, a woman will become pregnant immediately after she has stopped taking the pill. Some evidence suggests that a woman is much more fertile at this stage. If a woman has miscarried before, or has had experience of low fertility, then it is possible that this way could be ideal for her.

A woman who thinks that she may be pregnant while still taking the pill should see her doctor. This is because some types of pill contain very high doses of progestogen, which could interfere with the development of the embryo in the first few weeks.

Intrauterine device

This method is sometimes abbreviated to IUCD or IUD, or called 'the coil', and works by irritating the lining of the uterus, so that it is almost impossible for a fertilised egg to implant itself on the lining.

It is recommended that the IUD is removed before conception, as removing it after the woman is pregnant could increase the risk of a miscarriage. If the woman becomes pregnant while the IUD is in place, it usually comes away with the placenta after the birth.

Existing medical conditions

Certain illnesses and medical conditions can affect pregnancy. Women who have epilepsy, kidney disease, diabetes, heart disease, multiple sclerosis, thyroid disease or any long-term illness should discuss it with their GP before becoming pregnant. This will help them to cope with both the disease and the pregnancy in the best possible way.

Contact with animals

Certain animals can carry bacteria that are harmful to the developing baby. Toxoplasmosis is an infection that is caused by a parasite. In the mother, this would cause mild flu-like symptoms, but it can also cause foetal brain damage and blindness, and may even lead to miscarriage or stillbirth.

Eating raw or undercooked meat is actually the most common source of this infection, but it can also be present in cat faeces, and infected soil or litter trays used by cats. It is important to always wear rubber gloves if cleaning cat litter or when gardening.

KEY WORDS

Bacterium a single-cell microorganism; some are **pathogenic** (i.e. they can cause disease in humans)

Parasite an organism that lives off the cells of another organism

Virus a parasite that can cause disease; smaller than bacteria

QUESTIONS

Question 1

a What are the two main causes of sexually transmitted diseases?

b Chlamydia is the most common sexually transmitted disease among young people. What are the possible symptoms?

c Why is chlamydia particularly serious for women?

d Name two other sexually transmitted diseases.

Question 2

What do the following stand for:

a HIV?

b AIDS?

Question 3

a Why is rubella a dangerous disease to catch?

b Why are women who want to become pregnant advised to stop taking the contraceptive pill two to three months before trying for a baby?

c Name four medical conditions that can affect pregnancy.

Question 4

Why should pregnant women avoid contact with animals?

17 Genetics and Genetic Counselling

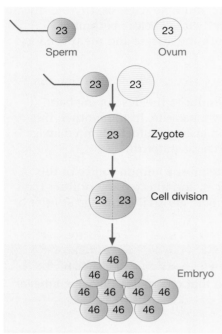

Chromosones in sex cells and fertilisation

Genetics is the study of heredity, and heredity is the process by which characteristics are passed on from one generation to the next.

All human cells have 46 chromosomes except the sex cells, the sperm and the ovum.

The sex cells contain only 23 chromosomes and at conception they join together to become one, forming a zygote with a complete set of 46 chromosomes.

Each individual chromosome is a thread-like structure that carries information that will determine the appearance, growth and function of a new life. Each chromosome carries several thousand genes and each gene is responsible for part of the human make-up (e.g. hair colour, hair texture, height).

Of the 46 chromosomes, two will determine the sex of the child. Some sperm contain a Y chromosome and some an X chromosome, while the ova always contain an X chromosome. When the egg and sperm join together, if an X and a Y chromosome meet, a boy baby is formed.

Sperm chromosome	+	Ova chromosome	=	Sex of baby
Y	+	X	=	YX boy baby
X	+	X	=	XX girl baby

Just as the colour of our hair or eyes, or the shape of our nose, can be inherited from our parents so, sometimes, can abnormalities. Abnormalities in the make-up or numbers of chromosomes can lead to common disorders such as Down's syndrome or Turner's syndrome.

Most babies are born healthy. A very few are born with a major birth defect and this is known as a congenital abnormality. Congenital abnormalities can be caused by environmental or genetic factors, or a combination of both.

Genetic abnormalities can be inherited from one or both parents. They are usually passed on by either the sperm or the egg. Very occasionally an abnormality might happen for the first time in just a particular sperm or egg for no apparent reason.

If there is any possible risk of a baby being born with a congenital abnormality or a life-threatening disease, a couple should ask their GP about genetic counselling. This should be considered for any of the following reasons:

- if there is a history of repeated miscarriages
- if there is a blood relationship between the mother and her partner – for example, they may be cousins
- if a woman has previously given birth to a child with a genetic disorder (e.g. cystic fibrosis) or a child with a chromosomal disorder such as Down's syndrome
- if a woman has a previous child born with a congenital defect (e.g. a club foot)
- if there is a family history of inherited disorders or birth defects (e.g. haemophilia, cystic fibrosis)
- if either partner belongs to an ethnic group in which a genetic disorder occurs frequently (e.g. sickle cell disease is common mainly in people whose families

come from Africa, the Caribbean and the eastern Mediterranean; and thalassaemia among people from Mediterranean, Asian and Far Eastern countries)
- if there is a high rate of some forms of cancer within families (e.g. breast cancer)
- if the couple are having problems conceiving.

Genetic counselling will help to ensure that the risks are known and understood so that the couple can make their own decision about whether or not to try for a baby.

Fertility and infertility

Fertility is the ability to have children. In women it is the ability to become pregnant and in men it is the ability to make a woman pregnant.

Infertility means being unable to conceive. Infertility is often defined by doctors as the inability to conceive after at least one year of trying.

There could be many reasons why people are infertile, and it could affect either partner, but when it happens it can cause a lot of stress and unhappiness. Nowadays many 'infertile' couples can be helped by assisted-conception treatments.

Reasons for infertility

Male	Female
A blockage of one or both of the vas deferens – the tubes that connect the testicles to the seminal vesicles (sperm is stored here). This blockage could be the result of a sexually transmitted disease.	Damaged or blocked Fallopian tubes, which can stop the sperm and egg meeting.
Very low sperm count. This could occur if the man works with pesticides or metals such as lead, mercury, etc. Tight underwear and overheating are two other causes.	Hormonal imbalance. An ovarian cycle is almost completely dependent upon the correct balance of hormones. If there is too much or too little of either one of them, an egg will not be produced.
Testicular failure. This is a rare condition when the semen contains no sperm.	Fibroids. These are totally benign (non-cancerous) growths within the uterine walls. They are more likely to occur in women aged 35 and over.
Poor diet. A poor or unhealthy diet can result in a low sperm count.	Endometriosis. This is a condition where patches of the lining of the uterus are found in the ovaries, the pelvis, Fallopian tubes, etc.
Mumps.	The cervical mucus in the neck of the womb is too thick and the sperm cannot pass through.
Testicular cancer or cancer treatment.	Ovarian cancer and related cancer treatment.
	Age. Fertility decreases as a woman gets older. Also, some women begin the menopause very early, which affects ovulation and this can reduce their chances of becoming fertile.

Treatments for infertility

Tubal surgery

If a woman has blocked or damaged Fallopian tubes, or a man a blockage in the vas deferens, microsurgery can open the tubes and any areas of damage may be removed.

Hormone therapy (fertility drugs)

If a woman has problems ovulating, fertility drugs may be prescribed. These drugs promote ovulation by stimulating hormones in the brain to get one or more eggs ready and release them from the ovaries each month. Hormone drugs can also be used to treat men in some situations.

IVF (in vitro fertilisation)

The woman's ovaries are encouraged to produce eggs by using fertility drugs. These are collected and mixed with sperm, and monitored until they begin to divide into cells. Two or three 'embryos' are then transferred into the woman's womb where it is hoped that at least one will implant and start to develop into a baby.

IVF can be used if the woman has blocked Fallopian tubes, endometriosis, thick cervical mucus or sometimes premature menopause. It can also be used when the man has a low sperm count.

GIFT (gamete intra-Fallopian transfer)

This is similar to IVF, but after the eggs and sperm have been mixed together they are surgically injected into the Fallopian tubes so that fertilisation can happen naturally.

ICSI (intra-cytoplasmic sperm injection)

This is used when the man has a low sperm count or the sperm are of poor quality. A single sperm is injected into an egg. Then, after fertilisation, up to three embryos are replaced in the uterus.

Egg donation

This is similar to IVF, but instead of the woman's own eggs being used, the eggs to be fertilised are taken from a donor and fertilised with the man's sperm. This way the baby carries the genes of the father, but not of the birth mother.

Sperm donation

This is a where the egg of a female is fertilised, using artificial insemination techniques or IVF with sperm from a healthy male that has been donated and kept frozen in a sperm bank. This gives a couple the chance to conceive a child who has genetic characteristics of one of the parents, and the mother can experience pregnancy.

Surrogacy

This is where another woman carries a couple's embryo or a donor embryo. A surrogate mother conceives after being artificially inseminated with the man's sperm (the man is usually the biological father). She then goes on to carry the baby to term.

REMEMBER!

Fertility can be improved and chances of conception increased by:

- having a healthy diet and lifestyle
- not being overweight
- keeping fit
- avoiding alcohol, smoking and drugs
- checking for sexually transmitted infections.

 QUESTIONS

Question 1

a What do the following mean:

  (i) genetics?

  (ii) heredity?

b What is a congenital abnormality?

c Give five possible reasons why a couple might ask their GP about genetic counselling.

d How can genetic counselling help a couple when they are planning to have a family?

Question 2

a What is infertility?

b Give three possible causes of male infertility.

c Give three possible causes of female infertility.

Question 3

Describe the following:

a IVF

b GIFT

c surrogacy

d sperm donation.

18 Pregnancy

Pregnancy is the time between conception and birth and usually lasts for 280 days (40 weeks) from the first day of the last menstrual period.

Some of the signs of pregnancy

Some women may know within a few days of conception that they are pregnant, but most do not suspect until after a few weeks when some or all of the following signs will be obvious:

- a missed period, although it is possible for some women to have a very light period
- a metallic or 'strange' taste in the mouth
- sickness, sometimes in the morning but it can occur at any time of the day or night
- desire to urinate more frequently
- feeling dizzy and even fainting
- tiredness
- constipation
- slightly increased vaginal discharge
- unable to consume certain drinks or food – for example, tea, coffee, chocolate (this may last the whole pregnancy or for the first few weeks)
- breasts become larger and more tender; the veins can look very obvious and 'blue'; the nipple and areola can go from a pink colour to a much darker pink.

All of the above symptoms are caused by the increase in the pregnancy hormone progesterone. The symptoms often become milder or disappear around the 12th week of pregnancy.

Confirmation of pregnancy

For couples who have planned a pregnancy, confirming it can be an euphoric time, filled with excitement and anticipation. For others it may be a more difficult time, particularly if the pregnancy is unplanned.

How to test for pregnancy

All pregnant women begin to produce a special hormone called gonadotrophin (hCG) as soon as the fertilised egg has implanted in the uterus. This can be found in the blood or urine.

The most common way of detecting a pregnancy is by obtaining a urine sample in a clean container from the mother after she has missed the first day of her period. The urine is mixed with various chemicals and this permits detection of the presence of the pregnancy hormone gonadotrophin. If the hormone is present this will be called a positive test. These tests are almost always correct. However, a negative result may not be correct and a re-test may be required two weeks later. This is because there may have been insufficient levels of gonadotrophin for the test to read.

A test can be carried out by a GP or, for a small charge, by Brook Advisory Centres, the British Pregnancy Advisory Service or a family planning clinic. Local chemists will charge a fee for a test.

Home pregnancy tests

Home pregnancy testing kits are now widely available and can be purchased from

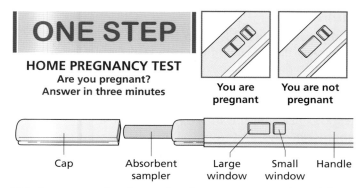

ONE STEP

HOME PREGNANCY TEST
Are you pregnant?
Answer in three minutes

You are pregnant   You are not pregnant

Cap   Absorbent sampler   Large window   Small window   Handle

This is an example of a modern home pregnancy test giving an accurate result from the very date a female should have started her period

chemists and large supermarket chains. The advantages of these tests are that they give instant results, using a midstream sample of urine. They also enable women to carry out the test in private. However, the test instructions must be read and followed accurately or a false reading may occur. A disadvantage is that they are rather costly.

Earlier tests

Modern technology means that it is possible to confirm pregnancy as early as five or six weeks from the last period by having an internal or vaginal scan.

It is also possible to carry out a blood test before a period is missed to look for gonadotrophin (hCG) in the bloodstream

Pick out the date of the first day of the last period from the figures in light type. The due date is immediately underneath in blue type.

January	1 2 3 4 5 6 7 8 9 10 11 12 13 14 15 16 17 18 19 20 21 22 23 24 25 26 27 28 29 30 31
Oct/Nov	8 9 10 11 12 13 14 15 16 17 18 19 20 21 22 23 24 25 26 27 28 29 30 31 1 2 3 4 5 6 7
February	1 2 3 4 5 6 7 8 9 10 11 12 13 14 15 16 17 18 19 20 21 22 23 24 25 26 27 28
Nov/Dec	8 9 10 11 12 13 14 15 16 17 18 19 20 21 22 23 24 25 26 27 28 29 30 1 2 3 4 5 6 7
March	1 2 3 4 5 6 7 8 9 10 11 12 13 14 15 16 17 18 19 20 21 22 23 24 25 26 27 28 29 30 31
Dec/Jan	6 7 8 9 10 11 12 13 14 15 16 17 18 19 20 21 22 23 24 25 26 27 28 29 30 31 1 2 3 4 5
April	1 2 3 4 5 6 7 8 9 10 11 12 13 14 15 16 17 18 19 20 21 22 23 24 25 26 27 28 29 30
Jan/Feb	6 7 8 9 10 11 12 13 14 15 16 17 18 19 20 21 22 23 24 25 26 27 28 29 30 31 1 2 3 4
May	1 2 3 4 5 6 7 8 9 10 11 12 13 14 15 16 17 18 19 20 21 22 23 24 25 26 27 28 29 30 31
Feb/Mar	5 6 7 8 9 10 11 12 13 14 15 16 17 18 19 20 21 22 23 24 25 26 27 28 1 2 3 4 5 6 7
June	1 2 3 4 5 6 7 8 9 10 11 12 13 14 15 16 17 18 19 20 21 22 23 24 25 26 27 28 29 30
Mar/Apr	8 9 10 11 12 13 14 15 16 17 18 19 20 21 22 23 24 25 26 27 28 29 30 31 1 2 3 4 5 6 7
July	1 2 3 4 5 6 7 8 9 10 11 12 13 14 15 16 17 18 19 20 21 22 23 24 25 26 27 28 29 30 31
Apr/May	7 8 9 10 11 12 13 14 15 16 17 18 19 20 21 22 23 24 25 26 27 28 29 30 31 1 2 3 4 5 6 7
August	1 2 3 4 5 6 7 8 9 10 11 12 13 14 15 16 17 18 19 20 21 22 23 24 25 26 27 28 29 30 31
May/Jun	8 9 10 11 12 13 14 15 16 17 18 19 20 21 22 23 24 25 26 27 28 29 30 31 1 2 3 4 5 6 7
September	1 2 3 4 5 6 7 8 9 10 11 12 13 14 15 16 17 18 19 20 21 22 23 24 25 26 27 28 29 30
Jun/Jul	8 9 10 11 12 13 14 15 16 17 18 19 20 21 22 23 24 25 26 27 28 29 30 31 1 2 3 4 5 6 7
October	1 2 3 4 5 6 7 8 9 10 11 12 13 14 15 16 17 18 19 20 21 22 23 24 25 26 27 28 29 30 31
Jul/Aug	8 9 10 11 12 13 14 15 16 17 18 19 20 21 22 23 24 25 26 27 28 29 30 31 1 2 3 4 5 6 7
November	1 2 3 4 5 6 7 8 9 10 11 12 13 14 15 16 17 18 19 20 21 22 23 24 25 26 27 28 29 30
Aug/Sep	8 9 10 11 12 13 14 15 16 17 18 19 20 21 22 23 24 25 26 27 28 29 30 31 1 2 3 4 5 6
December	1 2 3 4 5 6 7 8 9 10 11 12 13 14 15 16 17 18 19 20 21 22 23 24 25 26 27 28 29 30 31
Sept/Oct	7 8 9 10 11 12 13 14 15 16 17 18 19 20 21 22 23 24 25 26 27 28 29 30 1 2 3 4 5 6 7

Pregnancy calendar

Estimated date of delivery

The first thing parents usually want to know is when their baby will be born. Calculating the estimated delivery date (EDD) of the baby will require a pregnancy calendar like the one reproduced above. Calculations are made using an average 28-day cycle, so offer only a rough guide.

- A pregnancy lasts about 266 days from conception to birth.
- Conception, on average, takes place on the 14th day of the cycle.
- To calculate the EDD, count 266 days + 14 from the first day of your last period = 280 days.
- An average pregnancy is 40 weeks, although it can range from 38 to 42 weeks.

Miscarriage

The medical term for miscarriage is spontaneous abortion. This means the loss of the foetus from the uterus before the 24th week of pregnancy or before the baby is, by law, considered viable. A foetus that is viable would be able to survive outside the uterus without support from medical intervention.

The majority of miscarriages occur within the first ten weeks of pregnancy. Also, a woman may miscarry without knowing that she was ever pregnant. Therefore a number of women may not seek medical advice. However, it is estimated that approximately 30 per cent of all pregnancies end in miscarriage.

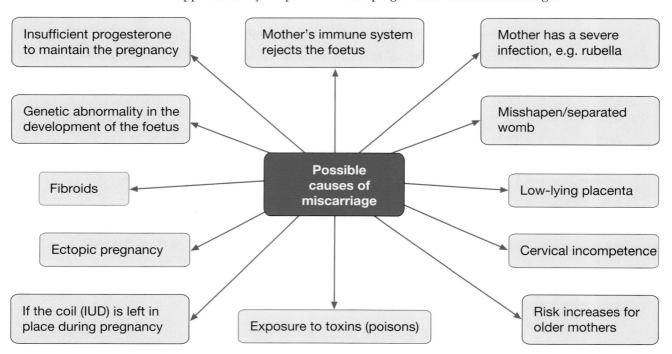

Signs and symptoms of miscarriage

- Bleeding from the vagina.
- Cramp-like period pain, which may be mild or severe.
- Light bleeding may occur, caused by a low-lying placenta or cervical erosion. These pregnancies may continue until full term.
- Spotting blood accompanied by severe pain may indicate a miscarriage or an ectopic pregnancy (where the implantation has taken place in the Fallopian tube). This is a most serious condition.

- A gush of clear or pinkish fluid may indicate that the amniotic sac has ruptured (broken).

There are different types of miscarriage.

- Threatened abortion – the foetus remains alive and does not come out of the uterus despite vaginal bleeding.
- Inevitable abortion – the foetus has died and is therefore expelled (sent out) from the uterus. Sometimes it is not complete and the foetus/placenta do not all come away.
- Missed abortion – despite the foetus having died it remains intact in the uterus with the placenta.

Prevention of miscarriage

When a woman is in danger of having a miscarriage she will be advised to have complete bed rest to reduce the blood loss. However, in some instances there may be little that can be done to stop it happening.

If the cervix is incompetent (unable to hold in the contents of the uterus) the woman would have the cervix stitched shut to make it stronger. Bed rest will be recommended as well as medication that may help the uterus to relax.

Women who have more than three miscarriages will be investigated to find out the possible cause.

If a miscarriage occurs the hospital will carry out an ultrasound scan to find out if the foetus has died. This may result in a short hospital stay where the woman will have her uterus cleared under a general anaesthetic.

Parents' feelings

When parents suffer the loss of a baby, even during the early weeks of pregnancy, it may be traumatic, particularly if the baby was desperately wanted.

- A mother may worry whether or not she will ever have a normal, healthy baby.
- A mother may feel guilty: was there something she did to cause the miscarriage?
- A mother may want to try to become pregnant again immediately, although some doctors advise waiting for at least three menstrual cycles.
- Some parents may be realistic about the loss and feel that it was not preventable.
- Parents can contact their local miscarriage support group.
- Other people may not understand the need to mourn and come to terms with the miscarriage.

Most women who have had a miscarriage will go on to have a normal healthy pregnancy.

KEY WORDS

Ectopic pregnancy when the foetus develops in the Fallopian tube	**Miscarriage** the natural loss of the foetus from the uterus
EDD estimated date of delivery	

QUESTIONS

Question 1

List ten possible signs of pregnancy.

Question 2

Which hormone is known as the 'pregnancy hormone'?

Question 3

As soon as the fertilised egg implants in the uterus a special hormone is produced and can be detected in the blood or urine. What is the name of this hormone?

Question 4

a Explain how a pregnancy can be detected.

b What might cause a negative test result to be incorrect?

Question 5

a What does 'EDD' stand for?

b How is the EDD worked out?

Question 6

a What is a miscarriage?

b When do the majority of miscarriages occur?

c Suggest five possible causes of miscarriage.

d List five signs and symptoms of miscarriage.

e What are the three different types of miscarriage?

Question 7

a How can a woman try to help prevent a miscarriage?

b Describe some of the feelings parents might have when they experience a miscarriage.

 RESEARCH ACTIVITY

Find out what support is available for parents who may have experienced a miscarriage or several miscarriages.

19 Antenatal Care

Antenatal care is the care of the mother and her unborn baby/babies before the birth takes place – that is, during pregnancy. Antenatal care is very good in the UK – it is free, widely available to all pregnant women and employers must, by law, allow pregnant women to attend antenatal classes without losing pay.

The main purpose of antenatal care is to monitor (check) the health of the mother and development of the baby regularly throughout pregnancy. Various tests are offered and carried out on a regular basis and these, along with advanced technology, can detect possible problems with the mother and/or her unborn child at an early stage. Often treatment can be given at an early stage to prevent further complications and ensure that the pregnancy is healthy. However, this is only one aspect of antenatal care. Just as important are regular meetings with the health carers, which also give the pregnant woman the opportunity to ask questions about the pregnancy and the birth of the baby, and to talk over any worries or concerns. This is especially important for first-time parents and for those who already have a family but may have experienced a difficult pregnancy.

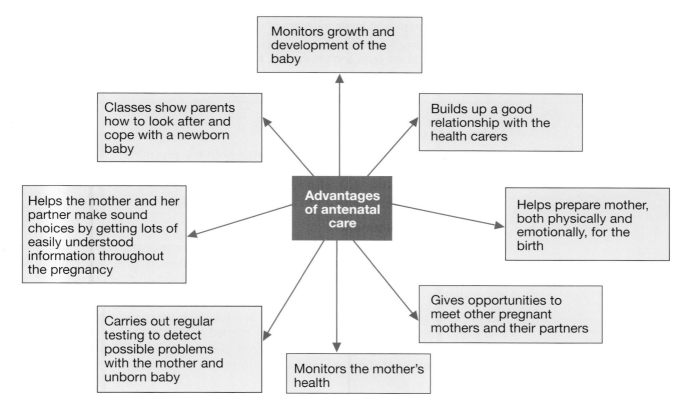

Types of antenatal care

There are different types of antenatal care available, depending on the area in which you live, as noted in the table below.

Shared care	Most women are cared for by their GP (general practitioner) and community midwife during pregnancy but they may see a consultant obstetrician at their local maternity hospital at the beginning and the end of the pregnancy or if there is a complication. This means that some antenatal checks will take place at the local doctor's surgery or health clinic and others at the hospital, where more specialist equipment is available.
Full consultant care	If a pregnancy is complicated in some way (e.g. if mother has diabetes) care will be given by a hospital-based consultant obstetrician. This means that all the care will be carried out in hospital, although more often than not a team of junior doctors and midwives will care for the mother. It is only when problems arise that the consultant will become more involved. Some women may choose to have private medical care with an obstetrician.
Community-led midwife care	This is where the antenatal care takes place at the health centre or GP's surgery. Routine appointments are carried out by a team of community and hospital midwives, and the local GP will be involved only if there is a complication. Many GPs' practices have doctors with a special interest in antenatal care. The mother often gets to know the team of midwives well.
Independent midwives	Some women choose to have an independent midwife to look after them during pregnancy, at the birth and afterwards, especially if they want to have a home birth. These midwives are fully qualified but work outside the NHS and will charge a fee.

Antenatal visits

These will take place on a regular basis throughout the pregnancy. The first visit – the 'booking-in visit' – usually happens around the eighth week of pregnancy and is the longest. After that, visits are usually once every four weeks until 28–30 weeks, then every two weeks until 36 weeks, then weekly until the baby is born.

The booking appointment

Once the pregnancy has been confirmed, the GP will arrange the booking appointment. It is at this point that the type of antenatal care will be decided, although this could change if complications arise, or if certain types of care are not available.

The booking appointment may take place at a hospital, antenatal clinic, home or at the GP's surgery. It is usual for this to be carried out by a midwife. The midwife will ask a lot of questions at this visit and it is her role to gather as much information as she can about the mother and her medical history, and so on.

The diagram below notes some of the information collected at the booking appointment.

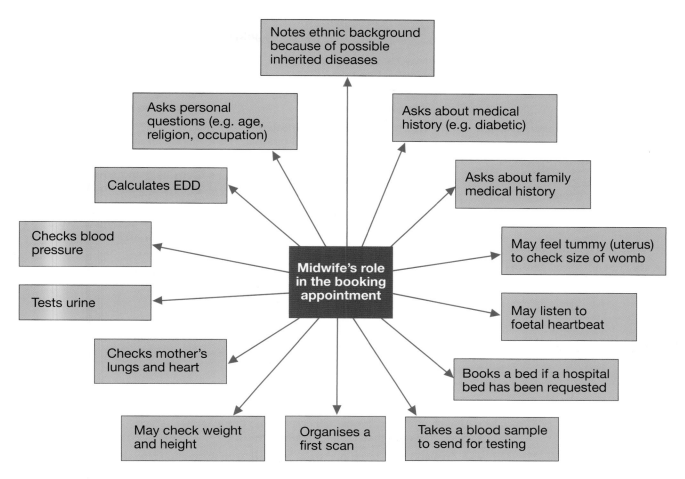

Midwife's role in the booking appointment

- Notes ethnic background because of possible inherited diseases
- Asks personal questions (e.g. age, religion, occupation)
- Asks about medical history (e.g. diabetic)
- Calculates EDD
- Asks about family medical history
- Checks blood pressure
- May feel tummy (uterus) to check size of womb
- Tests urine
- May listen to foetal heartbeat
- Checks mother's lungs and heart
- Books a bed if a hospital bed has been requested
- May check weight and height
- Organises a first scan
- Takes a blood sample to send for testing

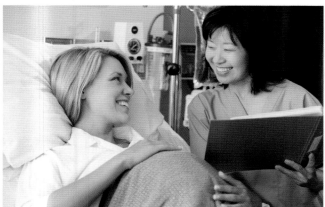

The midwife will support the pregnant woman through her pregnancy

The midwife

While there are many other healthcare professionals involved with the pregnancy, it is the midwife who is likely to have the most contact with the expectant mother, her partner and family, especially during the pregnancy.

It is most likely that a midwife will deliver the baby unless complications arise, and it would be at this point that an obstetrician would be brought in to perform sections, forceps and ventouse deliveries (see Chapter 28).

The role of the midwife

Midwives are highly qualified and skilled practitioners whose role is to look after an expectant mother through a normal pregnancy and labour, and after the birth. They are also qualified to give drugs. Most work in both the community and hospital alongside other health carers to meet the needs of all individuals, such as teenage mothers, disabled mothers and mothers from all types of ethnic background.

Role during pregnancy	Role during labour and birth	Role after birth
• Mainly responsible for running antenatal clinics • Carries out the booking appointment • Carries out all routine tests and monitors health • Books scans and specialist tests • Establishes a relationship with the mother • Helps to draw up birth plan • Gives advice and support • May run antenatal classes	• May deliver baby at a home birth • May deliver in hospital (if no complications) • Helps and encourages mother during labour and actual birth • May give requested pain relief • Cleans baby and passes baby to mum • Carries out Apgar testing • Checks placenta • Checks for excess bleeding • May stitch if episiotomy needed	• Looks after mother and baby on the post-natal ward • Visits the mother and new baby during first ten days after birth • Helps parents to adjust to their new role • Gives help and advice on feeding and caring for the baby • Checks the general health of the mother and baby

There are a number of other specialist people that the pregnant woman may come into contact with, depending on her health and medical history. The table below summarises the role of each healthcare professional that may be involved in the primary health care team.

GP (General practitioner)	• The family doctor • Usually the person who will confirm the pregnancy • Some GPs run their own antenatal clinics.
Health visitor	• A qualified registered nurses or midwife with special qualifications in community care • Supports families with young children from 10 days after the birth until child is 5 years old.
Obstetrician	• A doctor who is specialised in the care of babies and children • Will often deliver a baby when there are complications.
Paediatrician	• A doctor who is specialised in the care of pregnant women during pregnancy labour and birth • A baby born in hospital will be thoroughly checked by a paediatrician soon after birth.
Dietician	• A person qualified to give nutrition advice on any special diet or need • Particularly involved with women who are diabetic or develop diabetes during pregnancy.
Physiotherapist	• An obstetric physiotherapist is trained to help look after any physical problems of pregnant women during labour and postnatally • They often attend antenatal and aqua-natal classes and give advice on beathing techniques and exercises to tone muscles and regain shape after birth

Recording the antenatal information

During the antenatal period the information gathered about the mother and her unborn child needs to be recorded to measure progress. This information could be vital and therefore must be carried with the mother at all times.

Pregnancy notes (hand-held notes)

All the information about the pregnancy is recorded in the pregnancy notes. These are often called 'hand-held notes'. They are very detailed and contain all the information gathered from the booking-in date at the antenatal clinic until the birth is complete. They give the woman access to all the information about herself and her baby.

Advantages	Disadvantages
✓ More information can be written in detail. ✓ All information is kept within one booklet. ✓ The woman has access to all the information regarding herself and her unborn baby.	✗ If the notes are lost they cannot be replaced, although duplicate copies of scans and tests are kept by the hospital.

The pregnancy notes are made up of approximately 22 pages, although this can vary from area to area. Some pages are used for recording ongoing information while others give information about different aspects of the pregnancy, so that the pregnant women knows what is involved and can make an informed choice.

What would a typical set of notes contain?

A typical set of notes would contain:

- personal details, family history and ethnic origin
- a birth plan, with arrangements for the birth
- history of menstrual cycles, previous pregnancies and the woman's general health
- record of antenatal appointments
- information gathered related to the woman, e.g. blood group, urine tests, blood pressure, any swelling of feet and hands, and weight
- information gathered related to the unborn baby, e.g. position in the uterus, heartbeat, movement
- growth charts to record fundal height and estimated foetal weight
- ultrasound scan reports and pictures
- details of any hospital admissions
- general pregnancy and health information, e.g. choices about labour and birth, pregnancy complications, smoking, diet, information on breast-feeding.
- post-natal period.

The notes and birth plan should be available for the midwife if it is a home birth, or taken into hospital with the woman when she goes into labour.

Making a birth plan

The birth plan is an important part of the pregnancy notes. It is designed to enable the woman and her partner to make informed choices about labour and the baby's birth. The midwife will discuss with the expectant mother, and possibly father, what options are available and the woman will write down her preferences on the chart.

The birth plan is meant to be the ideal situation, although births do not always go according to plan. If the plan has to be changed for any reason this will also be recorded in the notes. It is a good idea to discuss options with partner and carers before making choices. The diagram below shows what might be included in a birth plan.

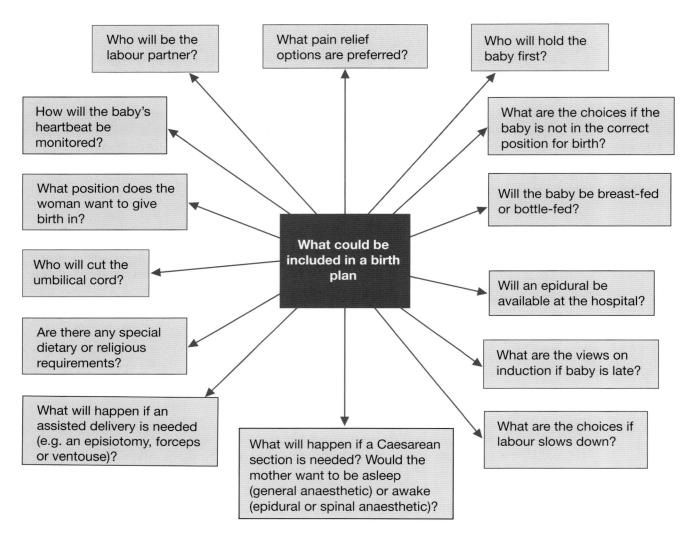

The woman and her partner may make several choices in response to the birth plan, but it is also a good idea to keep an open mind so that changes can be made if the need arises.

Antenatal/parentcraft classes

The purpose of antenatal classes is to prepare the expectant mother and her partner for the pregnancy, birth and beyond. The classes give them the chance to meet other expectant couples in an informal atmosphere and to ask any questions about things that may be worrying them. They provide advice and give information on a range of topics both about labour and birth, and about coping once the baby is born, such as:

- diet
- feeding baby

- bathing baby
- labour and birth
- pain relief
- exercise.

They may also organise visits to hospital.

Partners

Some partners do not wish to be involved in antenatal classes because they may feel daunted by all the pregnant mothers, embarrassed about the nature of childbirth, scared of 'blood', and so on. However, partners should be encouraged to support expectant mothers and to be prepared for the weeks ahead. Partners can learn how they can help throughout the pregnancy.

Who runs the classes?

Most classes are free, last for about six weeks and usually take place during the day at either local health centres or hospitals. Classes are run by:

- national midwives and health visitors (most common)
- obstetricians
- birth teachers from the National Childbirth Trust (NCT).

KEY WORDS

Antenatal before birth

General practitioner a qualified family doctor

Gynaecologist a specialist doctor who cares for women of any age and their reproductive organs

Health visitor a qualified nurse who opts to look after the health of the family in the community

Midwife a highly qualified practitioner (may be a nurse) who looks after the pregnant woman

---

RESEARCH ACTIVITY

Carry out further research into the importance of antenatal care. Plan and carry out a questionnaire about the importance of antenatal care. Use this to help you plan and make a fact sheet or PowerPoint presentation that would encourage young girls to understand the importance of attending antenatal classes and clinics.

? QUESTIONS

Question 1

a What is antenatal care?

b List six advantages of antenatal care.

c How often should a pregnant woman attend antenatal clinic?

Question 2

There are different types of antenatal care available. Name and describe three of these.

Question 3

a What is a booking appointment?

b Where would the booking appointment take place?

c What is the midwife's role at the booking appointment?

Question 4

What is the role of the midwife:

a during pregnancy?

b during labour and birth?

c after birth?

Question 5

Describe the role of the following healthcare professionals:

a gynaecologist

b general practitioner

c health visitor

d paediatrician

e obstetrician

f physiotherapist

g dietitian.

Question 6

a What are pregnancy notes sometimes called?

b Name one advantage and one disadvantage of hand-held notes.

c List five pieces of information that would be found in a typical set of notes.

Question 7

a What is a birth plan?

b Suggest four things a pregnant woman might want to include in her birth plan.

Question 8

Antenatal or parentcraft classes are an important part of antenatal care. List six ways these classes can help the pregnant woman and her partner.

20 Testing During Pregnancy

Throughout pregnancy a wide range of different tests is available for the pregnant woman to have. The purpose of the testing is to enable healthcare professionals to find out if:

- the baby is developing as it should be
- the woman continues to be healthy.

The main types of test

There are three main types of test:

1 routine tests, which are carried out regularly during antenatal visits – these can include screening tests (e.g. blood test)
2 screening tests, which are carried out at specific times during the pregnancy
3 diagnostic tests, which are offered and carried out if screening tests indicate possible problems.

We will look at the first of these in this chapter. Screening and diagnostic tests are looked at in detail in Chapter 21.

Some of the tests carried out do not harm the baby in any way, others may cause the woman discomfort, and more invasive tests carry a small risk of miscarriage.

However, the technological equipment available today can pick up problems before a baby is born and can sometimes treat a baby while it is still in the uterus.

Routine tests

Routine tests are those carried out during the antenatal period to monitor the baby and woman, and to check that everything is progressing as it should be.

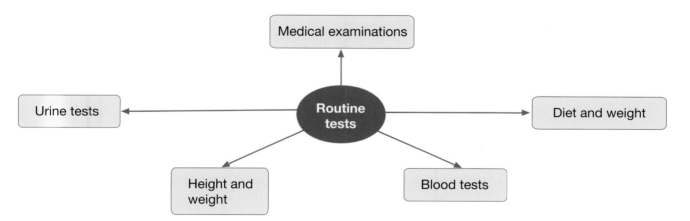

These routine checks are carried out at each antenatal visit and compared with those done at the booking-in visit. The results are compared to look for any changes that may indicate early signs of more serious problems, and to see if the woman and baby are growing and developing as they should.

Blood tests

Some women are scared at the thought of blood tests but when they realise the importance of them and experience only a minor discomfort they may believe that the knowledge gained from these results outweighs any discomfort.

What happens

A small sample of blood is taken at the first antenatal appointment. A further sample may be taken later in the pregnancy.

Information about the following potential problems can be found out from a routine blood test in pregnancy.

- **Anaemia:** a lack of haemoglobin in the blood due to lack of iron, causing the woman to be tired and listless. The woman is often treated with folic acid and iron tablets.
- **German measles (rubella):** whether the woman is immune to this disease. Rubella could be very dangerous to the unborn child, causing brain damage, blindness and deafness.
- **Blood sugar:** this indicates if the woman has diabetes, which can develop in pregnancy and disappear when it is over.
- **Sexually transmitted diseases (e.g. syphilis):** if these are evident they can cause untold damage to the foetus, and the mother can be treated to prevent this.
- **Blood group:** in case the woman bleeds excessively (haemorrhages) at birth or during the pregnancy. A transfusion can be given quickly if the blood group is known.
- **Rhesus factor:** if the woman has rhesus positive or rhesus negative blood.
- **Hepatitis B and C:** this virus causes liver disease. Both are treatable if the woman is found to have the infection.
- **HIV:** the woman can pass this to the baby via the placenta or during breast-feeding. Advice can be offered.

Blood tests can also be used to estimate the risk of Down's syndrome and neural tube defects such as spina bifida.

Urine tests

What happens

A small sample of urine is tested by the midwife.

Information about the following potential problems can be found out from a routine urine test in pregnancy.

- **Protein (albumen):** sign of infection or possibly a more serious condition later on in pregnancy, such as pre-eclampsia (see page 121).
- **Glucose (sugar):** may indicate diabetes (known as gestational diabetes during pregnancy). It is controlled by diet and possibly insulin.
- **Ketones:** may happen when the woman has hyperemesis (excessive vomiting), which will require hospital treatment. The woman may be dehydrated, requiring a drip to replace fluids and glucose. If left, the woman could go into a coma and die (ketosis).

Height and weight

What happens

The mother's height often gives the midwife an indication of her pelvic size. Height over 160 cm (5 ft) and more than size-three shoe indicate a normal-sized pelvis. The weight will be taken initially to use as a baseline to compare the weight of the woman as the pregnancy progresses (some areas do not weigh the woman).

- **Weight loss:** baby may have stopped growing, mother may be ill.
- **Weight gain:** sign of pre-eclampsia if excessive (most women will gain between 10 and 12.5 kg (22 and 28 lbs) during a normal pregnancy).

Blood pressure

What happens

The midwife or doctor will measure (and record) blood pressure (BP) at every antenatal check-up, usually electronically. This is then compared with the blood pressure measured at the booking-in visit and is done so that they know what is normal for the woman.

- The average BP range for a healthy young woman is 110/70 to 120/80.
- If your BP is above 140/90 on at least two occasions within a week, and you usually have normal BP, your doctor will make a diagnosis of pre-eclampsia.

Foetal heartbeat

What happens

Baby's heartbeat will be monitored at each visit to check it is alive and that the heartbeat is normal. This can be done in two ways:

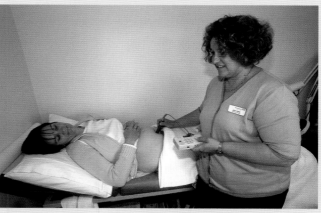

1. using a special ear trumpet called a pinard stethoscope

2. using a portable ultrasound called a **Doppler** or **Sonicaid**, which is placed against the abdomen.

Normal heartbeat for a foetus is 110–115 beats per minute.

Medical examination

This is usually carried out by the midwife and involves:

- **feeling the abdomen,** to check the position and size of the foetus, and whether it fits with the EDD
- **checking legs,** to look for swelling and signs of varicose veins.

 QUESTIONS

Question 1

What are the three *main* types of test available for the pregnant woman?

Question 2

Name five routine tests carried out during the antenatal period.

Question 3

What information can be found out from a routine blood test during pregnancy?

Question 4

What might the following found in a pregnant woman's urine indicate:

a protein?

b glucose?

c ketones?

Question 5

a What might it be a sign of if a pregnant mother gains excessive weight?

b How much weight does an average woman gain during a normal pregnancy?

Question 6

Name the serious condition that high blood pressure causes?

Question 7

a Name two ways that the baby's heartbeat can be found.

b What is the normal heartbeat per minute for a foetus?

21 Screening and Diagnostic Tests

Testing for abnormalities

Improved technology has enabled doctors to develop tests to detect and diagnose some abnormalities of the developing foetus. This may sound a straightforward procedure; however, it can involve the woman and her partner in many weeks of worry, waiting to find out the results of the tests.

The tests can, however, confirm that the baby is developing well and without abnormalities, which is reassuring for the parents. If a problem is detected the woman and her partner may have to decide whether or not to go ahead with a termination (to get rid of the unborn foetus). Some parents would not consider this option and therefore choose not to have further tests, which may carry a risk of miscarriage.

Women have the right to refuse screening tests. Some do, because they would not consider a termination. Others choose to have the tests even though a termination would be out of the question, so that they can prepare themselves and their family for the future.

The differences between screening and diagnostic tests

Screening tests

The following are the main screening tests used during pregnancy:

- ultrasound scans
- nuchal translucency test
- AFP (alphafetoprotein) test
- serum screening.

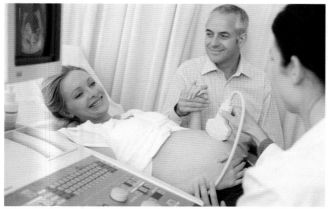

Ultrasound scan

Ultrasound scan

This is usually given at 11–13 weeks (sometimes called a 'dating scan') and 18–23 weeks, although an eight-week scan may also be offered.

What is it?

An ultrasound scan will give a picture of the baby on a TV-type screen. The picture will be in black and white, and the parents may find it difficult to identify the baby. Usually the woman requires a full bladder, she will lie on her back, gel will be placed on her abdomen, and a hand-held scanner will be rubbed back and forth on the abdomen until a picture appears on the screen.

Why is it given?

8 weeks	11–13 weeks	18–23 weeks
To: • confirm date of pregnancy • see if the baby is growing normally • see how many babies there are • see if it is an ectopic pregnancy.	Because the baby is bigger the face, limbs, spine and sex organs are seen more clearly. This scan will: • check the same things as the eight-week scan • determine the sex of the baby • confirm the number of babies present • see if there is a chance of Down's syndrome, if used to give a nuchal fold measurement (see below).	This is often called an anomaly scan. It looks in detail at features such as the heart, brain, kidneys, face, arms, legs, etc. This scan can: • check the position, size and function of the placenta • detect spina bifida, hydrocephalus (water on the brain), serious heart and kidney abnormalities, abnormalities of the baby's digestive system, cleft lip or abnormalities of the palate.

Advantages	Disadvantages
✓ It is very safe and does not affect or harm the baby. ✓ Does not hurt the woman – there is only the discomfort of a full bladder. ✓ Exciting for the parents to see the heartbeat and shape of their baby. ✓ Encourages the woman to bond early in the pregnancy as it becomes reality. ✓ Enjoyable experience.	✗ Accuracy depends on the quality of the machine being used and the skill of the person doing the scan. ✗ Ultrasound scans don't always pick up possible heart problems.

Doppler ultrasound scanning

Doppler scanning measures the blood flow between the placenta and the baby through the umbilical cord. It can usually be done at the same time as the 18–23-week scan and is useful for women who may have a risk of problems such as pre-eclampsia or very small babies.

3D and 4D scanning

3D and 4D scanning are now available, although they are expensive and often only available in private clinics. These allow lifelike and moving pictures of the baby to be seen.

Nuchal fold translucency (ultrasound) scan

This is a more accurate screening test for Down's syndrome. It may be offered at the same time as the 11–13-week scan.

What is it?

Using an ultrasound scan, this test measures the fold of skin on the back of the baby's neck as this is thicker in babies who have Down's syndrome. The measurement is fed into a computer along with the mother's age and any blood test results to work out if there is a risk of abnormality. If there is a positive result a CVS diagnostic test would be offered (see below).

Advantages	Disadvantages
✓ It is not invasive to the woman. ✓ No risk of miscarriage as a result of the test. ✓ It claims to have approximately 90 per cent detection rate (in combination with specific blood tests).	✗ It is not conclusive. ✗ It indicates only that Down's syndrome is possible. ✗ Not available everywhere, so the woman may need to have it done privately.

AFP (alphafetoprotein) test

What is it?

This is a blood test usually done between the 15th and 18th weeks of pregnancy to check how much alphafetoprotein is in the woman's blood.

High AFP could mean:

- may be more than 18 weeks pregnant
- may be more than one baby
- in rare cases, a problem with the spinal cord called spina bifida.

Low AFP could mean:

- may be less than 15 weeks pregnant
- the baby may have Down's syndrome (a higher risk with older women).

Advantages	Disadvantages
✓ May indicate the need for a diagnostic test without going straight to this risky procedure. ✓ It's like a warning test. ✓ Woman has not put her baby at risk. ✓ It's a simple blood test procedure.	✗ It suggests only that Down's syndrome is a possibility. ✗ The only way to be certain is to have cells from the foetus collected and tested. ✗ Could cause worry to the woman for no reason.

Serum screening

What is it?

This is also a blood test, which is used along with the mother's age to identify the possible risk of Down's syndrome. It is also known as Bart's, double or triple test.

The test measures the levels of three substances:

1. AFP
2. estriol (see AFP test)
3. human chorionic gonadotrophin.

If the results are negative it means that it is unlikely that Down's syndrome is present. A positive result means a higher chance of Down's syndrome. If a woman is at a higher risk she will be offered an amniocentesis test (see below).

Diagnostic tests

The main diagnostic tests used during pregnancy are:

- amniocentesis
- CVS (chorionic villus sampling)
- cordocentesis.

The amniocentesis test is more widely available than the CVS and there has been concern about the risk factors involved with it. Some evidence suggests the risk of miscarriage with CVS is similar to that with amniocentesis.

Amniocentesis test

What is it?

This test is usually carried out between the 15th and 17th weeks of pregnancy. It is done with the help of an ultrasound scan because it is very important that the position of the baby and the placenta are known. A hollow fine needle is passed through the skin of the abdomen, uterus wall and amniotic sac, and some amniotic fluid is drawn off. This is sent away to be tested. If the needle was to penetrate the placenta or foetus it might cause abnormalities.

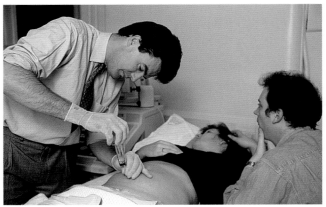

Amniocentesis

When is it offered?

It is usually offered to women over the age of 37 due to their higher risk of carrying Down's syndrome babies, or if there is a history of genetic disorders such as Down's syndrome. It will also be offered if the ultrasound scan has detected an abnormality or if the AFP, serum screening or nuchal translucency tests have indicated that there is a high risk of Down's syndrome.

What can it detect?

It can detect:

- Down's syndrome
- viral infections
- the sex of the baby (important for some sex-related genetic disorders
- lung developments of the foetus
- neural tube defects (e.g. spina bifida).

Advantages	Disadvantages
✓ If abnormality detected parents can prepare appropriately for the birth of the child. ✓ Some problems may be sorted out in the uterus. ✓ Parents have the choice to terminate. ✓ Parents may continue the pregnancy in a relaxed manner if the baby is proven to be free of some abnormalities.	✗ Takes two to five weeks to get the results and this is likely to be very worrying for parents. ✗ Once an abnormality is detected the foetus could be 20 weeks and the woman will have felt movements in the uterus, which may make termination of the pregnancy harder for her. ✗ A termination at this stage would require the woman to go through labour. ✗ As membranes are punctured there is a risk of miscarriage of a healthy baby. ✗ Foetus or placenta could be pierced or damaged. ✗ If the woman does not believe in termination, she may refuse an amniocentesis rather than risk a miscarriage.

Cordocentesis (foetal blood sampling)

What is it?

This is a test carried out when urgent information is needed round about 18–20 weeks of pregnancy. Like the amniocentesis test it is carried out with the help of an ultrasound scan. A hollow fine needle is passed into the umbilical cord to take a sample of the baby's blood, which is then tested.

When is it offered?

It is usually offered when other tests show that there is a high risk of the baby having an abnormality.

What can it detect?

It can detect:

- chromosomal problems
- blood diseases such as haemophilia, sickle cell and thalassaemia
- rhesus disease, in which case a blood transfusion is required.

Advantages	Disadvantages
✓ No anaesthetic needed. ✓ Results available within 48 hours.	✗ There is a 1–2 per cent risk of miscarriage. ✗ Small risk of infection. ✗ Can cause baby's heart to slow temporarily. ✗ May be a little uncomfortable for the mother. ✗ Can be done only later on in the pregnancy.

CVS (chorionic villus sampling)

What is it?

This is the only diagnostic test widely available to women between 10 and 11 weeks of pregnancy. As with the other diagnostic tests, it is carried out using an ultrasound scan. It involves taking a tiny sample of the placenta by inserting a fine needle through the wall of the abdomen or via the cervix. The sample is sent away to a laboratory and the results are usually received within seven to ten days.

When is it offered?

It is usually offered when other tests show that there is a high risk of the baby having an abnormality.

What can it detect?

It can detect:

- the same information as an amniocentesis test
- haemophilia and cystic fibrosis.

Advantages	Disadvantages
✓ Results are usually known within seven to ten days, therefore it is quicker than amniocentesis. ✓ If abnormality detected parents can prepare appropriately for the birth of this child or choose to terminate the pregnancy.	✗ There is a 1–2 per cent risk of miscarriage.

 KEY WORDS

Screening test a type of risk assessment; highlights the chance of having a baby with an abnormality such as spina bifida or Down's syndrome

Diagnostic test carried out if a screening test shows there is a possible risk, to find out if the baby actually does have a specific abnormality.

QUESTIONS

Question 1

a What is the difference between screening tests and diagnostic tests?

b List four of the main screening tests used during pregnancy.

Question 2

a What is an ultrasound scan?

b An ultrasound scan will be given at different stages of the pregnancy. Name two pieces of information an ultrasound scan will give at:

(i)   eight weeks of pregnancy

(ii) 11–13 weeks of pregnancy

(iii) 18–23 weeks of pregnancy.

c Outline three advantages of having an ultrasound scan.

Question 3

a What is Doppler ultrasound scanning?

b What is a Nuchal fold translucency test (ultrasound)?

c Name two advantages and two disadvantages of having this test.

Question 4

A blood test is carried out to detect the amount of AFP (alphafetoprotein) in the pregnant woman's blood. What could it mean if she has:

a a high level of AFP?

b a low level of AFP?

Question 5

Name the three main diagnostic tests used during pregnancy.

Question 6

a What is an amniocentesis test?

b Who would be offered an amniocentesis test?

c List five things that this test may show about the unborn baby.

d Name three advantages and three disadvantages of having this test.

Question 7

a What is a cordocentesis test?

b Give two advantages and two disadvantages of having this test.

Question 8

a What does CVS mean?

b What can this test detect?

c Name one advantage and one disadvantage of having this test.

RESEARCH ACTIVITY

Use the information in this chapter to produce an information leaflet about the importance of screening and diagnostic testing.

22 Problems During Pregnancy

The majority of women enjoy a healthy and trouble-free pregnancy and a safe birth. Occasionally the physical and emotional changes taking place can cause minor problems that need to be monitored so that they don't develop into more complicated issues.

The table below describes some of the more common minor physical problems that a pregnant woman may encounter.

Minor problem	Possible cause	Solutions
'Morning' sickness (which can actually happen at different times of the day or night)	• Hormone imbalance (disappears after the 12th week of pregnancy) • Severe sickness known as **hyperemesis** is more serious; a doctor should be consulted and urgent treatment is required	• If during the morning, eat a dry biscuit before getting up slowly • Eat little and often • Try eating crystallised ginger or drinking flat cola • If serious, hospitalisation may be needed
Feeling faint	• Lowered blood pressure • Moving quickly can have a brief effect on the blood supply to the brain • Blood sugar level may have dropped	• Eat smaller meals more frequently • Don't eat too many high-sugar foods as these cause a rise in blood sugar, extra insulin and then a rapid blood-sugar drop • Put head between the knees or lower than legs
Heartburn	• Burning feeling from the stomach into the throat caused by too much acid • Hormonal effects	• Take care taking antacids – consult a doctor first • Sit up in bed • Eat lots of small meals • Avoid pies and fatty foods
Urine leakage	• Towards the end of pregnancy and after the birth, coughing, sneezing and laughing can cause urine to leak • Weak pelvic floor muscles	• Pelvic floor exercises • Aqua-natal classes – exercise strengthens the pelvic floor
Frequent urination	• Passing water more often can be caused by hormones in early pregnancy • During later months, pressure on the bladder • With pain or burning may indicate an infection	• Empty bladder regularly • Visit doctor if pain or burning present
Swollen ankles	• More common in later months • If other swelling (i.e. face and hands) could be pre-eclampsia	• Put feet up • Don't wear tight socks, etc. • Walk • Rotate ankles • See GP if other swelling occurs
Backache	• More common in later pregnancy • Extra weight and enlarged uterus cause muscular strain • Hormones • Could be a kidney infection	• Avoid straining the back • Pick things up sensibly, bending at the knees • Sit in a straight, high-backed chair • Use lots of pillows • If kidney infection, consult GP • Exercise
Thrush	• A thick, white discharge from the vagina • Itching • Soreness • Bleeding • Painful to urinate	• A pessary and cream from the GP • No soap • Plain yoghurt • No tight clothing around the vagina

Complications with the pregnancy

There are occasions when some women during their pregnancy may have or develop complications that require close monitoring and special care. It is possible, through antenatal care, that a serious condition may be discovered; this could save both the woman's and the baby's life. This highlights the importance of attending antenatal clinics and classes.

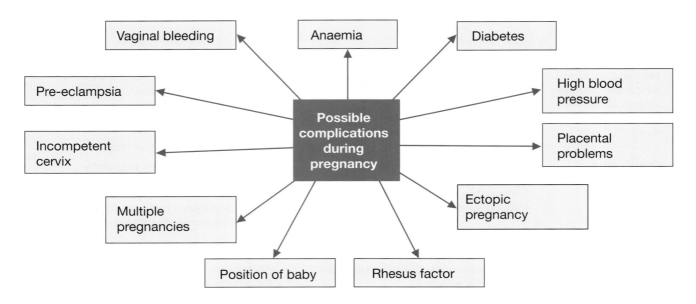

Anaemia

The problem

Mother feels very tired and lethargic. This can be quite mild or severe, and is caused by a lack of iron, which is needed to help make the red blood cells that transport oxygen to the cells of the body to reuse energy.

Treatment

- Iron and folic acid tablets.
- More foods containing iron, e.g. red meat, cabbage, spinach.

Diabetes

The problem

Diabetes occurs when the body has a problem producing insulin, which controls blood-sugar levels. If not treated it can make the diabetic nauseous or even pass out, and in extreme cases go into a diabetic coma.

Some women develop diabetes only during pregnancy and it disappears when the baby is born.

Diabetics have a higher risk of miscarriage and some risk of foetal abnormality.

Treatment

- It is important for known diabetics to consult their GP before planning to have a baby. They need to be carefully monitored during pregnancy as insulin will need to be adjusted to keep blood-sugar levels even.
- Diabetics need to be careful with their diet.

Ectopic pregnancy

The problem

Sometimes the fertilised egg implants itself into one of the Fallopian tubes (and sometimes into the abdomen) instead of the uterus, and begins to grow. As this is not the correct place it is very dangerous, and can cause a great deal of pain as well as vaginal bleeding.

Treatment

- This is a serious condition, which can cause internal bleeding. It will require hospital treatment and may lead to removal of the Fallopian tube.
- An ectopic pregnancy is not usually capable of surviving and in most cases will spontaneously miscarry.

Incompetent cervix

The problem

This is where the neck of the uterus – the cervix – is weak and cannot hold in the contents of the uterus, causing a miscarriage.

Treatment

- A small stitch will be put across the cervix to keep it closed. This will be removed towards the end of the pregnancy.

High blood pressure and pre-eclampsia

The problem

Some women already have high blood pressure while some develop it during pregnancy. Sometimes this is known as pregnancy-induced hypertension and may be a sign of pre-eclampsia.

Other symptoms include:

- swelling of face, hands and legs
- protein in the urine
- excessive weight gain
- severe pain in the abdomen later on in the pregnancy
- severe headaches.

Pre-eclampsia reduces the flow of blood to the placenta and can be quite dangerous for the unborn baby. If it is not checked it can lead to **eclampsia**. This is more dangerous because the woman may develop fits (convulsions), which can cause the baby to have a reduced oxygen supply.

Treatment

- Complete bed rest (sometimes in hospital) and tablets to lower blood pressure.
- Often women with pre-eclampsia may need to be induced to deliver the baby early, or may even need a Caesarean section to prevent eclampsia.

Multiple pregnancies

The problem

Although twins and triplets are not uncommon, fertility treatments can result in multiple births. This means the woman's body has to cope with additional work. There is a greater risk of anaemia, pre-eclampsia and babies lying breech, or transverse. Babies are often smaller and born prematurely, so will need special care.

Treatment

• Regular antenatal care and monitoring.

Position of baby

The problem

Most babies are born head first, with the back of the head facing the mother's abdomen. Sometimes babies settle into more unusual positions – for example:

• breech

• transverse

• posterior (see page 141).

Treatment

• Doctors and midwives will monitor this so that they will know how to deal with the birth.

Placental problems

The problem

Vaginal bleeding at about 28 weeks into the pregnancy can mean that there is a problem with the placenta. As this is the baby's lifeline it needs to be checked immediately. There are two possible problems:

1. **placenta praevia** – where the placenta lies across the cervix, blocking it

2. **placenta abruptia** – where some of the placenta becomes separated from the uterus.

Treatment

• Placenta praevia – hospitalisation and immediate care. Usually a Caesarean section will be needed to deliver the baby.

• Placenta abruptia – this is a very serious condition and requires immediate hospitalisation because the oxygen supply to the baby can be seriously affected. The baby may have to be induced or an emergency Caesarean section may be needed.

Rhesus factor

The problem

Blood can be either rhesus (Rh) positive or rhesus negative. If both partners have the same rhesus factor, there's no problem. If the mother is rhesus positive and the father is rhesus negative, there are no concerns either. However, if the mother is rhesus negative and the father is rhesus positive, it could lead to problems if the baby is also rhesus positive.

During pregnancy a small amount of the baby's blood crosses the placenta and Rh positive blood enters the woman's blood. The woman's blood thinks that there is something foreign in the blood and produces antibodies to fight it. There are not enough antibodies to harm the first baby but any further babies could be seriously affected.

Treatment

• A blood test for the rhesus factor early in pregnancy.

• If the first baby is Rh positive and the woman is Rh negative, the woman will be given a protective vaccination called Anti-D to destroy any of the baby's blood cells in her blood, so that they cannot harm any other babies.

Vaginal bleeding

The problem

This can be a sign of miscarriage if it is before 24 weeks. Later in pregnancy it could be a sign of an incompetent cervix or placenta praevia.

Treatment

• The woman must consult her doctor so that she can receive the appropriate treatment.

QUESTIONS

Question 1

a What is a possible cause of morning sickness?

b What is hyperemesis?

Question 2

What steps could the mother take to prevent the following minor physical problems:

a feeling faint?

b heartburn?

c swollen ankles?

d backache?

Question 3

Copy the table below and complete the information boxes.

Question 4

a Explain the problems that can be caused by a mother who has rhesus negative blood and a father who has rhesus positive blood?

b When is a blood test carried out to detect for the rhesus factor?

c Why would a woman be given an Anti-D vaccination?

Complication	Description of the problem	Treatment
Anaemia		
Diabetes		
Ectopic pregnancy		
Incompetent cervix		
High blood pressure		
Position of the baby		
Bleeding from the vagina		

23 A Healthy Diet During Pregnancy

One of the best starts to any pregnancy is to have considered and put into practice all the sound advice discussed in the chapters of this book that cover pre-conceptual matters (see pages 80–87). Much of that advice should be applied throughout the pregnancy together with the information presented in this chapter.

Eating your way through pregnancy

During pregnancy it is important to eat a varied and well-balanced diet because the growing baby will take all the nutrients it needs from its mother. If she doesn't eat a healthy diet she may have problems herself, although there is no need for a woman to 'eat for two' as this would lead to her putting on too much weight.

The following are the main nutrients that will contribute to a healthy pregnancy.

Animal protein

Why needed

Protein is needed for growth and repair.

Check it out!

✓ Always choose lean cuts of meat.
✓ Always cook meat thoroughly.
✓ Grill meat and fish rather than fry it.
✓ Eggs should be fresh and thoroughly cooked.
✓ No soft cheeses.
✓ A good idea is to read the label of pre-packed foods to check if they are suitable.

Animal proteins

Plant protein

Why needed

Protein is needed for growth and repair.

Check it out!

✓ The Department of Health advises that peanuts and peanut products be avoided while pregnant and breast-feeding as there may be a higher risk of the baby developing a peanut allergy.
✓ A dietitian would be able to give the woman specific advice about the best foods to eat to supply the protein she needs.
✓ A good idea is to look for a 'suitable for vegetarians' logo.

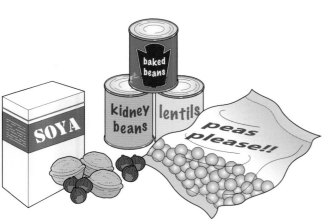

Plant proteins

✓ Another good idea is to steam or microwave fresh vegetables; better still, eat them raw, to preserve the vitamin C. Try smoothies and fresh fruit salad.

Vitamin C

Why needed

Aids the absorption of iron into the bloodstream and will also help to build a strong placenta. Assists with healthy gums; prevents them from bleeding.

Check it out!

✓ Vitamin C is lost during storage, preparation and cooking.
✓ Eat fresh fruit and vegetables.
✓ Twice as much vitamin C is required during pregnancy.

Iron

Why needed

✓ Important in the production of haemoglobin, which produces the red blood cells responsible for carrying oxygen to all living cells in the body.
✓ The foetus takes iron from the woman to store in its liver for after the birth; this lasts from four to six months (the reason for this is that there is no iron in milk!).
✓ During pregnancy more iron is needed by the mother, unborn baby and placenta.
✓ To prevent anaemia.

Check it out!

✓ Liver is an excellent source of iron but should be avoided because it contains very high amounts of vitamin A, which could harm the baby.
✓ A good idea is to eat iron-rich foods at the same time as foods high in vitamin C as this will help get the most iron from the food for the baby.

Calcium

Why needed

Calcium makes sure the bones and teeth of the foetus develop correctly. These start to form in the eighth week of pregnancy. Pregnant women need it because the calcium in their bones and teeth is used up by the baby.

Check it out!

✓ 'Fortified' means foods that are enriched by adding certain nutrients. It could be a legal requirement or carried out by manufacturers because they choose to.
✓ Many breakfast cereals are fortified with calcium.
✓ Twice as much calcium as normal is needed during pregnancy.
✓ A good idea is to choose dairy products that are low in fat (e.g. skimmed milk, low-fat cheese).

Folic acid

Why needed

Folic acid helps to form the neural tube correctly, which itself forms the spine and brain. It can prevent a condition known as spina bifida, where the spine can split and cause various degrees of disability (see pages 82–83).

Foods containing folic acid

Check it out!

✓ It is important to have lots of folic acid before conception and during the first 12 weeks of pregnancy when the baby's spine is developing.

✓ The Department of Health has produced a report recommending that all flour be fortified with folic acid to reduce further the number of children with spina bifida.

Fibre (NSP – non-starch polysaccharides)

Why needed

Fibre is not a nutrient but is important because it prevents constipation. Constipation can be a problem for the pregnant woman due to hormones causing the bowel to be sluggish. After the birth it can be traumatic if the mother is constipated while she has a sore perineum due to stitches.

Check it out!

✓ It gathers and collects all the waste material from the digestive system and helps to get rid of it on a regular basis from the body.

✓ Bran can stop your body absorbing essential nutrients.

The vegetarian mother

More and more women are opting for a vegetarian diet, and as long as they are sensible and aware of the potential dangers, there is no reason why they cannot continue with such a diet.

If a mother is on a vegetarian diet, as long as she eats dairy products, both she and the baby can remain healthy. However, she should increase both her protein and calcium intake. This can easily be achieved by eating more dairy products (e.g. at least three or four eggs per week and a pint of skimmed milk per day).

A very real problem arises if the mother is a vegan. A vegan does not eat animal products or by-products, and these are rich in vitamin B12. Since this vitamin is vital for the growth and wellbeing of a foetus, as well as being essential for the mother during breast-feeding, the mother must either add milk and eggs to her diet or take vitamin B12 supplements. This will have to continue throughout pregnancy and breast-feeding.

Tips for a healthy diet during pregnancy

- Eat a well-balanced diet.
- Avoid foods that are high in saturated fats.
- Try to grill or roast foods rather than fry them.
- Look for labels with 'healthy eating' logos and choose lower-fat foods where possible.
- Avoid excessive amounts of sugar and chocolate.
- Drink lots of water and fresh fruit drinks.
- Avoid alcohol and caffeine.
- Avoid processed foods, which are high in salt, sugar and fat, and have lots of added colourings, flavourings and preservatives.
- Avoid cook-chill foods and pre-cooked chickens (see page 129).
- Look for low-salt products, since salt is related to problems such as sweating and pre-eclampsia.

Foods that may harm the unborn child

The foods listed in the diagram below, and looked at in more detail in the table that follows it, should be avoided or prepared and cooked correctly, otherwise they could cause serious problems for the unborn child.

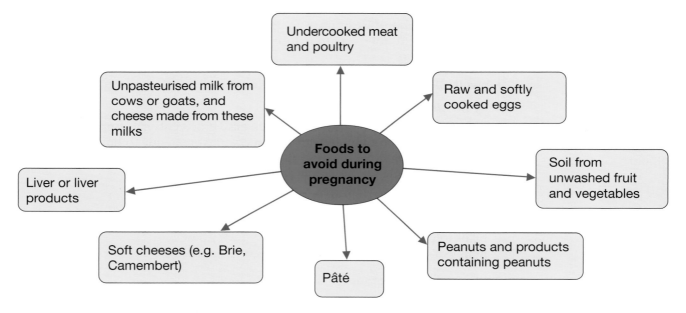

	Harmful foods	
Food	**Cause and problem**	**Possible effect on unborn baby**
Raw meat and poultry	Meat that is not cooked thoroughly may contain a parasite called **toxoplasmosis**. This can infect the pregnant woman, causing mild flu-like symptoms, but could severely damage the unborn baby. When eating cooked meat no blood should be visible and special care should be taken at barbecues.	• Miscarriage • Stillbirth • Hydrocephalus • Eye damage
Fruit and vegetables	The parasite toxoplasmosis is also found in soil. If raw fruit and vegetables or salads are eaten without being washed thoroughly the pregnant woman can become infected and the baby harmed. Care should be taken when eating in restaurants and cafés.	• As above
Eggs	Eggs contain **salmonella** bacteria, which can cause severe food poisoning. If eaten raw or only lightly cooked (e.g. softly cooked eggs), the bacteria will not be destroyed. Foods containing raw eggs (e.g. cheesecakes, meringues and mayonnaise) should be avoided.	• Miscarriage • Premature birth
Pâté Unpasteurised milk (from goats and cows) Products made from unpasteurised milk (e.g. goats' cheese, Brie, Camembert, Stilton)	These foods contain **listeria** bacteria. When being made they are not always heated to a high enough temperature to destroy this. Listeria can also survive at temperatures above 4°C. The temperature of home fridges is usually 1–4°C.	Listeriosis is a very rare disease, which can cause severe problems for the unborn baby, including: • miscarriage • stillbirth • meningitis
Cook-chill products	If cook-chill products are not reheated thoroughly they may contain bacteria such as **salmonella**, which could be harmful.	• Miscarriage • Premature birth
Liver and liver products (e.g. pâté)	Liver contains a lot of vitamin A. If too much vitamin A is eaten it remains in the body and will have a toxic effect on the baby.	Birth defects
Peanuts and products containing peanuts	Eating these can cause an allergic reaction. If there is a family history of allergy, or parents or children have hay fever, eczema or asthma, peanuts should be avoided during pregnancy and while breast-feeding.	Risk of passing on the allergy to the baby

QUESTIONS

Question 1

Why are the following nutrients needed in the diet and particularly during pregnancy:

a protein?

b vitamin C?

c iron?

d folic acid?

Question 2

Fibre is not a nutrient.

a Why is it important for the pregnant mother to have a good supply of fibre?

b What is another name for fibre?

Question 3

What dietary problems may arise for a pregnant vegan mother?

Question 4

Name six foods to avoid during pregnancy.

Question 5

a Which foods may contain the following:

   (i) toxoplasmosis?

   (ii) salmonella?

   (iii) listeria?

b What possible effects can the following have on the unborn baby:

   (i) toxoplasmosis?

   (ii) salmonella?

   (iii) listeriosis?

   (iv) too much vitamin A?

   (v) allergy to peanuts?

Question 6

Match the first and second halves of the sentences below.

1 Protein is required	to help form the spine and brain.
2 Folic acid is taken before conception	reaction, which can pass to the baby.
3 Calcium is required	and cook-chill products cause listeriosis.
4 Vitamin C helps	during pregnancy to prevent constipation.
5 Liver is an excellent source of iron	carry a parasite that causes toxoplasmosis.
6 Fibre, or NSP, is very important	iron to be absorbed in the bloodstream.
7 Listeriosis can cause	but should be avoided as it contains too much vitamin A, which is harmful to the baby.
8 Unwashed fruit, vegetables and raw meat	for healthy bones and teeth.
9 Peanuts can cause an allergic	a miscarriage or stillbirth.
10 Pâté and unpasteurised milk	for growth and repair.

24 A Healthy Lifestyle During Pregnancy

While a healthy diet during pregnancy can help to ensure that the mother remains healthy and provides all the nutrients needed for the baby to grow, develop and maintain good health, other factors need to be considered too, as noted in the diagram below.

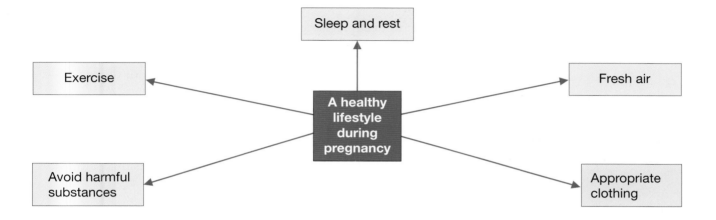

Harmful substances		
Substance	**Effect on foetus**	**Prevention**
Smoking – nicotine and other poisonous substances	• Reduces the amount of oxygen and nutrients received. • Greater risk of miscarriage, premature birth and stillbirth. • Greater risk of low birth weight. • Higher risk than normal of foetal abnormalities. • Possible breathing problems, bronchitis, pneumonia and other chest infections. • Increased risk of cot death. • Possible poor growth and learning difficulties.	Give up smoking before conception. Avoid passive smoking.
Alcohol	• Greater risk of miscarriage and stillbirth. • Possible retarded growth. • May damage the brain and nervous system. • Risk of being born addicted. • Risk of foetal alcohol syndrome (see page 86).	Avoid alcohol. Drink in moderation. Try fruit, juices and smoothies.
Illegal drugs (e.g. heroin, amphetamines, cannabis)	• Greater risk of miscarriage and stillbirth. • Greater risk of low birth weight. • Greater risk of abnormalities in development. • May be born addicted and suffer from withdrawal symptoms.	Stop using before conception. Seek medical advice.
Medicines and prescribed drugs	• May cause abnormalities.	Seek medical advice.

Couples who have followed the guidelines for a healthy lifestyle as part of pre-conceptual care (see pages 80–87) should continue to take the same care throughout the pregnancy. In particular, it is important that the pregnant woman avoids taking any harmful substances that could cross the placenta and affect the unborn baby.

A hop, skip and jump through pregnancy

Exercise and rest

It is important not to treat pregnancy as an illness. Sensible and regular exercise throughout the pregnancy will keep the body fit and muscles supple, which will be good preparation for labour and birth. It can also help to reduce stress and limit the amount of weight gained, making it easier after birth for the mother to get her figure back.

When exercising, especially during pregnancy, it's important not to push the body too far, and to start gently. Also, choosing something that is enjoyable means that it's more likely to be done regularly!

Swimming, cycling and walking are all excellent, and many health clubs run aerobic classes specifically for pregnant women.

Aqua-natal classes

These must not be confused with *antenatal* classes.

They are usually held at the local swimming pool and are led by an obstetric physiotherapist with the assistance of community midwives.

Because the exercise is done in water it is less strenuous on the joints and easier to concentrate on the places that matter (e.g. strengthening the pelvic floor muscles).

Other advantages

They:

- are a good way of meeting other mums-to-be and making friends
- are usually held when there are few other people in the pool
- concentrate on breathing exercises that assist with labour
- are a good way of getting to know community midwives.

An aqua-natal class

Pelvic floor exercise

The term 'pelvic floor' refers to the 'hammock' of muscles that support the bowel, bladder and uterus. These muscles come under a lot of strain during pregnancy, labour and birth. They often become weaker with the pressure of the baby as it grows. This can cause problems such as:

- urine leaking out when sneezing, coughing and/or laughing
- a heavy feeling between the legs.

It is therefore very important to exercise these muscles to keep them strong, both before and after the birth.

- Try to exercise the muscles frequently throughout the day; this can be done anywhere.
- Try to imagine stopping the urine coming out in mid-flow.
- Try to imagine stopping a bowel movement; squeeze the muscles.
- Hold the muscles for a few seconds, then let go.

Posture and backache

During pregnancy the posture of the expectant mother changes and this can cause her to stick out her bottom, causing the back to overarch. This contributes towards backache, and together with the pregnancy hormones that cause the muscles and ligaments to relax, the back muscles could very easily be strained.

Check it out!

✓ Protect the back by not making sudden movements.
✓ Don't bend over to pick up something – kneel or squat instead.
✓ Roll on to the side from a lying-down position and get up gradually.
✓ Stand tall, tuck in bottom, lift chest.
✓ Carry objects or lift from a squatting position.
✓ Sit up straight in a chair, supported by a cushion.

Rest, relaxation and sleep

Rest is particularly important during pregnancy and the pregnant woman should try to put her feet up for about an hour each morning and each afternoon, especially towards the end of the pregnancy. A good night's sleep is also essential.

The pregnant woman may feel very tired during the first trimester (first 12 weeks) of the pregnancy as the baby develops fully. She may feel unable to carry out everyday tasks, particularly if she is suffering from sickness. This is a time to listen to the body and to sleep as much as possible.

Often the second trimester (12–24 weeks) is the one where the woman 'blooms', has most energy and sleeps quite well. However, during the third trimester (24–40 weeks) the baby is growing fast and often decides to wake up at night, which disturbs the woman's sleep as the baby kicks and pushes. Also, the bladder requires emptying more regularly, so this also disturbs sleep. The mum-to-be should try adopting some relaxation positions, using lots of pillows to support the bump and legs. She should try to have a sleep in the afternoon or put her feet up, close her eyes and listen to some pleasant music.

Ways to relax	
• Watch television	• Phone a friend
• Read books	• Got out for a meal with partner
• Listen to music or the radio	• Join a local group
• Take exercise	• Go shopping – 'retail therapy'
• Have massage/reflexology	• Gentle yoga
• Walk in the park	• Talk over worries with partner
• Visit friends	

Clothing

During pregnancy the woman's body shape changes a lot. The breasts enlarge and the abdomen expands. Because of this, at some point clothing will be needed that is loose and stretchy, especially around the waist and across the abdomen.

Clothing will always be a matter of personal choice and, as well as comfort, pregnant women also want to look attractive and fashionable. However, it's important to remember that pregnancy clothes will only be worn for a reasonably short period of time, so it's best not to buy too many expensive items.

A well-fitting bra that gives good support is important. It should have wide straps, be adjustable and be the correct cup size.

It's also important to have comfortable, well-fitting shoes, as feet tend to ache and swell slightly during pregnancy. Ones with low or medium heels are best and will also help to prevent backache.

? QUESTIONS

Question 1

Describe five factors needed to ensure that the mother maintains a healthy lifestyle during pregnancy.

Question 2

a Give five effects of smoking on the foetus.

b What effect could alcohol have on the developing foetus?

c Illegal drugs can increase the risk of miscarriage. Name three other effects on the developing foetus of a pregnant woman taking illegal drugs.

Question 3

a Name three forms of exercise that would be suitable for a pregnant woman.

b What are aqua-natal classes?

c What is the 'pelvic floor'?

d Name two problems that can occur when the pelvic floor becomes weak.

Question 4

a Why can the back easily be strained during pregnancy?

b Give four ways to prevent back problems during pregnancy.

c Rest and sleep are very important for the pregnant mother. List six ways she could try to relax.

Question 5

Clothing is a matter of personal choice for the pregnant woman. Explain why she will need:

a a well-fitting bra

b comfortable, well-fitting shoes.

🔍 RESEARCH ACTIVITY

Design and produce a 'healthy pregnancy' booklet aimed at pregnant women. Include the following information.

The importance of:

- exercise
- sleep
- rest
- fresh air
- a healthy diet
- avoiding harmful foods.

25 *Where to Have the Baby*

One of the first issues an expectant mother faces once she has adjusted to the fact that she is pregnant is where to have her baby. What are the choices available and which will be the best for her?

The choices may depend on a number of factors:

- complications with previous deliveries
- complications with the health of the expectant mother, e.g. if she is diabetic
- personal circumstances, such as living on her own (there may not be anyone to help with the baby)
- the expectant mother's personal feelings
- medical advice.

There are two main choices of where to have the baby: at home or in hospital.

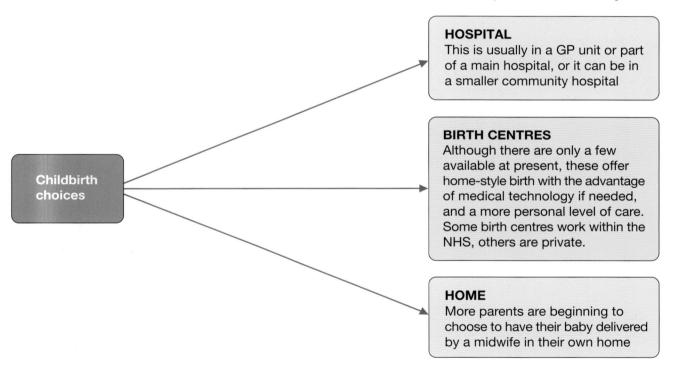

Childbirth choices

HOSPITAL
This is usually in a GP unit or part of a main hospital, or it can be in a smaller community hospital

BIRTH CENTRES
Although there are only a few available at present, these offer home-style birth with the advantage of medical technology if needed, and a more personal level of care. Some birth centres work within the NHS, others are private.

HOME
More parents are beginning to choose to have their baby delivered by a midwife in their own home

There are many advantages to having the baby at home or in hospital, and it would seem that the birth centre combines most of the advantages of both. However, there are circumstances where medical advice will be given to the expectant mother that may make her seriously consider the option of delivering the baby safely in hospital. These are listed in the diagram below.

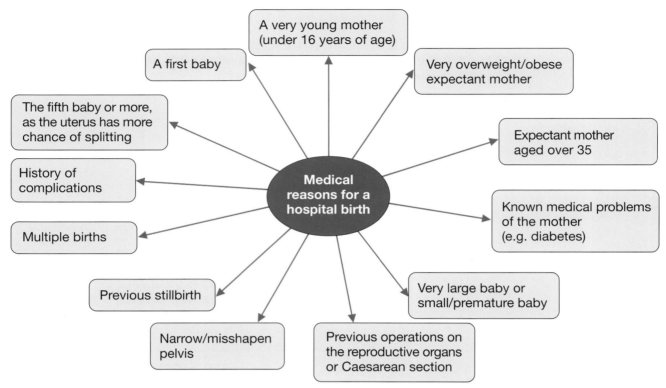

Medical reasons for a hospital birth:

- A very young mother (under 16 years of age)
- A first baby
- The fifth baby or more, as the uterus has more chance of splitting
- History of complications
- Multiple births
- Previous stillbirth
- Narrow/misshapen pelvis
- Previous operations on the reproductive organs or Caesarean section
- Very large baby or small/premature baby
- Known medical problems of the mother (e.g. diabetes)
- Expectant mother aged over 35
- Very overweight/obese expectant mother

Home birth

In Britain during the 1950s approximately one-third of all expectant mothers chose to have their babies at home. By the mid-1980s the number had dropped to around 1 per cent. Today this figure has risen very slightly because expectant women are considering home birth as an option. It is still more unusual, however, and the trend is to have babies in hospital.

Arrangements for a home birth

Some GPs are reluctant to support this and only agree if no complications have occurred with a previous birth and the expectant mother is in excellent health.

The following are requirements for a home birth:

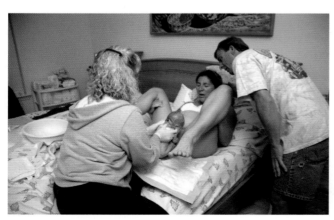

Midwife at a home birth

- a room that is clean, hygienic and has good temperature control
- a midwife must be booked
- a table is available for the midwife's equipment, which will include
  - a birth delivery pack (bought one month prior to the EDD)
  - oxygen
  - gas and air
  - resuscitation equipment to clear a baby's airways and assist breathing
- a comfortable bed for the mother
- a cot and equipment for the baby
- plastic sheets to protect the floor, carpet, etc.
- two buckets – one for waste and another for the placenta
- plenty of hot water.

Advantages of a home birth

✓ The family can be involved, particularly if there are other children.
✓ The woman will be more relaxed in her own home with familiar surroundings and without lots of people watching the birth.
✓ No transportation is required (unless a complication arises).
✓ The midwife can bring a TENS machine, gas and air, and pethidine to the house.
✓ There is the possibility of hiring a birth pool to have a water birth at home.
✓ Minimal monitoring is needed by the midwife.
✓ There is the freedom to move about anywhere within the home.
✓ A midwife could perform an episiotomy if required, and stitch and repair the wound at home.
✓ The mother can determine her own routines and mealtimes.
✓ She may experience less interference from medical staff and be able to deal with her newborn baby as she sees fit.
✓ She can build up a good relationship with the midwife who will deliver the baby at home.

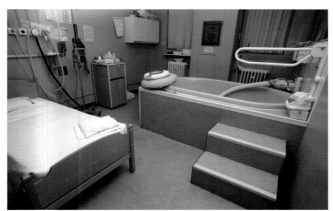

Delivery room in hospital

Hospital birth

By the end of the 1950s, over half of all births were taking place in hospital and, by the mid-1980s, 99 per cent of women were having their babies in hospital. The main reason for this change was the development and availability of a lot more advanced technological equipment in case complications arose during birth. There is always the worry with a home delivery that, if something goes wrong, there may not be enough time to get to hospital to save the mother or baby.

Different types of hospital care

The different types of NHS hospital care available will often depend on where you live. There is also the choice of care in a private hospital or with an independent midwife who will be able to link to NHS facilities if needed.

Advantages of hospital birth

✓ Trained staff are available, which is particularly important if a problem or emergency arises.
✓ If a baby becomes distressed, then the equipment and staff will immediately be available to deal with the situation, which could save the baby's life.
✓ Forceps, ventouse and Caesarean deliveries would have to be carried out in hospital.
✓ It is possible to have an epidural as pain relief only in hospital. This has to be administered by an anaesthetist.
✓ An emergency Caesarean section to save the baby's, and possibly the mother's, life could take place only in a hospital. This may require a general anaesthetic.
✓ The mother and her partner feel reassured by the 'safe environment' and secure in the knowledge that if an emergency arose they would be in the best place.
✓ After the birth the mother has the constant support of the midwives to assist with breast-feeding and any worries.
✓ Midwives can give the mother a break by taking the baby to the nursery.
✓ The mother will not become exhausted by having too many visitors.
✓ She will be comforted by the other mothers and they will have shared experiences and worries.
✓ There are none of the worries of home life – the telephone ringing, visitors arriving unexpectedly, shopping, cooking, cleaning, etc.

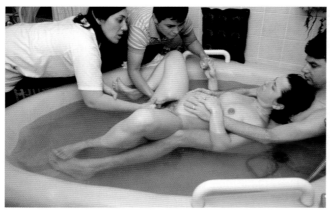

A birthing pool in a birth centre

Birth centres

Birth centres are small maternity units staffed and usually run by midwives. They may also be known as 'midwife-led units', 'birthing centres', 'maternity homes', 'maternity hospitals' or 'GP units'.

Most birth centres are independent, but more hospitals are now opening midwife-led birth centres alongside 'consultant-led' maternity units. Some centres can handle emergencies and, if necessary, it will be possible to transfer to a hospital. Currently, there are about 90 birth centres in England, and many more in Scotland and Wales.

Advantages of birth centres

- ✓ They may offer family accommodation.
- ✓ They often offer facilities not always available in local hospitals, such as family accommodation, water pools, complementary therapies and comfortable, low-tech birthing rooms.
- ✓ The mother is more likely to have one-to-one care from a midwife than in a busy hospital.
- ✓ Most centres offer antenatal care; some have regular clinics with a visiting obstetrician.
- ✓ They offer a high level of post-natal care.
- ✓ They offer a lot of support for breast-feeding.
- ✓ Research has shown that women giving birth in a birth centre are less likely to be induced, need pain relief, need forceps or a Caesarean or have problems breast-feeding.

Preparing for a birth centre or hospital birth

The expectant mother must prepare herself a few weeks prior to the EDD in case the baby arrives early. It is a good idea to prepare a bag even if a home delivery is planned, in case of an emergency. The following diagram lists the things that should be packed in this bag.

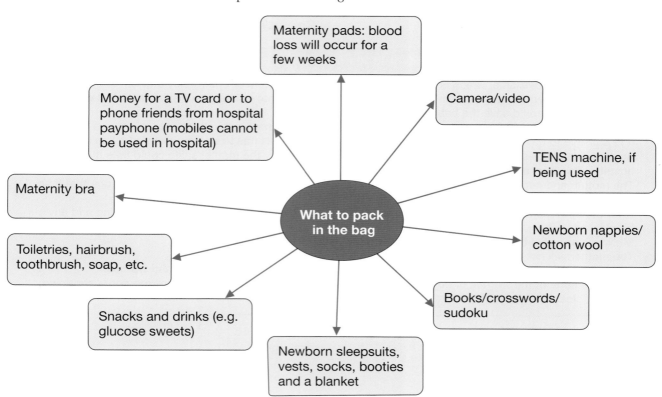

Maternity pads: blood loss will occur for a few weeks

Camera/video

Money for a TV card or to phone friends from hospital payphone (mobiles cannot be used in hospital)

TENS machine, if being used

Maternity bra

What to pack in the bag

Newborn nappies/ cotton wool

Toiletries, hairbrush, toothbrush, soap, etc.

Books/crosswords/ sudoku

Snacks and drinks (e.g. glucose sweets)

Newborn sleepsuits, vests, socks, booties and a blanket

KEY WORD

Obstetrician a doctor who specialises in the care of pregnant women during labour and immediately after birth

QUESTIONS

Question 1

There are two main choices of where to have a baby: at home or in hospital.

a Suggest five factors that may influence the choice of where to have a baby.

b Where is a woman most likely to have her baby today?

Question 2

A mother may choose to have her baby at home.

a List five requirements for a home birth.

b Give six advantages of having a baby at home.

Question 3

List eight advantages of having a hospital birth.

Question 4

a What are birth centres?

b Give four possible advantages of having a baby in a birth centre.

Question 5

What should an expectant mother pack in her hospital bag?

26 The Birth

The word 'labour' suggests physical and mental hard work. In this case it is used to describe the process of childbirth from the start of uterine contractions to the delivery of the baby.

It is also a time when the mother may go over the EDD and begin to worry whether everything is all right. In fact, the EDD is only a guideline and very few babies actually arrive on this date. *It is quite normal for a baby to be delivered between 38 and 42 weeks of pregnancy.*

Labour is divided into three stages (see pages 142–144). It is triggered by chemical messages, which cause a hormone called oxytocin to be released. This helps the cervix to soften ready for dilation.

The main aim of labour is to ensure that the muscular contractions of the uterus cause the cervix to open to 10 cm (4 in) in diameter, which enables the baby's head to drop down to the vagina and for the baby to be born.

Signs of labour

There are three main signs that labour is about to start.

1 Contractions: the woman may begin to have regular contractions as the muscles of the uterus begin to tighten and then relax. These will gradually occur closer and closer together, and become longer and stronger.
2 Waters breaking: this is when the bag of water (amniotic fluid) surrounding the foetus bursts. It may produce a trickle or a large gush. At this stage the woman will be advised to go to hospital to prevent risk of infection.
3 Show: this may happen as labour starts. It is a blood-stained plug of mucus that comes away from the cervix as the cervix becomes wider (dilates). There should not be a loss of blood. The purpose of this plug is to seal off the uterus during the pregnancy. As the cervix dilates the plug comes away.

Other signs may include:

• diarrhoea
• backache (a mild, period-type pain, which will increase and become more regular)
• nausea or vomiting.

Braxton Hicks contractions

These are sometimes called practice contractions and can sometimes be felt in the last three months of the pregnancy. As with 'real' contractions, the muscles of the uterus will tighten and relax – however, Braxton Hicks contractions usually last for only about 30 to 60 seconds.

Most women will recognise the signs of labour; however it would be advisable to telephone the hospital or midwife if there is any doubt. At this point an expectant woman will either go to the hospital or, if she has arranged a home confinement, the midwife will make a visit, to prepare for the first stage of labour.

Hospital confinement

• The expectant woman (and her partner) will report to the admission desk.
• She will either be admitted to the antenatal ward if she is in the early stages of labour or the delivery suite if the labour is more advanced.

- The expectant woman will be assessed by a midwife. She will have her temperature and blood pressure taken and her abdomen felt, and will be connected to a foetal heart monitor, which will record the baby's heartbeat as well as her own.
- A vaginal examination will establish how dilated the cervix is.
- The midwife will examine and discuss the birth plan, the chosen options for pain relief and the position the expectant mother wishes to give birth in.
- A midwife will ask her to put on a hospital gown or an old one of her own.

Position of the baby

Before the birth of a baby the midwife will be able to feel the mother's abdomen to find out what position the baby is in. An ultrasound scan will also give this information.

The usual position for a baby to be delivered is with the head down and the back of the head towards the mother's abdomen (see the illustration below). The head becomes engaged in the pelvis ready to descend down the birth canal.

However, there are other positions that the baby may lie in and although it may be possible for the doctor to attempt to turn the baby, sometimes it will resume its original position.

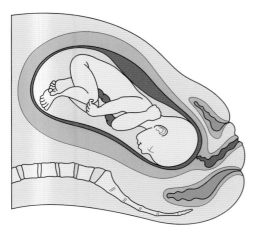

Normal birth position

Alternative positions

- Breech: babies in the bottom or feet-first position can be delivered vaginally although they can cause problems. Often forceps are used to deliver the head quickly.
- Transverse: the baby lies across the abdomen instead of vertically.
- Oblique/posterior: the baby lies at an angle in the abdomen, often with face and limbs towards the mother's abdomen.

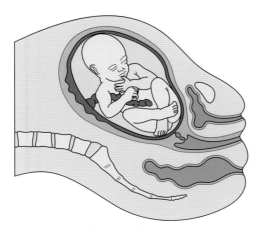
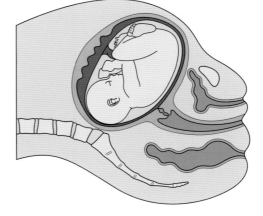

Breech and transverse birth positions

It is obvious that babies presenting themselves in the above positions may require assistance during the delivery. A transverse or oblique presentation would require a Caesarean section, as might the breech baby if the delivery was proving difficult or the mother requested it.

Positions during labour

Unless she has been hooked to a monitor or given an epidural, the mother should try to keep as mobile as possible. While it is more common to see women lying on their beds during labour there are other positions that may be more comfortable, as noted in the table below.

Standing up and moving around	This is especially good during the first stage of labour. It is easier to push, and gravity helps the baby move down the birth canal.
Sitting	This could be on a chair or birthing ball, and allows the expectant mother to 'bear down' more easily.
Kneeling on a bed or cushion	Either on a bed or on cushions on the floor, leaning forward on to a birthing ball. This can help when contractions are strong.
On all fours	This helps to protect the back and is a good position when tired. It is thought to be the best position as it helps to deliver the baby's head slowly.
Lying down	This should not be on the back but on the left side in the recovery position, with upper arms and legs resting on pillows.
Squatting	Leaning with the back against birth partner or bed/chair. This helps to open the pelvis and makes pushing more effective.

The three stages of labour

No two births are the same but all women go through three stages when giving birth, as detailed in the following table.

The first stage

This begins with early symptoms showing that labour has started. Its purpose is to open up the cervix gradually.

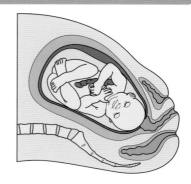

- With a first baby, this stage could take 12 to 15 hours until delivery.
- The waters (amniotic fluid) may break.
- Contractions tighten and shorten, become stronger, more regular and last longer; at this stage more pain relief is required.
- The mother is asked to be as active as possible, to try to remain upright and take a warm relaxing bath.
- The mother may adopt various positions rather than lie on her back, although she may be restricted by the type of pain relief she has chosen.
- Contractions gradually open up the cervix until it is fully dilated to a width of 8–10 cm (3–4 in).
- If the head has not already engaged in the pelvis it will do so now.
- Towards the end of this stage the contractions can become intense and the mother may become agitated.
- This stage can cause sweating, vomiting, shivering and loss of bladder and bowel control caused by the pressure from the baby's head.

The transition stage links the first and second stages of labour and it is at this point that the contractions speed up and become very intense.

The second stage

This begins when the cervix is fully dilated and ends with the birth of the baby. This stage can take about an hour and can be exhausting for the mother.

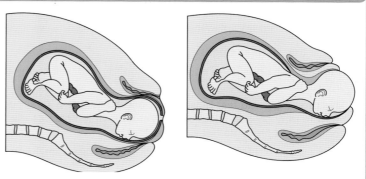

- The partner can rub the mother's back, massage her and offer words of encouragement.

- Once the cervix has fully dilated to 10 cm (4 in) the vagina and cervix become one and are called the **birth canal**.

- The baby's head will now be able to move down the birth canal.

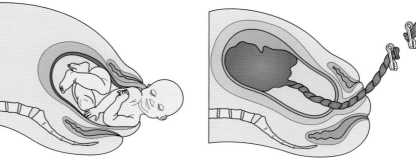

- During this stage each time a contraction starts the mother will push down. This is helping the baby move along the birth canal.

- The mother should rest between contractions.

- Once the head can be seen, the midwife will ask the mother to stop pushing and blow out to allow the baby's head to be born gradually. When the head can be seen at the vaginal opening this is known as **crowning**.

- It is important for the head to be born slowly so that the perineum (skin between the vagina and the rectum) does not tear. Sometimes an **episiotomy** (cut) might be needed.

- Once the head has been delivered, the hard work is over.

- Some babies require the mucus to be cleared from their mouth and nose, and others require some oxygen.

- The baby's body will be turned to allow one shoulder at a time to be delivered.

- The rest of the body then slides out easily.

- The umbilical cord is clamped and cut, and this ends the second stage of labour.

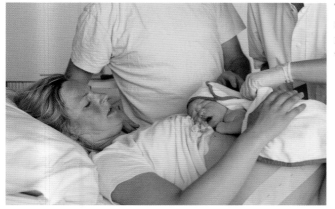

Mother and baby immediately after the birth

The baby can be placed straight on to the mother's stomach if that is what she has requested. The baby may be a little messy with blood and perhaps the white greasy substance called vernix will be evident.

The third stage

This stage begins when the baby is born, and is completed after the membranes, cord and placenta have been delivered.

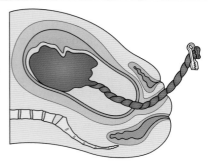

- This is the shortest stage.
- After the baby has been born, more contractions will push out the placenta (afterbirth).
- This process could last between 20 and 60 minutes. To speed it up, the midwife may give an injection of **syntocin**, which causes the uterus to contract and prevents heavy blood loss.
- At this stage if a tear has occurred or a cut (episiotomy) was required because the perineum would not stretch, the midwife will carry out stitching using a local anaesthetic.

Examination of the placenta

A thorough examination of the placenta will take place once it has been expelled (pushed out). It will be dark red, like liver, weigh 470 g (1 lb) and be the size of a large dinner plate. It should be intact (complete) as it is dangerous to leave any inside the mother as this could cause an infection or a haemorrhage (large blood loss). The placenta belongs to the mother and if she wishes to keep it she can. However, it is most common in this country that the hospital will dispose of the placenta.

The role of the birth partner

For many couples, sharing the experience of the birth of their child is exciting and very special. Some men, however, are naturally nervous about being present throughout the birth. They may:

- worry about how they will react to seeing their partner give birth
- be concerned about the safety of both their partner and the baby
- be concerned about what role they can play and whether they will be 'in the way'.

Although most women want someone to be with them, some are not comfortable with the idea of their partner seeing them give birth. For various reasons, others may not be able to have their partner with them. For these reasons some couples may decide to have another birth partner present – perhaps a close relative or friend.

Birth partners are welcomed in most maternity units and can also stay if the woman is having a Caesarean section. However, if there are serious complications, they may be asked to leave.

How the birth partner can help

The birth partner can help by:

- giving encouragement and support
- monitoring the number of people involved
- offering cool drinks/ice cubes/snacks
- reminding the expectant mother to go to the toilet
- making sure that the nurses/doctors are aware of what the mother has included in her birth plan

- talking/playing simple games to occupy the time
- helping with breathing and relaxation techniques
- massaging back, shoulders and legs
- suggesting different positions to stay comfortable
- sponging down face, neck, arms
- timing contractions.

KEY WORDS

Birth canal when the vagina, cervix and the uterus become one channel

Contractions shortening and tightening of the muscles of the uterus during labour

Crowning where the baby's head can be seen at the entrance to the vagina

Dilation the widening of the cervix during labour

Perineum the skin between the vagina and the anus

Transition stage the stage of labour that links the first and second stage

RESEARCH ACTIVITY

1. Carry out a survey of mothers to discover:
   - who was present at the birth
   - what role the partner played during the birth
   - how the partner supported the mother.

2. Interview three mothers about their childbirth experiences. Record your findings as a case study.

QUESTIONS

Question 1

a During childbirth what does the word labour mean?

b What is the main aim of labour?

c Name and describe the main signs that labour is about to start.

d What is a Braxton Hicks contraction?

Question 2

When the expectant mother arrives at the hospital to have her baby she will report to the admission desk.

a Describe where she will go from there.

b What assessments will be carried out by the midwife?

c What will the midwife discuss with the mother and her partner?

Question 3

a What is the usual position for a baby about to be delivered?

b Name and describe three other positions the baby may be lying in.

Question 4

a Labour is divided into three stages. Describe what happens during the:
   (i) first stage of labour
   (ii) second stage of labour
   (iii) third stage of labour.

b Why is the placenta examined after it has been pushed out of the body?

Question 5

Many women choose to have a birth partner with them. How can a birth partner help during labour?

27 Types of Pain Relief

Everybody's labour is different and so everybody's need for pain relief varies.

The main purpose of pain relief during labour is to ease the pain and discomfort the expectant mother may experience, ensuring that the baby is unharmed.

As the EDD (estimated delivery date) gets closer an expectant mother will begin to focus on such questions as:

- Will labour hurt?
- Will I show myself up by screaming with pain?
- How will I cope with the pain?
- How will I make the best choice for the baby and myself?

Some expectant mothers aim to have as little interference as possible during labour whereas others are happy to consider as many pain relief options as possible. There is no doubt that the more relaxed and active a woman can be during labour, the more easily labour will progress, since tension can cause greater pain as the muscles contract.

Pain relief options

There is a wide variety of pain relief options and these can be discussed during antenatal classes, clinics and parentcraft classes.

Methods of pain relief generally fall into two categories:

1 those that use drugs
2 those that are drug-free.

There are a number of advantages and disadvantages to consider when selecting the type of pain relief for labour. Although an expectant mother and her partner may have investigated fully all the options available, written them into the birth plan and felt happy with their choice, it may be wise for them to keep an open mind, since their views may change as labour progresses.

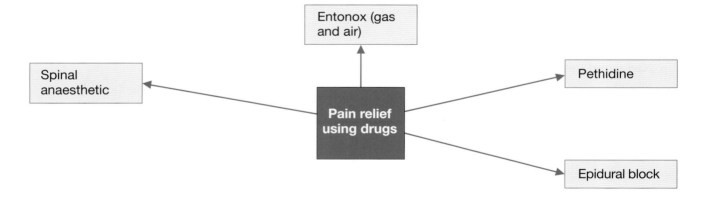

Pain relief using drugs

Pethidine

How it works

This is an opiate drug that is given by injection. It makes the mother feel very sleepy and relaxed, but it does not take away all the pain.

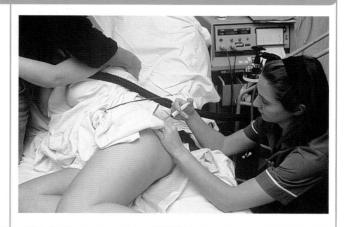

Advantages

✓ It can be given quickly and it works quickly.
✓ It makes the muscles relax.
✓ The pain is more bearable because the mother feels confident.
✓ It is more useful during the early stages of labour, allowing the mother to rest and sleep.

Disadvantages

✗ The drug crosses the placenta and if given too close to the birth causes the baby to be sleepy, which can delay breast-feeding and may also affect the baby's breathing.
✗ The mother does not feel in control.
✗ Can cause the mother to feel drowsy, nauseous and disorientated.
✗ Does not completely take away the pain.
✗ Should not be given too close to the birth as the mother needs to be alert.

Spinal anaesthetic

How it works

This is similar to an epidural but involves injecting local anaesthetic beside the spinal nerves, which results in total pain relief in the lower part of the body.

Advantages

✓ A smaller amount of anaesthetic is needed.
✓ It works within five minutes, therefore it is useful in emergencies (e.g. Caesarean and forceps).

Disadvantages

✗ It is not suitable during labour as it is usually effective for only about an hour and a half before wearing off.

Entonox (gas and air)

How it works

A mixture of nitrous oxide (laughing gas) and oxygen is inhaled through a mask or via a mouthpiece. It can act quickly and wears off quickly but it does not take away all the pain.

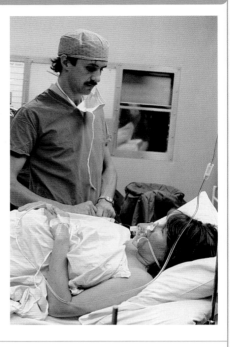

Advantages

✓ Mother controls how much of the drug she wants.
✓ The feeling quickly wears off when the mother stops breathing it in.
✓ Takes only a few seconds to start working.
✓ It can be used safely as pain relief in a water pool.
✓ Provides a distraction for the mother.
✓ It will not harm the baby.
✓ It can also be used when an epidural is being administered and when a mother is being stitched after an episiotomy.

Disadvantages

✗ Does not take away all the pain.
✗ Some women do not like the feeling of a mask over their face (sometimes a mouthpiece can be used).
✗ It can make the mother feel sick, light-headed and a little 'drunk'.
✗ Not as effective during the second stage of labour where the mother has to push her baby out.
✗ Cannot easily move around.
✗ Can be difficult to get the timing right.

Epidural anaesthetic

How it works

This is carried out by an **anaesthetist**, a doctor specialising in giving pain relief.

The mother will be asked to curl up in a ball or lie on her side and keep very still.

A local anaesthetic will be injected at about waist level. The anaesthetist will then find the correct space in the spine to place a hollow needle. This needle contains a fine plastic tube (catheter), which will be left in place and taped to the mother's back. The needle is removed.

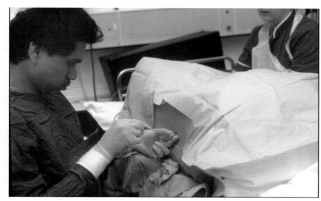

The liquid anaesthetic is then injected into the space in the spine where the nerves of the uterus, birth canal and spinal cord meet.

The mother will not feel pain because the brain will not receive the messages.

It can take up to an hour before the mother feels completely numb from the waist down, therefore it may need to be planned in advance.

This method is useful during a long, difficult and painful labour.

Advantages

✓ Takes away all the pain from the waist down.
✓ The mother will be calmer and feel less stressed, which will benefit the baby.
✓ Unlike the after-effects of pethidine the mother will not feel drowsy after the birth.
✓ A mobile epidural, which uses less local anaesthetic, enables a mother to move about and possibly walk with help. These are now more widely available in hospitals.
✓ If timed correctly the epidural can begin to wear off and a mother can assist with the second stage of labour.
✓ If the epidural is still effective after the birth, the mother could be stitched if necessary.
✓ A Caesarean section could be given under epidural.

Disadvantages

✗ The mother cannot feel contractions and therefore has to rely on the midwife to tell her when to push.
✗ After labour some mothers wished they had experienced how a contraction felt and feel cheated.
✗ Often forceps are required to assist delivery for Caesarean sections.
✗ A complication may occur that can cause the woman to have a very severe headache, which can last for a week. This could affect the early days with the newborn baby, particularly if the mother is attempting to breast-feed.
✗ Electronic foetal monitoring will be required (see page 155). This means that it is more difficult for the mother to move about. This can slow down labour and the baby's oxygen supply.
✗ An intravenous drip will be needed because epidurals lower the blood pressure and the drip will help to keep the blood pressure high.
✗ A catheter may need to be fitted in the urinary tract because the mother will not be able to pass urine.
✗ Some women suffer from backache for a long time afterwards.
✗ Epidurals are not always effective.

Drug-free pain relief

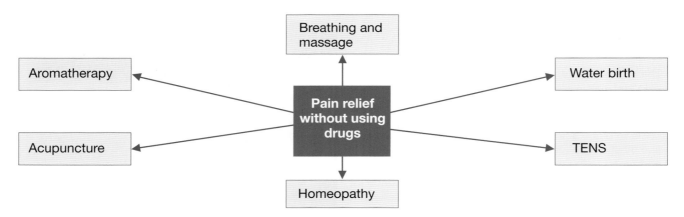

Breathing techniques

How it works

A mother may learn to control the timing of contractions and the breathing techniques through aqua-natal classes, and other antenatal classes, yoga, etc.

Advantages	Disadvantages
✓ Gives the mother a focus, and can distract from the pain and help her to feel relaxed. ✓ It does not affect or harm the baby or mother. ✓ The partner can assist with such techniques prior to and during the birth.	✗ This will not take away the pain. ✗ If a mother panics she may totally forget all that she has learnt.

TENS (transcutaneous electrical nerve stimulation)

How it works

This uses small electrical impulses to block pain.

Four or six small electrodes are attached to the back where nerve messages travel. Using a small monitor the mother can control pain by pushing a button that causes electrical impulses to be sent through the electrodes.

The impulses interfere with the pain messages and **endorphins** are released. These are the body's natural pain-relieving chemicals.

A TENS machine may need to be hired if it is going to be used at home.

Advantages	Disadvantages
✓ It is drug free. ✓ It is useful during the early stages of labour, giving the mother something to focus on. ✓ It can be used at home. ✓ The mother can control it. ✓ There are no side effects to the mother or baby as it is external. ✓ The mother can move about freely.	✗ The TENS machine can become less effective as the first stage of labour progresses. ✗ If the pain becomes intense it may have little effect. ✗ The mother is unable to take a bath or shower. ✗ TENS cannot be used during a water birth. ✗ It cannot be used by women with heart conditions or pacemakers.

Water birth

How it works

The mother enters a special pool provided by the hospital (or the pool can be hired privately), which is filled with warm water and kept at a constant temperature.

When a baby is born into water it still gets oxygen through the umbilical cord and doesn't need to breathe until lifted out of the water, usually within 30 seconds of being born.

Advantages	**Disadvantages**
✓ The muscles of the back and abdomen relax. ✓ Encourages the release of endorphins. ✓ The partner can enter the birthing pool and help.	✗ There is a possible risk of infection. ✗ The midwife may not be able to monitor the baby as effectively. ✗ It does not take away all the pain.

Homeopathy

How it works

These are natural products that may use herbs. An example is caulophyllum (blue cohosh), which reduces the length of labour.

Advantages	**Disadvantages**
✓ Before the birth a homeopath can supply a number of natural remedies to be used during labour.	✗ None are known.

Aromatherapy

How it works

This is the use of essential oils.

Advantages	**Disadvantages**
✓ Before the birth a homeopath can supply a number of natural remedies to be used during labour.	✗ The oils must be mixed by a qualified aromatherapist as some are considered unsafe for use during birth.

Acupuncture

How it works

At specific energy points fine, sterilised needles are placed under the skin.

The needles are placed along **meridians** (lines in the body) where the Chinese believe the chi (life force) energy flows.

Advantages	Disadvantages
✓ This helps to relieve pain and relax the body. ✓ It encourages the production of endorphins. ✓ In some areas acupuncture is available through the NHS.	✗ The angle of the needles makes it difficult to sit or lie down.

KEY WORDS

Anaesthetic a substance that prevents the feeling of pain

Anaesthetist a doctor who specialises in giving anaesthetics

Endorphin the body's natural pain-relieving chemicals

Injection giving a medicine or drug in liquid form directly into the body through a vein

Local anaesthetic an anaesthetic that takes away the feeling of pain in a small area only (e.g. the back)

RESEARCH ACTIVITY

1. Carry out a survey to find out which type of pain relief was the most used by pregnant mothers during labour. Find out how effective the pain relief was for them.

2. Find out more about different methods of pain relief. Use your research to design and produce a PowerPoint presentation on the benefits of different types of pain relief during labour and birth.

QUESTIONS

Question 1

a Pain relief for a mother giving birth falls into two categories. What are they?

b List four types of pain relief using drugs.

Question 2

Copy the chart below and identify four types of pain relief that are available without using drugs. Explain how each works and name two advantages and two disadvantages of these methods.

Question 3

a Describe how a TENS machine works.

b Name two advantages and two disadvantages of using a TENS machine.

Question 4

a What is a water birth?

b List three advantages and three disadvantages of using a water birth for pain relief.

Drug-free pain relief	How it works	Two advantages	Two disadvantages

28 Technology and Medical Assistance During the Birth

Technology can be defined as 'scientific knowledge and skills that can be applied practically'. Today technology helps to ensure that all babies have a very good chance of being born safe and well. It is because of advances in technology that few women nowadays lose their child, or their own lives, while giving birth. The infant death rate in the early 1900s was very high and many women had large families – perhaps nine or ten children – but only a few of these would survive until their first birthday.

While childbirth is one of the most natural aspects of life, it is possible for complications to occur and for science to be needed.

Reasons to assist with the delivery

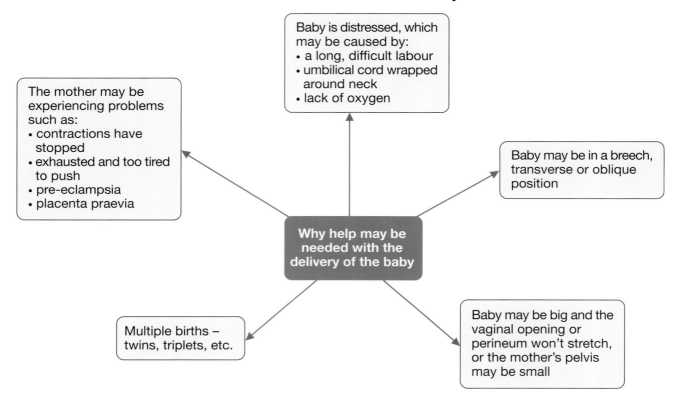

Baby is distressed, which may be caused by:
- a long, difficult labour
- umbilical cord wrapped around neck
- lack of oxygen

The mother may be experiencing problems such as:
- contractions have stopped
- exhausted and too tired to push
- pre-eclampsia
- placenta praevia

Baby may be in a breech, transverse or oblique position

Why help may be needed with the delivery of the baby

Multiple births – twins, triplets, etc.

Baby may be big and the vaginal opening or perineum won't stretch, or the mother's pelvis may be small

How delivery might be assisted

Induction

Sometimes a doctor will decide that a woman needs to have her labour artificially started. This is called induction or being induced.

This usually happens if:
- the mother's contractions have started and then either slow down or stop
- the mother has high blood pressure
- the baby is failing to grow and thrive
- the mother has gone over her EDD (estimated delivery date) by one to two weeks; after this time the placenta becomes less efficient in supplying oxygen.

Membrane sweeping

Once a doctor decides that a baby might need to be induced it is now common for a membrane sweep to be offered first. This can be done by a doctor or midwife. While a routine internal examination takes place they will simply 'sweep' a finger around the cervix (neck of the womb). The idea is to separate the membranes around the baby from the cervix – this releases hormones, which often start off labour within 48 hours. If this does not happen, induction will be carried out.

How induction takes place

1 By pessary or gel, which is inserted into the vagina. This works by softening, or 'ripening', the cervix. This can take more than one attempt. Once labour has been triggered it usually progresses as expected.
2 The hormone syntocin (an artificial form of oxytocin) is given through a drip into the mother's arm. This can have quite a dramatic effect, causing the mother to go into labour quickly without a gradual build-up of pain. Labour can be slowed down by controlling the flow of the drip.
3 Breaking the waters: an instrument called an amni hook is used to break or rupture the membranes surrounding the baby to allow the amniotic fluid (waters) to be released and trigger labour. This does not hurt as the membranes contain no nerves.

Episiotomy

An episiotomy is a cut in the perineum to avoid a tear into the rectum. Many women are frightened at the prospect of having an episiotomy. This is not performed unless necessary and may prevent the risk of a serious tear to the perineum. It may also be used to speed up the delivery if the baby is distressed or lacking oxygen.

A local anaesthetic will be given in the perineum prior to the cut being made. The cut will be stitched up after the third stage of labour.

Monitoring during labour

When a mother goes into the early stages of labour, she will be monitored by the midwife either at home or in hospital to ensure that the baby's heartbeat is regular and that it is not distressed. The midwife will know if the baby is distressed because its heartbeat will be too fast or too slow. The heart rate of a

Listening	Continuous external foetal monitoring	Internal foetal monitoring
• The midwife listens using a foetal stethoscope, which looks like a trumpet, or a hand-held Doppler ultrasound. • Where the mother is having a water birth, a hand-held waterproof ultrasound monitor will be held against her abdomen. • Only the midwife can hear the heartbeat, not the mother.	• Two electrodes are strapped to the mother's abdomen using stretchy bands. • This measures the baby's heart rate. • It also measures the contractions – how long they are and the gap between them. • The mother will have to lie down or sit for the monitoring.	• A tiny electrode is placed through the vagina onto the scalp of the baby (or its bottom if breech). • This can be used only if the waters have broken. • The mother will have to lie quite still for this type of monitoring.

baby is approximately twice the speed of the mother's. If the heartbeat slows it may be that the blood vessels of the placenta are being squashed.

There are three main ways to monitor the heartbeat, as outlined in the table below.

The issue of monitoring can be discussed with the midwife during antenatal classes and can be included in the birth plan.

If all is going well then monitoring may be needed only from time to time. However, if any doubt exists about the baby's condition the internal foetal monitor will gave a clearer, more accurate picture of what is happening.

There are a number of advantages and disadvantages to monitoring, as listed in the table below.

Advantages	Disadvantages
✓ If there is a problem with the heartbeat and the baby is distressed, emergency treatment such as a Caesarean section can be carried out immediately to save the baby's life. ✓ When mother feels tired it can reassure her and keep her going. ✓ It gives an indication that all is well, which can be very comforting.	✗ It can prevent mother being active and walking about. ✗ The heartbeat monitor can affect people emotionally and make them feel scared. ✗ The internal monitor can be painful to insert for the mother and has to be placed on to the baby's scalp.

Forceps

The main reasons for using forceps are:

- the mother is exhausted

- the mother and/or baby are showing signs of stress

- the baby is in a breech position, or it is very small or a premature birth, and the baby's head requires protection

- the mother has had an epidural and can't feel when to push the baby out.

The forceps are two curved metal instruments a little like sugar tongs. The mother will be given a local anaesthetic and an episiotomy. The forceps are placed into the birth canal and around the baby's head, allowing the doctor to pull gently with each contraction and assist the delivery.

This instrument can leave some bruising and red marks on the baby's face. The mother's cervix must be fully dilated to use it.

Ventouse extraction

Sometimes known as a vacuum suction, this can be used for similar reasons to a forceps delivery although the cervix does not have to be fully dilated.

It is not suitable for a breech or premature baby because in such deliveries the baby's head needs to be protected.

A small cap connected to a vacuum pump is placed on to the baby's head and used to pull out the baby. This may cause a slight swelling and bruising on the baby's head, and sometimes the top of the head may be a little misshapen. All such symptoms will gradually subside.

Vacuum extractors used in ventouse extraction

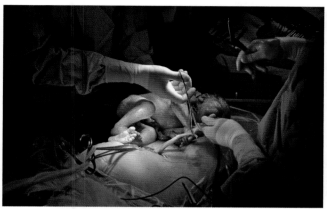

Caesarean section

Caesarean section

A Caesarean section is a surgical operation that usually takes 30–40 minutes. The operation is named after Julius Caesar, whose own mother died during childbirth and her uterus was opened to pull him out.

Where possible, doctors prefer to perform Caesareans under epidural or spinal anaesthetic as there are fewer risks to mother and baby.

A bikini-line cut is made into the mother's abdomen and uterus, and the baby is lifted out. The mother is given an injection of oxytocin to help delivery of the placenta and the wound is then stitched.

The scar from a Caesarean usually fades within three to six months and most parents feel that it was worth the discomfort to ensure the safe delivery of their child.

Sometimes a Caesarean may be planned during the pregnancy because some problem has been identified. This is known as an elective Caesarean.

If labour has started and the doctor decides that a Caesarean is needed because there is a problem, this is known as an emergency Caesarean.

Elective Caesarean section

This is a planned Caesarean and can be carried out using a local anaesthetic, such as an epidural or spinal block. This means that the mother will be conscious (awake) for the operation but will feel nothing from the waist down.

Elective Caesareans may be planned for the following reasons:

- if the mother is having a multiple birth
- if the baby is too large to pass through the pelvis (this sometimes happens with diabetic mothers)
- if the mother's pelvis is misshapen or deformed
- if the placenta is covering the entrance to the birth canal and the baby cannot emerge without the placenta tearing and haemorrhaging (bleeding); this is known as placenta praevia
- if the mother is HIV positive; this is to protect the baby from infection
- if the mother has active genital herpes (cold sores on the vagina); this can seriously affect newborn babies
- if the baby is in a difficult position
- if the mother has fibroids or an ovarian cyst.

Advantages	Disadvantages
✓ No after-effects of a general anaesthetic (e.g. sickness, drowsiness).	✗ The mother has not experienced a 'normal' delivery and may feel cheated.
✓ The father or partner can be present.	✗ She is likely to be very sore after the operation and may find breast-feeding uncomfortable.
✓ The baby can be held by the mother straight away.	✗ The mother may be unhappy to have a scar but these usually heal quickly and are rarely permanently visible.

Emergency Caesarean section

An emergency Caesarean section may be needed for the following reasons:

- the foetal heart rate could drop, which may cause a lack of oxygen to the foetus
- the mother may be very distressed after a long labour that is not progressing
- if the mother is bleeding this might indicate placenta problems
- if the mother has very high blood pressure
- if the umbilical cord falls down ahead of the baby.

If the mother has had an epidural as a form of pain relief for her 'normal' delivery and it is still effective, then she could go ahead with an emergency Caesarean section as previously mentioned. However, there is not always time to set up an epidural and a general anaesthetic is given instead.

Advantages	Disadvantages
✓ The baby is delivered safely. ✓ The mother's life may have been saved. ✓ If the mother was scared she would know nothing about the operation.	✗ The parents may miss the birth completely. ✗ They may feel robbed of those first precious moments. ✗ The mother may feel sick and drowsy after the anaesthetic.

 QUESTIONS

Question 1

a List five reasons why help might be needed with the delivery of the baby?

b What is 'membrane sweeping' and when might it be done?

Question 2

a What is induction?

b List four reasons why induction may take place.

c Describe three different ways induction might be carried out.

d What is an episiotomy?

e Explain why an episiotomy might be carried out.

Question 3

a Why does the midwife monitor the baby's heartbeat?

b Name and describe three ways of monitoring the baby's heartbeat.

c List three advantages and three disadvantages of monitoring the baby's heartbeat.

Question 4

a Give four reasons why forceps are used.

b Describe what forceps look like and how they are used.

Question 5

A ventouse extraction is carried out for similar reasons to a forceps delivery.

a Who is the ventouse extraction not suitable for?

b Describe how a ventouse extraction takes place.

Question 6

a What is a Caesarean section?

b Describe the following:

(i) an 'elective' Caesarean

(ii) an 'emergency' Caesarean.

c Give four reasons for a planned Caesarean.

d List two advantages and two disadvantages of having a Caesarean using a local anaesthetic (e.g. an epidural).

e A general anaesthetic may have to be used to perform an emergency Caesarean section. What are the advantages and disadvantages of this type of Caesarean section?

29 The Newborn Baby

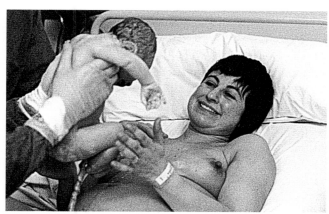

Mother and her newborn baby

A newborn baby will usually be handed straight to the mother so she can hold her baby closely. It is a very emotional time for both parents and their child, and if all appears well the medical personnel will give the parents a few moments with their baby before the first health check is carried out.

The appearance of a newborn baby

All babies look beautiful to their parents but in truth a newborn baby is at its least attractive immediately after birth. Many look strangely old with a wrinkled face and skin, and some look bruised if they have had a difficult birth. Within a few hours they begin to look quite different.

Characteristics of a newborn baby

Fontanelle	This is on the top of the head. It is a soft spot where the four pieces of bone that form the top of the skull have not yet joined together. There is a pulse that can be seen beating beneath the scalp.
Umbilical cord	The stump of the umbilical cord can be seen. It will shrivel quickly and will drop off within a few days.
Head	The head is big compared to the rest of the body – about a quarter of the size of the overall body length. It is often misshapen because of the journey through the birth canal.
Eyes	May be puffy and closed most of the time.
Milia	These are small white spots on the face. They are caused by the temporary blockage of small sebaceous glands. They will disappear of their own accord within a few days.
Arms and legs	These will remain bent and drawn up close to the body as if the baby were still in the uterus.
Vernix	The skin may be covered in a whitish lard-like substance called vernix – especially in the folds of skin. During pregnancy this acts as a natural barrier cream to protect and lubricate the baby's skin.
Lanugo	There may be a fine covering of downy hair on parts of the body. This is called lanugo and will soon fall off.
Hair	Some babies have a lot of hair when born while others are bald.
Genitals	A new baby's genitals may be large in proportion to the rest of the body. This is because of the effects of hormones from the mother that have crossed the placenta.
Birthmarks	Birthmarks are harmless and do not cause the baby pain. Most birthmarks are just abnormal collections of small blood vessels under the skin. They often need no treatment and disappear in time. The most common are stork bites, strawberry marks and Mongolian spots.

Immediately after birth babies will be given a number of routine checks. These checks are carried out by an experienced midwife or a doctor.

Apgar testing

Between one and five minutes after they are born, babies will be examined to check their Apgar score. The Apgar test is carried out to ensure the lungs and heart are functioning and the responses are sound. Each of the five elements shown in the diagram below is given a score of nought to two. A score of over seven means the newborn baby is in excellent condition. If the score is under four the baby may require some resuscitation.

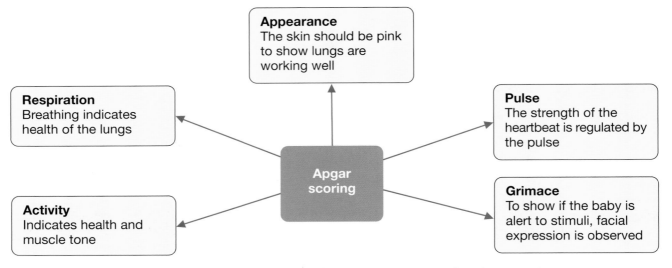

The table below shows the scoring system used in Apgar testing.

	0	1	2
Appearance	Blue or pale arms and legs	Body pink and blue	Completely pink
Pulse	No pulse	Under 100 beats per minute	Over 100 beats per minute
Grimace	No response to stimulus	Small movement or whimper to stimulus	Vigorous crying
Activity	Limp and floppy muscles	Some movement, bending of arms and legs	Active/moving
Respiration	Absent	Slow and irregular	Breathing well

Other checks

Other checks that take place immediately after birth are:

- making sure the facial features and body proportions are normal
- checking the spine for defects
- examining the anus, legs, fingers and toes
- checking the umbilical cord has two arteries and one vein
- weighing the baby (average 3.5 kg/7.5 lb)
- measuring head circumference (average 35 cm)
- measuring body length (average 50 cm)
- checking the baby's temperature (average 37°C).

When these initial tests have been carried out babies will be left to get used to their new world.

Birth weight

As noted above, the average weight of a newborn baby is 3.5 kg (7.5 lb). The weight is always recorded because it helps the doctor to see how the baby is progressing.

It is not unusual for a newborn baby to lose between 5 and 10 per cent of its weight (about 175–350 g) in the first few days of life. This is mainly because of loss of fluids until the mother's milk supply is established. Most regain this weight within ten days and then gain 150–200 g per week.

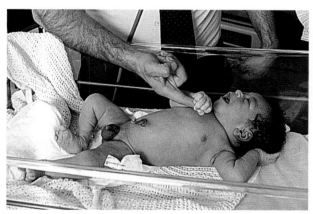

A paediatrician carries out checks on a one-day-old baby

Other tests

Within 24 hours a paediatrician will carry out a more detailed examination. The parents will be encouraged to attend the examination so they can ask the doctor questions and discuss any queries they may have. The examination generally begins at the head and works its way down to the toes.

Head and neck

The neck will be checked for cysts or swellings, and the mouth for abnormalities such as a cleft palate. Although rare, some babies are born with a tooth. If this happens the tooth is likely to be removed because there is a risk it may fall out and be swallowed. The eyes, ears and nose will be checked, and the fontanelle and skull bones looked at. The fontanelle is generally known as the 'soft spot' and is an area where the skull bones have not yet fused together, in order that the head may pass easily down the birth canal.

Chest and heart

The heart and lungs will be checked with a stethoscope. Many babies' hearts make odd sounds in the days immediately after birth because the workload of the heart increases substantially when they are controlling their own circulation. These odd sounds will normally disappear very quickly.

Arms and hands

Each arm will be checked for a pulse and for strength and movement. The doctor will look at the palms of the hands. Two major creases are normal. If there is only one then the doctor will look for other physical abnormalities.

Abdomen

By pressing gently on the abdomen the size and shape of the liver and spleen will be assessed. It is not unusual for these to be slightly enlarged. The lower spine and anal area will also be checked for congenital abnormalities.

Hips, legs and feet

The test to check the hips is called Barlow's test. It is used to find out whether the head of the thighbone is unstable or lying outside the hip joint.

The test is carried out by laying the baby on his or her back with the feet pointing towards the doctor. Each leg will be checked for size and length, and then each hip will be gently flexed and moved away from the midline of the body with backward pressure. If the hip is prone to dislocation a click can be felt. If the hips do dislocate, treatment will begin to correct the problem because if left untreated it can lead to problems later in life.

Treatment usually includes manipulation and perhaps a splint. Barlow's test does not hurt the baby but many babies cry at the unusual movement. Sometimes a baby's ankle may be turned in. This can also be corrected by manipulation or a cast.

Nerves and muscles

The baby's arms and legs will be put through a range of movements to check they are not too stiff or too floppy. This tells the paediatrician about the condition of the nerves and muscles. The paediatrician will also check that the baby's inborn reflexes are present and that head control is normal.

At the end of the first week two further tests are likely to be carried out on the baby: the PKU, or Guthrie, test and the thyroid function test.

PKU, or Guthrie, test

PKU stands for phenylketonuria. This is a rare disorder that prevents the baby from metabolising a chemical called phenylalanine, which is present in most protein foods, including milk.

Babies are given the Guthrie test routinely to check the levels of phenylalanine in the blood by pricking the heel and obtaining a blood sample. If phenylketonuria is diagnosed the baby will be given a special milk substitute, and at weaning a very low-protein diet will be recommended.

Thyroid function test

The thyroid function test is carried out to check if the thyroid gland is producing the hormone thyroxin. Thyroxin is needed for normal growth and development. Low levels of thyroxin may lead to poor growth. The condition is easily remedied by giving the baby regular supplements of the hormone as early as possible. Like the PKU test, this is a simple blood test.

Vitamin K and the newborn

A small number of newborn babies are at risk of a rare disease called Vitamin K deficiency bleeding. Half of babies that suffer this may die or suffer brain damage due to bleeding into the brain. This disease can easily be prevented by an injection of vitamin K (which helps blood to clot), which is given immediately after birth. It can also be given 'by mouth' (orally).

Reflex actions

Babies display a number of movements called reflexes, or involuntary reflex actions. Movements of this kind are inborn and made automatically without thinking. The most important reflexes are:

- swallowing and sucking
- rooting
- grasp
- walking
- startle
- falling
- blinking.

The swallowing and sucking reflex

When a finger is placed in the mouth babies will automatically suck, so when the breast or teat is put in the mouth they respond by sucking, then swallowing.

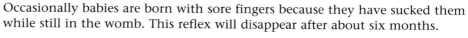

Occasionally babies are born with sore fingers because they have sucked them while still in the womb. This reflex will disappear after about six months.

The rooting reflex

When a finger is gently stroked across the face, babies will turn their head as if in search of a nipple or teat. This reflex will disappear after six weeks.

The grasp reflex

Babies will automatically curl their fingers round an object when it is placed in the palm of their hand. This reflex will disappear at about three months.

The walking reflex

When held in a standing position with the soles of the feet touching a firm surface babies will make stepping movements and attempt to straighten their bodies.

This same reflex will cause babies to 'step up' if their shins are placed against a firm surface. This reflex will have disappeared by six months.

The startle reflex

When loud noises or bright lights startle babies they will close their hands into fists, bend the elbows to bring the arms towards the shoulders and they may cry.

The falling/Moro reflex

The falling reflex is also known as the 'Moro' reflex. Sudden movements affect the neck and make babies feel that they may be dropped. This feeling causes them to open their hands wide and throw their arms back, then bring the arms together as though they were catching a ball.

The blinking reflex

Newborn babies respond to light and touch by blinking. When a light is shone directly into babies' eyes they will blink.

The senses of a newborn baby

The newborn baby uses the senses to begin to learn about the world it has been born into.

Senses collect information and bring it to the central nervous system. At birth a baby possesses the following senses:

- vision/sight
- hearing/sound
- smell
- taste
- touch.

These senses will become more refined as the baby develops.

Vision/sight

It is believed that babies' eyes have been developing since the very early weeks of pregnancy and by the 26th week they can be opened and shut. At birth babies can see but eyesight is limited: they can focus on objects between 25 and 30 cm away, so it is very important to hold babies close when talking to them. Outside this range, objects may appear to the baby as blurred and fuzzy.

In the early days babies like to look at faces, lights and patterns, and strong contrasting colours will attract them. Newborn babies with white skin usually have blue-grey eyes, while babies with dark skin usually have brown eyes. The colour of the eyes will change over the first few months. True colour may not be defined until as late as 12 months.

The eyes will be examined as part of the six-week developmental check. Babies at this stage will be expected to focus on a face and follow a moving object. Many babies appear to have a squint, where the eyes move independently of each other. This is normal as they are still gaining control of their eye muscles.

Newborn baby's hearing being checked

Hearing/sound

Long before babies are born they are able to hear and can recognise familiar sounds. These sounds will be very comforting during the birth and will be recognised among the great jumble of sounds after the birth. The most recognisable and comforting sound for babies is their mother's voice and they can easily pick this out from other voices.

To encourage the development of hearing it is important that babies are talked to. Hearing is an essential part of speech development. Babies quickly begin to copy the mouth movements of whoever is speaking to them and by the age of six months babies will be able to associate sound with a cause, and be able to locate the direction from which sound is coming.

To check babies are hearing well, stand behind them and clap your hands, ring a bell or click your fingers – they should turn round in response to the sound.

Smell

Newborn babies are sensitive to smell. They recognise the scent of their own parents/carers quickly and will be comforted by familiar smells. Babies who are breast-fed will smell the milk when near the breast and try to root for the nipple. If babies come into contact with an unpleasant smell they will try to turn away from it.

Taste

Babies show that they find tastes pleasant or unpleasant by facial expression or by trying to expel the taste from their mouths.

Touch

New babies are very sensitive to touch. As we know, they are comforted by close human contact, and like to be cuddled and stroked.

Needs of the newborn

New babies are very vulnerable, and need lots of love and care. They also need the things noted in the following diagram.

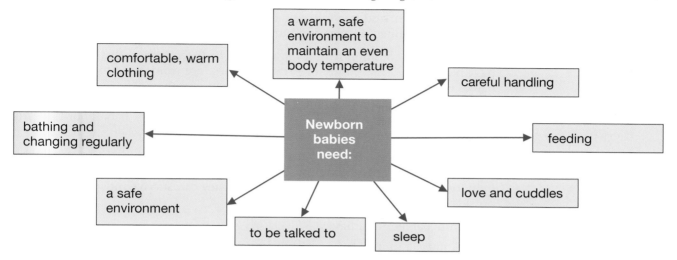

Newborn babies need:
- comfortable, warm clothing
- a warm, safe environment to maintain an even body temperature
- careful handling
- bathing and changing regularly
- feeding
- a safe environment
- love and cuddles
- to be talked to
- sleep

KEY WORDS

Cleft palate a slit in the roof of the mouth

Congenital abnormalities abnormalities that are present at birth

Paediatrician a doctor who specialises in the treatment of diseases in children

Dislocation when bones meeting at a joint are displaced (put out of position)

Manipulation skilful handling

Metabolising when food is broken down by chemical and physical changes, enabling the body to grow and function

Splint a rigid support to maintain the hips, legs or feet in a set position

QUESTIONS

Question 1

What are the following:

a the fontanelle?

b lanugo?

c milia?

d vernix?

Question 2

a Name and describe the five different elements of the Apgar test.

b Explain how the Apgar test is scored.

Question 3

a What is the average weight and length of a newborn baby?

b Other than weight and length, describe four other checks that are carried out immediately after the birth.

Question 4

a What is Barlow's test and why is it carried out?

b Describe four other tests carried out by a paediatrician.

c Why is a vitamin K injection recommended for newborn babies?

Question 5

a Name and describe the seven reflex actions.

b Name the five senses.

c Why is it important to hold babies close when talking to them?

30 Special Care Babies

Some babies need extra care when they are born and may be taken to a special care baby unit (SCBU), also known as a neonatal intensive care unit. Here they can be kept warm and free from infection, and the most up-to-date technology and specially trained doctors and nurses can help them survive.

By far the most common reason for babies to be taken into special care is if they have been born prematurely or pre-term. These are words used to describe babies who are born *less than 37 weeks* into the pregnancy. One in 18 babies in Britain is premature. Today, with the great advances in technology and the highly skilled and dedicated teams in special care baby units, babies born as early as 22 weeks can survive.

From approximately 12 weeks into pregnancy babies are already formed but the next 28 weeks are spent maturing. Therefore, babies born early are going to need help for their maturation to continue before they can survive independently outside the womb.

Premature babies often have:

- weak muscle tone and do not show much movement
- low calcium, iron and blood-sugar levels
- sealed eyes
- underdeveloped lungs, which cause breathing difficulties; this is known as respiratory distress syndrome (RDS)
- an inability to suck and swallow
- difficulty in digesting milk
- difficulty in regulating body temperature because they have little body fat
- a yellow tinge to the skin (jaundice)
- red and wrinkled skin
- a disproportionately large head in comparison to the rest of the body
- a weak immune system, which means the body cannot defend itself adequately and there is an increased risk of infection.

If the parents have been to antenatal classes they will probably have been shown the special care baby unit, so if their baby needs special help they will already be familiar with it.

Special care baby units can initially be very daunting places with so many incubators, monitors and IV lines (see below), and with a high ratio of doctors and nurses to babies.

Effect on the family when a baby is in a special care baby unit

Having a baby in the special care baby unit can be traumatic for parents, who after months of waiting for the arrival of their newborn child, with hopes and dreams of taking the baby home to the newly decorated nursery, find that life becomes centred around hospital visits and nights spent sleeping at the hospital bedside. The diagram below notes some of the effects on the family this might have.

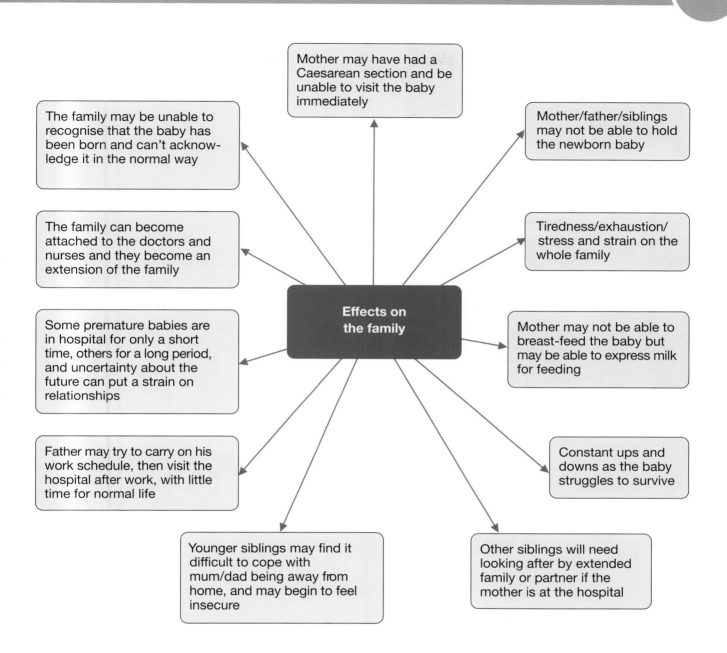

Mother may have had a Caesarean section and be unable to visit the baby immediately

The family may be unable to recognise that the baby has been born and can't acknowledge it in the normal way

Mother/father/siblings may not be able to hold the newborn baby

The family can become attached to the doctors and nurses and they become an extension of the family

Tiredness/exhaustion/ stress and strain on the whole family

Effects on the family

Some premature babies are in hospital for only a short time, others for a long period, and uncertainty about the future can put a strain on relationships

Mother may not be able to breast-feed the baby but may be able to express milk for feeding

Father may try to carry on his work schedule, then visit the hospital after work, with little time for normal life

Constant ups and downs as the baby struggles to survive

Younger siblings may find it difficult to cope with mum/dad being away from home, and may begin to feel insecure

Other siblings will need looking after by extended family or partner if the mother is at the hospital

Special care baby unit equipment

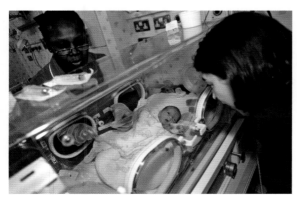

Incubators

An incubator is an enclosed, thermostatically controlled cabinet made of transparent material with a 'lid' that opens and 'portholes' in the side. The incubator filters and humidifies the air, and maintains a constant temperature. Babies may lie on sheepskin or a soft sheet to keep them warm and protect their delicate skin.

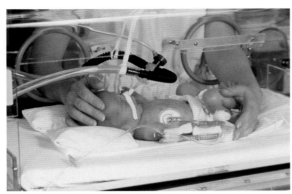

Ventilators

Ventilators help babies to breathe until their lungs are mature enough to cope on their own.

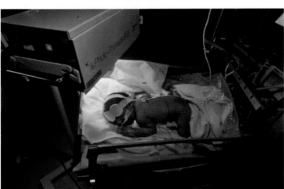

Monitors

Monitors are soft sensors that can be attached to the baby's skin. These sensors can monitor breathing, the heartbeat and the amount of oxygen in the bloodstream. The sensors are linked to monitors/display screens. If the signals suggest the baby needs attention, an alarm bell sounds to alert staff.

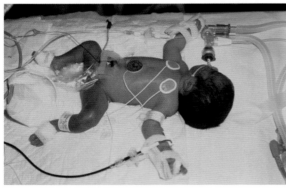

Intravenous (IV) lines

IV lines, as they are commonly known, are needles connected to tubes that pass measured doses of fluid and drugs directly into the baby's system. The tubes are connected to a pump that regulates the flow. Babies who are unable to digest food naturally may be fed intravenously.

Nasogastric tube

If a baby is unable to suck and swallow, food may be given by a tube, which goes up through the nose and down into the stomach. If the mother of a premature baby wishes to breast-feed her baby she can express (squeeze out) her milk and it can be fed to the baby in this way.

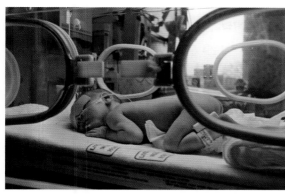

Light therapy

Light therapy units are usually placed above an incubator and are used to treat jaundice. Jaundice is not a disease but is caused by the breakdown of red blood cells a couple of days after the birth.

This causes an excess of bilirubin in the blood, which may give the skin a yellowish tinge. Bilirubin is usually excreted by the liver but the premature baby's liver may take a week or so to be working fully and so clear the jaundice.

Low birth weight babies

Low birth weight babies are those who weigh less than 2.5 kg (5.5 lb) at birth. Some low birth weight babies may be full-term but are naturally small. Premature and undernourished babies may well need special care.

? QUESTIONS

Question 1

a What is another name for a special care baby unit?

b What is a meant by a premature, or pre-term, baby?

c Describe the problems a premature baby might have.

d What is the term used to describe a baby whose birth weight is under 2.5 kg (5.5 lb)?

Question 2

a How can the following equipment help premature babies:

(i)   incubator?

(ii) ventilator?

(iii) monitor?

b Describe six ways the family might be affected if a newborn baby has to stay in a special care baby unit.

31 Crying and Sleeping

A crying baby can be very stressful

Newborn babies cry!

Babies do not cry to exercise their lungs. It is their way of communicating with parents and carers. A carer will quickly learn to distinguish between different cries (see table below).

Reasons babies cry	To comfort babies
Hunger	If babies are bottle-fed and it is more than two hours since the last feed, they may be hungry again and could need another feed. If babies are breast-fed it is difficult to judge how much food they have had and they should be offered a feed.
Thirst	Babies often cry because they are thirsty, not hungry. A new baby can be offered a drink of previously boiled water from a bottle.
Temperature	If babies are too hot or too cold they may cry. If a baby looks hot, loosen any tight-fitting clothing and fold back or take off some covers.
Soiled nappy	Some new babies do not like lying in a soiled nappy. Change the nappy to make them comfortable.
Tiredness	Sometimes babies become over-tired and are fractious and irritable. Some babies respond to being picked up and loved while others prefer to be left alone to fall asleep.
Colic (abdominal pain)	This is one of the most common causes of crying in the early days. It often occurs in the evening, when babies may have continuous bouts of screaming, pulling their legs up to their tummy. The baby will probably find comfort in being held closely and being soothed. Infant colic usually stops at around three months old.
Fear/insecurity/loneliness	Babies can cry if they are frightened by a loud noise. They may be bored if put in a pram or cot where they are not able to see anything. They will respond if picked up and cuddled tightly then sat in a bouncing cradle or propped up in a pram or pushchair.

Hints on soothing a baby

If young babies continue to cry for no apparent reason, carers can:

- rock them in their arms or in a rocking chair
- hold them tightly and talk or sing quietly
- lay them across the knee and gently rub their back
- play some music (low noises are preferable to high-pitched sounds)
- offer a comforter (a sterile dummy).

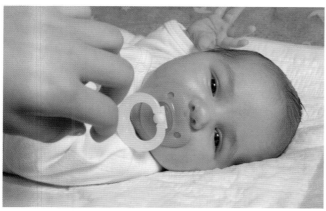
Dummies can help soothe a baby

The benefits of a comforter

In the early days a dummy often provides a form of comfort to a baby. As long as the dummy does not replace human forms of comfort such as love and cuddles it is not harmful. A comforter can be a great source of security when no one is around – for example, a baby may wake in the night and be comforted with the dummy without disturbing anyone else, before drifting back to sleep. After the first few months babies often have a favourite blanket, garment or soft toy that acts as a comforter (see pages 313–314).

Sleep and the newborn baby

The amount of sleep a newborn baby needs varies from baby to baby, and probably from day to day. Babies are individuals and will adopt their own routine. Although babies rarely sleep for longer than three to five hours it is not unusual for some to sleep for 20 of the 24 hours in each day, waking only if they are hungry, cold or uncomfortable.

Initially babies are not aware of night and day but they gradually notice that there are more sounds and movements during the day and use this as a wakeful time. Night-time is seen as a quieter time but parents should be warned that baby's evenings may not begin until after 10 pm.

Where should babies sleep?

Over the first few weeks it is ideal if the baby can sleep in a seat, carrycot or crib that is portable. This will enable the baby to be moved around the home, and taken out shopping and visiting without being disturbed.

Some newborn babies are likely to share their parents' bedroom for the first couple of months. The parents are sure they can always hear if the baby needs comfort, and giving night feeds is easier if the baby is close at hand.

If and when babies have their own room, it must be kept warm because babies cannot regulate their body temperature. A suitable room temperature is between 16°C and 20°C. A night light or dimmer switch is useful so babies can be checked without switching on a main light, which might disturb them.

In the daytime it is good for babies to sleep outdoors. They should be wrapped up according to the weather and should be visible at all times. If it is sunny the pram should be in the shade, or a sun canopy or parasol should be used. The hood of a pram can act as a windbreak and a cat net should always be used.

Tips to settle babies to sleep

- For the first weeks babies like to be swaddled (wrapped up tightly). The feeling of being tightly enclosed, as they were in the uterus, makes them feel secure.
- Give a comfort suck of breast or bottle.
- Darken the room.
- Have a musical mobile over the cot.
- Gently rock the pram/cot or lovingly stroke the head, back or limbs.
- Some babies settle if they are carried around, being held closely so they feel the warmth and the heartbeat of the person carrying them.

Baby's bedtime routine

It is a good idea to try to start to establish a bedtime routine (see table below), even for a young baby, as soon as possible. This will make it easier as the baby gets older.

Suggested bedtime routine
Bath or 'top and tail' baby. Put on a clean nappy and nightclothes.
Say goodnight to other family members.
Carry up to the bedroom, talking gently and saying what is happening.
Give a last breast- or bottle-feed.
Possibly sing or nurse until beginning to go to sleep.
Settle the baby in the cot and say goodnight.
Leave the room.

Newborn baby sleeping on back

Sleeping position

Young babies should be placed on their back to sleep with their head turned to one side, so any regurgitated milk (milk that has been swallowed then brought back into the mouth) can trickle from the mouth. Once babies are able to turn over and move around in the cot they will adopt the position in which they feel most comfortable.

Sudden infant death syndrome (SIDS)

Sudden infant death syndrome is commonly known as cot death and is the sudden and unexplainable death of a baby under six months old. SIDs is more common in male babies, babies born with a low birth weight or prematurely.

As the cause of cot death is not known it is impossible to give carers advice on prevention. Risk factors have been identified and continuing research will perhaps ultimately give an answer, which will prevent the unexpected deaths of over 300 babies in the UK each year.

The following guidelines are recommended to reduce the risk of cot death:

- always place babies on their back to sleep
- place babies in the 'feet to foot position' in the cot; this means placing them with their *feet* touching the *foot* of the cot to prevent them from wriggling down under the covers
- have the baby's cot in parents' bedroom for first six months
- don't smoke during pregnancy (both parents) as it is believed that babies whose parents smoke before birth are at greater risk of SIDS
- don't let anyone smoke in the same room as the baby
- buy a new mattress for each new baby, or buy a special mattress cover
- do not let babies become overheated, either from the heat of the room or too much clothing or bedding
- don't give babies a pillow until they are at least two years old
- use a sheet and cellular blankets instead of duvets, quilts or cot bumpers as these may cause overheating

- don't share a bed with a young baby especially after drinking alcohol, taking drugs or medication that can cause drowsiness, or if you are a smoker
- if babies appear to be feverish take off clothing or blankets to cool them down
- use a dummy when baby goes to sleep but wait a month if breast-feeding
- always seek medical advice if you think the baby is unwell.

QUESTIONS

Question 1

a Suggest seven reasons why babies might cry.

b Describe three ways parents might soothe a crying baby.

Question 2

a Describe six ways parents might try to encourage a baby to sleep.

b Describe, with reasons, how a baby should be placed in a cot to sleep.

Question 3

a What is another name for sudden infant death syndrome (SIDS)?

b Give ten guidelines to help reduce the risk of SIDS.

RESEARCH ACTIVITY

1. Carry out some research into the possible causes and prevention of cot death. Use this to make an illustrated fact sheet for the parents of young babies.

2. Use a variety of different sources (e.g. textbooks, websites, health visitors, parents) to find out more about why children cry and how to cope with a baby who cries a lot.

   Analyse and compare the advice given and present your results as a report, stating the sources used.

32 Post-natal Care

Post-natal means the first six weeks after the birth of the baby.

During pregnancy, most expectant mothers will have imagined what life with a newborn baby will be like. It is easy to imagine, but sometimes reality is a little more difficult to live with. A baby can take up a great deal of time and energy, but new mothers also need to care for themselves and keep fit and healthy. They must never be afraid to seek help and advice from partners, from family or from medical personnel.

If the baby has been born in hospital, a midwife will always be on hand to offer help and advice. When the mother returns home, a midwife attached to her general practitioner's (GP's) practice will visit daily until the baby is ten days old. The midwife who makes a home delivery will continue to visit the mother and baby for the next ten days. After the first ten days the care of the mother and baby becomes the responsibility of the health visitor. If the mother has had a difficult time or requires more support the midwife can visit up to 28 days after the baby is born.

The role of the health visitor

A health visitor is a nurse who has midwifery experience and has also gained further qualifications in family health and child development. The health visitor will make an initial visit and will then call from time to time to check all is well. He or she will give the mother a contact number where advice can be asked for, if there are any problems.

Remember, health visitors are there to help. The new mother must never be afraid to ask questions, however simple they may seem. Finding out the answer to a problem will give the new mother added confidence.

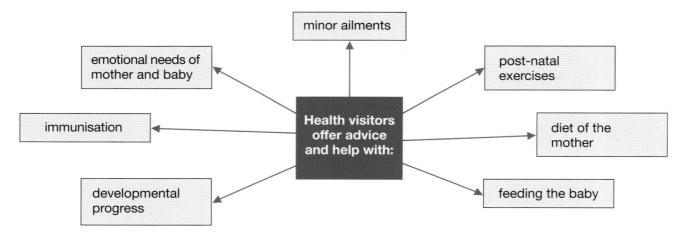

In addition, the health visitor will encourage parents to attend a local baby clinic, which is usually run by the general practitioner or local health authority. Parents can go once a week, if they wish. A health visitor will be present to offer advice and weigh the baby.

The baby clinic is a good place to meet other parents and make new friends. Parents will be encouraged to take along their 'Personal Child Health Record' booklet (see page 248).

Registration of the baby

The parents have six weeks after the baby is born (three weeks in Scotland) to register the birth. A birth certificate will then be issued to the parent or parents.

The family and the new baby

Whether it is a first baby for the parents or a second or third, a new baby brings with it lots of pleasure and enjoyment but also a lot of changes as each member of the family has to adapt to the new arrival. The parents may become very tired with the responsibility of looking after the baby, and this may put a strain on their relationship. Other children in the family may feel they are being left out, and may start to misbehave as they seek the parents' attention.

Father and baby bonding

Bonding

Bonding is the process in which strong psychological and emotional ties are established between a parent and a newborn child. It is an essential and very basic part of a baby's emotional development.

Bonding is a two-way process in which baby and parent respond to each other's gestures and expressions. Bonding is not instant – it is built up during the first months of life.

Some mothers find it difficult to bond with their new baby and this is not unusual. It may be because:

- the baby is very ill or was premature and is in a special care baby unit where it is not easy for the parents to hold, cuddle and feed their baby
- the mother has had a difficult and tiring labour and birth
- she is trying to breast-feed and is finding it difficult
- she is worried that she may not be able to look after her baby properly
- she did not have a close, loving relationship with her own parents and family, and may find it difficult to show emotions
- the baby was unwanted.

It is widely believed that lack of bonding at this very early stage can lead to emotional difficulties for the child in later life.

One of the most instinctive feelings a mother has when her baby is born is to hold the baby to the breast. The baby's rooting and sucking reflexes begin, creating a close skin-to-skin contact with the mother. This can be an overwhelming experience for the mother, creating a special bond. However, this close bond will also occur with the baby who is bottle-fed, since skin-to-skin contact is made with a simple gesture such as touching cheek to cheek.

Baby blues and post-natal depression

It is very common during the week following the birth for the new mother to feel miserable and down for a day or two. This is not post-natal depression. This is commonly known as the 'baby blues' and it comes about because the mother's hormones are trying to return to their normal pattern, which has changed during pregnancy. She is also getting little sleep and may be very tired after a long, hard labour, and she may be worrying about how she is going to cope with a new life.

Baby blues usually disappear as rapidly as they appear and, as long as she has plenty of love and understanding around her, the new mother will realise her feelings are natural. A partner can be very supportive during these early days and it is sensible for him to take paternity leave when the mother and baby return home, rather then when they are in hospital. Paternity leave is a statutory right for working fathers. They are currently allowed to take one or two weeks away from work and receive Statutory Paternity Pay, which is the same as the standard rate of Statutory Maternity Pay.

If the baby blues continue for more than a few days and the new mother appears to show the signs described in the diagram below she may be developing long-term depression, known as post-natal depression.

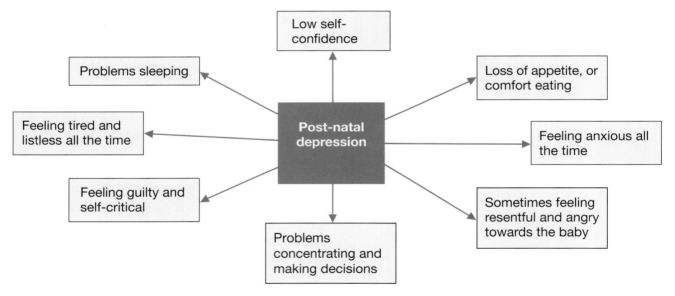

Post-natal depression (PND) is when the mother feels extremely sad and low. She is overtaken by a feeling of hopelessness, often does not want to, or feels she cannot, take care of her baby, and feels she cannot cope with the simplest of tasks.

The most important stage in treating post-natal depression is accepting that there is a problem and talking to a GP or health visitor. They will suggest ways to treat it.

Possible treatments

It is very important that a woman suffering from post-natal depression has the understanding, help and support of her partner and family.
Self-help groups can be very useful in providing encouragement and support, and health visitors or GPs will be able to provide information about these.
Some websites (e.g. raisingkids.co.uk) have forums where mothers suffering from PND can share their fears and feelings with others who are suffering, or have suffered, in the same way. This can be good for people who might find it hard to talk to their partner or family.
Antidepressants are often prescribed by GPs. These can be effective, but usually have to be taken for four to six months and can take two to four weeks to work.
St John's wort is a herbal remedy that can be taken for depression; however, it should not be used if breast-feeding
Regular exercise, such as jogging or swimming, is believed to help.

If the post-natal depression continues and the mother is not responding to treatment she may be admitted to a psychiatric hospital for more intensive treatment. Most psychiatric hospitals have a mother-and-baby unit so that mother and baby do not have to be separated for any length of time, as this could seriously damage the bonding process that may have already been affected by the post-natal depression.

Puerperium

The period from birth to six weeks is known as the puerperium. During the puerperium:

- the uterus is expected to have shrunk back to normal size
- any soreness around the perineum should have disappeared
- any stitches should have dissolved and wounds healed
- post-natal bleeding should have cleared
- minor problems like constipation, backache and haemorrhoids will have cleared up

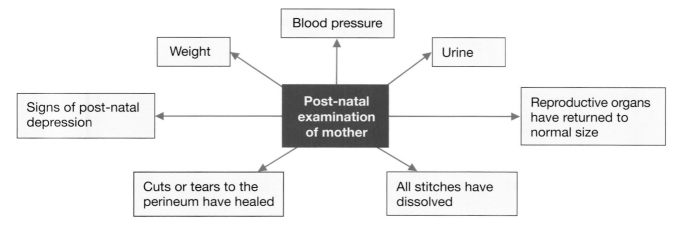

• post-natal exercise should be done to help pelvic and abdominal muscles to return to normal.

At the end of the puerperium the mother and baby will have a check-up known as the post-natal examination. This examination can be carried out by a GP or by a doctor at the hospital where the baby was delivered. Babies are checked to ensure they are in good health and thriving.

The post-natal examination of the mother will check the things outlined in the diagram on page 177.

The doctor will also offer a routine smear test and volunteer contraceptive advice.

After the first six weeks everyone tends to leave the mother and baby to settle into a routine. It is advisable to adopt a routine that suits both the mother and baby and to be flexible. No one expects her to be perfect and to know all the answers, so she still has the support of the health visitor and her GP, but words of encouragement from partners, relatives, neighbours and friends are always needed. Mothers still need time for themselves and time to spend with their partner, so they should arrange for someone reliable to look after the baby occasionally.

KEY WORD

Post-natal refers to the first six weeks after the birth of the baby

---

QUESTIONS

Question 1

a What period of time does post-natal usually refer to?

b What is the role of the health visitor after the birth of the baby?

Question 2

a What is bonding?

b Suggest four reasons why a mother may find it difficult to bond with her new baby.

Question 3

a It is common for a new mother to suffer from the 'baby blues'. What are 'baby blues'?

b What is the difference between 'baby blues' and post-natal depression?

c List five signs that may indicate a mother is suffering from post-natal depression.

d Describe four ways of treating post-natal depression.

Question 4

a When is a post-natal check-up carried out?

b List five checks that will be carried out at the post-natal visit.

Web Links	
www.bbc.co.uk/parenting/childcare	A huge range of articles and information on all aspects of child development and caring for children, including having a baby.
www.brook.org.uk	Information and advice relating to contraception and pregnancy testing.
www.childdevelopmentinfo.com	Information on being a new parent, plus lots on development and learning, parenting, health and safety issues.
www.fpa.org.uk	Family Planning Association. Information on family planning, sexual health and contraceptive methods.
www.fsid.org.uk	Foundation for the Study of Infant Deaths. Advice on reducing the risk of cot death; support and information for bereaved parents.
www.dh.gov.uk	Department of Health. Lots of information on infant care, pregnancy and childbirth, including immunisation, reducing the risk of cot death, weaning, breast-feeding and antenatal care.
www.food.gov.uk	Food Standards Agency. Lots of information on food, dietary advice relating to disease and allergy, healthy lifestyles, eating for breast-feeding, current guidelines and legislation.
www.milk.co.uk	The Dairy Council. Bright, concise material in an appealing format. Lots of free publications – leaflets and posters. Dietary advice from conception to toddlers, to teenagers and sports people.
www.nctpregnancyandbabycare.com	National Childbirth Trust. Information on conception, antenatal care, pregnancy, birth and care of children.
www.uk-sands.org	Stillbirth and Neonatal Death Society. Run by parents for parents who have lost a baby or soon after birth.
www.vegsoc.org	Vegetarian Society. Nutritional stages/requirements for mothers, from pre-conception through to birth.

PART 3

DIET, HEALTH AND CARE OF THE CHILD

This part of the book is about caring for children. It includes information about:

- the importance of a healthy diet
- feeding babies and young children
- food-related health problems
- the importance of hygiene
- childhood illnesses, immunisation and how to look after a sick child.

 REMEMBER!

From the moment of birth, a parent becomes a carer, nurse, teacher, provider and protector. Help is available from a wide variety of sources.

33 Nutrition and Healthy Eating

What is healthy eating?

A healthy diet is one that includes the right balance of nutrients, from a variety of foods, in the correct amounts. A healthy diet also requires water and dietary fibre to maintain healthy functions within the body.

A healthy diet will help to prevent a number of diseases, such as cancer, diabetes and heart disease.

Why do we need a healthy diet?

It is important to follow a healthy diet, not only for our general health and well-being but to prevent problems and diseases such as cancer, obesity, diabetes and heart disease, which *can be* caused by poor diet, lack of exercise and other lifestyle choices.

The government has been very concerned about the health of the nation for some time. There are now a large number of children in the UK who are not only overweight but obese. This means that they are very overweight, to the point that this could have a serious effect on their health.

While this is mainly due to poor diet there are other reasons, such as:

- some families may be on low incomes
- poor cooking skills and lack of freshly prepared meals
- increased consumption of ready-made convenience foods high in fat and salt
- diet lacking in fibre
- lack of nutritional knowledge
- the media encouraging children to eat foods that are associated with current trends/films.

Healthy eating for the future

The aim of the government to improve the health of young children and tackle obesity has been highlighted in the Every Child Matters programme, which aims to ensure that all children have a healthy, balanced diet and regular physical activity (see Chapter 64).

Other initiatives have been introduced to support families, and help to improve diet and health. These include:

- the 'Five-a-Day' programme, which aims to encourage people to eat at least five portions of fruit and vegetables a day
- the 'Let's Get Cooking' programme, which is a network of cookery clubs taking place after school that will give children the chance to learn how to cook healthy dishes
- the 'Licence to Cook' initiative, which aims to ensure that all children aged 11–14 years will leave school with the ability to cook healthy meals; it will be compulsory in schools from 2011
- Healthy Start vouchers to buy milk, fresh fruit and vegetables, infant formula and vitamins
- improved school meals that must comply with the 'Healthy Schools' initiative
- the control of advertising to prevent children being influenced by the media and pressurising parents to buy unhealthy, gimmicky foods
- free entrance in some local authority areas to leisure facilities, to improve physical fitness.

About nutrients

Food contains five nutrients, which are essential to life. These nutrients listed below are found in a variety of foods and do different jobs (functions) in the body.

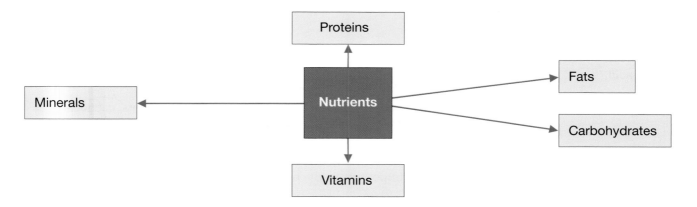

The table below lists the functions and main sources of the proteins, fats and carbohydrates in the British diet.

Nutrient	Function	Source
Protein	• For growth and repair • Second source of energy • Healing	Animal sources • Meat, poultry, fish, cheese, eggs, milk Plant sources • Cereals, pulses, nuts, Quorn, soya
Fat	• Provides a store of energy • Protects the vital organs • Insulates the body (keeps it warm)	• Fat on meat, bacon, oily fish, butter, margarine, oil, suet, chips, crisps, chocolate cakes, biscuits, egg yolk
Carbohydrate	• Provides energy	• Pasta, flour, breads, cereals, fruit, vegetables, sugar, jam, honey, cakes, biscuits

Vitamins

Vitamins cannot be made by the body. They must be obtained from food that is eaten. They have many functions in the body but are required only in small amounts.

Nutrient	Function	Source
Vitamin A	• Helps to see in dim light • Keeps skin healthy	Animal • Egg yolk, oily fish, dairy, milk, butter, fish, liver, oils Vegetable • Carrots, apricots
Vitamin D	• Makes strong bones and teeth • Helps to absorb calcium	• Milk, margarine, oily fish, sunlight
Vitamin E	• Helps prevent heart disease	• Found in most foods, particularly vegetable oils, peanuts, wheat germ, seeds
Vitamin K	• Helps the blood to clot	• Green leafy vegetables

Vitamins B and C are water soluble. This means that they will dissolve into water, so care must be taken when preparing and cooking foods containing them.

Nutrient	Function	Source
Vitamin B group	• Releases energy • Helps growth	• Cereal products • Meat • Eggs • Milk • Cheese
Folic acid	• Provides energy • Helps to make red blood cells	• Dark green vegetables • Potatoes
Vitamin C	• Helps to make strong bones and teeth • Helps to keep skin and blood healthy	• Citrus fruits, blackcurrants, cabbage, peas

Minerals

Minerals are also important to the body and are needed in small amounts.

Minerals are found in the soil, in plant-eating animals and dissolved in the water we drink. The most important minerals are listed in the table below.

Nutrient	Function	Source
Calcium	• Makes strong bones and teeth • Clots blood	• Milk, cheese, yoghurt, bread, cereals, green leafy vegetables
Iron	• Helps to make red blood cells, which carry oxygen around the body and release energy to other cells	• Liver, cocoa, green leafy vegetables, white bread
Fluoride	• Helps to make enamel on the teeth	Tea, water, fish

Fibre

Fibre is a non-starch polysaccharide and is sometimes called NSP. Fibre is important because it helps the faeces move easily out of the body, which helps to prevent constipation.

Some foods that are high in fibre are listed in the diagram below.

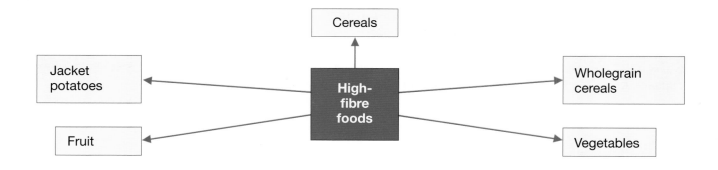

Water

Water is essential to life. A total of 70 per cent of the body is made up of water, which is also needed to keep the membranes healthy and to lubricate the joints.

A balanced diet

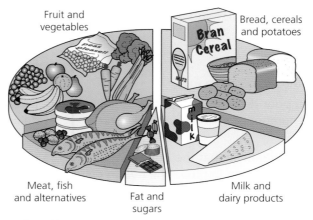

The balance of good health

A balanced diet is one that provides all the nutrients needed by the body in the right amounts. To do this, when planning and preparing meals for children, it is important to choose a variety of different foods. This will ensure that they are receiving a good balance of all the nutrients needed.

The 'balance of good health' pie chart shows how foods should come from all the different food groups to achieve this balance in the diet. The five main food groups are:

1 milk and dairy products
2 fruit and vegetables
3 cereals and bread
4 meat, fish or alternatives
5 fats and sugar.

 RESEARCH ACTIVITY

Record a typical day's meals for yourself, including drinks and snacks. Analyse your diet to see if it has a good balance of foods from the main nutrient groups.

QUESTIONS

Question 1

a What is meant by a 'healthy diet'?

b Name three problems or diseases that could be caused by a poor diet and lack of exercise.

Question 2

a What does the word obese mean?

b Other than a poor diet, suggest five reasons why a large number of children in the UK are now obese.

c Describe four initiatives that the government has introduced to try to improve the health of children and reduce obesity.

Question 3

a List the five main nutrient groups.

b What are the functions of protein in the body?

c Give two examples of animal proteins and two examples of vegetable proteins.

d List three reasons the body requires fat.

e Which nutrient is the main source of energy in the diet?

Question 4

a Design a table to show the functions and sources of vitamins A, B, C and D.

b Explain why folic acid is an important vitamin.

c Describe why children need a good supply of calcium, iron and fluoride in their diet.

d Explain why fibre is an important food in the diet.

e Name three foods rich in fibre.

Question 5

a What is meant by a 'balanced diet'?

b List the five food groups that make up 'the balance of good health'.

34 Advertising, Labelling and Packaging of Food

Food choices are very much influenced by the advertising, labelling and packaging of the food.

Advertising

Both parents and children are influenced by advertising, especially on TV. Companies often target adverts for food at children, hoping they will persuade their parents to buy the products.

Clever marketing techniques using popular characters from TV shows and films are often used to promote and sell food products, with little consideration of their nutritional value.

Advertising in supermarkets often includes special offers such as 'buy one, get one free' or 'three for the price of two'. While these might seem good value, they are often products high in fat and sugar (e.g. biscuits, crisps and sweets).

The government has recently introduced measures to limit the amount and type of food adverts shown on TV channels for children in the hope that this will stop them demanding so-called 'junk foods'. These are foods that contain a lot of fat, sugar and additives, and children should be discouraged from eating them. Parents and children who cook with fresh ingredients will know exactly what the food contains.

Labelling and packaging

Food packaging is important because it can help to protect and preserve the food. It carries information about the food, makes it look attractive, and advertises it. It also causes an environmental problem as it makes up a third of all household waste.

Parents should take great care when buying food for children. It is important that they look beyond the photo and colourful packaging, and understand the information and symbols on the label (see pages 188–189). These can tell them:

- the ingredients the food contains
- how healthy it is (the type and amount of nutrients it contains)
- the colourings, flavourings or other additives used.

Some information on labels must be included by law.

Labelling and the law

The label should include:

- the name of the food product
- a description of the product
- ingredients, listed in descending order of weight
- name and address of manufacturer
- 'best before' date
- net weight
- cooking/heating instructions
- the process used to produce the product
- storage information.

Labels often include logos and symbols that can help parents make a healthy choice. These can show if the packaging can be recycled and if the food is:

- additive-free
- suitable for vegetarians
- gluten-free
- recyclable
- suitable for freezing
- a healthy option.

Nutritional labelling

Existing nutritional labels on food give a lot of information about amounts of nutrients but are often difficult to understand without a good knowledge of nutrition. Most people simply want to understand quickly when they pick up a product and read the label if it is healthy, low in fat and sugar, etc. As a result of this, the Food Standards Agency has adopted a 'traffic light' system for labelling food products, and many of the large supermarkets have now introduced this system.

The 'traffic light' labelling system

This gives a simple red, amber and green guide to nutrition. Below is an example of the labels that you could see on food products.

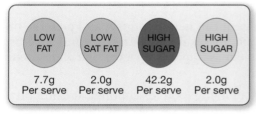
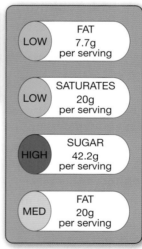
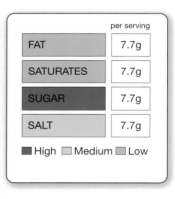

Traffic-light labelling

This system is a quick and easy way for people to tell at a glance if the product is healthy or not. Parents should select more of the foods with a green label, a few with an amber label and only occasionally buy those with a red label.

Large supermarkets have opted for this system. The Diabetes UK society has supported this system, saying it is the 'quickest and easiest way for consumers to know what the food contains'.

The GDA labelling system

GDA stands for **guided daily amounts** – that is, the amount of calories, sugar, fats and salt that should be eaten daily for a healthy diet.

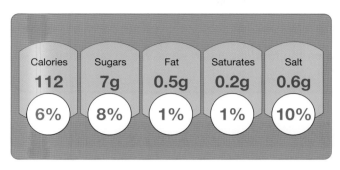

Calories	Sugars	Fat	Saturates	Salt
112	7g	0.5g	0.2g	0.6g
6%	8%	1%	1%	10%

GDA labelling

This system of labelling shows the percentage of these amounts each serving of the food will provide. This helps shoppers to make healthy choices.

Additives

Parents should be aware of the additives that foods contain as children can often have an intolerance or allergic reaction to them and this can affect their health (see Chapter 39).

Additives are used in the food industry for a number of reasons. In general, they are used to preserve a food to keep it longer, or to add colour, texture and flavour to the food. They can be either chemical additives such as tartrazine – an artificial orange colouring found in orange juice – or natural, such as sugar, which is from a plant.

E-numbers are a way of identifying different chemical food additives. An E-number is given only if the additive has passed all safety tests. The ingredients list on the label must gives details of what additives a food contains.

> **E-number codes**
>
> E100–E180: colours
>
> E200–E283: preservatives
>
> E300–E322: antioxidants
>
> E400–E495: emulsifiers and stabilisers
>
> E953–E962: sweeteners

Processed foods

A processed food is one that has gone through many stages from the raw ingredient to the final product that arrives on the supermarket shelf. During this process additives may have been used and the nutritional content may have been reduced. Parents should avoid foods that have been processed as they are often high in additives and fat, and low in fibre.

Organic foods

Many people are now choosing to buy organic foods, especially fruit and vegetables but also things like tea and flour.

Organic means that the crop, or the food made from it, has been grown without using:

• pesticides
• substances that make crops grow faster
• man-made fertilisers.

Farming the organic way is a return to more traditional methods, relying on natural manure and natural pest control.

Parents may wish to buy organic foods for their children, believing that they are healthier and more natural.

REMEMBER!

It is important that a parent looks at the information on the food label and uses this to give their child a balanced, healthy diet.

 QUESTIONS

Question 1

a Suggest three ways advertising can influence the types of food parents choose to buy.

b What are so called 'junk foods'?

c What steps is the government taking to try to reduce the amount of 'junk foods' bought by parents?

Question 2

a Why is food packaging important?

b What are the environmental problems caused by food packaging?

Question 3

a The labels on food packages give very important information. List the information that a label must include by law.

b Give five other pieces of information that a label might include.

c Nutritional labelling can sometimes be difficult to understand. What is the name of the simplified labelling system recently introduced by the Food Standards Agency?

d Explain how the GDA labelling system could make it easier for parents to buy healthier foods.

Question 4

a What are additives?

b Explain what E-numbers are.

c How might some additives affect children?

Question 5

a What are organic foods?

b Why might parents choose to buy organic foods for their children?

RESEARCH ACTIVITY

1. Investigate how food adverts on TV target parents and children. You could compare the length of the advert, the people/characters in the advert, the type of music/song used, the 'message' the advert is giving, etc.

2. Carry out a comparative investigation into the packaging and labelling of food for young children. Look at the packaging and labelling on the following items: a jar of baby food; a packet of dried baby food; a children's yoghurt or dessert; a cook-chill meal for a toddler.

    Using the information on the packaging, compare the following:
    a system of nutritional labelling
    b type of packaging material
    c ingredients and additives in the food
    d symbols and logos.

    Decide which of the products seems to be the most healthy, the easiest to understand, the most environmentally friendly, the most eye-catching, and explain why.

    Present your findings as a report.

35 Breast-feeding

Breast-feeding

Breast-feeding is considered to be the best and most natural method for feeding babies. Some mothers and babies may, however, struggle to breast-feed and alternate infant formula feeds may have to be bottle-fed to the baby.

Successful breast-feeding does not depend on the size of the breasts, so every woman is capable of breast-feeding their baby. However, it is a matter of personal choice as to whether she chooses to breast- or bottle-feed her baby. In making her choice she needs to think carefully about what is best for her baby and for herself.

Occasionally a baby may refuse to take breast milk. This often happens during the first few weeks after the birth. There could be many reasons, for example:

- the baby was not particularly hungry
- the breasts were too full of milk, making it difficult for the baby to suck.

Patience, time and encouragement are needed if the mother is determined to breast-feed.

If planning to breast-feed, is very important for the mother to have a healthy well-balanced diet. Although it is not necessary to have 'special foods', the mother should make sure that she has a good balance of proteins, iron, calcium, fresh fruit and vegetables. This, together with plenty of fluids, will help her to produce a good supply of milk.

The average mother can produce approximately 800 ml of milk per day and it requires 500 kcals (2090 kj) to produce it. This is the equivalent of approximately 1.5 pints per day.

Breasts and breast milk

During pregnancy, the mother's breasts change. They become enlarged and the glandular tissue within each breast develops to prepare them for milk production. Milk production actually starts a few days after the birth.

The structure of the breasts

Each breast contains between 15 and 20 sections of milk-secreting glands. Each gland is connected to the nipple by milk ducts. The milk is made within these glands. The dark area around each nipple is called the areola.

First milk

During pregnancy, the expectant woman's placenta and ovaries produce very high levels of both oestrogen and progesterone. These two hormones work together to stimulate the milk glands to produce a substance called colostrum. This is the milk produced in the first few days after the birth, although it is produced at least 12 weeks before the end of the pregnancy. At first it is very clear and almost colourless. Later it becomes yellowish in colour.

The colostrum provides the baby with water, proteins, sugar,

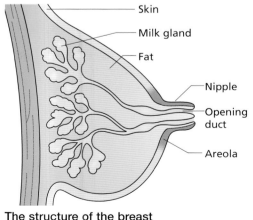

The structure of the breast

- Skin
- Milk gland
- Fat
- Nipple
- Opening duct
- Areola

vitamins, minerals and also antibodies to give extra protection from various infections.

The birth is the signal for the breasts to stop producing colostrum and to make a start on milk production. Milk production begins between three to five days *after* the baby is born. This process is called lactation.

Mature milk

Two or three days after the birth, mature milk is produced. This actually includes two kinds of milk: foremilk and hindmilk.

- Foremilk is high in lactose (milk sugar) but low in fat. It is thirst-quenching.
- Hindmilk is higher in fat and very important for the baby's growth.

Nutrition and breast-feeding

Breast milk is an ideal food for the baby. The human body produces milk with the correct balance of nutrients, as outlined in the table below.

Nutritional content of 100 g of breast milk
• 289 kj (69 kcal) of energy
• 1.3 g protein
• 4.1 g fat
• 7.2 g carbohydrate (mainly lactose)
• 34 mg calcium
The baby stores vitamin D and iron before it is born.

Breast milk contains:

- the right amount of water to satisfy a baby's thirst so that they do not need extra
- the right amount of the right quality protein, in a form that is easily absorbed and digested
- fat for energy, which can be easily and completely absorbed by babies and contains a high concentration of fatty acids
- more carbohydrate than cow's milk; carbohydrate is an extremely important source of energy
- vitamins and minerals in the right amounts
- a low salt (sodium) content.

Babies are born with a good iron supply, which is stored in the liver. There is no risk that the milk is too concentrated in one nutrient or another, and the breast milk changes during a feed and from day to day as the baby grows.

Advantages and disadvantages of breast-feeding

Advantages	Disadvantages
For the baby	**For the baby**
✓ Babies are less likely to become obese (fat).	✗ Occasionally, the baby does not get enough milk from the breasts because the mother is tense and/or overtired.
✓ Research suggests that babies' brains develop better if they have been breast-fed.	✗ A baby who is fed entirely on milk for six months may find it difficult to take to 'new' foods when weaning starts.
✓ Breast milk does not need to be sterilised.	✗ Some babies have an intolerance to the lactose in the milk.
✓ Gastroenteritis and other common ailments of babies are less likely in babies who have been breast-fed.	✗ Certain foods, drugs and alcohol can be passed from the mother to the baby and cause harm.
✓ Breast milk is less likely to give the baby eczema or nappy rash.	
✓ Babies fed on breast milk are less likely to suffer allergies than those babies who are bottle-fed.	
✓ Breast milk cannot be prepared wrongly and its quality is always the same.	
✓ Breast milk contains natural antibodies that help to ward off infections.	
✓ Breast milk is easier for the baby to digest than bottle milk.	
✓ Breast milk never causes indigestion.	
✓ The milk changes as the baby grows to match the age and needs of the baby	
For the mother	**For the mother**
✓ She has a chance to sit down and rest.	✗ It can be tiring as babies often feed more frequently.
✓ Breast milk requires no equipment for preparation.	✗ The baby can be very demanding of the mother's time.
✓ The production of the hormone oxytocin when breast-feeding causes the uterus to return to its normal size more quickly.	✗ She may feel 'tied' to the baby and find the loss of freedom difficult.
✓ Breast-feeding can delay the return of periods.	✗ She may get sore or cracked nipples or suffer from mastitis.
✓ It helps to increase the mother's natural bonding.	✗ She will need to avoid alcohol, drugs and strongly flavoured foods because these will be passed on to the baby.
✓ It is cheaper than formula milk.	✗ Some mothers feel too embarrassed to feed their babies in public.

Using a breast pump

Expressing milk

Mothers who choose to breast-feed can **express** breast milk so that someone else can feed the baby. This can give the mother's partner more opportunity to be able to bond and interact with the baby. Expressing breast milk can be done by hand or using a breast pump.

As with all feeding of young babies, it is important that all equipment used when expressing and storing the milk and feeding the baby is sterilised (see pages 197–198).

Hygiene rules for feeding with expressed breast milk

- Sterilise all equipment.
- Express milk into a sterilised bottle.

- Cap the bottle immediately.
- Store in a fridge for up to 24 hours.
- Freeze and store in the freezer compartment of the fridge for up to one week.
- Freeze and store for up to three months in a freezer.
- Thaw breast milk in a fridge or in warm water.
- Use within 24 hours.
- Never re-freeze breast milk.

KEY WORDS

Areola the dark area surrounding the nipple

Colostrum the first milk from the breasts, which is rich in nutrients and antibodies

Foremilk the first part of the breast milk, which is thirst-quenching

Hindmilk the second part of the breast milk, which is higher in nutrients

QUESTIONS

Question 1

a How much breast milk can a mother produce in one day?

b What should a breast-feeding mother include in her daily diet to help her produce a good supply of milk?

Question 2

a What is colostrum?

b Why is it important for a new baby?

c What is the difference between foremilk and hindmilk?

Question 3

a Give five reasons why breast milk is the ideal food for babies.

b Breast milk does not contain iron. Why is this not a problem?

Question 4

a Give four advantages of breast-feeding for the baby.

b Give four advantages of breast-feeding for the mother.

c Give five important hygiene rules for breast-feeding. Explain why each is important.

RESEARCH ACTIVITY

Carry out a survey of how many people in your class were breast-fed or bottle-fed. Present your results in a table and see what pattern emerges.

Ask your parents why they decided to bottle-feed or breast-feed.

36 Bottle-feeding

For mothers who are unable to breast-feed or choose not to, bottle-feeding provides an alternative method of feeding the baby.

There is no reason to suggest that a baby who is bottle-fed cannot be as healthy, and grow and thrive in the same way, as a baby who is breast-fed. Bottle-feeding is perfectly safe as long as the mother is careful to follow closely the manufacturer's instructions on how to make up the feed.

For bottle-feeding, commercially produced infant formula is used. This is usually made from cows' milk. Because this was designed for feeding calves it is very different to breast milk and has to be altered in order to be used for babies.

Although cows' and breast milk have almost the same number of calories, the balance of nutrients is different.

- Cows' milk has more protein; this is of a different kind and is harder to digest.
- It has less lactose (milk sugar).
- Fat does not adjust to the baby's needs and is not as easily absorbed.
- Most importantly, cows' milk does not contain antibodies to protect babies against allergies and infections.
- Vitamins and minerals are not absorbed as easily.

A father bottle-feeding his son

As mentioned above, cows' milk has to be modified to make it suitable for babies – it is diluted, and extra lactose, vitamins and iron are added.

Although most infant formulas are based on cows' milk, soya milk formulas are also available. These are important for babies who cannot tolerate the protein in cows' milk.

If the mother is unsure which one to use for her baby, she should first consult her doctor, health visitor or midwife.

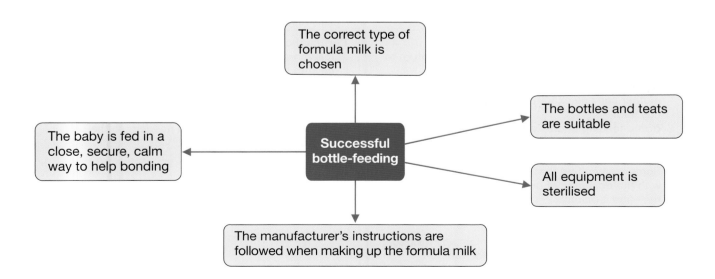

The correct type of formula milk is chosen

The bottles and teats are suitable

The baby is fed in a close, secure, calm way to help bonding

Successful bottle-feeding

All equipment is sterilised

The manufacturer's instructions are followed when making up the formula milk

Different types of milk

Type	What it is	Suitable for
Infant formula	Cows' milk that has been modified	Birth to 12 months
Follow-on formula	Similar to infant formula, but has higher amounts of protein, iron and other nutrients	Six months onwards
Growing-up milk	Formula milk with extra nutrients, especially vitamins and iron, sometimes flavoured with vanilla	12 months to three years
Soya-based formula	Made from soya beans, modified, and with added vitamins, minerals and nutrients	Birth to five years for babies with lactose intolerance or cows' milk protein intolerance; otherwise not suitable for under 12 months
Full-fat milk	Cows' milk with 3.9 g fat per 100 ml	Can be used in cooking from six months and as a drink from 12 months
Semi-skimmed milk	Cows' milk with 1.7 g fat per 100 ml	Can be used from two years onwards
Skimmed milk	Cows' milk with 0.2 g fat per 100 ml	Can be used from five years onwards
Goats' and sheep milk		Unsuitable for under 12 months

Advantages and disadvantages of bottle-feeding

Advantages	Disadvantages
For the baby ✓ Formula feeds, although not perfect, are a good substitute for mothers unable to breast-feed. ✓ Babies are extremely sensitive to the person giving the feed. A mother who is relaxed giving a bottle-feed is better than a mother who is tense and anxious or afraid while breast-feeding.	**For the baby** ✗ Bottle milk does not have the same protection against allergies and infections as breast milk. ✗ The closeness between mother and baby may not be as intense while bottle-feeding. ✗ Babies who are bottle-fed tend to suffer more from constipation. ✗ Babies who are bottle-fed often swallow more air than breast-fed babies, and they need to be 'winded' more often. ✗ Babies may burp more and bring up a little milk. This is known as 'posseting'.
For the mother ✓ It is useful for those women who wish to return to work before the baby is weaned. ✓ Bottle-feeding can be reassuring because the mother can see exactly how much milk the baby has had. ✓ Bottle-feeding affords a better quality of milk for those babies of women whose nutritional and dietary way of life is not very good. ✓ Some women find that they cannot physically cope with the demands of breast-feeding, especially if they find it painful. ✓ The bottle can be given by other people and that takes the pressure off the mother. ✓ The mother's breasts do not contain any milk so are not uncomfortable and cannot leak. ✓ The mother can feed the baby anywhere. Breast-feeding might make her feel embarrassed in public areas.	**For the mother** ✗ It is more expensive as the equipment and formula have to be bought. ✗ It makes extra work as equipment has to be sterilised and feeds made up. ✗ The mother may find it difficult to work out the correct quantities of formula needed, so the baby may be overfed or underfed.

REMEMBER!

Babies who are bottle-fed must never be left to feed themselves. Allowing this to happen might make the baby choke.

Also, if not being supervised closely, the baby could be sucking on a flattened teat or empty bottle. Either way, the baby is taking in air.

Cleaning and sterilising equipment

Infant formula milk is not sterile – it may contain micro-organisms which can cause infection, although this is rare. Newborn babies are most at risk, especially if they are pre-term, and these babies should be given ready-for-feed liquid formula milk.

When preparing and using formula milk, hygiene is very important, and cleaning and sterilising must be a vital part of the bottle-feeding routine. All equipment used for bottle-feeding must be scrupulously clean to prevent any chance of the baby coming into contact with harmful germs and bacteria. If this is not done it can result in tummy upsets or, more seriously, the baby may get gastroenteritis.

Gastroenteritis is an inflammation of the stomach and intestines, which causes vomiting and diarrhoea. In a young baby this can cause excessive fluid loss and hospital treatment may be needed.

Equipment should first be rinsed with cold water then thoroughly cleaned with hot, soapy water. A bottle brush and teat cleaner are useful gadgets for this initial process.

The detergent should then be rinsed off the bottles, teats, caps, etc., and the equipment sterilised using one of the following:

- an electric steam steriliser
- a microwave steriliser
- a cold-water steriliser.

Types of sterilising equipment

Electric steam steriliser	
These are very convenient and easy to use, but storage may be a problem if there is not a great deal of space in the kitchen. The steamers are electric and the cycle needed to sterilise bottles and teats takes approximately 10–15 minutes. All the carers have to do is add cold water and turn on.	

Microwave steam steriliser

In a microwave, sterilised water is added to the container and the equipment; the lid is then fitted and the steriliser put into the microwave. The microwave then needs to be operated on full power for about eight minutes.

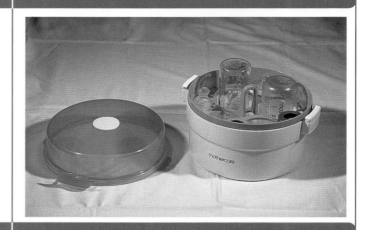

Cold-water steriliser

For this method of sterilising, all equipment has to be submerged in cold water with sterilising tablets or sterilising solution for at least half an hour. Once made up, the solution can be used several times. Cold, previously boiled water should be used to rinse the equipment just before use.

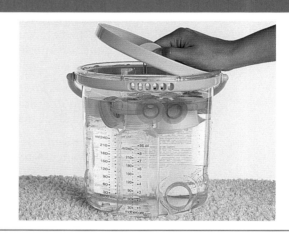

How to make up a formula feed

	Stage	Why
	Clean and sanitise work surface; wash hands thoroughly, then dry with a clean towel	To kill any harmful bacteria
	Boil a kettle, allow it to cool and use within 30 minutes of boiling; water should be no cooler than 70°C	This temperature will kill harmful bacteria

	Stage	Why
	Pour the correct amount of water into the graduated bottle	Accurate measuring is very important
	Put the required number of scoops of formula milk powder into the bottle; use the scoop provided with the formula, and level off	Feeds that are too concentrated could damage a baby's kidneys; too weak a feed means baby is not getting enough nutrients
	Put the teat and cap on to the bottle; shake well to mix together the water and milk powder	To ensure even mixing
	Cool the bottle quickly by holding it under cold running tap water and use immediately	The longer milk is kept, the greater the risk of bacteria growing
	Check the temperature on the inside of the wrist	To avoid burning the baby's mouth

	Stage	Why
	Throw away any unused feed within two hours	The longer it is kept, the greater the risk of bacteria growing

Storing bottle feeds

While it is safest to make up bottle feeds as they are needed, sometimes it is necessary to make up feeds for later use. These should be made up in individual bottles, cooled quickly and put straight into a refrigerator at no higher than 5°C. The milk should be thrown away if not used within 24 hours.

Reheating bottle feeds

1. Take the bottle from the fridge just before it is needed.
2. Place it in a jug of warm water for no more than 15 minutes. Shake the bottle occasionally to heat evenly.
3. Check temperature.
4. Never reheat more than once.
5. Never use a microwave to reheat bottles – they can cause 'hot spots', which can scald a baby's mouth.

? QUESTIONS

Question 1

a What is infant formula food?

b Describe five ways the balance of nutrients in formula milk differs from that in breast milk.

c Suggest four guidelines for successful bottle-feeding.

Question 2

a What is follow-on milk?

b Which type of milk should not be given to children under the age of five?

c Why might a baby need to be given soya-based formula feed?

d At what age can semi-skimmed milk be given to a child?

e What type of milk can be used in cooking from six months and as a drink from 12 months?

Question 3

a Give two advantages of bottle-feeding for the baby.

b Give two disadvantages of bottle-feeding for the baby.

c A baby should not be left to feed from a bottle on their own. Give two reasons for this.

Question 4

a A bottle-feed must be prepared safely and hygienically. Explain why this is important.

b Name and describe three types of sterilising equipment.

c Sometimes bottle-fed babies may suffer from gastroenteritis. What are the symptoms of gastroenteritis?

Question 5

a Design and make a leaflet explaining the importance of good hygiene at each stage of making up a formula feed.

b How should a formula feed be stored?

c How should formula feeds be reheated?

37 Weaning

Weaning is the name given to the stage of feeding when babies change from an all-milk diet to milk and solids diet.

Weaning should be a gradual process and, to be successful, needs to be done slowly so that the digestive system can develop correctly.

When to start weaning

Weaning starts when the baby is not satisfied on a diet of breast or formula milk. This varies from baby to baby. Usual signs for the mother are if the baby:

- is still hungry after a milk feed
- wakes up hungry before the next feed is due
- chews his/her fists.

The Department of Health strongly suggests that babies are not weaned before six months. By this age nearly all the iron supply in their body has been used up. Since iron is a vital nutrient that is *not* found in milk, babies need to be given food to supply this.

Eating from a spoon is a new skill for a baby

The reasons for not starting weaning early are as follows.

- It can lead to obesity.
- The kidneys cannot cope with the salt content.
- The ability to swallow foods with a thick consistency or bits has not developed.
- The baby cannot properly digest the solid foods.
- Avoiding unhealthy foods (e.g. sugar) in the diet for as long as possible.
- It can cause some allergies and food refusal.

Weaning is the first stage in developing social skills and introducing the baby to family mealtimes.

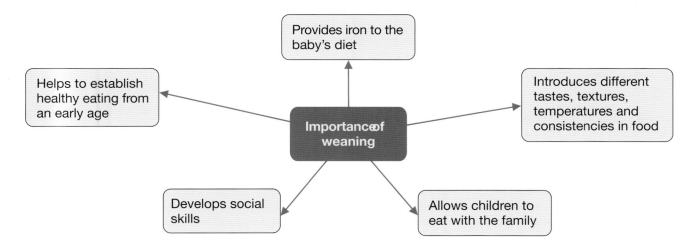

Provides iron to the baby's diet

Helps to establish healthy eating from an early age

Introduces different tastes, textures, temperatures and consistencies in food

Importance of weaning

Develops social skills

Allows children to eat with the family

Stages of weaning

Because weaning should be a gradual process it usually happens in four main stages, as outlined in the table below.

Stage 1

This stage usually begins at six months. Its purpose is to get the baby used to taking food from a spoon. It is best to offer food only once a day to begin with and usually before, or halfway through, the lunchtime feed.

The food should be a very smooth purée, and just one teaspoon should be given. Most of the nutrients needed still come from breast or formula milk.

Parents need to be very patient and not expect too much. Babies have to get used to new tastes and textures as well as learning to suck, move the food to the back of the throat and swallow.

Suitable foods: smooth and runny

- Puréed fruit and vegetables, e.g. carrots, parsnips, bananas, apples
- Purées of lentils, sweet potato or split peas
- Baby rice mixed to a fine purée with breast milk, bottled milk or water that has been boiled

Stage 2

Once babies are used to feeding from a spoon at one mealtime, they can be offered food at a second meal and different foods can *slowly* be introduced. Food still needs to be puréed or mashed.

As more solid food is given, the amount of milk will gradually decrease, but it is recommended that approximately 600 ml should still be given daily until one year.

Suitable foods: puréed foods progressing to mashed

- Fish (no bones)
- Beans and pulses, lentils, dhals, stews, casseroles – all mashed and well puréed
- Mashed banana, custard, milky puddings (e.g. rice)

Stage 3

By this stage babies will be used to a variety of foods and will be able to cope with chewing and swallowing foods with a thicker and lumpier texture. Finger foods can be given at this stage, but parents must supervise children when feeding because of the risk of choking.

Suitable foods: mashed moving to chopped food

As above plus:

- bread, e.g. toasted fingers, pitta and low-sugar rusks
- sticks of fruit and vegetables, e.g. apple and carrots

Stage 4

Babies will now be more used to eating solid foods and should be learning to fit in with family mealtimes. They should be eating three meals a day, plus milk. Fruit and healthy snacks can also be given when needed.

Suitable foods: foods from each of the following groups are needed for a healthy balanced diet

Cereals, bread, chapatti, rice, pasta and potatoes	2–3 servings per day
Fruit and vegetables	5 servings a day
Meats, fish, poultry, eggs, lentils and beans	2 servings a day
Breast or formula milk and dairy foods, e.g. yoghurt and cheese	Up to 500 ml per day

The iron store a baby is born with will have run out by the time they are six months old, therefore it is important to give them iron-rich foods, such as beans, lentils, broccoli, green leafy vegetables and breakfast cereals fortified with iron, during the first stage of weaning. Giving something containing vitamin C along with iron-rich foods helps the body to absorb the iron.

Vitamin drops are suggested for children between the ages of six months and two years. This is to help prevent a vitamin D deficiency, which can cause rickets (bone malformation).

Cutting down on milk

Once a baby starts to have solid foods the amount of milk given will need to be reduced, but this needs to be done very gradually and health visitors will help mothers through this stage.

Reducing feeds too quickly could make the baby dehydrated, but gradually the number of milk feeds can be reduced and the baby will learn to drink from a feeding cup. They will need to have extra fluids to make up for the water they are not getting from the milk, and can be given cool, boiled water or diluted fruit juice (not squash) after food.

It is important at the weaning stage that the baby begins to eat with the rest of the family, although the food will not be the same to begin with. Gradually, as the baby becomes more used to different flavours and textures, she/he will be able to eat similar foods to the rest of family, in a mashed or puréed form.

 REMEMBER!

If the baby demands more solid food, a small piece of banana mashed in milk could be given at teatime. Also, some small pieces of puréed vegetables mashed in boiling water could be tried at lunchtime.

Foods to avoid during weaning

During the weaning process certain foods should be avoided as they may cause harm to the baby. This will also help the child to develop healthy eating habits from a very young age.

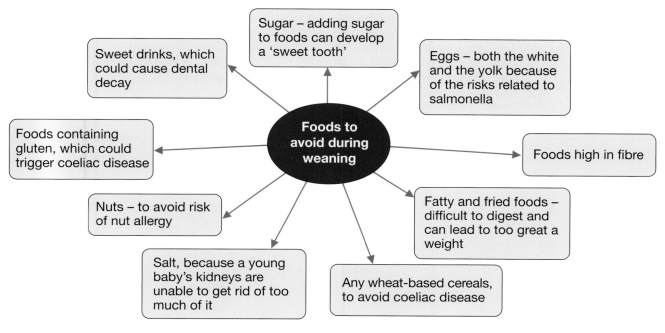

Home-made vs bought baby foods

When starting to wean babies, new parents often worry about preparing and cooking food – whether it is suitable, whether it is the right consistency, if it contains the right nutrients, and how much should be given.

Nowadays there is a wide range of different brands of commercially produced baby foods in many different forms available for every stage of weaning, and through to the toddler stage and beyond. Clever marketing and labelling implies that the food is 'perfect' for the baby, nutritionally balanced and additive-free. However, all this food has to be processed in some way, which can often destroy some nutrients. Additives and preservatives often need to be added to food for a variety of reasons (see page 189) – these must by law be shown on the label and some additives can affect the behaviour of children.

While bought baby foods are very useful at certain times, they are expensive and it is better for parents to give their babies home-cooked, puréed or minced food as much as possible, not least because it encourages babies to get used to home cooking!

Advantages and disadvantages of home-made and bought baby foods

	Advantages	**Disadvantages**
Home-made baby foods	✓ Fresh foods and ingredients used ✓ More interesting and varied diet for baby ✓ Less expensive ✓ Baby gets used to eating the same food as the rest of the family ✓ Less chance of food refusal/fussy eating later ✓ Amounts can be frozen for later use, so less wastage ✓ No additives ✓ Parent knows what is in the food	✗ Parents may be unsure of how to cook foods properly ✗ Parents may be unsure about how much to give ✗ Uncertainty about what foods are suitable for what age ✗ Lack of knowledge about nutrition ✗ May need to buy equipment to purée and blend food
Bought baby foods	✓ Quick and easy to prepare ✓ Convenient for travelling, holidays or when shopping ✓ Useful when only small amounts needed ✓ Wide range and types to choose from ✓ Produce adequate levels of nutrients ✓ Some have added nutrients ✓ Many do not have added colours, flavours or preservatives ✓ Hygienically prepared and packaged ✓ Easier to know how much to give ✓ Clearly labelled with the weaning stage	✗ More expensive than home-made ✗ May be a lot of wastage when only small amounts needed ✗ Bland taste, so may lead babies to reject home-made food ✗ They are processed, so some nutrients will be lost ✗ Short storage/careful storage needed once opened

Safe preparation of food

Safe preparation and handling of food are very important to prevent cross-contamination and food poisoning.

Dos and don'ts of food safety

DO:	DON'T:
✓ wash hands before handling food	✗ reheat food more than once
✓ keep food covered and check labels for storage instructions	✗ re-freeze defrosted food
✓ check temperatures of fridges and freezers	✗ allow raw fish, meat and eggs to come into contact with other food
✓ reheat food thoroughly to a high temperature	✗ allow pets onto kitchen surfaces
✓ cook food thoroughly according to the manufacturer's instructions	✗ allow pets to feed in the kitchen
✓ defrost frozen food, especially chicken, thoroughly before using	✗ use foods from tins that are 'blown', dented or rusted
✓ wash fruit and vegetables before eating raw or in salads	✗ cough or sneeze over food
✓ check expiry and best before dates carefully	✗ lick fingers when handling food
✓ use different preparation areas or chopping boards for different foods to avoid cross-contamination	✗ handle food if suffering from sickness or diarrhoea.
✓ keep the kitchen, all food preparation surfaces and cooking equipment clean	
✓ change dishcloths and tea towels frequently and wash at high temperatures.	

KEY WORD

Weaning the stage of feeding when babies change from an all-milk diet to a milk-and-solids diet.

RESEARCH ACTIVITY

1. Visit a local chemist or supermarket and carry out a survey on the different types of bought baby foods available. Present your findings in a table. For example:

Type of food	Sunshine breakfast cereal		
Sweet/savoury	Sweet		
Packet, jar, tinned or frozen	Packet mix		
Cost	£1.12		
Age suitable for	Six months		
Storage instructions	Cool, dry cupboard		
Other useful information on the package	Gluten-free, salt-free		

Analyse and evaluate your results.

QUESTIONS

Question 1

a What does the term weaning mean?

b List three signs that a baby might be ready for weaning.

c Why should weaning not begin before a baby is six months old?

d Give three reasons why weaning is important.

Question 2

a How many stages of weaning are there?

b What consistency should food be during the first stage of weaning?

c Suggest three foods suitable for the second stage of weaning.

d At what stage can finger foods be given to a baby?

e Why should babies be supervised when they are given finger foods?

e What should babies be eating at Stage 4 of weaning?

Question 3

a Why do babies need to be given iron-rich foods?

b Suggest three iron-rich foods they could be given.

c Once a baby starts to eat solid foods what should happen to the amount of milk they are given?

d Suggest, with reasons, five foods to avoid during weaning.

Question 4

a Parents often buy ready-made baby foods. Discuss the advantages and disadvantages of these.

b Suggest six advantages of using home-made baby food.

c Design and produce a set of guidelines for parents about safe preparation of foods for babies and toddlers.

 CHILD STUDY ACTIVITY

If studying a child aged between six and 12 months try to observe the child eating at two different mealtimes. Comment on the types of food being eaten and how the child's fine motor skills have improved and developed.

38 Feeding the Young Child

Toddlers soon begin to develop their own likes and dislikes about food but, like adults, they need to have a balanced diet. This is especially important as good habits developed at this age are more likely to remain with them.

Seven guidelines for a healthy diet

1. Enjoy your food.
2. Eat a variety of different foods.
3. Eat the right amount to be a healthy weight.
4. Eat plenty of foods rich in starch and fibre.
5. Eat plenty of fruit and vegetables.
6. Don't eat too many foods that contain a lot of fat.
7. Don't have sugary foods and drinks too often.

What makes up a healthy diet?

The 'eatwell plate' (see below) can help parents to plan healthy meals as it shows the types and balance of foods needed for a healthy diet. However, children under the age of five years will need a slightly higher fat content and less fibre.

The plate is divided into different sections, as shown in the illustration.

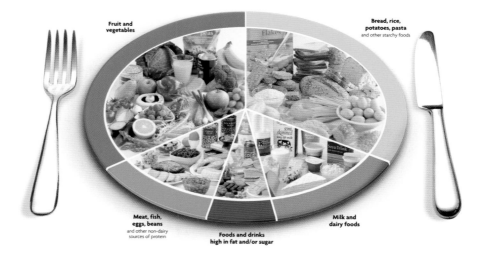

The 'eatwell plate'

Children should choose, or be served, foods from the following five groups of food each day:

1. milk and dairy foods
2. fruit and vegetables
3. bread, cereals and potatoes
4. meat, fish and alternative proteins
5. fats and sugars (this group should be eaten in moderation).

Milk and dairy foods

Milk and dairy foods

Children should drink milk or eat food made with milk to ensure they have sufficient calcium for bones and teeth. They should try to eat two to three servings a day. Butter, eggs and cream do not fall into this food group and should be eaten only in small amounts.

Fruit and vegetables

Fruit and vegetables

Children should be encouraged to eat more of all fruits and vegetables. The aim is to eat five portions of fruit and vegetables a day. This supports the government's 'Five-a-Day' campaign.

Bread, rice, potatoes, pasta and other starchy foods

Bread, cereals and potatoes

Children should be encouraged to eat foods that are carbohydrate based and starch based, not sugars. About one-third of the total intake of food should come from this group at each mealtime (e.g. potato with chicken, pasta with sauce).

Meat, fish and alternative protein foods

Children need to eat foods that are high in protein, which include meat, poultry, fish, eggs and alternatives. These foods are essential for the child's growth and repair. Children should avoid eating meat products such as sausages, beef burgers and salami, which are often very high in fat. The government recommends that some protein is eaten each day, and fish is eaten twice a week.

Meat, fish,
eggs, beans
and other non-dairy
sources of protein

Fats and sugars

Both fats and sugars should be eaten in moderation.

Fats

Generally the guideline is to consume less fat, and in particular saturated fats. Fats are high in energy, and foods that contain low fat or reduced fat will help to reduce cholesterol and the risk of heart disease.

Eat less animal fat and replace with fats from plants.

Some fats are important for young children as they provide vitamins A and D.

Foods and drinks
high in fat and/or sugar

Sugars

Sugar can be hidden and found in lots of other products – for example, in fizzy drinks, cakes, biscuits, puddings, ice cream and jam. These foods will provide a lot of energy. However, if too many sugary foods are eaten, this could lead to obesity and tooth decay.

Healthy snack foods and packed lunches

Children often take packed lunches to school rather than have school dinners. Parents need to make sure that these are as well balanced as all other meals, and not high in fats, sugar or salt.

There are many advantages of children taking their own healthy lunch or snack to school, as parents know what they are providing.

A healthy packed lunch

Some suggested snack/lunchbox foods for children are:

- fresh fruit, small bananas, plums, cherry tomatoes, fruit yoghurts, low-fat fromage frais, plain yoghurt with fresh fruit
- wholemeal bread, wraps, pitta breads
- salads, celery, cucumber and carrot sticks
- crackers, rice cakes and breadsticks.

Drinks

Children should avoid fizzy drinks and fruit juices, all of which are high in sugar and will contribute to obesity and tooth decay. Milk and water are the best drinks for children.

Food refusal

Growing toddlers often become more fussy with foods as they begin to become independent and know what they like and don't like. This can result in food refusal.

Food may not be the most important thing in their mind as they would rather be playing. A child's appetite will often vary depending on how active they have been that day. One day they might eat a great deal, other days hardly anything.

Also, they will go through phases when, for a little time, they will really like a specific item of food. Then, when it suits them, they will go off it. This is natural and only to be expected.

Food refusal is a stage many children go through

Children will rarely starve and it is important not to force-feed them. Children enjoy fuss and attention, so this will only make matters worse.

Coaxing may help, but under no circumstances should sweets, chocolate or cakes be given as a bribe. Children will eat when they are hungry. They have smaller stomachs than adults and can, therefore, consume only small quantities.

All the parents can do when this happens is to continue to provide healthy, nutritious and attractive-looking food.

Food can be fun and educational

As children get older, as well as enjoying eating food they will also enjoy helping to prepare and cook foods – this is important as it can help to improve all areas of development.

Physical

Fine motor skills are developed when using spoons and forks. Gross motor skills will improve when mixing and stirring, and hand–eye coordination when weighing and measuring. Food also helps sensory development – especially taste and touch.

Cognitive

Both cooking and eating food help children to learn many concepts, e.g. hot and cold, shapes and sizes. It can also help with number skills and understanding weight and volume.

Language

Eating together at mealtimes will help to develop children's language skills. When they are making food they can also learn new words.

Emotional

Food is enjoyable and something to look forward to. It often makes us feel better and can be comforting. Preparing and making food is fun but it can also help children to cope with negative emotions, e.g. frustration at having to wait for things to cook or cool down.

Social

Children can learn to feed themselves and to become independent – they also learn how to share and how to behave at mealtimes. Mealtimes are a good way of spending time together as a family.

Religion and culture

Children may have special dietary requirements that are not medically related. Children may not eat certain foods due to religious or cultural reasons, for instance.

The table below offers a basic guide to the most common food restrictions and requirements.

Culture/religion	Restrictions	Requirements
Jewish	• No pork or bacon • No shellfish • No gelatine	• Meat must be slaughtered under Jewish law (kosher meat) • Fish have scales and fins • Meat and milk should not be eaten together
Islamic (Muslim)	• No food from a pig (e.g. bacon, pork) • No alcohol	• Meat must be slaughtered using a ritual method (halal meat)
Hindu	• No beef • No alcohol • No eggs • No fish or other meat	• Vegetarian
Sikh	• No beef • No alcohol	• Meat slaughtered by one blow to the head
Rastafarian	• No preserved or pre-packed foods • No meat or poultry • No eggs or dairy • No salt • No coffee	• Eat natural foods

Children's diets will be greatly influenced by their parents and the types of food they buy. Many people now follow a vegetarian diet.

Vegetarians and vegans

Lacto-ovo vegetarians will not eat meat, poultry or fish but will eat some of the following foods:

Vegans eat *only* plant foods – no animal products, no eggs, no dairy products and no honey. They also will not wear or use *any* animal products (e.g. leather, silk, wool, lanolin, gelatin).

Although it is perfectly possible to bring up children on a vegan diet, great care has to be taken to make sure that they are getting a good balance of nutrients.

 REMEMBER!

In the first year, children eat what is given to them and always seem to be hungry. However, this hungry phase gradually gives way to children not always being hungry, and adopting a fussier attitude towards food.

By 12 months they know what they like and what they don't like. At this stage children will have 'food fads', where they will eat a certain food one day and refuse it the next.

 RESEARCH ACTIVITY

1. Find out about the types of foods that children will not be able to eat because of their beliefs as members of different religious groups and cultures.

QUESTIONS

Question 1

a Why is it important to develop good eating habits when children are young?

b List seven guidelines for healthy eating.

Question 2

The 'eatwell plate' helps parents to plan healthy, balanced meals for the family.

a Name the five groups of food from this plate that children should choose from, or be served, each day.

b How many portions of fruit and vegetables should a child eat each day?

c Which group of foods should be eaten in moderation?

d What proportion of the total intake of food should come from carbohydrates?

e Which meat products should children avoid eating?

Question 3

a Suggest different types of healthy foods that would be suitable for a child's lunchbox.

b Name two drinks that would be suitable for a child to have with their packed lunch.

Question 4

a Children often become fussy eaters and will sometimes refuse food that they usually like. Why might children refuse food?

b How can children be encouraged to eat when they are going through the stage of food refusal?

Question 5

a Describe how children's development can benefit from helping to prepare and cook food.

 CHILD STUDY ACTIVITY

1. Plan and carry out a cooking activity with the child you are studying. Discuss it with the parents and ask for their permission. Make sure that the recipe you choose is simple, with not too many stages or ingredients, so that the child can actually make the dish. Plan the activity carefully, thinking about safety.

2. Collect lots of pictures of different types of foods. Use these to make a 'Healthy Foods' book or a 'Healthy/Good Foods Plate' and an 'Unhealthy/Bad Foods Plate' with the child. Think about what areas of development this could encourage, and use these as your expectations.

39 Food-related Problems

In recent years there has been a big increase in the number and type of food-related problems affecting even very young children. More and more children are developing intolerance to a variety of different foods; there has been a big increase in childhood obesity and also in type 2 diabetes, as well as chronic fatigue syndrome (CFS) and conditions such as attention deficit hyperactivity disorder (ADHD).

The two main factors causing this are:

1. a poor, unhealthy diet
2. lack of exercise.

Obesity

The number of cases of childhood obesity is increasing dramatically. Recent research suggests that one in ten children in England is obese by the time they start primary school and that 25 per cent of children aged four to five years are either obese or overweight.

Overweight children often grow into overweight adults who have a greater risk of suffering from heart disease, stroke, high blood pressure, certain types of cancer – and dying at a younger age!

Obesity, however, does not only affect health – it can seriously affect a child's physical, intellectual, social and emotional development. Many obese children are:

- teased, bullied and called names by other children
- often ignored by other children, which affects their social development
- unwilling or unable to join in physical games and play
- shy and unwilling to mix with other children
- lacking in self-confidence and self-esteem.

Type 2 diabetes

This is an illness that used to mainly affect people of about 50 years old. Nowadays, because of the increase in the number of overweight and obese children, it is becoming a very serious health issue for younger children.

Type 2 diabetes results in the body not being able to control the amount of glucose in the blood. Although the symptoms might not be severe at first, if high levels of sugar in the body are not controlled it can lead to irreversible damage to the eyes and kidneys, and to earlier death.

Diabetes can be controlled in two ways:

1. a diet low in glucose
2. injecting insulin.

Causes of obesity and type 2 diabetes

Both obesity and type 2 diabetes are mainly caused by poor diet and lack of exercise. Parents have a responsibility to encourage children to develop healthy eating habits from an early age. Yet children today are eating more snack foods high in sugar, salt and fat, more refined carbohydrates and more sweet fizzy drinks. Parents are buying more convenience foods, fast food, takeaways and processed foods, all of which are high in additives and E-numbers (see page 189). In addition, families use cars to transport children even for small journeys, therefore children are walking less.

Ways of reducing obesity

Obesity can be reduced by:

- breast-feeding rather than bottle-feeding
- allowing children to have occasional treats – if they are forbidden foods by the parents they often then eat these foods excessively
- encouraging children to sit down with the family and eat with utensils, as they are more likely to develop good eating habits from their parents
- children should be offered a balanced diet with increased fruits and vegetables, less fat and fewer fizzy drinks, and encouraged to enjoy freshly prepared foods
- encouraging children to prepare healthy foods with their parents
- providing opportunities for spontaneous play where children can increase their physical activity
- reducing snacks, convenience foods and takeaway meals, which are often very high in energy and fat.

By supporting children in these ways, parents are helping to keep them healthy.

Tooth decay

Because children are having more and more sugary foods and fizzy drinks there has been an increase in tooth decay and other oral health problems.

What causes tooth decay?

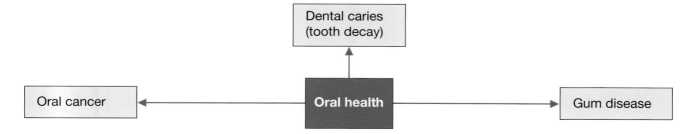

- Tooth decay is caused by eating food and drinking drinks that contain sugar.
- A layer of plaque forms on the surface of the mouth. When sugar enters the mouth the plaque bacteria produce acid, which dissolves the surface of the teeth.
- If sugar is taken in frequently during the day a dental cavity can form.

Prevention of tooth decay

- Reduce the number of times drinks or foods containing sugar are taken in during the day.
- Brush teeth twice a day using a fluoride toothpaste (this prevents the acid from the sugar attacking the enamel).
- Visit the dentist regularly.
- Fluoride is added to drinking water.

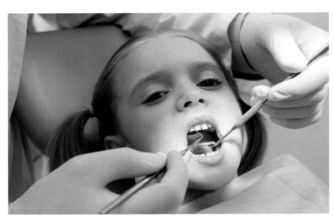

Regular visits to the dentist are a must

Food intolerance

Some children (and adults) are not able to eat certain foods without becoming ill. A food intolerance is a condition where a person can suffer a number of physical reactions caused by food, and there are different types of food intolerance.

Food allergies

Some people can react strongly to a food substance that has been eaten. The immune system, which helps to protect the body from harmful substances, reacts to the substance that the body has taken in. This substance is known as an allergen.

Children can be allergic to many foods. Some of the most common allergies are to cows' milk, eggs, shellfish and nuts. The diagram below lists some of the symptoms that a child may experience when having an allergic reaction

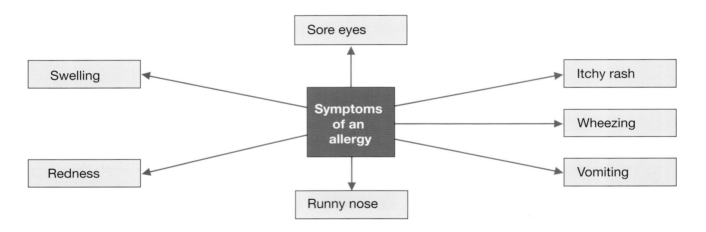

Peanuts can often trigger a nut allergy. A peanut allergy can be very serious and can lead to anaphylactic shock (see the box below).

> **Peanut allergy**
>
> Symptoms of anaphylactic shock are:
> - swollen mouth and throat
> - sore, red eyes

Inability to absorb nutrients

Sometimes the body cannot absorb some nutrients. For example, some people are sensitive to gluten. This causes a condition known as coeliac disease. Gluten is a protein found in wheat, oats, barley and rye – because these are used to make many different kinds of foods, such as bread, cakes, biscuits, pasta, sauces and gravy, great care needs to be taken when buying and preparing foods, and especially when eating out.

Nowadays a good range of gluten-free products can be bought in supermarkets, and parents can also get these on prescription from their GP.

A child who has coeliac disease will display the symptoms noted in the diagram below.

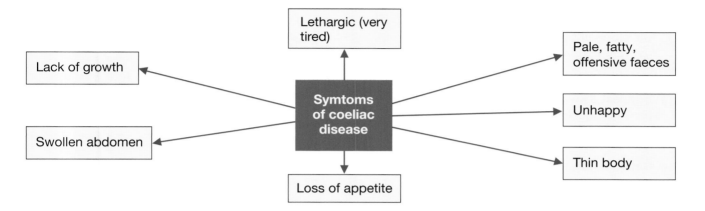

Hyperactivity – ADHD (attention deficit hyperactivity disorder)

Children who suffer from ADHD cannot concentrate for long periods of time and their behaviour is often hyperactive. Research has shown that artificial colourings, flavourings and preservatives often make hyperactive children worse.

Parents need to avoid foods with lots of additives in them, and check labels carefully (see page 189).

 RESEARCH ACTIVITY

1. Discuss how parents could prevent a child from becoming obese. Then produce a fact sheet for parents, entitled 'Steps to Prevent Childhood Obesity'.

2. Rachel has invited her friend, Olivia, to a birthday party. Olivia has coeliac disease and may not be able to eat some of the food at the party. Find out about the gluten-free products that can be bought at the supermarket. Suggest gluten-free foods that Olivia could take to eat at the party so she does not feel left out.

QUESTIONS

Question 1

a Name three types of food-related problem that have increased in recent years.

b Describe how obesity might affect the development of a young child.

c What is type 2 diabetes?

d How can this be controlled?

e Suggest six ways parents could help to prevent obesity.

Question 2

a Suggest three possible causes of tooth decay.

b Describe three ways parents could help to prevent tooth decay in young children.

Question 3

a What is food intolerance?

b Name three of the most common foods that can cause allergies.

c Describe some of the symptoms a child might experience with an allergic reaction.

d What can happen to a person with a peanut allergy?

Question 4

a What is coeliac disease?

b List five of the symptoms a child will display if they have coeliac disease.

c What sort of foods should parents avoid giving children suffering from ADHD?

40 Hygiene Is Important

Bathtime

Bathtime for young babies and toddlers must be fun. New parents often fear bathtime, but if everything is prepared and everyone is relaxed there shouldn't be any problems. There is no correct time to bath a baby but it is generally accepted that before a feed is best. Some parents prefer to bath their baby in the morning and others prefer early evening. This is a matter of personal choice, although some people feel that bathing the baby in the evening helps to settle him/her to sleep.

Bathing a young baby

Collect together all the equipment you will need and make sure the room being used is warm (18–21°C is ideal). Prevent draughts by closing windows and doors. Remember that new babies are not able to regulate their body temperature.

What do you need?

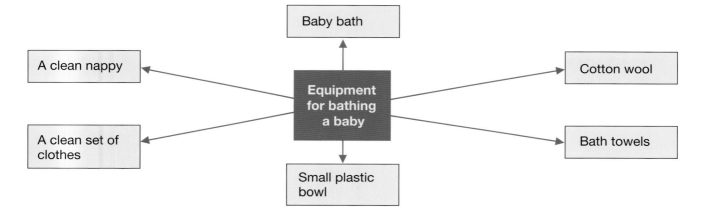

Baby bath

A clean nappy

Cotton wool

Equipment for bathing a baby

A clean set of clothes

Bath towels

Small plastic bowl

Steps to bathing a baby

Step 1

Always put cold water in the baby bath first and then add the hot water. Test the temperature of the water using a thermometer, elbow or wrist.

Keep the water shallow (5–8 cm is deep enough).

Testing bath temperature

Step 2

Undress the baby, apart from nappy, and wrap in a towel.

Clean the face with damp cotton wool using cooled boiled water.

Clean each eye separately, wiping from the inside out and using a new cotton wool ball for each eye to prevent the risk of spreading any infections.

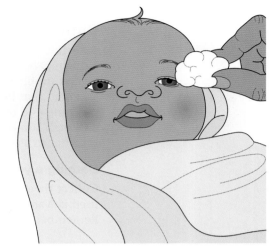

Washing the eyes and face

Step 3

Hold the baby carefully under one arm to support the back and head, and wash the baby's head.

In the first few weeks it is not necessary to use lotions, shampoos or soap.

Washing the scalp

Step 4

Unwrap the baby, remove nappy and clean bottom. Gently lower into the bath, supporting the head and neck.

Wash the baby gently, paying particular attention to areas where there are folds and creases in the skin.

Bathing the baby

Step 5

Lift the baby from the bath, wrap them in a warm towel and dry them thoroughly.

Though babies do lose body heat quickly, if the room is warm they often like a few moments of freedom without their clothes before they are dressed.

Drying the baby on a towel

Bathing an older baby

It is highly likely that by the age of six months a baby will have outgrown a baby bath and will be ready to be introduced to a normal bath. To get babies used to this it is a good idea to put the baby bath in the 'big bath' so that they become familiar with the surroundings.

When using the full-size bath, place a non-slip bath mat on the base of the bath. Add the cold water first and then top up with the hot. Check the temperature with an elbow. Keep the bath water relatively shallow (10–13 cm). Turn the taps off very tightly and cover the hot tap with a flannel. Touching a hot tap can burn little hands.

Do not let babies stand up in the bath. Apart from the obvious danger they may frighten themselves and not want to bath again. Children and toddlers must never be left alone in the bath.

Playing in the bath

Once babies can sit up unsupported they will enjoy extra moments in the bath to play. There are many bath toys available on the market but an empty shampoo bottle or plastic cup will give hours of pleasure. Remember, however, that loose caps, etc., should be removed before bottles and suchlike are used as toys.

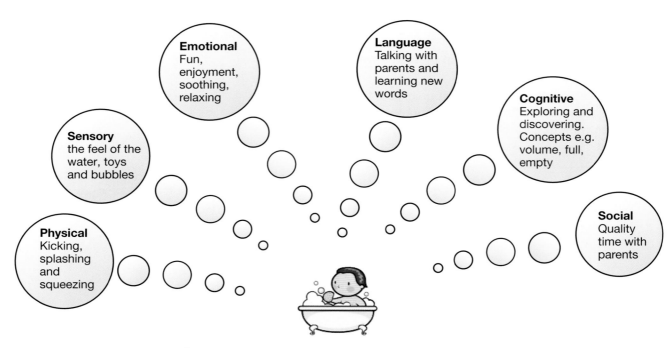

Steps to topping and tailing

Topping and tailing

It is not always convenient to bath a baby on a daily basis. Difficult times may be when travelling or on holiday, for instance. On these occasions a baby should be 'topped and tailed'. This means cleaning the baby's face and nappy area thoroughly.

It is important to use either two separate bowls or a divided 'topping and tailing' bowl to prevent infection spreading.

For topping and tailing you will also need the following:

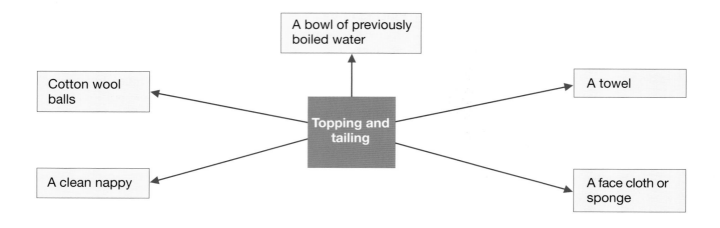

1. Undress the baby but leave on the baby's vest and nappy. Lay the baby on a towel.

2. Using the cool boiled water moisten a cotton wool ball and clean the baby's eyes. Remember to use one cotton wool ball per eye and wipe from the inside out, as described in the section above on bathing a baby.

3. Using a facecloth, gently wash the baby's hands and feet, and towel them dry.

4. Remove the nappy and cleanse the nappy area with baby lotion/water and cotton wool, or with baby wipes.

5. Put on a clean nappy and dress the baby.

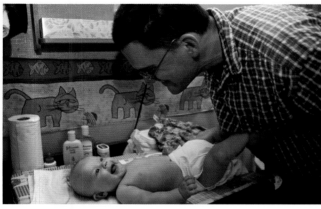

Nappy changing

Changing a nappy

As it is possible that a baby may need to be changed up to 12 times a day it is important that there is an area of the home that is warm and convenient to keep all the equipment needed close at hand.

Nappy liners, pins and waterproof pants for reusable nappies

A changing mat

Clean nappies

Bucket for dirty reusable nappies

Clean clothes if the baby has soiled the ones she/he is wearing

To change the baby you will need

Nappy sacks (for disposables)

Nappy rash/barrier cream

Baby wipes/cotton wool/tissues

Bowl of warm water

Step-by-step guide to changing a nappy

1. Make sure all the equipment needed is to hand.

2. Wash your hands thoroughly.

3. Lay the baby on the changing mat and remove the soiled nappy by holding the baby's ankles with one hand and lifting the nappy away with the other.

4. If the nappy is a dirty one, use cotton wool, tissues or wipes to clean the baby's bottom.

5. Use warm water and cotton wool to clean the bottom thoroughly.

6. Dry the bottom thoroughly and put on a thick layer of barrier cream.

7. Open out the new nappy and slide it under the baby using your free hand to lift the baby's ankles.

8. Put the baby's legs down, then fasten the nappy securely with nappy pins or Velcro tabs.

Nappy rash

Nappy rash (ammonia dermatitis) is a common skin complaint that affects the area covered by the baby's nappy. Nappy rash occurs when the tender skin of the baby is left in contact with urine and faeces. Bacteria in the faeces react with the urine and ammonia is released. This causes burning and irritation. The baby's skin becomes red and inflamed, and is warm to the touch.

Most babies have nappy rash at some stage in their first year. It is essential therefore that the nappy is changed regularly and the nappy region is washed and dried thoroughly.

Many babies do suffer from nappy rash but the following factors increase the likelihood of the baby being infected:

- a few days after an immunisation injection
- a change of diet from breast to bottle
- if the baby has an upset tummy causing excessive bowel movements or diarrhoea
- if the baby is teething
- if the baby is generally 'off colour'.

Most causes of nappy rash can be treated at home but if the soreness continues for more than a week it would be wise to consult a doctor.

Ways to prevent nappy rash

• Baby's skin should be kept dry.
• Reusable nappies should be washed and rinsed thoroughly.
• Use nappy rash cream at the first sign of soreness.
• Do not wash the skin with soap and water as this 'de-fats' the skin.
• Use a fairly thick application of barrier cream at each nappy stage.
• Try never to leave a baby in a wet nappy.
• Leave the baby without a nappy (lying on a towel) when possible, to let the air reach the skin.

If nappy rash does develop, barrier cream should not be used until the bottom is no longer sore. It is not advisable to use talcum powder on babies' bottoms.

Care of teeth

From an early age it is important to care for, and encourage children to care for, their teeth.

Cleaning the teeth

As soon as teeth appear they need to be cleaned. If they are not, plaque will stick to the teeth and begin to cause them to decay.

- When babies are able to hold an object let them have a soft toothbrush – they will learn to imitate others they see cleaning their teeth.
- From about a year old, children can be taught to brush their own teeth – it is a difficult skill and they will need help until they are about seven years old.

Young children need to be encouraged to clean their teeth from an early age

- Add a small amount of children's toothpaste containing fluoride to the toothbrush even if they have no teeth; this can still get rid of bacteria in the gums.
- Brush teeth after breakfast and before going to bed.

Meals and snacks

A healthy diet will promote healthy teeth and gums. Sugar causes decay and can damage the teeth before they come through.

- Children need foods with a lot of calcium, phosphorous, fluoride, vitamins A, C and D, and foods that are crisp and need biting and chewing, such as carrots, apples and celery.
- Parents should avoid giving sweets as treats.
- Don't give sweet drinks in baby bottles and feeders, or dip dummies in honey or jam, as this concentrates the sugar on the teeth.
- If a child needs medicine, make sure it is sugar-free.

Dentists

Regular visits to a dentist are a must. These should start as soon as teeth come through. If children start these early:

- they are less likely to be afraid
- any problems can be dealt with immediately.

Children should visit the dentist every six months.

'Smiling for Life'

'Smiling for Life' is a national programme on nutrition and oral health for child carers. This programme has been produced by the Health Education Authority and is being taken into nurseries and pre-schools to support the promotion of good oral health.

Hair and nails

Care of the hair and scalp

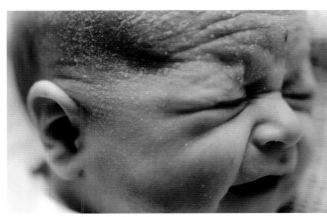

Baby with cradle cap

A baby's hair/scalp should be washed daily if possible. It is not necessary to use soap or lotion for the first few weeks. Cradle cap is extremely common in small babies. This is when scaly patches, often red in colour, appear on the scalp. Cradle cap is harmless and will clear up without any special treatment. Do not be tempted to pick off the scales. Wash the scalp regularly and gently massage a little baby oil into it. This loosens the scales and they will then wash off easily.

When shampoo or lotions are used for hair washing it is very important to use non-sting varieties and to ensure they don't get near the baby's eyes. Only a small amount of shampoo is needed, which should be worked into a lather and rinsed away almost immediately. Some adults apply two lots of shampoo, but one wash is enough for babies.

To dry the hair, rub gently with a towel. Try not to cover the baby's face as he/she will be frightened. A good investment may be a shield that prevents water and soap running over the baby's face while the hair is being washed.

Care of nails

Babies have fast-growing nails. In order to stop babies scratching themselves, nails should be kept short.

Using a small pair of blunt-edged scissors, cut the nails when they are soft. The best time to do this is after bathtime. However, if you feel nervous or it is difficult to keep the baby still, cut the nails when she/he is sleeping.

Toiletries

The skin of new babies is delicate and it is not advisable to use soaps or wipes for the first six weeks.

After six weeks, special baby toiletries can be used as these are unlikely to irritate the baby's skin. Many are hypo-allergenic.

 QUESTIONS

Question 1

a What room temperature is ideal when bathing a baby?

b Why is it sensible to put cold water into the bath first then add hot water?

c Why must a clean piece of damp cotton wool to be used to cleanse each eye?

d What is meant by topping and tailing?

e What is cradle cap?

Question 2

Describe five ways that playing in the bath can encourage an older baby's development.

Question 3

a What is nappy rash and how can it be caused?

b What is another name for nappy rash?

c Suggest six ways to prevent nappy rash.

Question 4

a When should parents begin to clean a baby's teeth?

b A baby can be encouraged to use a toothbrush and toothpaste even before they have teeth. Why will this benefit the child?

c A healthy diet can help to prevent tooth decay. What sort of foods should children be encouraged to eat?

d Sugar is one of the main causes of tooth decay. Suggest three ways that parents could limit the amount of sugar in the diet.

e Why should children start to go to the dentist as soon as their teeth come through?

 RESEARCH ACTIVITY

Interview the parents of the child being studied about how they encourage care of the teeth. Try to find out what food and snacks are given, how often the child goes to the dentist, whether the child cleans his/her own teeth, what type of toothbrush/toothpaste is used, etc.

CHILD STUDY ACTIVITY

1. If you are studying a baby, observe them being bathed. Record this routine activity, the equipment used and what emotions the baby showed. In particular, comment on what the baby enjoyed/did not enjoy about the activity.

2. For an older baby or toddler, bathtime can offer an excellent opportunity to observe a child playing with a selection of toys. Observe the toys the child plays with in the bath. What areas of development did you observe with this water play?

41 Clothing and Footwear

Clothing

Once babies start to become more mobile they tend to need different types of clothes for different situations. They will need clothes for both indoors and outdoors and for hot, cold and wet weather.

Whether choosing clothes for babies, toddlers or pre-school children, the general points outlined in the box below should be remembered.

> **Clothing should be:**
> - comfortable and easy to move around in
> - easy to put on and take off, especially for nappy changing or going to the toilet
> - hardwearing and give protection, especially when babies are learning to crawl and starting to walk
> - washable (as it will get dirty quickly), easy to dry, and should need minimum or no ironing
> - made from a fabric that suits the purpose of the garment (e.g. stretch fabrics allow for movement, denim or heavy cotton material for play, and so on)
> - easy to fasten for both child and parent – zip fasteners, Velcro and popper studs are much easier than buttons or ties, and waist and wrist bands are much easier to manage (and often more comfortable) if they are elasticated.

Because children grow very quickly, it is often sensible to buy sizes that are slightly too big for them, to allow for growth and comfort, but they should not be so big that they make movement difficult.

Unisex clothing is useful because it can be handed down from one child to another and, often, home-made clothes can be cheaper than bought ones.

As children get older and begin to be more independent they will want to choose for themselves what they want to wear. They will also want to dress themselves, although shoes may go on the wrong feet and clothing may be put on back to front. This can often be frustrating for parents as it can take so long, but it is an important stage in developing independence. Choosing clothes that are easy to put on and fasten will make this stage slightly easier.

Clothes for different situations

Underwear and nightwear

Nightwear should be soft and comfortable, and should suit the temperature and time of year. Because young children often kick off bedclothes when they sleep, a sleep suit can keep them warmer than pyjamas and nightdresses; however, the latter are easier if children need to go to the toilet. A fleecy dressing gown with a zip opening is also useful.

Legal requirements for nightwear

The law requires that all nightdresses and dressing gowns should be made from material that does not flare up or burn easily. (See Chapter 5.)

Clothes for outdoors

The sort of clothing needed for outdoors will depend on the time of year, the weather and the activity.

When playing out in winter children need to be warm but able to run around

In winter or very cold weather, children should wear several warm layers of clothing, rather than just one or two heavy garments, to allow warm air to circulate between the layers. These garments should be warm and protective without being heavy and bulky so that they don't restrict movement.

Often, clothing that is lined, padded or quilted will add extra warmth. Knitted hats, gloves and scarves are a useful addition for cold weather. If it is raining or snowing, garments should be waterproof and elasticated at the wrist, and hoods should be fastened with either fasteners or zipped up under the chin, never with drawstrings.

During warm weather clothing should be lightweight and absorbent. T-shirts are ideal but should have long sleeves to protect against the sun, and hats that protect the neck and ears should be worn.

Footwear

Children do not really need shoes until they start walking and, in fact, letting children go barefoot (provided there is nothing around to hurt them) will allow the feet to develop naturally.

The bones of a child's foot are very soft and can very easily be damaged. If children are allowed to wear shoes or even socks that are too tight, the bones and muscles will not develop properly. This can result in deformed feet, corns and other foot problems.

Children's feet grow very quickly – about two to two-and-a-half sizes each year – until approximately the age of four years. As a result, a child will outgrow his/her shoes about once every three months. Feet should always be measured professionally so that they are the correct size, length and width. New shoes should be fitted to leave 12–18 mm growing space between the end of the longest toe and the end of the shoe. Shoes should also be wide enough to allow the toes to wriggle inside.

Some useful points to remember when either buying shoes for the first time or simply buying a new pair of shoes are noted in the diagram overleaf.

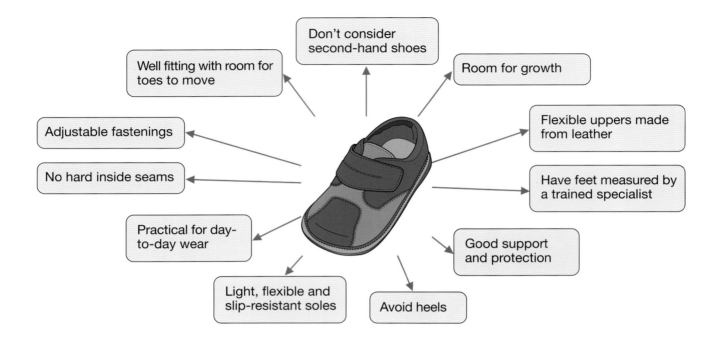

Don't consider second-hand shoes

Well fitting with room for toes to move

Room for growth

Flexible uppers made from leather

Adjustable fastenings

No hard inside seams

Have feet measured by a trained specialist

Practical for day-to-day wear

Good support and protection

Light, flexible and slip-resistant soles

Avoid heels

Other types of footwear

Whenever possible, children should wear good-quality, well-made and well-fitted shoes. However, there may be circumstances where a toddler or child will wear other types of footwear, possibly to suit the weather (e.g. sandals, slippers, wellington boots or trainers). These are fine for short spells only, because they are not usually made to the same standard as shoes and may not give the support and protection feet need.

? QUESTIONS

Question 1

a What points should be considered when choosing clothing for young children?

b Describe, with reasons, suitable clothing for children to wear outside.

Question 2

a Why is it best to let children go barefoot for as long as possible?

b The bones in a child's foot are easily damaged. Explain why.

c How often should children's feet be measured?

d Why should shoes be measured professionally?

e Give six points to consider when choosing shoes for young children.

42 Child Health

All children will be unwell at some time, and by the time babies are about nine months old they have already experienced their first cold or sniffles. Most parents are capable of dealing with this, whereas the onset of a rash might make them feel less confident.

From time to time young children will suffer from colds, flu, upset stomach, earache, toothache and so on, but these can usually be dealt with by the parent.

Young children will rarely pretend to be ill so, if they are ill, they will show signs of being unwell or display different behaviour.

Signs of good and poor health

Good health	Poor health
✓ Good eating habits	✗ Poor appetite
✓ Alertness	✗ Signs of apathy
✓ Normal opening of bowels	✗ Constipation
✓ Always interested in surroundings	✗ Being miserable, crying, unhappy
✓ Contented child	✗ Breathing difficulties
✓ Breathing normally through the nose	✗ Dull eyes
✓ Very bright eyes	✗ Very poor sleeping habits
✓ Sleeping well	✗ Skin has a pallor, almost white-looking
✓ Good, clear and firm skin	✗ Muscles tend to be flabby
✓ Well-developed muscles	✗ Constantly runny nose
✓ No constantly runny nose	✗ Child not progressing and developing as expected
✓ 'Normal' progress and development for the age group	✗ Below average weight and height for age group
✓ Weight and height 'average' for the age group	

Causes of ill health

There are three main causes of illness:

1. microbiological
2. genetic
3. environmental.

Microbiological

Microorganisms are commonly known as germs and cannot be seen by the human eye. Microorganisms can be divided into three main groups, as outlined in the table below.

Bacteria	• Not all bacteria are harmful. Some live naturally in the human body. • Bacteria multiply very quickly. • When bacteria multiply this creates harmful toxins (poisons) in the body; the sufferer will show signs of being ill with the infection or disease.
Viruses	• They are very small in size. • They live and reproduce in other living cells. • They multiply within the cell until it bursts then spread the infection to other cells. • A virus cannot be treated with antibiotics.
Fungi	• They are small plant organisms. • They cause irritations and conditions such as athlete's foot and ringworm.

Genetic

Genetic disorders can cause a child to have some health problems. Examples of these are outlined in the table below.

Cystic fibrosis	• Breathing difficulties • Chest infections • Food is not digested and absorbed properly • The child fails to gain weight
Down's syndrome **Sickle cell anaemia**	• Heart, chest and sinus conditions • The disease can be made worse by getting a cold

Environmental

The environment a child is brought up in and the parental guidance a child receives could affect their health. Some environmental factors are noted in the diagram below.

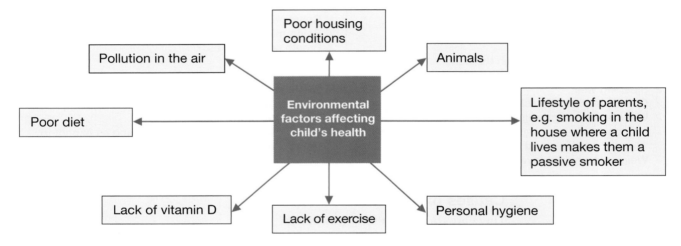

 RESEARCH ACTIVITY

Investigate how lack of exercise could affect a young child. What steps could a parent or carer take to increase the amount of exercise the child does?

? QUESTIONS

Question 1

a List five general signs that a child is well.

b List five general signs that a child is not well.

Question 2

a What are the three main causes of illness?

b What are microorganisms commonly known as?

c What do bacteria produce that is harmful to the body?

d How does a virus spread infection?

Question 3

a What health problems can be caused by cystic fibrosis?

b Name two other genetic disorders that can cause a child health problems.

Question 4

a List six environmental factors that can affect child health.

43 Infectious Diseases and Immunisation

Infectious diseases are caused by both bacteria and viruses.

The diagram below notes some infectious diseases; the colour coding shows which ones are caused by bacteria and which by a virus.

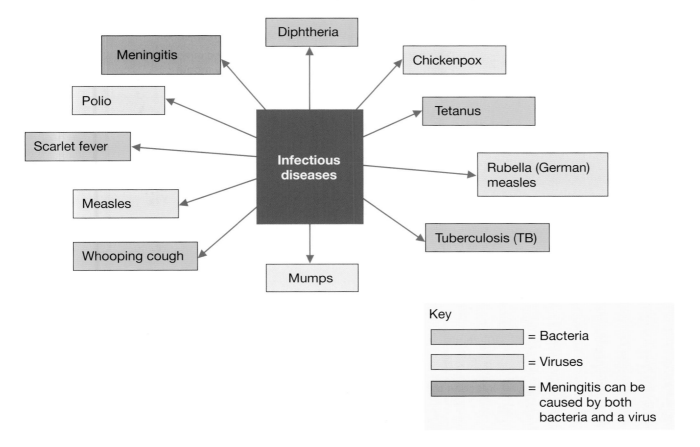

Diphtheria

Meningitis

Polio

Scarlet fever

Measles

Whooping cough

Infectious diseases

Chickenpox

Tetanus

Rubella (German) measles

Tuberculosis (TB)

Mumps

Key

☐ = Bacteria

☐ = Viruses

☐ = Meningitis can be caused by both bacteria and a virus

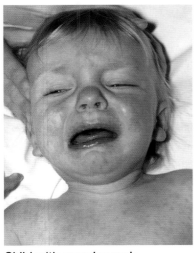

Child with measles rash

Many infectious diseases are contagious. This means that they are spread from one person to another by direct contact. This could be by touching or kissing an infected person, or by using the towel of someone with the disease.

What is immunisation?

Immunisation involves giving children a vaccine, usually by injection. The vaccine contains a very small, weak amount of the bacterium or virus that causes the disease, or small amounts of the toxin of the disease. It does not give the child the disease but it triggers the body's immune system to produce antibodies that will fight the disease.

Children can be vaccinated against many infectious diseases, but not all of them (e.g. there is no vaccination for chickenpox or scarlet fever).

The table below lists the recommended immunisation programme for young children.

Age	Vaccination	How given
Birth	BCG (Bacillus Calmette Guerin)	One injection
Two, three, four months	Diphtheria, whooping cough, tetanus and HIB Meningitis Polio	One injection One injection By mouth
12–15 months	Measles, mumps and rubella (MMR)	One injection
Three to five years	Diphtheria and tetanus Polio MMR	One injection By mouth One injection

Infectious diseases

Disease	Bacterium or virus	Symptoms	Immunisation
Diphtheria	B	A white layer forms on the throat, which may block the airway; it produces poison that damages the heart and nervous system	Yes
Whooping cough (pertussis)	B	Long bouts of coughing that may end with a 'whoop', and vomiting	Yes
Tetanus (lockjaw)	B	Muscles of the neck, back and limbs tighten and the jaw may lock	Yes
HIB (haemophilus influenzae type b)	V	Depends on the part of the body infected	Yes
Poliomyelitis (polio)	V	Infection of the spinal cord, which may result in paralysis	Yes
Tuberculosis	B	A general feeling of being unwell. A persistent cough sometimes resulting in blood being coughed up. Damage to lungs. Swollen glands in the neck	Yes
Measles	V	Fever, severe cold and cough. Four to five days later a red rash appears on the face and spreads downwards	Yes
Mumps	V	Painful swelling near the jaw or one or both sides	Yes
Rubella (German measles)	V	A mild disease with a red rash and usually with swollen glands	Yes
Chickenpox	V	Small red spots that turn to painful blisters	No
Meningitis	V or B	May include fever, convulsions, sickness, listlessness, crying. A very distinctive rash that will not disappear when pressed. Stiff neck, painful joints, can't bear bright lights. Bulging fontanelle in a baby	Meningitis A and C can be vaccinated against

Key

☐ = Bacterium

☐ = Virus

☐ = Meningitis can be caused by both bacteria and a virus

Immunisation protects children against serious illness

The importance of immunisation

It is important to immunise children against certain diseases so that they can fight off that disease if they come into contact with it, instead of becoming ill and perhaps dying from it.

In most cases, once a child is vaccinated they should have lifelong protection from polio, and probable lifelong protection against measles, mumps, rubella and meningitis C.

It is because of immunisation that many of the most serious diseases, such as smallpox and polio, have almost disappeared. However, the more parents who decide not to immunise their children against diseases such as measles and mumps, the more outbreaks of the disease there will be and more children will be at risk of being ill.

Choosing not to immunise

Recently there has been a lot of concern among parents about the MMR (measles, mumps and rubella) vaccine because of possible links with autism. As a result more parents are now choosing not to give their children this vaccine. This has led to a serious situation in the UK, where the number of people catching measles in England and Wales has risen from 56 in 1998 to just under 1000 in 2007. Measles is a serious disease because it can lead to complications. There is now a national campaign to encourage people to be immunised against measles, to stop it spreading across the country.

While a small number of children might have a reaction to vaccines, it is important to remember that, overall, the risk of harmful, lasting complications is extremely small, while the risk of harmful effects from catching the disease are much higher – and much more serious.

Why parents might decide not to have children immunised

- Doctors themselves and other experts are divided about possible effects of vaccines.
- Fear of the unknown – whether their child will be one of the few who have a serious reaction.
- Having an injection is upsetting – for both the parent and child – and it seems cruel.
- There is no obvious benefit of immunisation – it doesn't 'make the child better' in a way that medicine does because the child is actually healthy!
- Because parents don't know anyone who has had measles, polio or meningitis it is difficult to understand why it is needed.

It's a hard decision to make, but certainly a child should not be immunised:

- if they are really ill or have a very high temperature
- if they have had a reaction to previous vaccines
- if they are taking medicines or antibiotics
- if they are receiving chemotherapy or radiotherapy.

KEY WORDS

Antibodies substances the body produces to try to control/destroy the disease

Contagious disease disease that spreads from one person to another by contact

Infectious stage when germs can spread from one person to another

Immunisation protection against infection and disease by vaccination

Immunity a person's ability to resist infection

Symptoms act like signposts because they signal that something is wrong

Vaccine very small, weak amount of a bacterium or virus that triggers the body's immune system to produce antibodies that will fight the disease

QUESTIONS

Question 1

a Infectious diseases are caused by both bacteria and viruses.

   (i) List four infectious diseases caused by a bacterium.

   (ii) List four infectious diseases caused by a virus.

b What is a contagious disease?

Question 2

a What is a vaccine?

b Describe how immunisation helps to fight against disease.

c What are antibodies?

d What vaccinations are offered to children of two, three and four months?

e What vaccinations are offered to children aged from three to five years?

Question 3

a Describe the symptoms of the following:

   (i) chickenpox

   (ii) meningitis

   (iii) measles

   (iv) mumps.

b What are the technical terms for the following infectious diseases:

   (i) whooping cough?

   (ii) polio?

   (iii) German measles?

   (iv) lockjaw?

Question 4

a Why is it important to immunise children?

b Give four reasons why parents may choose not to immunise their children.

RESEARCH ACTIVITY

There has been much debate over the uptake of the vaccination for measles, mumps and rubella (MMR). There is a suggestion that the MMR vaccination could be linked to autism. There have also been recent outbreaks of measles.

Carry out research into the reasons why some parents choose to opt out of this type of vaccination, and why others support the MMR immunisation programme.

CHILD STUDY ACTIVITY

Often children can regress during prolonged periods of ill health. Find out from the parents if the child has had any childhood ailments or illnesses that may have affected her/his progress and development.

44 Care of the Sick Child

Children often show symptoms of not being well and can sometimes recover quickly from an illness. They can appear very poorly one day and free of symptoms the next.

Young children will often get a cold, stomach upset, earache, etc., particularly when they start mixing with other children.

Parents are usually very good at knowing when their child is displaying a change in their usual behaviour or showing different eating and sleeping habits. It is sometimes hard, however, for a parent to know when a child is feeling unwell and when the situation changes to a more serious nature.

The following diagram lists some of the symptoms a child may show if they are unwell.

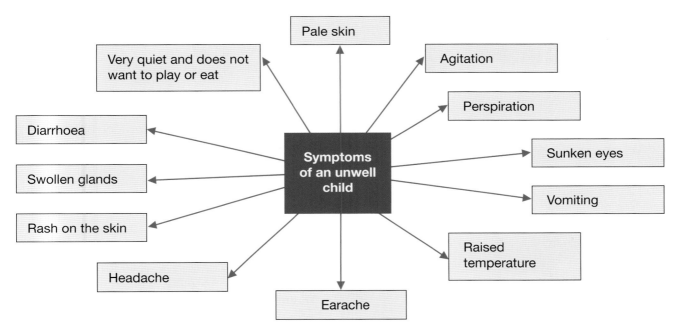

The sick child at home

When a child is at home and unwell the parent will be the first person to treat them. Usually the parent would:

- take a child's temperature; if raised the parent may give them liquid paracetamol to reduce the temperature and pain
- try to encourage the child to drink plenty of fluids to avoid dehydration
- try to keep the child cool and comfortable
- monitor their temperature regularly with a thermometer
- give them lots of hugs and reassurance
- notice any changes in their symptoms.

It is, therefore, important that a medicine box containing a thermometer is kept in the house, in either a lockable box or cupboard, out of the reach of a young child.

There are three different types of thermometer available, all of which record the temperature of the body, which should normally be around 37°C. If the temperature is raised, then this is a good indication that a child could be ill and, if very high, it may indicate a serious illness.

> **Forehead thermometer**
>
> This is a strip that is placed on the child's forehead. The strip is made of plastic and the liquid crystals in it will react with the temperature recorded on the forehead. This changes the colour of the strip, which tells you the temperature of the body. This does not cause the child any distress and is very quick and easy to use.

Forehead thermometer

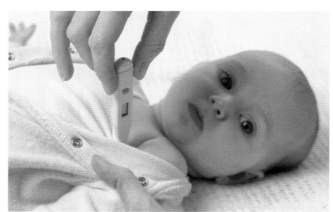

Digital thermometer

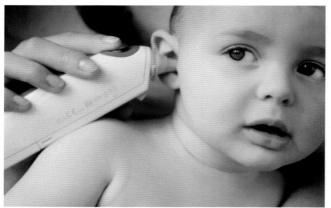

Ear thermometer

> **Digital thermometer**
>
> This is a safe and easy-to-read thermometer. It is placed in the mouth and when the thermometer bleeps the accurate reading can be taken.

> **Ear thermometer**
>
> This type of thermometer is placed into the ear and accurately records a result in a very similar way to the digital thermometer. This is useful when a child is sleeping or doesn't like having a thermometer in their mouth.

Mercury thermometers should never be used as they are easily broken and the mercury is poisonous.

When to call a GP/doctor

If parents are worried about their child's condition, or if the symptoms change and become more serious, it may be time to seek advice from the doctor. It is always better to ask advice if in doubt, particularly with a baby, who is unable to describe any symptoms.

Emergency situations

The diagram below lists some of the situations that will require a doctor (GP) or the child being taken into hospital.

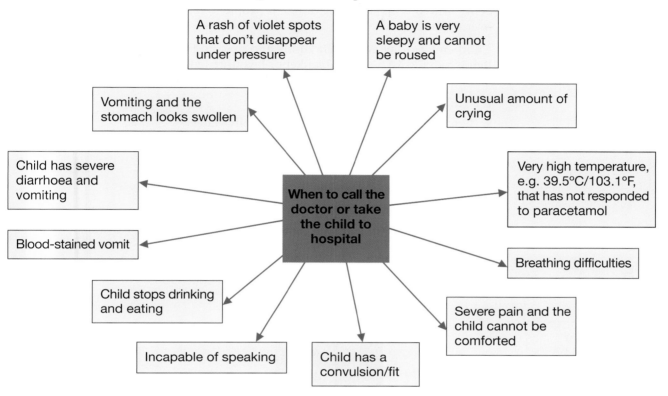

Giving medicines

At some point, parents might need to give medicine to a baby or young child, either because a doctor has prescribed it or if the child has a toothache or high temperature.

Guidelines for giving medicines
- Check with the pharmacist to make sure the medicine is suitable for the age of child.
- Check labels – especially if the child has a known allergy.
- Use the spoon provided with the medicine and measure accurately.
- Never give more than the required dose.
- Follow manufacturer's/doctor's instructions.
- Check the 'use by' dates of all medicines.
- Make sure the spoon in clean and/or sterilised.
- Store all medicines correctly and out of the reach of children.
- Complete the course.
- Use a small syringe to give medicine to babies.
- Only give liquid medicine – tablets can cause choking.
- Check for any reaction and seek medical advice immediately.
- Do not give children other people's medicines.

Looking after the sick child at home

There are many reasons a child may be unwell and can be treated at home by the parents, grandparents, friends or relatives. Children often love the attention of being unwell. This can bring different people to talk to them and make a fuss over them.

Children like to be near their family and may find comfort on the sofa, in the living room, with a special blanket or favourite teddy. Sometimes children may need to be in bed where they may be more comfortable.

If a child has to stay in bed make sure that:

- they have plenty of cool drinks, especially water
- they have regular but small meals
- the bed is kept clean and is changed regularly
- windows are open to allow in some fresh air
- the bedroom is kept at an even temperature
- the child is kept clean.

As well as being kept comfortable the child should have some distractions to avoid boredom, as outlined in the diagram below.

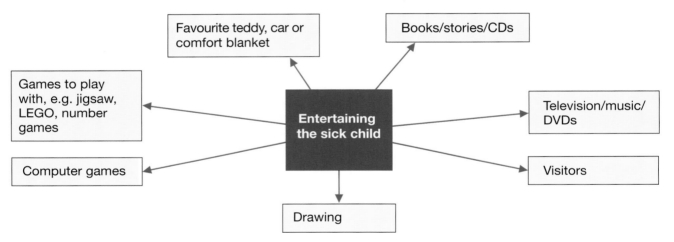

Coping with the sick child in hospital

Children may have to go into hospital as an emergency, which leaves little time to prepare them for what will happen to them. There are occasions when children go into hospital for an operation or treatment, so it is possible to prepare the child for what could be a traumatic and emotional time.

The following suggestions may help the child.

- Explain to the child that the nurses and doctors in the hospital are there to make them feel better.
- Tell them that they will be able to take their favourite toy, and encourage the child to pack their own suitcase with other favourite items, e.g. pyjamas, story book, slippers.
- Read a story with the child about a child going into hospital.
- Try to visit the hospital beforehand to let them see what it is like.
- Reassure the child that they will not be left on their own and that parents are allowed to stay in the hospital and be near to them.

- Role play doctors, nurses and being at hospital with the child.
- Tell them that friends and family can come and visit them.

Parents can be reassured that children are usually admitted to either a children's hospital or a children's ward in a general hospital where the staff are normally specially trained to deal with children.

QUESTIONS

Question 1

a List six signs that a child may not be well.

b How can a parent or carer treat a sick child at home?

Question 2

a What is the normal body temperature?

b What can a raised temperature indicate?

c There are different types of thermometer that record body temperature. Name and describe three of these.

d Why is it dangerous to use a mercury thermometer?

Question 3

Children can quickly become quite poorly.

a List six situations where you would call for a doctor or take a child to hospital.

b Produce a checklist to guide parents about the correct use of medicines.

Question 4

a List five ways a sick child could be kept comfortable.

b When children are ill they may become bored and frustrated. Suggest five different activities that could be used with sick children.

c Describe six ways parents can prepare a young child for going into hospital.

Web Links	
www.allergyuk.org	Information on allergies relating to diet.
www.abm.me.uk	Association of Breastfeeding Mothers. Information, advice and support in connection with breast-feeding.
www.asthma.org.uk	Information, support and leaflets about asthma.
www.bbc.co.uk/parenting/childcare	A huge range of articles and information on all aspects of child development and caring for children.
www.breastfeedingnetwork.org.uk	Useful leaflets and support with breast-feeding.
www.babycentre.co.uk	Wide range of articles and information on all aspects of pregnancy, birth, and care of babies and toddlers.
www.childhealth.co.uk	Information and advice on all sorts of child health problems.
www.cry-sis.org.uk	Information and support for families with excessively crying, sleepless, demanding children.
www.dh.gov.uk	Department of Health. Lots of information on infant care, pregnancy and childbirth, including immunisation, reducing the risk of cot death, weaning, breast-feeding and antenatal care.
www.hacsg.org.uk	Hyperactive Children's Support Group. Information on and support with hyperactivity.
www.milk.co.uk	The Dairy Council. Bright, concise material in an appealing format. Lots of free publications – leaflets and posters. Dietary advice from conception to toddlers, to teenagers and sports people.
www.nctpregnancyandbabycare.com	National Childbirth Trust. Information on antenatal care, pregnancy, birth and care of children. Useful A–Z of topics.
www.nhsdirect.nhs.uk	Health information and advice, including self-help, immunisations, infectious diseases, and various NHS job roles.
www.food.gov.uk	Food Standards Agency. Lots of information on food, dietary advice relating to disease and allergy, healthy lifestyles, eating for breast-feeding, current guidelines and legislation.
www.laleche.org.uk	La Leche League. Help and information for breast-feeding women or those who wish to breast-feed.
www.vegsoc.org	Vegetarian Society. Nutritional stages/requirements for mothers, from pre-conception through to birth. Weaning information for veggie babies.

DEVELOPMENT OF THE CHILD

This part of the book looks at how children acquire the skills that will help them to progress through life.

During their first five years, children grow and develop more than at any other stage in their life. This development is usually divided into four main areas: physical, intellectual, emotional and social (PIES). These areas often overlap and development in one is often closely linked to development in others, as the diagram below demonstrates.

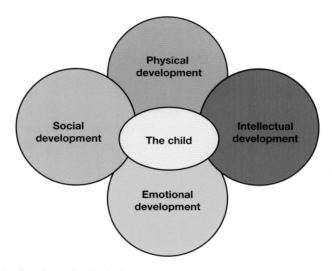

This part of the book includes information on:

- physical, intellectual, social and emotional development
- the importance of play
- play malnourishment
- toys and books
- technology and play.

 REMEMBER!

- All children will develop at their own pace.
- All areas of development are interlinked.

45 Physical Growth

Physical development is one of the easiest areas of development to observe and recognise in children because changes in development can be *seen*.

There are two separate strands to physical development.

1. Growth is about the physical changes in the child – the increase in size, height and weight. This is usually checked using percentile and centile charts (see below).
2. Development is about how children begin to develop and control physical actions, so that they can do more complex activities and become more independent. This is usually assessed using developmental milestones (see pages 255–260).

Growth and development are very closely linked, because the ability to develop and improve skills will very much depend on size and muscular strength.

Looking at growth

Growth is about size, height and weight. It is easy to recognise, easy to measure and easy to record.

Children usually grow at around the same rate – sometimes referred to as the norm. For example, a newborn baby will measure, on average, 50 cm; by one year old he will have grown to about 75 cm, and by five years old will have more than doubled in length/height to 110 cm. Children tend to grow faster in the spring and summer. This is probably because they can go out more and get fresh air and exercise.

As part of developmental screening tests, health visitors and doctors will measure children's height and weight, usually using centile charts (see below).

In this way, children's patterns of growth can be checked, and any problems can be detected and dealt with.

Percentile and centile charts

Centile charts are used by health professionals to compare the growth patterns of individual children with those of other children in the same age range.

Different charts are used for boys and girls as boys tend to grow slightly taller than girls, and are usually heavier at birth.

Measuring height

At birth, an average baby measures 50 cm and its head measures a quarter of the whole body length. During their first two years, children grow very quickly and, as they get older, their muscles, bones and limbs grow, becoming stronger, and the body and head look much more in proportion.

At birth, the brain is only one-third of its adult size, but by two years of age it is almost fully grown.

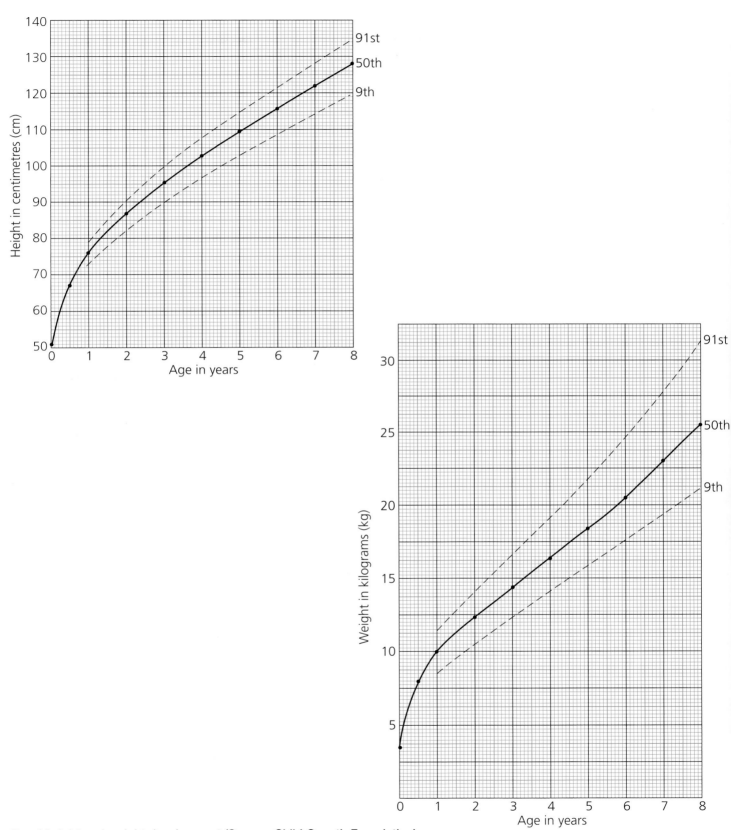

Boys' height and weight development (Source: Child Growth Foundation)

Measuring weight

At birth the average weight of a baby is 3.5 kg (7.5 lb). Babies will double their birth weight within the first six months and triple it by the end of the first year. After this, weight gain will slow down but still continues steadily.

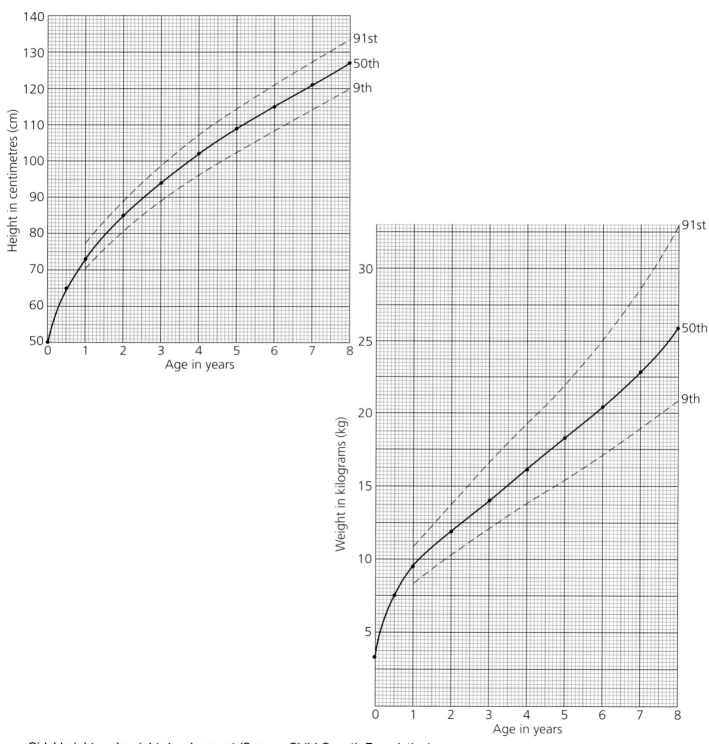

Girls' height and weight development (Source: Child Growth Foundation)

Using centile charts

Each chart shows the normal range of weight or height for girls and boys, and has three lines marked on it, as follows.

1. The middle line (red) is known as the 50th centile. This means that 50 per cent of children have a weight or height around this line.
2. The top line (green) is known as the 91st centile. This means that 98 per cent of children have a weight or height below this line.
3. The bottom line (blue) is known as the 9th centile. This means that only 2 per cent of children have a height or weight below this line.

Therefore, only 4 per cent (four in every 100) of all children will not follow a normal growth pattern.

How tall children grow depends largely on the genes they inherit from their parents.

Weight may also depend on genetic inheritance, but will also be influenced by:

- diet
- exercise
- environmental factors.

Recording a child's height using centile charts

1. Find the child's age in years and/or months along the bottom axis.
2. Identify the child's height along the vertical axis.
3. Where the two lines cross is the child's height in comparison to other children of that age.

In the example shown, the boy is aged three years six months and measures 100 cm. This falls on the 50th centile line, so the child is of average height for that age.

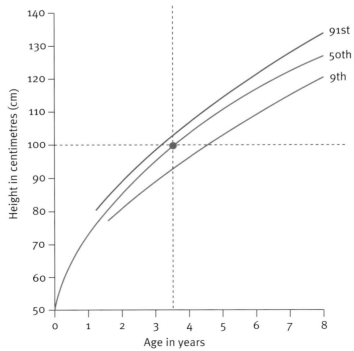

Age and height

The 'Personal Child Health Record'

The health visitor will give the parents a 'Personal Child Health Record' book.

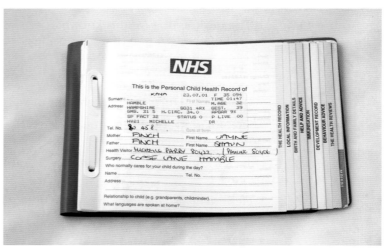

Personal Child Health Record

This book will be filled in regularly at each check-up, usually up to the age of five years. It is an important document for the parents and medical staff, who will record some of the following information in it:

- height and weight
- head circumference
- developmental milestones
- general health
- any health problems
- feeding habits
- general care of the baby
- vaccinations given.

New guidelines for health visitors (and GPs) mean that height is no longer measured regularly between 18 months and school age. Parents are advised to measure their child's height every six months from about 18 months. If the child's height does not stay on their normal centile line over a period of 18 months, parents are advised to check with their GP.

Teeth

From around the age of six months, a child's primary (milk) teeth will start to appear.

There are three different types, as outlined in the table below.

Incisors	There are mainly used for biting and are 'chisel shaped' with sharp edges.
Canines	These are used to tear food into manageable pieces. They are sharp and pointed.
Molars	These are used to grind and crush food to make it easy to swallow. They are strong and have a wide, flat surface area.

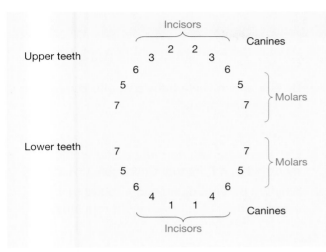

The primary teeth

There are 20 **primary teeth**, and they usually appear in the order shown in the illustration below.

Occasionally, a baby may be born with a tooth already through. Usually children will have all 20 primary teeth by the time they are three years old.

Permanent teeth usually begin to come through at around six years of age, and there are 32 of these.

From an early age it is important for parents to care for, and encourage their children to care for, their teeth (see pages 224–225).

As soon as teeth appear they need to be cleaned. If they are not, **plaque** will stick to the teeth and begin to cause them to decay.

KEY WORDS

Centile charts another name for percentile charts

Development the ability to use more complex skills

Developmental screening tests regular testing of young children's development, carried out by health professionals

Growth a change in size

Percentile charts charts used to compare the growth of individual children with expected average growth

CHILD STUDY ACTIVITY

Measure the child's weight and height at both the start and end of the study. Compare these to the charts on pages 245–247 to try to see if the child is growing at the expected rate.

Find out how many teeth the child has.

QUESTIONS

Question 1

a What is the difference between 'growth' and 'development'?

b Explain how and why growth and development are closely linked.

c Suggest two factors that might affect the growth of a child.

Question 2

a What are 'centile charts' and why are they used?

b Why are there different centile charts for boys and girls?

c What is the average length/height of:

(i) a newborn baby?

(ii) a one-year-old?

(iii) a five-year-old?

d What is the average weight of a newborn baby?

e By how much will a baby's weight increase in the first six months?

Question 3

a List six pieces of information that would be recorded in a Personal Child Health Record.

b Why are parents being encouraged to measure their children's height regularly?

Question 4

a What is another name for milk teeth?

b How many milk teeth do children have?

c Name and describe the three different types of milk teeth.

46 Looking at Physical Development

Physical development is a much more complex process and much more difficult to measure and record than growth.

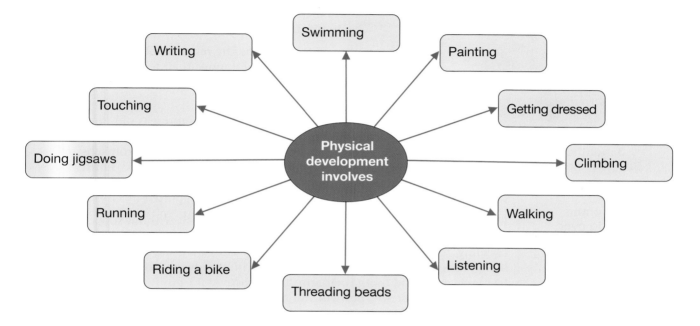

As children's bodies become more mature they gradually learn to control and use different muscles and make different movements.

In doing so, they learn to do more complicated and difficult physical tasks more skilfully and easily. However, this control may be learnt at different rates by different children – so one child may learn to walk at nine months, another at 12 months and another at 18 months. For this reason, instead of using charts and norms for development, professionals tend to refer to developmental milestones: points at which a child masters a skill that can broadly be linked to an age.

Newborn babies have little control over their bodies. They are born with a number of involuntary reflexes (see page 162), which are designed to keep them alive, and which they cannot control. As they get older, these reflexes disappear and babies begin to develop voluntary skills: movements they can control.

To gain complete control, children need to master two different types of skill:

1. gross motor skills
2. fine motor skills and hand–eye coordination.

Physical development also includes sensory development.

Understanding gross motor skills

Children need to learn to control the muscles used for balance and large movements, such as walking, climbing and throwing and kicking a ball. These are known as gross motor skills. Control of these muscles develops from the head down to the shoulders and arms, and finally to the legs.

At birth babies hardly move at all, but they will soon start to wriggle and move their legs and arms almost non-stop as they gradually start to learn how to control their movements.

By the time they are three months old they will have begun to control their neck muscles. They will be able to lift their head and turn it from side to side if lying on their stomachs, and should be able to push up on their arms. By the time they are six months they will be kicking strongly and can usually roll over from their back to front. They will also be able to sit for a reasonably long time if supported by cushions.

By the time babies are 12 months not only can they sit without support for long periods, they are also becoming very mobile and can move around quickly by crawling, 'bear walking' or bottom shuffling. They may also begin to 'cruise' along, using furniture, and some children will have begun to walk – with their feet wide apart and using their arms to balance. At 15 months they should be walking independently, but will still need to use their arms to balance. They should also be able to throw a large ball but may lose their balance.

3 months
Supports head

↓

6 months
Rolling over

↓

9 months
Sitting

↓

12 months
Crawling and walking

↓

15 months
Walking and throwing a ball

↓

18 months
Running

↓

2 years
Climbing up and down stairs

↓

3 years
Hopping and jumping

↓

4 years
Riding a tricycle

↓

5 years
Dancing rhythmically

At 18 months their gross motor skills will be quite well developed – they will be able to walk without using their arms to balance, and may even run although they will often bump into things as they are not yet skilful enough to avoid them. From this stage skills develop very quickly.

At two years old they can run, jump, kick a ball, walk up and down stairs with two feet to a step, and push themselves along on a tricycle, while at three years old they are even more skilful and are able to hop and jump, walk on tiptoe, throw a ball overarm and pedal a tricycle. They will also have good spatial awareness and will be able to run around without bumping into things.

Four- and five-year-olds are becoming experts!

By **four years old** they will have learnt to walk up and down stairs like an adult, and will be able to climb ladders, ride and control a tricycle, and be much more skilful at ball games – they should be able to throw, catch, bounce and kick a ball, and use a bat. Finally, at five years old, they will be very agile and show good coordination; they will enjoy running around and playing 'chase'. They will be able to play ball games and dance rhythmically to music; they will enjoy playing on equipment such as swings, slides and climbing frames.

Understanding fine motor skills

3 months
Finger/hand play

↓

6 months
Whole-hand palmar grasp

↓

9 months
Primitive pincer grasp

↓

12 months
Tripod grasp

↓

15 months
Palmar grasp

↓

18 months
Mature pincer grasp and tripod grasp

↓

2 years
Uses preferred hand

↓

3 years
Improved tripod grasp

↓

4 years
Mature pincer grasp

Children need to learn to develop and control the smaller muscles of the hands and fingers (and feet) so that they can do more delicate tasks, such as drawing, fastening buttons, threading beads and playing with some toys. These are the fine motor skills. Children learn to coordinate 'inwards to outwards' – so they learn to control arms, then hands, then fingers.

Being able to control the hands is one of the most important skills a baby has to learn. To do this they have to learn about hand–eye coordination, how to reach out and then grasp an object, then to hold it and control it – whether it is a toy, a pen, a spoon, a toothbrush or a remote control.

At birth, although babies have a grasp reflex they have not developed any fine motor skills, but this quickly changes. At three months they will be fascinated by their own hands and enjoy playing with them.

They will start to reach out and touch things like a mobile, often 'swiping' at them to try to grasp them, but these movements are still very uncoordinated.

By six months they will be able to grab hold of toys using a whole-hand palmar grasp, and will enjoy playing by passing toys from one hand to the other. At nine months they can pick up small objects using their thumb and first finger (primitive pincer grasp) and will also use their index finger to point. Although they can let go of toys, they cannot yet put them down and place them voluntarily.

At 12 months they are becoming much more skilled and will be using a variety of grasps.

They can now use a fine pincer grasp to pick up small objects, and will drop and throw toys deliberately. They will enjoy banging bricks together using a tripod grasp and will also hold crayons using a palmar grasp, as well as turning several pages of a book at once.

By **15 months** they will try to scribble with a crayon and use their hand–eye coordination to build a tower of two blocks if shown how to. They will also want to feed themselves and should be able to pick up a drink using two hands, as well as using a spoon – even if they do turn it upside down! At **18 months** children can pull off their shoes, and they become fascinated by buttons and zips. They can turn knobs and handles, and will use a mature pincer grasp to pick up objects. They will also be beginning to use a tripod grasp when using pencils.

At **two years**, toddlers will have a good hand–eye coordination and will be quite skilful at using a mature pincer grasp to pick up and place objects. They can also hold a pencil firmly to make circles, dots and lines on a page.

Three-year-olds can use toy scissors to cut, and will control a pencil with the thumb and first two fingers to draw a face and colour in more neatly.

By **four years old**, the fine motor skills are well developed and will continue to improve. They can now hold a pencil like an adult, using a mature tripod grasp, and build a tower of ten cubes or more. Children should now be able to use different grasps with increased precision and accuracy when handling different things.

While all this is happening, children are also learning to develop and use their **sensory skills** – the skills of taste, touch, vision, hearing and smell (see the table below).

During their first two years especially, children will use all of these senses to explore and learn about their world. Sensory development is closely linked with all areas of development.

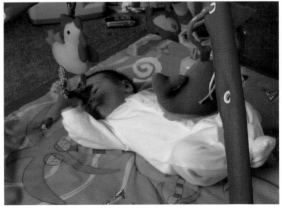

Baby gyms will help sensory development

| **Vision** is closely linked to **fine motor skills** and the development of **hand–eye coordination**. |
| **Hearing** is closely linked to **language development**. |
| **Taste** and **touch** are closely linked to **intellectual development**. |
| **Smell** is closely linked to **social** and **emotional development**. |

Developmental milestones for physical development

Children's physical development usually follows the same sequence, although the age at which different points are reached may vary. However, there are some children who may grow at the same rate as other children, but whose control and development do not follow the expected pattern – perhaps because of some disability (see Chapter 63).

KEY WORDS

Developmental milestone a point or stage where an average child should have mastered a skill

Fine motor skills the use and control of hands and fingers

Gross motor skills the use and control of the whole body and larger muscles

Involuntary movement an automatic movement that cannot be controlled

Hand–eye coordination the ability to use the hands and eyes together to make precise movements

Palmar grasp using the whole hand

Pincer grasp using thumb and first finger

Sensory to do with sight, hearing, touch, taste and smell

Tripod grasp using the thumb and two fingers

Voluntary movement a movement that can be controlled

Age	Gross motor skills	Fine motor skills
Newborn	• When held standing will make walking or stepping movements. • When lying on back (supine) head is turned to one side. • When lying on tummy the knees are tucked up, bottoms are in the air and head is to one side. • Limbs are curled up to body. • Head is floppy. • If held in a sitting position head will 'lag' behind body. • When held in a sitting position back is rounded.	• If a finger or object is placed in their hand they will grasp it tightly. • Hands are usually closed. • Thumb is often tucked under fingers.
3 months	• When lying on front, can lift head and turn from side to side. • When lying on front can push up on arms and raise shoulders. • Can kick legs strongly. • If held in a sitting position head will lag a little. • When held can sit with a straight back.	• Looks at hands and plays with hands and fingers. • Can hold a small toy for a short time before dropping. • Grasp reflex may have disappeared.
6 months	• Can lift head and chest clear of floor, using arms for support. • Can sit for long periods if supported by cushions. • Can sit for short periods without support but will topple over. • May try to roll over from back to front. • May try to crawl. • When lying on back, grasps legs and feet and puts feet into mouth. • Kicks strongly when lying on back. • May hold out hands to be picked up.	• Puts all objects to mouth (mouthing). • Grabs toys using whole-hand palmar grasp. • Begins to reach out for small toys. • Can pass toys from one hand to another. • Has learnt to drop things.
9 months	• Tries to crawl by rocking backwards and forwards. • Can pull self into a standing position, by going on to knees first. • May begin to 'cruise' (side-step) around furniture. • May begin to crawl upstairs. • Can sit unsupported for long periods of time. • When sitting, can turn to look sideways and stretch to reach toys. • May take some steps if held. • Can stand when holding on to furniture.	• Uses primitive pincer grasp (thumb and first finger) to pick up small objects. • Can release a toy by dropping it but cannot put it down voluntarily. • Will begin to look for dropped or fallen objects that are out of sight. • Uses index finger to point. • Pokes objects with index finger.

Sensory skills	Suitable toys and activities	How parents/carers can help
• Startled by sudden noises and bright lights. • Turns towards sound. • Begins to recognise main carer's voice. • Cannot focus on objects more than 25 cm from eyes. • Blinks at sudden bright lights.	• Mobiles over cot and pram. • Light rattles and squeaky toys.	• Use bright, colourful furnishings to provide stimulus. • Spend lots of time with the baby – talking and giving lots of physical contact. • Allow children to lie without a nappy to move and kick.
• Finds hands and brings them to mouth. • Begins to move head to look at things when hearing a voice. • Will turn towards a sound. • Fascinated by faces.	• Baby gyms. • Rattles and squeaky toys. • Pram toys. • Activity mats with different textures. • Bath toys to kick.	• Give baby time and opportunity to lie on back and kick, and to lie on front to strengthen neck and back. • Play finger and hand games. • Give time for play at bathtime.
• Still 'mouths' objects. • Looks around curiously. • If a toy falls out of sight will not look for it. • Watches what people are doing.	• Stacking beakers/blocks. • Bricks to hold and bang. • Rattles. • Simple picture books. • Teething rings. • Mirrors. • Textured (feely) toys.	Because baby is learning through using the senses s/he needs toys and activities that will encourage this. For example: • textured/feely toys • peek-a-boo • finger rhymes • clapping games.
• Looks in correct place for falling or fallen toys. • Begins to recognise familiar pictures. • Enjoys joining in games such as 'peek-a-boo'.	Any object that will encourage sensory skills: • bricks • safe household objects • plastic bath toys • squeaky toys.	• Play simple games, e.g. peek-a-boo. • Point to toys and objects. • Give baby time to explore toys on floor.

Age	Gross motor skills	Fine motor skills	
12 months	• Becoming very mobile – either by crawling, shuffling, 'bear walking' or bottom shuffling. • Can 'cruise' along furniture. • Can walk a few steps if held. • May start to walk but will tend to fall or sit down suddenly. • Can sit unsupported for long periods. • Tries to crawl upstairs forwards and downstairs backwards. • Can stand alone.	• Uses neat pincer grasp (thumb and first finger) to pick up small objects. • Points at objects of interest with index finger. • Uses both hands but may begin to show preference for one. • Puts small objects into a container, e.g. bricks into a beaker. • Drops and throws toys deliberately. • Uses tripod grasp to hold and bang together bricks. • May hold a crayon in a palmar grasp. • May try to turn pages in a book but usually several at once.	
15 months	• Walks independently using arms to balance. • Can crawl upstairs safely and downstairs, feet first. • Throws a large ball but may fall over. • Can kneel without support. • Can get into a standing position without using the help of people or furniture.	• Claps hands together. • May build a tower of two blocks if shown how. • Can pick up and drink from a cup using two hands to hold it. • Makes a mark with crayon using a palmar grasp. • Turns pages in a book but will turn several at once. • Tries to eat with a spoon but will turn it upside down.	
18 months	• Can walk confidently without using arms to balance. • Can pick up toys by bending from waist. • Can 'squat' to look at things without losing balance. • May be able to walk upstairs and downstairs without adult help. • Runs, but sometimes bumps into obstacles. • Can push and pull toys when walking. • Can crawl backwards downstairs.	• Can turn knobs and handles on doors. • Can build a tower of three cubes. • Can string together four large beads. • Uses mature pincer grasp to pick up objects. • Beginning to use the tripod grasp when using pencils and crayons. • Can pull off shoes. • Fascinated by buttons, zips and fastenings.	
2 years	• Can walk up and down stairs confidently, two feet to a step. • Enjoys climbing on to furniture. • Can kick a large ball that is not moving. • Enjoys toys that are put together and pulled apart, e.g. Duplo, Sticklebricks. • Walks and runs more steadily. • Pushes and pulls large, wheeled toys. • Can sit on a tricycle and use feet to move it.	• Can turn the pages of a book one by one. • Has good hand–eye coordination. • Can build a tower of five or six bricks. • Uses mature pincer grasp to pick up and place small objects. • Holds a pencil firmly and can form circles, lines and dots. • Can zip and unzip a large zipper.	

Sensory skills	Suitable toys and activities	How parents/carers can help
• Watches people, animals and moving objects for long periods. • Drops and throws toys deliberately and watches them fall. • Recognises familiar people and sounds. • Turns towards sound. • Looks in correct place for toys that fall out of sight.	• Rattles. • Stacking beakers/bricks. • Push and pull toys. • Wheeled toys. • Large balls. • Cardboard books. • Baby swings. • Shape sorters.	• Allow baby the time and opportunity to develop gross motor skills. • Play games that will help fine motor skills, e.g. playing with shape sorters or building with bricks. • Give lots of praise and encouragement.
• Looks with interest at pictures in a book and pats them. • Stands at a window and watches what is happening for long periods of time.	• Picture books. • Shape sorters. • Large chunky crayons and paper. • Musical toys. • Cause-and-effect toys, e.g. jack-in-the-box.	• Spend time playing with children and showing them how toys work.
• Hand–eye coordination is good. • Picks up small objects such as beads on sight with delicate pincer grasp. • Enjoys simple picture books. • Recognises and points to brightly coloured items on a page. • Recognises familiar people at a distance.	• Push and pull toys. • Threading toys. • Picture books in card or fabric. • Simple tricycles. • Rocking horse.	• Children like to spend time playing alone, so need to be allowed to do this. • They will enjoy repetitive games, e.g. putting small objects such as bricks into a box. • They are becoming more independent and like to try to take off shoes, socks, etc. They need to be allowed to do this.
• Enjoys looking at picture books. • Recognises fine detail in favourite pictures. • Recognises familiar adults in photographs. • By two and a half may recognise self in photographs.	• Ride-on and sit-on toys. • Large Duplo/Sticklebricks construction toys. • Bricks. • Crayons and paper. • Play-Doh. • Picture books.	• Parents need to provide children with a wide variety of toys to play with and explore, especially as concentration spans are limited. • Children are beginning to have favourite toys and activities.

Age	Gross motor skills	Fine motor skills
3 years	• Can walk and run forward with precision. • Can walk on tiptoe. • Can kick a ball forwards. • Can throw a ball overhand. • Can catch a large ball with extended arms. • Pedals and steers a tricycle. • Walks upstairs with one foot on each step. • Can hop on one foot. • Can manoeuvre around objects, showing spatial awareness.	• Holds a crayon with more control and can draw a face. • Can colour in more neatly and more within lines. • Can eat with a spoon or fork without spilling. • Can put on and take off coat. • Can build a tower of nine or ten bricks. • Cuts with toy scissors. • Uses improved tripod grasp.
4 years	• Can walk or run alone upstairs and downstairs, in adult fashion. • Can walk along a straight line, showing good balance. • Climbs ladders and trees. • Pedals and controls a tricycle confidently. • Is becoming more skilled at ball games – can throw, catch, bounce, kick and use a bat.	• Can build a tower of ten or more cubes. • Can build three steps with six bricks if shown how. • Uses a mature pincer grasp. • Can fasten and unfasten buttons. • Can put together large-piece jigsaw puzzles. • Can colour in pictures but not always between the lines.
5 years	• Can skip with a rope. • Very skilful at climbing, sliding, swinging, jumping, etc. • Can use a wide variety of large equipment confidently. • Can throw a ball to a partner, catch, hit a ball with a bat with some accuracy. • Can balance on one foot for several seconds. • Can hop. • Can dance rhythmically to music.	• Dresses and undresses with little help. • Can complete more complex jigsaw with interlocking pieces (20+ pieces). • Cuts out shapes using scissors more accurately. • Can use a knife and fork when eating. • Has good pencil control. • Can colour in pictures neatly, staying within outlines. • Can construct complex models using kits. • Can copy several letters, e.g. V, T, H, O, X, L, A, C, O and Y.

Sensory skills	Suitable toys and activities	How parents/carers can help
• Knows names of some colours. • Can match two or three main colours, usually red and yellow. • Listens eagerly to favourite stories and wants to hear them over and over again. • Can thread large beads.	• Large outdoor toys such as swings, slides and climbing frames. • Paints and crayons. • Tricycles. • Dressing-up clothes. • Sand and water.	• Children are becoming more social and willing to play with other children. • They may be ready for play or nursery school. • They will enjoy practical activities such as baking.
• Matches and names four main colours. • Follows storybooks with eyes, and identifies words and pictures.	• Any materials or objects for creative activities, e.g. collage, junk toys. • Paints and crayons. • Jigsaw puzzles. • Construction toys, such as LEGO. • Climbing frames, slides and swings.	• Children at this age are more independent and need less help from parents. • They can play with other children, usually cooperatively. • They still need a wide variety of opportunities for playing.
• Matches 10–12 colours. • Vision and hearing developed to adult level. • Picks up and replaces very small objects.	• Bicycle with stabilisers. • Balls. • Rollerblades. • Creative materials. • Construction toys. • Board games.	• Children are now beginning to understand and enjoy games with rules, but they need adult help – both in terms of explaining and acting as peacemaker! • They will play independently and make up their own games.

RESEARCH ACTIVITY

Investigate how the indoor and/or outdoor toys that the child has can encourage physical development.

Use a chart to record your results and give each toy a rating according to how well it encourages:

- fine motor skills
- gross motor skills
- sensory development.

If possible, use ICT/PowerPoint to present your results as a report.

CHILD STUDY ACTIVITY

1. Plan and make a jigsaw or simple book with or for the child being studied. You could use photographs, pictures from catalogues, old birthday or Christmas cards, or even the child's own drawings. Observe and evaluate how this activity helps the child to develop fine motor skills and compare your observations to expected milestones.

2. Plan a 'feely bag' or box for the child being studied. Use a cardboard box or a bag – preferably a cloth one, such as a shoe bag. Put a number of different objects inside – both familiar and unfamiliar – and try to include items of different textures. Make sure the items chosen are suitable for the age of the child.

   Encourage the child to talk about and describe what they can feel.

   This will help both language and sensory skills.

 QUESTIONS

Question 1

a What is meant by a developmental milestone?

b Why should care be taken when using 'milestones' to assess children's development?

Question 2

What is the difference between an 'involuntary movement', or reflex, and a 'voluntary movement'?

Question 3

a Explain the difference between 'gross motor skills' and 'fine motor skills'. Give three examples of each.

b Gross motor skills develop from the head downwards. Explain what this means and at what age each stage is achieved.

c Name and describe three different grasps a young child might use when playing with toys.

d Which of the following are examples of gross motor skills, and which are examples of fine motor skills: skipping; doing a jigsaw puzzle; painting; fastening a button; cutting shapes with scissors; swimming; riding a tricycle; reading a book; building with LEGO; playing with a shape sorter?

Question 4

a Name the five senses.

b How are the different senses linked to physical, intellectual, emotional and social development?

Question 5

a In your own words, describe the gross motor skills of:

  (i) a six-month-old baby

  (ii) a two-year-old child.

b Suggest, with reasons, three toys or activities that would be suitable for a six-month-old baby and a two-year-old child.

c Suggest four different toys or activities that would help to encourage fine motor skills in a three-year-old child.

47 Encouraging Physical Development

Dressing up

Almost every toy, game and play activity will involve some sort of physical movement, and will therefore help, in some way, to encourage different physical skills. For example, when children are playing at dressing-up they are using gross motor skills to put on the clothes, and fine motor skills to pick them up and fasten them. When handling them they will be feeling different textures, which is part of sensory development.

However, more toys and games tend to be used indoors and, therefore, concentrate on children's fine motor skills.

As children grow and become more mobile they usually have lots of energy, which some games and activities will not use up. Parents need to give children the chance to run around and burn off this energy, while at the same time allowing them to explore their own and new environments, and to learn more about the world around them.

It is important, for lots of reasons, to give children time to play outdoors – even on a cold day.

Why outdoor play is important

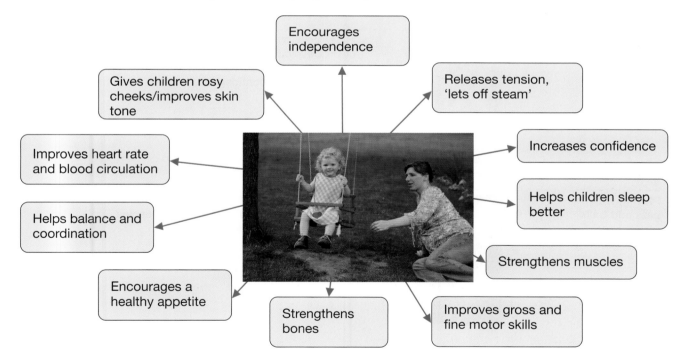

Encourages independence

Releases tension, 'lets off steam'

Gives children rosy cheeks/improves skin tone

Improves heart rate and blood circulation

Helps balance and coordination

Encourages a healthy appetite

Strengthens bones

Increases confidence

Helps children sleep better

Strengthens muscles

Improves gross and fine motor skills

Equipment for outdoor activities, such as swings, slides and climbing frames, can be expensive and take up a lot of space. It also needs to be safe, secure and checked regularly. However, this sort of equipment is usually readily available at parks and play areas. Regular visits to such places with parents will provide good play opportunities and children will get a lot of pleasure from just having the freedom to run around. It will also help parents and children to bond, and may provide opportunities for social development and a chance to explore a new environment.

Ideas for outdoor play

Activity		How it helps
Riding bicycle/ tricycle		• Helps to develop leg muscles and strengthen bones. • Improves balance. • Builds up stamina. • Helps coordination. • Increases confidence.
Playing hide and seek/tig/ chasing game		• Develops coordination and balance. • Builds up stamina. • Promotes spatial awareness. • Helps develop social skills.
Hopping/ skipping/ jumping/ trampoline		• Develops leg muscles. • Develops coordination and balance. • Improves stamina. • Builds up confidence.
Playing with bats and balls		• Develops hand–eye coordination. • Develops hand, arm and leg muscles. • Encourages cooperative play.
Climbing		• Improves balance and coordination. • Develops leg and arm muscles, and strength. • Increases confidence and independence. • Promotes spatial awareness.

When the weather is bad, and 'playing out' is not possible, parents can still provide opportunities to allow children to 'let off steam' by taking them swimming or to organised playgroups where there is still space to run around, or parents can even run a disco.

And, should it snow, there are endless opportunities for all sorts of physical development and to explore a totally new world!

 REMEMBER!

Physical growth and development are very closely linked – being able to learn and improve a new physical movement or skill will depend a lot on size and muscular strength.

Fresh air, exercise, rest and sleep

Once a child is able to get about on his/her own, he/she should be allowed to play outside in the garden as much as possible. Cold weather should not be used as an excuse – all children should be encouraged to go outside whatever the weather. A child who is kept indoors, and inactive for long periods, may ultimately become bad tempered, possibly naughty and could lose their appetite. If there is no garden, the parents should still ensure they take their child outside once a day for fresh air – perhaps taking them to a recreational area, a park or even to the shops. It will not only help give the child fresh air and exercise, but can help to educate them, especially if the parent is prepared to point things out to the child along the way. The fresh air and exercise will also help to make the child naturally tired and hungry, and this should help minimise both feeding and sleeping problems.

The importance of sleep

- Babies and young children need to have adequate amounts of sleep.
- Sleep allows the body to relax and to 'recharge the batteries'.
- While asleep, the body produces more of the hormone that stimulates growth, so sleep is important for children's growth and development.
- After a good night's sleep children are less likely to be overtired and irritable.
- Lack of sleep can affect memory and concentration.

The sleep pattern of newborn babies is often determined by their weight and height, as well as their need for food. So, generally, the less the baby weighs, the more often it will wake to feed.

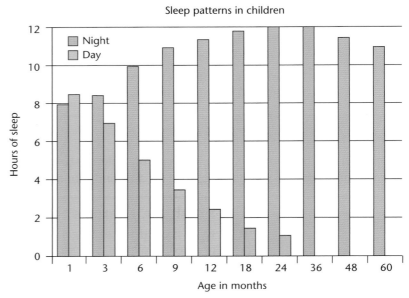

Sleep patterns in children

Young babies	Babies often sleep more than 16 hours out of every 24, and they tend to sleep in four-hour cycles. Their sleep pattern is often determined by their weight and height, as well as their need for food. Generally, the less the baby weighs, the more often she/he will wake to feed.
6 to 18 months	As the feeding pattern of babies changes, so does their sleep pattern. They begin to be awake more during the day and will gradually begin to sleep through the night.
Two years (24 months)	Gradually, the amount of daytime sleep decreases and they will sleep longer during the night. By the age of two, a child will be more mobile and active, and may sleep for 12 hours at night, but for only a short time during the day. This daytime sleep will usually be a mid-afternoon nap; in fact the child may not actually sleep at all but will be resting. This is just as beneficial, and not just for the child: it also gives parents a break!
Three years	By now daytime sleep is not usually needed.
Four to five years	The amount of night-time sleep needed is starting to drop but children still need to have at least eight to ten hours' sleep a night

It is important that children also have a regular bedtime routine, so that getting children to bed and to sleep does not become a battle.

Suggested bedtime routine for a toddler

Young children need plenty of sleep

Routine	Reason
Have a regular bedtime every night.	Child more likely to accept going to bed.
Reduce the level of activity.	Child will become calm and less excitable, and more likely to sleep.
Bath the child.	A warm bath is relaxing. It also allows the child to spend quality time with parents.
Give the child a warm drink.	This will help to calm and relax the child, and may encourage sleep.
Choose a suitable story to read.	This is quality time for parents and child – and the child may fall asleep during the story time. However, an active or frightening story may cause sleeplessness and nightmares.
Tuck child in and give a kiss and/or cuddle.	This will increase feelings of security and the child will settle more easily.
Let the child have a favourite toy or comforter.	This increases feelings of security and gives the child something to focus on.
Leave on a night light or lamp.	Many children dislike the dark and become apprehensive.
Check on child regularly.	Reduces 'separation anxiety'.

QUESTIONS

Question 1

Playing outdoors is important in helping children's physical development. Suggest eight reasons why.

Question 2

a Suggest three ways parents and carers could give children the opportunity to enjoy outdoor physical play.

b List three outdoor play activities suitable for a four-year-old child.

c Describe how playing a game of hide and seek could encourage development.

Question 3

a Why are fresh air and exercise important for young children?

b Give three reasons why sleep is important for young children.

c List three factors that might affect the sleep pattern of a newborn baby.

Question 4

a Why is a bedtime routine important?

b Explain how the following can help:

(i)   reading a story

(ii) leaving a light on

(iii) going to bed at the same time each night

(iv) giving the child a warm drink.

RESEARCH ACTIVITY

1. Find out what outdoor play facilities there are locally in your area for children under the age of five. Look at the range of facilities available, their condition, safety, ease of access, etc.

Present your findings as a report, using ICT where possible.

2. Plan and carry out a questionnaire to find out how parents and carers encourage outdoor physical play.

 CHILD STUDY ACTIVITY

Ask the parent of the child being studied to help you to set up a simple obstacle course in the garden (make sure it's on a soft area such as grass, and check with the parent for possible hazards).

Observe the child you are studying, and note the way in which gross motor skills are used.

48 Intellectual Development

Intellectual development is about learning – about how we use and organise our minds, thoughts and ideas to understand and make sense of the world we live in.

Understanding how children learn, how their thoughts and ideas develop, is very complicated. The diagram below shows some of the different ways children might 'learn'. In any one day, they could use all these different ways (and more) at some time.

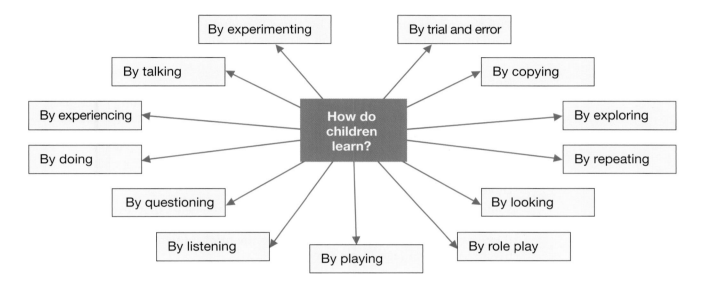

This means that it is sometimes difficult to separate intellectual development from the other areas of development.

- Children learn through their senses – by touching, tasting, listening and through active play (all physical experiences).
- Children play and relate to other children and people socially and emotionally.
- Children also need language and communication skills, the important tools of intellectual development.

The nature vs nurture debate

Are children born intelligent or does the 'environment' they are born into and grow up in develop their intelligence? This is the basis of what people call the nature vs nurture debate.

Some people believe that intelligence is determined at conception through the genes inherited from the parents. Others believe that the quality of the child's environment, including the people the child comes into contact with (especially when they are very young), has a greater influence on how their intelligence develops.

Initially, it was believed that children were born with a fixed level of intelligence and that this would never change – however, that view is no longer accepted, and it would seem that both 'nature' and 'nurture' have their part to play in the development of learning and understanding. Over the years psychologists (specialists in human behaviour) have studied the way children think and learn, and have produced some theories that help us to understand cognitive development.

Theories about how children learn

There are three main theories about how children learn:

1. Social Learning Theory
2. Behaviourist Theory
3. Developmentalist Theory.

Social Learning Theory

This theory was first developed by Alfred Bandura. He believed that children learn by looking at the behaviour of adults and other people they see, and then copy what they have seen.

Behaviourist Theory

Behaviourists are groups of psychologists who believe that learning takes place through actions and experiences, and that we will repeat actions and experiences that are enjoyable and avoid those that are not. The psychologist Burrhus F. Skinner believed that praise and reward (positive reinforcements) would encourage children to repeat the experience and develop learning.

Developmentalist Theory

Some psychologists have based their theories on the belief that learning is linked very closely to defined stages of development, and that children will go through these stages but at varying speeds. Perhaps the most influential of these psychologists was Jean Piaget (1896–1980).

As well as studying his own children, Piaget was involved with carrying out intelligence tests with young children. Through these tests, he discovered that children's answers followed a logical pattern, but that this was different to that displayed by adults and seemed to be based on their own experiences. He called these answers schemas.

He also believed that as children learned new concepts and had new and different experiences, they would adapt or change their schema. He called this assimilation (adapting) and accommodation (changing). Based on this Piaget decided that children went through four very different, but distinct, stages of learning (as described in the table below), and that these stages could be linked to approximate ages. He also believed that children would not move from one stage to another before they were ready, and would not 'skip' a stage.

Piaget's stages

Stage	Age	Title	Description of learning
1	0–2 years	Sensory motor (sensorimotor)	At this stage, children: • learn mainly through the **senses**, especially touch, taste and hearing • are **egocentric** – they see the world only from their own point of view • begin to be aware of **object permanence** – that a person or an object they cannot see still exists; this usually happens at about eight months • learn through trial and error • have only limited language skills.
2	2–7 years	Pre-operational	At this stage, children: • still learn through the sense of taste and touch but hearing becomes more important • are still egocentric • have better language skills, and begin to use these to ask questions and put their thoughts, ideas and feelings into words • use symbols in play – so teddy becomes a baby or a bus driver (for more on pretend play, see page 332) • believe that objects and animals have the same thoughts and feelings as themselves – **animism**. As children get towards the end of this stage they: • begin to learn about **concepts** • become more involved in pretend play • begin to understand right and wrong, but in a very simple way • use symbols more – in play, language and drawing.
3	7–11 years	Concrete operational	At this stage, children: • can see things from other people's point to view – they can **decentre** • begin to develop more complex reasoning skills – but they will still need to use objects to help them to understand and solve problems • understand that things are not always what they seem – they can **conserve** • understand that non-living things do not have feelings.
4	12–adult	Formal operational	At this stage, children: • can think logically • can think abstractly – that is, they can manipulate ideas in their head and don't need to use objects to help them to solve problems • can understand more complex concepts.

The two main strands of intellectual development are:

There is a strong and clear link between the two strands, and it is almost impossible to understand children's cognitive development without looking at how their language skills develop (see pages 282–283). Language is the tool that enables us to make sense of our world. It helps us to organise our thoughts, knowledge and understanding into concepts; these can be simple, such as size, shape and colour, or complex and abstract, such as time, silence and space. Language helps us to make connections and to ask questions about what we see. It helps us to develop and progress from simple understanding to more complex ideas.

? QUESTIONS

Question 1

a Describe what is meant by intellectual development.

b Children will learn in lots of different ways. List eight ways in which children might learn.

c Describe how and why intellectual development can be linked to physical, social and emotional development.

Question 2

a What is the difference between 'nature' and 'nurture'?

b Briefly describe the three theories about how children learn.

c According to Piaget, children aged between two and seven years are at the 'pre-operational' stage of development. Describe how you would expect a child to act and learn at this stage.

Question 3

Intellectual development involves two main strands. Name and describe these.

49 What Is Cognitive Development?

Cognitive development is about how we use our minds and organise our thinking to understand our world and our place in it.

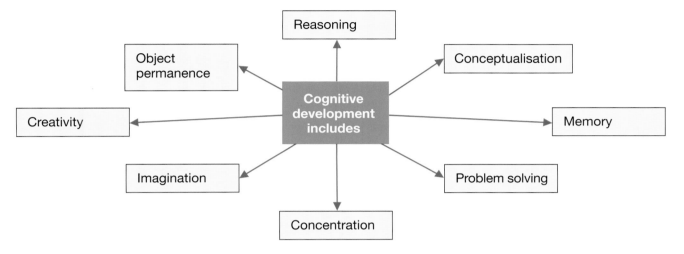

Imagination is the ability to picture things when they are not in front of us or when they do not exist.		

Imagination is the ability to picture things when they are not in front of us or when they do not exist.

Children use their imaginations to play pretend games and to tell stories. They also use it when drawing, painting, reading, dancing, making models and dressing up.

Problem solving is the ability to solve both simple and complex problems, e.g. putting shapes in a shape sorter and riding a bike. The ability to solve problems tends to follow a set pattern:

Trial and error
↓
Identify the problem
↓
Work out a solution
↓
Predict what might happen (hypothesise)

Creativity is the ability to express imaginative ideas in an individual and unique way.

Children are creative when they paint, make collages and junk toys, dance, make music and so on.

Memory is the ability to store and recall information, ideas and events. We have both:

- short-term memory, which allows us to remember things as we need to, e.g. shopping lists
- long-term memory, which allows us to store information until it is needed; we often need a 'trigger' to jog our long-term memory, e.g. a smell, a name, a picture.

Object permanence is the ability to understand that something still exists even when it is out of sight.

Children show their understanding of this when they play hide and seek, hunt the thimble, etc.

Conceptualisation is the ability to understand and use concepts. These are ideas we use to help organise information into an understandable form.

Children need to begin to learn to understand concepts of number, colour, shape, time, volume, speed, etc.

Concentration is the ability to pay attention to one particular task.

Children tend to concentrate more on things in which they are interested.

Children need to be able to concentrate so that they can learn, store and sort information.

Reasoning is the ability to understand that whatever actions we take have a cause and effect, e.g. if you press the button on the toy, the animal pops up.

Learning about concepts

Concepts are ways in which we organise our knowledge, information and thinking, so that we can understand and make sense of the world we live in. They are also important, because they allow us to communicate with other people and share ideas and opinions.

We need to **learn** concepts.

Some are quite simple and easy to understand, such as colour, size and shape, and children will learn these quite early. Others are more complex and will take a long time to understand, such as the concepts of space and time. Some concepts we may never fully understand.

Colour is one example of a concept.

Look at the pictures above.

The coat, bus, umbrella, bicycle, ball and flower are all yellow, and although they are all different shades, we can recognise them as yellow.

But, if we tried to explain how we *know* that they are yellow or what it is that makes them yellow or what exactly 'yellow' means, we would find it very difficult. We just know that they are yellow!

This is because, as adults, we have stored and sorted different pieces of information and ideas in our memories, which help us to recognise and identify yellow as yellow – whatever the shade.

Children need to learn many different concepts.

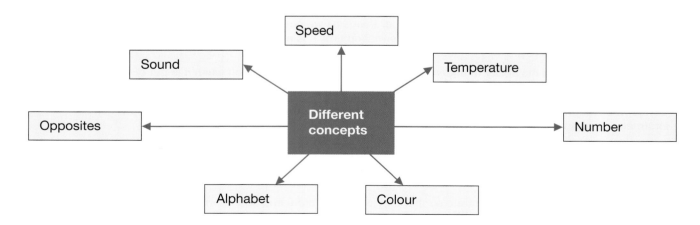

Children learn about some concepts just by seeing and experiencing, but to understand others they need the help of adults. It is important that parents, families and other adults who deal with children, such as carers and teachers, support or **facilitate** children's learning. They can do this by making sure that children have lots of opportunities to explore, discover and investigate, by playing with different toys, games and activities. They also need to spend time playing with children, talking to them, answering their questions and offering praise and encouragement.

More about number and maths concepts

Babies and young children are learning about numbers and maths all the time, often without parents realising it. From being born the first thing they see and remember is the **shape** of their mother's face!

Parents can help children to understand many number and maths concepts very simply through play and everyday activities, and often do so without thinking.

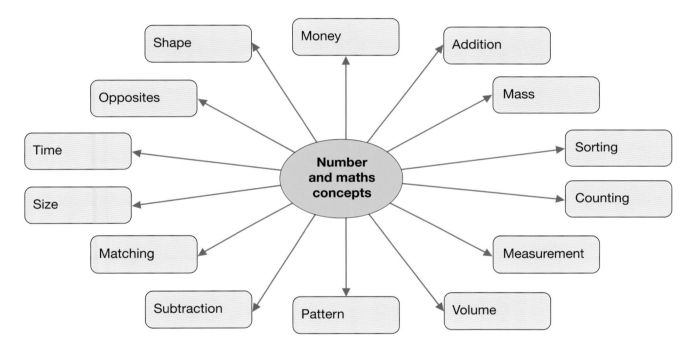

'Numbers' is probably the first concept children learn. Many parents say that their children 'know their numbers' or 'can count to ten'. What they really mean is that they can repeat the names of numbers in the right order! Children need more than this – they need to know what numbers really are and what the number system really means. This takes time.

The first stage is to understand that a number is the same no matter what it refers to, whether it is the number two, the letters that make up the number two, two socks, two flowers or two cars. Before they can understand numbers for things that can be seen, children need to play with real objects to check that the count is right each time.

Maths at home

Children have lots of opportunities at home to learn about numbers and maths.

Counting and money concepts

Weighing and measuring

Other activities to help could include those listed in the table below.

Activity	Concepts
Going shopping	Money and counting
Setting the table for tea	Time and counting out numbers of plates, forks, etc.
Putting away clothes or toys	Sorting, matching and size
Tidying away	Sorting out similar objects
Going to bed	Time and counting steps
Playing in the bath	Volume and size
Making pizzas and bread	Weighing, measuring, counting, temperature
Cutting a cake or an apple into pieces	Number and simple fractions
Playing with Play-Doh or making bread	Shapes, sizes and maths language
Activity books	Recognising numbers, matching, counting, shapes, sizes
Rhymes and songs	Learning numbers and sequences
Reading books	Counting

 REMEMBER!

Intellectual development has two main strands: cognitive skills and language skills. However, it is also closely linked to physical, social and emotional development. Intellectual development can be helped by parents spending time with children, and giving them lots of opportunities to play, investigate and explore.

Developmental milestones for cognitive development

It is not always easy to give specific milestones for cognitive development. The age and stage at which children may acquire knowledge and understand concepts depends on their own pattern of development, and the range and variety of play and opportunities they have – the nature vs nurture idea again.

However, cognitive development does depend on developing the ability to classify, store and remember information.

To do this, children need to have lots of opportunities to play with toys and games, and experience other activities that will help them to concentrate and develop their memories.

Age	Stage of development	Suitable toys and activities
0 to 12 months	• Uses mouth and touch to explore. • Watches and copies adults. • Repeats actions, e.g. dropping a rattle or brick. • Looks for an object that has been taken away. • Finds an object that has been seen and hidden. • Places an object, such as a brick, in a container when asked.	• Rattles. • Teething rings. • Soft squeaky toys. • Finger rhymes and actions. • Activity centres. • Mobiles. • 'Feely' toys. • Peek-a-boo game.
12 months to two years	• Points to parts of the body. • Learns about things through trial and error. • Recognises and points to a named picture or object. • Scribbles on paper. • Can take out objects one by one from a container.	• 'Feely' bags and boxes. • Activity mats. • Paper and large crayons. • Building bricks. • Musical toys. • Cause-and-effect toys, e.g. jack-in-the-box.
Two to three years	• Begins to show some reasoning skills but still learns mainly by trial and error. • Can copy a circle. • Can complete a simple three- to five-piece puzzle. • Recognises and matches different textures. • Can stack beakers in order. • Matches three colours. • Uses everyday objects in pretend play, e.g. wooden spoon may be sword, a cardboard box may be a car.	• Any safe household items. • Simple games and large puzzles. • Paints, crayons, paper. • Construction toys, e.g. LEGO. • Dressing-up clothes. • Any toys or objects for imaginative play. • Alphabet games. • Play-Doh/plasticine. • Simple cooking activities. • Trips to new places, e.g. zoos, farms. • Visits to library. • Musical instruments.
Three to four years	• Asks lots of questions. • Can sort out simple objects. • Recognises long or short objects. • Knows and names three shapes. • Can count ten objects with help. • Recognises letters and numbers. • Knows primary colours. • Can say which of two objects is heavy and light. • Can repeat a simple story.	• Jigsaw puzzles. • Magnetic boards with letters and numbers. • Toys for imaginative play, e.g. dolls. • House, farms, garages. • Construction sets. • Books. • Dressing-up toys. • Water and sand play.
Four to five years	• Can pick up a number of objects if asked, e.g. four sweets. • Can name five textures. • Can name eight colours. • Begins to understand use of symbols, e.g. letters and numbers in reading and writing. • Can count up to 20 by rote. • Uses reason based on experience. • Can understand simple rules in games. • Can name times of day, e.g. bedtime.	• Board games. • More complex jigsaws. • Matching games. • Simple card games, e.g. snap. • Dominoes. • Cardboard boxes to create cars, furniture, cartons, etc. • Items to make 'dens'. • Visits to zoos, museums, theatre, cinema. • Simple scientific toys, e.g. magnifying glass, binoculars.

Toys, games and other activities

As we have already seen, cognitive development depends on the ability to be able to group, sort, remember and recall information. Therefore, it is very important for parents not to just buy toys and games because they look attractive and interesting, but to think about how they will help children to learn.

They also need to plan different games and activities that will encourage these skills and, above all, spend time playing and working with the child.

Look at the activity in the illustration alongside. It shows how something as simple as threading beads can help cognitive development, as well as helping concentration and memory skills – and of course it improves fine motor skills.

- Helps learn about and understand concepts of size, shape and colour.
- Helps develop reasoning skills and memory.
- Helps to learn and understand sequence, pattern and colour.
- Helps to understand pattern and spatial awareness.
- Helps to develop concentration and memory.
- Helps to understand matching and sorting according to size and shape.
- Helps to understand sequence.
- Helps to understand numbers and counting.
- Helps to develop an understanding of pattern and spatial awareness.
- Helps to understand comparisons and order of things according to size.

While toys, game and activities can help to encourage cognitive development, it can be delayed, as the following chart shows.

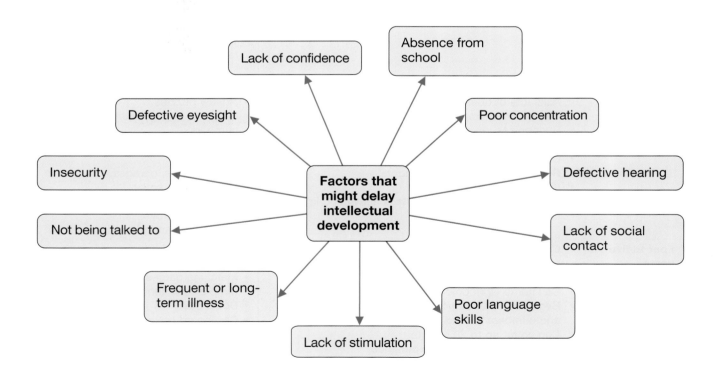

REMEMBER!

Toys, games and activities need not always be expensive or bought. Playing with safe household items will give lots of opportunities for cognitive development.

KEY WORDS

Cognitive to do with thinking and understanding

Concept a way of organising knowledge and information so it can be understood

Decentre seeing things from other people's point of view

Egocentric self-centred

Nature the talent and abilities we might inherit

Nurture outside factors that can influence development

Object permanence understanding that objects and people still exist even when out of sight

QUESTIONS

Question 1

a What is cognitive development?

b What is meant by each of the following:

(i) object permanence?

(ii) problem solving?

(iii) reasoning?

(iv) imagination?

c What is the difference between long-term and short-term memory?

Question 2

a What is a concept?

b Name two simple concepts.

c Name two more complex concepts.

Question 3

a List six different number and maths concepts.

b What is the first stage in learning about numbers?

c Suggest four different everyday activities parents could do with children that would help them learn about numbers and maths. State which number and maths concepts the activities would teach.

Question 4

a Parents and other adults, such as carers and teachers, need to 'facilitate' children's learning.

(i) What does this mean?

(ii) How could this be done?

b Cognitive development depends on the ability to do which three things?

Question 5

a List the cognitive milestones you might expect the following children to have reached:

(i) a 12- to 24-month-old child

(ii) a three- to four-year-old child.

b Give six ways in which cognitive development might be delayed.

RESEARCH ACTIVITY

Try to organise a visit to a nursery.

1. Draw a plan of the nursery showing the different areas and activities provided. From your plan and observations, identify which aspects of intellectual development are being encouraged and how.

2. Interview one of the staff in the nursery about how they plan activities to help children understand and learn numbers.

3. Make an inventory of the toys, books and games of the child you are studying. Think about how the child would play with them and which concepts they might encourage. Present your inventory as a table, using ICT if possible, and analyse and evaluate your results.

Use your findings to plan a visit using some of the toys. Evaluate how successful the toys are and comment on any other skills they help to develop (e.g. fine motor skills, social skills).

 CHILD STUDY ACTIVITY

1. Design and make a simple game such as lotto or dominos, or an activity book that would help to encourage concept development such as numbers, shape, size and colour.

2. Make some play dough or salt dough and use this to roll out and cut out shapes. Think about any other concepts this activity could encourage.

50 Language and Communication

Language is the use of symbols and is the main way that people communicate with each other, but it is not the only way. As well as speaking and writing words we also communicate through:

- body language
- facial expressions
- signs and gestures
- tone of voice
- painting and drawing.

The importance of language

People need to talk and communicate

As in all development the acquisition of language follows a distinct pattern, but the rate of progress will depend on the individual child. This often depends on the (chronological) age of the child, but the opportunities they have to work and experiment with and to use language are also very important.

Language is very closely linked to cognitive development. The world is a complex place – to be able to make sense of it we need to be able to organise our thinking from more than a simple understanding of what is there. We need to be able to predict and hypothesise; language allows us to talk about things that are concrete and abstract (e.g. silence).

All humans are born with a need to communicate – language is the tool that allows us to do this. It begins very simply with crying sounds, which are used to tell parents how the baby is feeling, and builds up quickly until by the age of five the child can use a huge range of words, put together in complex sentences, to describe, question, discuss, express feelings, and so on.

Learning to talk

Language has to be learnt. All babies babble in some way, even deaf babies. Language development begins at birth – a new mother's initial reaction when first holding her baby is to hold it close, look directly into the baby's face and talk to it. This is the surest way to give the baby a good start.

To be able to make speech sounds babies must learn to control many different muscles. They need to practise pushing lips and tongue forwards and backwards, and up and down, while at the same time taking in air.

Most children pass through two distinct phases of language development: pre-linguistic and linguistic.

Pre-linguistic/non-verbal communication

This phase usually lasts from birth to 12 months. During this time babies cry, smile, use facial expressions and make sounds such as cooing and grunting to attract attention. This is how they begin to communicate.

Linguistic verbal communication

This phase usually begins between 12 and 15 months. It is the phase when children begin to use recognisable words to communicate. They use these words as labels for familiar objects (e.g. dog, cup, ball), then gradually progress to simple, then more complex, sentences.

Stages of language development

Pre-linguistic stage: birth to 12 months

Approximate age	Level of development	At a glance
Birth	• Involuntary crying. • Begins to cry in different ways depending on needs, e.g. if hungry, tired, lonely. • Begins to make different vocal noises, e.g. coos, gurgles, grunts. • Begins to listen and tries to imitate sounds. • Will watch lip movement if held face to face. • Will start to respond with noises when spoken to.	Unintentional crying ↓ Tries to imitate sound ↓ Intentional crying ↓ **Cooing** and gurgling ↓ Babbling ↓ Repeats syllables ↓ Learns first words – **active vocabulary** ↓ Understands more words than can say – **passive vocabulary** ↓ **Jargon**
3 months	• Coos and gurgles to show contentment. • May smile when spoken to by carer. • Beginning to control muscles of lips, tongue and voice box. • May begin to babble.	
6 months	• Cooing may cease. • Babbling is more repetitive (e.g. 'da, da, da') and more tuneful (**echolalia**). • Laughs, chuckles and squeals. • Screams with annoyance. • May understand simple words, e.g. 'bye-bye', 'mama'. • Begins to imitate/repeat sounds.	
9 months	• Repeats syllables, e.g. 'dad, dad', 'mum, mum', 'ba, ba'. • Uses sound deliberately to express emotions. • Imitates sounds, e.g. smacks lips, blows raspberries. • May understand simple words, e.g. 'no', 'bye-bye'.	
12 months	• Imitates simple words • Recognises simple words, and points, showing **understanding**. • Babbling becomes more tuneful and similar to speech. • Learns first words (**active vocabulary**). • Understands more words than he/she can vocalise (**passive vocabulary**). • Talks incessantly in their own language (**jargon**).	

Linguistic stages: 15 months to 5 years

Approximate age	Level of development	At a glance
15 months	• Uses several words that parents can understand. • Points using single words to indicate items. • Beginning to use words to communicate.	Says more single words ↓
18 months	• Active vocabulary increases. • Words are used to mean more than one thing (e.g. 'cup' may mean 'Where is my cup?', 'I want my cup', 'I've dropped my cup' – **holophrase**). • Echoes and repeats words (**echolalia**). • Enjoys trying to copy rhythms and simple songs. • Words are symbolic, e.g. 'dog' is used for any four-legged animal (**holophrase**).	Holophrases ↓ Echolalia ↓ Vocabulary increasing ↓
2 years	• Is learning new words quickly. • Has a larger vocabulary. • May use **telegraphic sentences**, e.g. 'Me want ball'. • Begins to use pronouns, e.g. me, I, you. • Begins to ask questions. • Talks non-stop. • Begins to use negative, e.g. 'No teddy'.	Telegraphic sentences ↓ Talks non-stop ↓
3 years	• Vocabulary is large. • Sentences longer and close to adult speech. • Often holds long, imaginary conversations when playing. • Can describe past and present experiences. • Incessantly asks questions: why, when, where, what. • May use incorrect word ending, e.g. 'drawed', 'sheeps'.	Complex sentences ↓ Always asking questions ↓
4 years	• May use about 1500 words. • Talks about past and future. • Sentences are more grammatically correct but may still get endings wrong. • Uses a variety of questions. • Uses positional words, e.g. in, over, under. • May mispronounce words. • May mix up sounds like 'th' and 'f'.	May use 1500 words ↓
5 years	• Speech is grammatically correct and more fluent. • Enjoys jokes and riddles.	Speech is more grammatically correct

Encouraging language development

All children need to be talked to, listened to, praised and encouraged. They need to be given the chance to practise their skills and make mistakes.

Encouraging language and speech development can start before birth – research has shown that babies can hear and respond to the mother's voice while still in the womb, so during the pregnancy parents should talk to their unborn baby.

Once the baby is born it is important to spend time talking to her/him, especially when feeding, bathing and changing. Babies learn by copying, so it is important to hold babies close and make eye contact – they will watch the movement of

Babies learn by copying and listening

the lips and eventually try to copy. It is important for parents to talk simply, slowly and gently in a sing-song voice, which will hold the baby's attention. This is often called **motherese**.

Parents can help by:

- using different intonation
- speaking clearly
- speaking slowly
- always answering
- listening
- asking questions
- correcting sympathetically
- being patient.

There are some children who, in spite of all normal efforts, support and encouragement, do not begin to speak or whose speech is distorted. This could be due to emotional pressure and/or disabilities.

 KEY WORDS

Active vocabulary the words a child is able to use

Cooing the earliest sounds used to show contentment

Crying how a new baby communicates – changes in tone may indicate hunger, boredom, discomfort, etc.

Holophrase where one word may be used for more than one thing

Jargon the child's 'own' language, which may be understood only by those close to them

Monosyllabic babbling the repetition of single syllables with no meaning, e.g. 'ba ba ba ba'; this is sometimes called echolalia

Motherese used to describe the way in which adults speak to a baby in a simple, slow, clear rhythmic manner; it is not baby talk

Passive vocabulary the words a child may understand but cannot yet use

Polysyllabic babbling long strings of different syllables, e.g. 'do-da-dee-do'; this is sometimes known as 'scribble talk', when changes in tone and pitch may sound like conversation

Telegraphic speech when sentences are used without the linking words, e.g. 'Me want drink'

QUESTIONS

Question 1

Language is used by people to communicate with each other.

a List five other ways people can communicate.

b What must babies learn to do to be able to make speech sounds?

Question 2

a What is another name for pre-linguistic communication?

b Describe the main stages of verbal communication.

c List six ways that parents can help to encourage language development.

Question 3

Explain the meaning of the following:

a babbling

b jargon

c echolalia

d holophrases

e telegraphic sentences

e passive vocabulary.

 INVESTIGATION

Choose a selection of children's books and toys, and investigate how they encourage language development.

 CHILD STUDY ACTIVITY

1. Depending on the age of the child being studied, make a matching picture and word game to help to encourage language development.

2. Try to take a tape recorder with you at the start of the study. Use this to record your conversations with the child. Make a list of the words, phrases and sentences used, and check this against developmental milestones.

Repeat this again at different stages of the study so that you can see how the child's language and vocabulary are improving.

51 Drawing, Writing and Reading

Drawing, writing and reading are all closely linked, and developing and learning these skills is an important part of the development of language and communication.

Drawing and writing

Drawing helps develop fine motor skills

Most children love to draw and paint, and from an early age toddlers will enjoy making marks on paper although they will not represent any real meaning – this is often known as mark-making. Encouraging children to handle crayons, paintbrushes and pens will develop fine manipulative skills and good hand–eye coordination. Through trial and error they will eventually develop good pencil control and the drawing symbols will represent their thoughts more clearly. This process will develop a good foundation for writing skills where a child will be able to hold a pencil effectively, form recognisable letters, write their own name and form simple sentences.

Children will develop at their own rate and the ages and milestones stated in the table below simply offer a guideline to the child's progression.

Sequence of drawing and writing skills

Approximate age	Drawing	Crayon control
15 months		• Grasps crayon halfway up with the **palmar grasp** with either hand. • May use a crayon to scribble backwards and forwards.
18 months		• May still use either hand to draw. May begin to show a preference for right or left hand. • May hold a crayon with a **primitive tripod grasp** (thumb and first two fingers). • Can scribble backwards and forwards on paper and make dots.
2 years		• Attempts to hold the pencil close to the point in a **primitive tripod grasp**. May make a letter V. • May form vertical lines and circular scribbles.

Approximate age	Drawing	Crayon control
2½ years		• Holds a pencil or crayon with an **improved tripod grasp**. • May copy or make circular scribbles and lift hand off paper to make lines. • May copy horizontal lines. • May copy the letters V and T.
3 years		• Has quite good control of the crayon between first two fingers and thumb. • Shows preference for left or right hand. • Can copy a circle but it does not always join up. • Can form squares, lines and dots. • May copy the letters V, H and T. • Can draw a person and head with one or two features.
4 years		• Holds a pencil in the same way as an adult with quite good control. • Can colour in pictures but not always within the lines. • May now copy the letters V, H, T and O. • Begins to trace shapes, letters and numbers formed by dots. • Draws a 'potato person' with head, legs and trunk; may not have fingers or toes. • Talks about and names drawings.
5 years		• Has good control of a pencil. • Can copy circles, squares, triangles and the letters T, H, O, X, C, A, C, U, Y. May write own name and simple words. • Drawings are more complex and varied. • Can draw a house with windows, door, chimney and roof. • Pictures now have a background, e.g. sky, clouds, sun. • Can colour in a picture and stay within the outlines.

Once children have mastered the art of drawing a recognisable circle, they will then begin to represent a person by making markings within the circle to represent two eyes, a nose and a mouth, resembling a 'potato person'.

This will progress to more features representing arms and legs from the head. At first there will be no body mass. Finally a body appears and the legs have feet and toes. Clothes are then added to represent characters that are familiar to the child's environment. Eventually drawings will become more recognisable and will contain more complex detail.

From the age of five, drawings of houses look recognisable. Pictures usually have sky and grass with a simple tree. Animals look more realistic, with tails, and have their feet on the ground.

Also from the age of five children will have gained good pencil control and their writing will be more recognisable. At this stage children spell phonetically (how the word sounds literally) and their writing reflects this.

Drawings by a child aged five years

TO MUM I
LUV you veremuch
LUV from
James xxxxxx

James, writing aged five

Encouraging drawing and writing

A number of factors may affect a child's interest and development in drawing and writing:

- the amount of encouragement and praise from parents, guardians and siblings
- the availability of a wide variety of drawing implements, e.g. chunky wax crayons, crayons, washable felt-tip pens, chalk
- providing lots of cheap paper
- having a suitable table and chair at an appropriate height
- giving opportunities to copy good examples of how to hold a pencil
- providing books containing exercises such as join the dots, copying patterns and letter formation, can help to develop pencil control

Jumbo crayons and pencils are easier to hold

- letting the child paint freely, while wearing a protective apron
- providing colouring-in books to encourage skilful pencil control
- allowing a child to choose the preferred hand for writing
- going to playgroups, nurseries and childminders where they have the chance to draw and paint.

The skills of reading

Reading is one of the most important skills a child needs to learn.

Babies are born into a world where they are surrounded by words and symbols. Learning to read means being able to recognise, interpret and understand hundreds of symbols and combinations of symbols in a meaningful way.

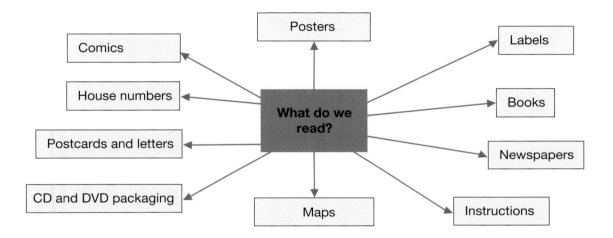

As with other aspects of development this process is gradual and continuous.

Pre-reading skills

Pre-reading skills are the skills children need to have *before* they can learn to read. Many of these are learnt naturally and can be encouraged by parents reading and talking to their children.

Children need to understand that symbols on paper have meaning.

• The recognition of **picture symbols**	
• Then linking **alphabet symbols** to picture symbols	**a**
• Finally, recognising combinations of alphabet symbols and linking these to picture symbols	**apple**

There are more practical skills that children also need to learn when reading books. For example:

- beginning to read at the top of the page
- holding the right way up
- reading from left to right
- turning the page from right to left.

This process takes time and 'real' reading (i.e. recognising and correctly interpreting the symbols) may not begin fully until a child is over four years of age.

Learning to read involves being able to remember and interpret symbols. Many shapes of letters look very similar (e.g. the letters d and b, and g, p and q). Some words also look similar (e.g. was and saw). Children have to learn to recognise the difference between these and to remember them. This is known as **visual discrimination**.

Looking at books is, of course, an important way of learning this.

However, there are many other fun activities parents could share with a child, which would make the process easier e.g. spot the difference:

Other activities parents could do with children are:

- picture lotto
- matching games
- snap
- dominoes
- rhymes
- threading beads
- sorting games.

The importance of reading books with children

Books are the most obvious and most effective tools we can use to help children learn to read. It is, therefore, important that from a very early age children have access to books. However, these are of little value if parents do not spend time with their children looking at pictures, telling stories, asking questions and having fun together.

Reading with children

When reading with children, parents must make sure they set aside a special time when they won't be interrupted. It is important to be comfortable and cuddle up together, to make sure the child can see the book the right way up, and that books are appropriate for the child's age, stage of development and interests (see pages 350–355).

Parents need to spend time reading with their children

Babies and toddlers

When reading with babies and toddlers:

- use a slow, sing-song voice
- speak slowly and simply
- point to pictures
- talk about the pictures before turning pages
- use different voices for different characters
- as the child gets older, say a name and ask the child to point to the item
- always praise them each time the child gets something right.

Two-to four-year-olds

When reading with two-to four-year-olds:

- ask questions about the story
- with favourite stories, encourage the child to join in and finish words and phrases
- ask them what they liked and didn't like
- always follow the words with a finger when reading
- let the child look at the pictures before starting to read the page.

Four-year-olds upwards

When reading with children aged four and upwards:

- proceed as with two-to-four-year-olds (see above)
- try shared reading – let the child read single words, a sentence or a phrase, then you read one.

Just as with learning to walk and talk, some children find reading easier than others. They will learn to read when they are ready and must be allowed to progress at their own pace. There should be no pressure from parents since this may put the children off books and reading.

 RESEARCH ACTIVITY

1. Find out more about how parents can help children to develop their pre-reading skills. As well as looking in books and searching the internet, you could interview teachers and parents to get ideas and information.

   Use your research to make a booklet or a PowerPoint presentation for parents and carers about the importance of reading with children.

2. Visit a local bookshop and look at the different types of drawing, puzzle and colouring books for children of different ages.

   Use some of these ideas to design and make an activity book that would encourage the drawing and writing skills of the child you are studying.

QUESTIONS

Question 1

a Why is it important to encourage children to draw from an early age?

b Suggest six ways a parent or carer could encourage children to draw and write.

Question 2

a At what age might a child be able to do the following:

   (i)   scribble backwards and forwards, and make dots?

   (ii)   copy or make circular scribbles?

   (iii) copy horizontal lines?

   (iv)   draw a head with one or two features?

   (v)   copy the letters V, H and T?

   (vi)   hold a pencil in the same way as an adult?

   (vii) colour in pictures, staying within the outlines?

   (viii) add background to pictures?

Question 3

a When learning to read, what do children have to be able to do?

b Other than books, list six different items children might need to read.

c At what age might real reading start?

Question 4

a Describe four practical skills children need to learn when reading books.

b What is visual discrimination?

c Suggest four activities parents could do with children to help to encourage visual discrimination.

d Suggest two guidelines for parents to follow when reading with:

   (i)   babies

   (ii)   a three-year-old

   (iii) a four-year-old.

 CHILD STUDY ACTIVITY

1. If the child is old enough, plan some different drawing or painting activities for one of your visits. Use these as an opportunity to look at their fine motor skills and their stage of drawing development. Talk to the child about her/his drawings.

2. Make up some word and picture cards. Choose simple everyday objects that the child will know and recognise (e.g. ball, sun, dog, flower, teddy). Draw each object and write each word on several cards. You could then use these to play snap or in a matching game.

52 Social and Emotional Development

Children are born into a world that they have to share with others. To do this they need to learn:

- to respect and understand others
- to cope with feelings and emotions
- to develop a positive self-image.

Social development is the process of learning these skills – it is sometimes called socialisation.

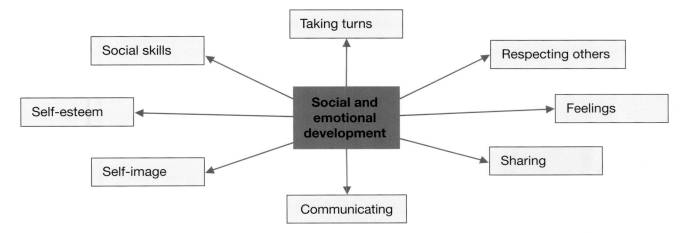

Social development and emotional development are very complex processes, and are very difficult to separate. For example, adults are expected to have more control over their own behaviour and feelings than are children. Yet the way some adults act, behave and treat others can depend on many different factors, such as whether they feel happy or sad, what someone has said to them and how it affected them, whether they feel ill or tired, or even what the weather is like.

All of these factors and many more can affect how we act. Learning to balance and control feelings and behaviour is a skill children need to develop – and this learning will go on throughout their childhood and adult life.

The theories

There are many different theories about how and why children develop their personalities and relationships with others. The three main ones are:

1. the Social Learning Theory of Albert Bandura
2. the Psychoanalytical Theories of Sigmund Freud and Erik Erikson
3. the Attachment Theory of John Bowlby.

Social Learning Theory

This theory is often used to explain how children act and behave. It is also used to explain how children's personalities develop, suggesting that children will copy and take on the characteristics of their parents. So, if parents are happy, outgoing and friendly, children will be more likely to develop similar characteristics.

Psychoanalytical Theories

These theories are more complicated. In very simple terms, Freud and Erikson believed that children's personalities and behaviour are shaped both consciously and unconsciously by their experiences at different stages of their development, and how they cope with the experiences.

Freud believed that physical needs were the main influence, while Erikson felt that stages of development were more linked to intellectual and social development. Erikson also believed that personalities carry on developing and changing all through life.

Attachment Theory

This suggests that children's main need is to have a strong and stable relationship with their primary carer – usually their parent(s). Their ability to develop and relate to other people is dependent on how secure this relationship is. Originally, this theory was used as the basis for the belief that mothers should not work, and should stay at home with their children. However, it has developed from this and it is now accepted that even very young children can have *more* than one close relationship and, as long as this exists, their social and emotional development will be secure.

Bonding with baby

The importance of bonding

Bonding describes the close two-way feelings and relationships that develop between a baby and an adult. Once the bond is made and becomes strong, the child will want to stay close to that adult and be cared for by them. When that adult is not with them, or leaves them, children may suffer from separation anxiety. They will become emotionally upset and distressed because they think the adult will not come back.

Bonding is a very important factor in a child's social and emotional development, and forms a main part of John Bowlby's Attachment Theory (see above). Bowlby believed that babies had a biological instinctive need to form an attachment to the person who fed and cared for them – initially the mother. His theory was developed further to show that babies could, in fact, form several attachments, and needed to for successful social and emotional development.

Factors that can encourage bonding

Although physical bonding will begin only at birth, there are other factors that can help, both before and during the actual birth process.

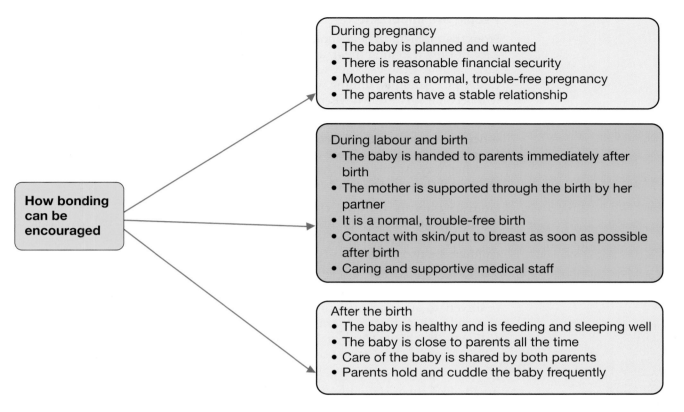

How bonding can be encouraged

During pregnancy
- The baby is planned and wanted
- There is reasonable financial security
- Mother has a normal, trouble-free pregnancy
- The parents have a stable relationship

During labour and birth
- The baby is handed to parents immediately after birth
- The mother is supported through the birth by her partner
- It is a normal, trouble-free birth
- Contact with skin/put to breast as soon as possible after birth
- Caring and supportive medical staff

After the birth
- The baby is healthy and is feeding and sleeping well
- The baby is close to parents all the time
- Care of the baby is shared by both parents
- Parents hold and cuddle the baby frequently

Encouraging social development

Giving children opportunities to mix and meet with other people, in different environments and situations, is very important for their social development. It gives them confidence, helps them to learn how to respect and be sympathetic to other people's views and feelings, to communicate, to share and to become independent. Initially, parents, close family and any regular carers (e.g. childminders) are the main influence on a child's social development – **primary socialisation**. From them children begin to learn the attitudes, values and behaviour patterns that are socially acceptable.

However, as they get older, children need wider social experiences. They need to be given opportunities to develop friendships of their own, mix with peers, have contact with young and old alike, experience contact with other cultures and those with special needs in situations where they will see broad gender roles. All of these will help children grow into socially developed adults.

Some examples of social experiences are:

- holidays
- mother/toddler groups
- activity clubs
- parks
- beach
- shopping trips
- swimming pool
- playgrounds
- visit to zoo
- nursery classes.

People are important

From the moment they are born, babies are aware of other people and will spend a lot of time watching them, although at this stage they don't understand about other people. However, they respond to the actions and feelings of parents and carers – for example, smiling when they smile. When they start to 'babble' they will become very excited when parents respond and talk back to them.

At the age of **five to six months**, babies will enjoy being in the company of other babies or young children, even if they are not actually 'playing with them'. However, they will love 'peek-a-boo' games and will take turns in doing this – in a limited way. At this stage they are still very reliant on close family for emotional support and will begin to show **separation anxiety** (see page 314).

From **six months onwards**, children begin to notice, and be more sensitive to, the actions and feelings of other people in their family. Separation anxiety can become greater and they become very afraid of strangers. This can last until children are two or three years of age, but does become easier as children become more confident and know that their parents will not leave them permanently.

As children become more mobile and confident, they begin to respond more positively to other people – they will love playing to an audience, will play alongside other children (**parallel play**) and may offer toys or sweets to others – although they are likely to grab them back! This is their first real attempt at socialisation.

By **two to three years of age** children are becoming more skilful. They can usually feed themselves, use the toilet independently and wash and dress themselves (after a fashion). They are also becoming more independent, wanting to try things for themselves and are very easily frustrated when things don't work out or they are told they cannot do something. The role of adults at this stage is very important – they have to try and make sure that children are successful but at the same time allow them to fail at times without damaging their self-esteem (see page 306). So, providing children with clothes and shoes that are easy to put on/take off, a step up to the toilet and suchlike will aid success. Being supportive and loving and not laughing at failures will prevent damage to children's confidence.

From **three years onwards** children are much more aware of other people, and their social circle needs to be much wider. Now is the time for them to attend playgroup or nursery on a regular basis. They need to learn how to react and respond to others, to be cooperative, to take turns, to share and to consider other people. They can do this only if they are around others regularly, but they will still need parent and family support and help.

Friendships and sharing

From around three years of age friendship will become increasingly important and children will, in many ways, become less socially dependent on their parents, family and carers.

They will begin to choose their own friends – by three years of age children can usually play cooperatively, although at this stage the actual play activity is more important than the other people playing it. By four years of age stable friendships are now being formed and 'having a friend' is very important. At this age, children will begin to choose same-sex friends and will become very attached to them. Some friendships made now will last a lifetime, some only a few days; some will cause tears and tantrums, some will give lots of hours of pleasure; all are important to the learning process.

Alongside developing friendships grows the ability to share – ideas, toys, attention, other people, etc. This is hard for children to do, as initially children are naturally **egocentric**. This means they want everything for themselves – if another child, even a brother or a sister, picks up a toy that belongs to them they may well throw a tantrum and become aggressive, even if they don't want to play with it.

It takes time to learn how to share, and they need to be with other children and adults to be able to learn this concept. Initially they may be able to share only for very short periods of time.

Play and socialisation

Children use play as a way of learning how to get along (socialise) with other children. Most children will go through the following stages as they learn to play together.

Stages of play

Very young children are quite happy to play on their own, as long as they know that there is an adult close by. As they become older, they become more interested in playing with other children – this is known as social play and is divided into four main stages, as outlined in the table below.

Solitary play

This is playing alone, and from birth to two years old is often the only type of play observed.

However, older children will continue to have times when they will enjoy playing alone.

Parallel play

By the time children are two years old, they will begin to enjoy parallel play. This is where they play alongside other children but not with them.

Looking-on play

Looking-on play occurs from about three years of age. It is when children will be happy to watch other children as they play and may copy them. At this stage they are often ready for nursery/ playgroup.

Cooperative play

This also happens at about three years old; children will be happy to play together, share activities and take on roles. However, arguments will occur.

Stages of social and emotional development

There are different and definite stages of social and emotional development and, although ages can be given as a guideline, the actual age at which children will reach each stage will vary greatly and depend on many factors.

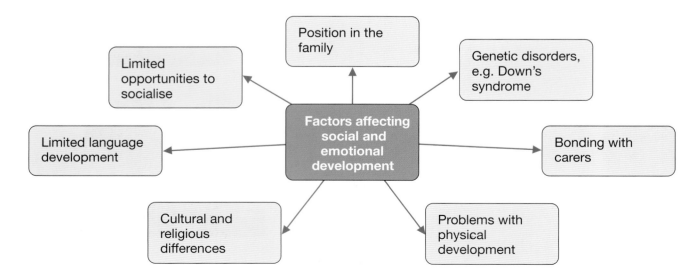

Position in the family

Limited opportunities to socialise

Genetic disorders, e.g. Down's syndrome

Limited language development

Factors affecting social and emotional development

Bonding with carers

Cultural and religious differences

Problems with physical development

Birth to one year

During this stage children are solely dependent on others. They are learning to communicate their needs and learning through play. Contact is sensory through touch and eye contact, and by cries, smiles and coos.

Newborn	• Watches parent's/carer's face. • Will maintain eye contact when feeding. • Turns towards carer's voice.
3 months	• Will smile and coo to show pleasure and enjoyment. • Likes to be cuddled.
6 months	• Will enjoy being played with. • Laughs.
9 months	• Can tell the difference between family and strangers. • Will show fear of strangers.
12 months	• Will show affection for parents and family. • Will want to be close to familiar people. • Will play on their own (**solitary play**). • Will wave 'bye-bye'.

Between one and two years

At this age children are very egocentric – this means that they see things only from their own point of view. They are often very demanding and can be defiant. They want their own way and they want it now!

15 months	• Will be more adventurous and want to explore *but* will still need a familiar adult near. • Will begin to use words to communicate. • Will have a stronger feeling of being an individual.
18 months	• Will show strong and different emotions – fear, anger, happiness. • Will have a greater vocabulary, so can communicate more easily. • Will still be shy of strangers and need a familiar adult close to them.

Between two and three years

At this age children are becoming more independent and adventurous, but because they still don't have total control over language and physical skills they are often frustrated at not being able to do what they want to. Emotions are strong and temper tantrums frequent, although they do occur less frequently as the child gets to three years old.

2 years	• Will play near other children (**parallel play**). • Will act out ideas and feelings through pretend play. • Will copy and imitate adults. • Prone to tantrums and shows strong emotions. • Still very egocentric. • Will have a strong sense of their own identity.
3 years	• Are beginning to understand gender and age. • Will begin to show interest in other children and to play with them. • Shows feelings and concern for others. • Becoming less egocentric and may not demand immediate and full attention from adults.

Between four and five years

At this age children are usually friendlier, more confident and more trusting. They are usually more social, and are beginning to make friends and lasting friendships.

4 years	• Will be very affectionate towards family, friends and people they see often. • Will begin to play with others (**cooperative play**). • Will play on their own for long periods of time without adult attention. • Will share toys.
5 years	• Beginning to choose their own friends. • Can understand rules and fair play. • Will play happily with other children (**cooperative play**). • More confident. • Will take turns in play activities. • Will respond to reasoning. • May start to play more with own sex.

KEY WORDS

Bonding the close feeling that develops between a baby and an adult

Cooperative play playing together and sharing/taking turns

Egocentric self-centred

Emotional development learning to handle and control feelings

Looking-on play watching other children and copying them

Parallel play playing alongside other children but not with them

Social development learning to live with others

Solitary play playing alone

QUESTIONS

Question 1

a What is meant by bonding?

b Why is bonding so important?

c Describe how bonding can be encouraged:

(i) during pregnancy

(ii) during labour and birth

(iii) after the birth.

d What is separation anxiety?

Question 2

a Why is it important for children to have plenty of opportunities to meet other people?

b Suggest six ways parents can encourage their children to meet other people.

c Discuss how and why people are important in encouraging social development.

d What is meant by 'egocentric'?

Question 3

a Name and describe the four stages of social play.

b List six factors that might affect social and emotional development.

c At what age might children:

(i) be able to tell the difference between family and strangers?

(ii) want to be with familiar people?

(iii) be shy of strangers?

(iv) play near other children?

(v) have temper tantrums?

(vi) take turns in play activities?

CHILD STUDY ACTIVITY

Try to organise an activity that involves a group of children. Look at the way the children react to one another, and comment on any social or antisocial behaviour or skills.

53 Social Skills: Feeding, Washing, Dressing and Toilet Training

The social skills of feeding, washing, dressing and going to the toilet are part of both social and emotional development. They are also very closely linked to physical development, as children need to have developed good gross and fine motor skills before they can manage these tasks.

Feeding

Once a child reaches the age of 12 months they will want to feed themselves – this is the first sign of independence. Providing baby-friendly spoons will help them to learn to do this for themselves – they will make lots of mess but this is all part of the learning process.

Once the child becomes more skilful it is important that the family sits down together for meals. This way, children will learn the following skills by copying:

- to eat alongside others
- to use cutlery
- to sit at the table
- good manners (e.g. saying 'please' and 'thank you')
- to drink from a cup.

Washing hands

Washing

As with other social skills, washing is mainly learnt by copying adults. It starts at bathtime by playing with a sponge or facecloth, then, as children get older, they will learn to wash their hands after using the toilet and before mealtimes. By the time they are three years old they should be able to wash their hands but not to dry them. By four years old, they can wash and dry their hands and face, and clean their teeth.

Dressing

Children learn to undress first – usually socks and shoes – often as a game. They will soon learn to help to get dressed by holding out hands or arms, or stepping into trousers. By the age of three years, children will probably be able to get undressed if clothing is unfastened, and will want to dress themselves, which they can usually do by four years.

Toilet training

Children have no control over the bowel and bladder until well into the second year of their lives. Young babies may perform on their potties at a younger age but it is just luck. The age at which children are able to control the workings of their bladder and bowels varies considerably but it is generally accepted that bowel control develops before bladder control, and girls are usually quicker to be completely clean and dry than boys. The most important thing to remember when encouraging bladder and bowel control is that a relaxed unhurried, undemanding, happy atmosphere will gain the best results.

Learning to get dressed takes time

Bowel and bladder control comes gradually. Toilet training can begin properly only when children begin to realise they can control the muscles that open the bladder and bowel.

Bladder and bowel control usually follows a general pattern. It begins when children become aware they are passing urine or having a bowel movement. They will then indicate to their parents that they are wetting or soiling their nappy. Next, children will learn to indicate they are about to wet or soil the nappy. This allows the parents to put the child on a potty or on the toilet.

When children have complete bowel and bladder control in the daytime they may still need a nappy at night. Children can be encouraged to be clean and dry at night by putting them to bed without a nappy, making sure nightclothes are easy to remove, leaving the potty by the bed and cutting out drinks before bedtime. Some parents lift the children onto the toilet or potty during the night. It is sensible to put a waterproof sheet under the ordinary bed sheet to protect the mattress.

Points to remember when helping children to gain bladder and bowel control

- Never force children to use a potty or the toilet. If they want to use the potty as a toy, let them. At some stage all children seem to like to use the potty as a hat.
- Always encourage and give praise. Be patient. Never chastise or ridicule children.
- Keep the potty handy. Take it with you when you go visiting or out in the car.
- If children like to sit on the potty, sit and read with them. This will relax them and encourage them to become familiar with using the potty.
- Accidents often occur. Make the minimum fuss and let children know it is not a problem.

Potty training

Developing social skills

Age	Skill development
6 months	• Drinks from a cup that is held for them.
12 months	• Uses fingers to feed themselves. • May try to help with feeding by holding the spoon. • May drink from a feeding cup themselves. • May help dressing by holding out leg/arm.
15 months	• Can hold a cup and drink from it without help. • Can eat using a spoon but may spill some food. • May be beginning to understand when they want to empty bladder but cannot control muscles. • Will need help with dressing and undressing but will try to do it themselves.
18 months	• Can use a cup and spoon well. • Can take off clothing quite easily and help to dress themselves. • Can give warning that they need the toilet, by words or action.
2 years	• Can feed without spilling a lot. • Can lift up a cup and put it down without spilling liquid. • Can put on some clothing themselves. • Can say when they need the toilet and manage to get the potty themselves.
2½ years	• Can use a spoon well. • Can pour themselves a drink. • Can unfasten buttons, zips and buckles. • Will be dry during the day. • May be dry at night.
3 years	• Can use a fork and spoon to eat. • Will go to the toilet on their own during the day. • Should be dry at night. • Can wash their hands but not dry them properly. • Becoming independent, wanting to dress themselves.
4 years	• Can feed themselves skilfully. • Can dress and undress themselves. • Can wash and dry hands and face, and clean teeth.
5 years	• Can use a knife and fork well. • Can easily dress and undress themselves. • May be able to tie shoelaces.

? QUESTIONS

Question 1

a What are social skills and why are they linked to a child's physical development?

b How do children learn most of their social skills?

c Why is it important for families of young children to sit down together to eat their meals?

Question 2

a At what age might it be possible to try to toilet train children? Explain why.

b Suggest five guidelines for parents to remember when toilet training their children.

Question 3

At what age might a child be able to:

a wash and dry hands and face, and clean teeth?

b use fingers to feed themselves?

c take off clothes easily and help to dress themselves?

d unfasten buttons and zips?

e be dry at night?

54 Understanding Emotions

Emotions are the feelings we have for and about people, objects, situations, etc. Everyone experiences strong feelings and emotions throughout their life. Adults can use words to try to explain how they feel, and this helps them to understand their feelings and control them. Children cannot do this so easily. They cannot understand themselves and they don't always have the words to be able to explain how they feel. So:

- they hit out when angry or frustrated
- they cry, scream and kick when they are refused
- they shriek with happiness.

Emotions such as happiness are positive emotions and parents need to work to encourage these feelings.

Emotions such as anger and sadness are negative emotions and need to be handled carefully, in a positive way: getting angry with a child who is angry will not work.

Encouraging positive emotions

Too often we can take positive emotions for granted – parents need to make sure that they consistently praise and encourage their children, not only when they succeed and when they do something well, but also when they try hard but perhaps fail. Then they won't grow up to be afraid of failure. Giving children lots of cuddles and smiles, pinning pictures on walls and suchlike can all help.

Coping with negative emotions

Emotion	Cause	Ideas for coping
Jealousy	Often occurs if there is a new baby because they feel insecure and not loved. It is one of the hardest emotions to control – even for adults.	• Give children love, attention and cuddles. • Be patient. • Try to respect how they are feeling. • If they are old enough, talk about feelings.
Fear	Children often develop irrational fears for no apparent reason, so it is often hard for adults to understand.	• Try to show that you understand the fear and accept that it is real. • Give lots of love. • Reassure them. • Avoid 'scary' stories or TV programmes.
Anger	This is one of the most common emotions and can be caused by lots of situations.	• Sometimes best to try to 'ignore' it. • Try to stay calm. • With a young child try to distract with a toy or activity. • Talk firmly but gently to the child about how they are feeling and why. • Give time and space to 'cool down'.
Sadness	This can also happen for no apparent reason – it may be because something hasn't worked, because a game has been lost or because a pet has died.	• Give plenty of love and attention. • Help them to talk about what has caused the sadness. • Try to distract with an interesting activity.

Self-image and self-esteem

How we relate to other people is very much affected by how we feel and think about ourselves.

Children's social and emotional development is very closely linked to their self-image and self-esteem.

Self-image and self-esteem can, and often do, affect how we behave, how successful we are, how we are able to get on with others and how we react to problems.

Self-image	

If we feel good about ourselves and believe in ourselves we have a positive self-image.	If we don't like ourselves and don't feel good about ourselves we have a negative self-image.
We will: • have high self-esteem • find it easy to make friends • be confident • not be afraid of failing, and willing to learn from mistakes.	We will: • have low self-esteem • find it harder to make friends • lack confidence • be afraid of making mistakes and failing.

Children learn about themselves and develop a self-image based mainly on the way adults treat them, talk with them and react to them. It is, therefore, very important that parents and carers encourage children to grow up feeling loved, valued and respected.

There are lots of different ways in which parents can do this, as outlined in the table below.

• **Praise and encourage** children when they do something well and succeed, *and* when they try!	• Have **realistic expectations** of children, remembering their age and stage of development.	• Give lots of **love and affection** so that children know they are loved and valued.
• Give children **opportunities to be independent,** to make mistakes and fail without criticism.		• Try to provide a **wide variety of toys and games,** especially those that encourage imaginative role play and feelings.
• Try to make sure children are brought up in a positive atmosphere – laugh with them but not at them.	• Make sure children have lots of **opportunities to socialise** with other children and make friends.	• Avoid attitudes, behaviour and experiences that promote **stereotyping**.

All these factors work together to help children develop a positive self-image, which in itself will influence their behaviour, feelings and attitudes towards others.

Above all, it must be remembered that children will often model themselves, both consciously and unconsciously, on the adults around them and copy what they say (see the section on behaviour, pages 310–317). So parents need to be very careful what messages they give to children through their own behaviour. In particular, parents should try to avoid any activity that might encourage stereotyping.

What is stereotyping?

Stereotyping is the expectation people may have of themselves and others, based on age, gender, race or disability.

Once children get to about three years old, they become more aware of their gender and need to work out for themselves what 'being a boy' or 'being a girl' is all about. They can do this in lots of ways but are mostly influenced by adults and their attitudes and behaviour. They see and copy.

Why is stereotyping harmful?

Stereotyping can damage children's development and self-esteem in many ways. It can stop children from achieving their full potential, because they may believe that they should not or cannot do something because of their gender.

- It can make them start to behave in certain ways that they think are expected of them – for example, girls are always expected to be caring and gentle, boys boisterous and adventurous.

- It may make boys afraid of showing affection or that they care, and girls afraid of being strong and daring.
- It can reinforce superior and inferior roles and attitudes towards others.
- It can make it difficult for children to mix with and relate to members of the opposite sex.

How can stereotyping be avoided?

- Allow boys and girls to play together.
- Do not buy gender-biased toys (e.g. dolls, prams and kitchens for girls and train sets and tractors for boys).
- Check books for gender bias (e.g. girls in 'caring roles' looking after home or boys having adventures and climbing trees).
- Share roles and jobs in the home.
- Avoid letting children watch TV programmes that reinforce gender roles.
- Don't dress children differently – especially in terms of colour choices (e.g. girls in dresses, boys in jeans; girls in pink, boys in blue).

Girls and boys should be allowed to play with any type of toy

 REMEMBER!

Social and emotional development depends on lots of factors. Above all, children need to be praised and encouraged, and brought up in a positive atmosphere. This will help them to develop a positive self-image and self-esteem.

 KEY WORDS

Bonding the close feeling that develops between a baby and an adult

Egocentric self-centred

Emotional development learning to handle and control feelings

Self-concept another term for self-image (see below)

Self-esteem how we feel about ourselves; sometimes called 'self-confidence'

Self-image what we think of ourselves; sometimes called 'self-concept'

Separation anxiety the emotional distress children feel when away from the parent/primary carer

Stereotyping expecting people to behave and act in a certain way – usually based on gender, race or disability

QUESTIONS

Question 1

a What are emotions?

b Give three examples of positive emotions.

c Give three examples of negative emotions.

d How can parents help to encourage positive emotions in children?

Question 2

How could parents cope with a child who:

a is jealous of a new baby?

b is afraid of going to bed at night?

c is sad because their pet has died?

Question 3

a What is meant by self-image and why is it important?

b Suggest six ways a parent could help a child to develop a positive self-image.

Question 4

a What is meant by stereotyping?

b Why might stereotyping be a problem?

c Suggest six ways in which parents could help prevent stereotyping.

55 Behaviour

As well as learning how to share, cooperate and respect other people, children also have to learn to behave in a way that is acceptable to others.

Parents have to help to develop these skills by making sure they set realistic expectations about what is acceptable and unacceptable behaviour, and using appropriate discipline when necessary.

Learning to behave is a gradual process – children are not born with self-control.

How children are expected to behave will vary and can depend on lots of factors, such as:

- cultural beliefs and traditions
- country
- parents' attitudes
- position in family.

Also the way children are expected to behave changes with time: 50 years ago children were expected to be seen but not heard, especially when with adults. Nowadays, children are expected and allowed to have views and opinions, and to show their feelings freely.

What is good behaviour?

Again this will vary from family to family and from society to society, but in general good behaviour means thinking of the feelings and needs of others, as well as our own. It means being able to share, take turns, listen to others, and be helpful and kind.

How do children learn to behave?

Different people have different theories (views) on how children learn to behave. The most common of these are:

- Behaviourist Theory
- Social Learning Theory
- Self-fulfilling Prophecy Theory.

Behaviourist Theory

This theory, developed by B.F. Skinner, is based on the idea that if good behaviour is recognised and rewarded in some way, children will learn that it is acceptable and will repeat it.

Rewards are called positive reinforcers and can be things such as attention from parents, praise, a treat, a sweet, and so on. However, children can sometimes use unacceptable behaviour to attract attention – this should be ignored. This is called negative reinforcement.

Good behaviour $\longrightarrow$ • Praise • Attention • Treat $\longrightarrow$ Good behaviour repeated

Social Learning Theory

This theory, developed by Albert Bandura, suggests that children learn to behave (as they do lots of other things) by watching and copying what happens around them, so they will learn to behave from their parents or primary carers.

Therefore, if a child is brought up by parents who swear and are aggressive, they will see this as 'normal' and copy. If, however, parents are polite, calm and considerate, then children will copy this and behave in a similar way.

Self-fulfilling Prophecy Theory

This theory suggests that the way adults *think* about their children will influence how the children behave. So, if a parent thinks a child is 'good' and 'kind' the child is likely to behave in that sort of way. If, however, a parent thinks the child is 'naughty', then the child is more likely to behave in that way. This theory holds that negative labelling of children can be very harmful.

Putting the theories into practice

None of these theories is perfect. However, all can give parents ideas about how they can help children to learn and show 'wanted' behaviour. Parents can do this by:

- staying calm
- creating a positive atmosphere and environment where children can see and feel that they are important and valued
- being a good role model
- praising and rewarding wanted behaviour, and ignoring unwanted behaviour
- having realistic expectations of children, depending on their age and stage of development
- being consistent in what is acceptable and unacceptable
- setting clear guidelines and boundaries about what is acceptable
- letting children know that they are loved, unconditionally
- being consistent in using any sanctions
- treating all children in the family the same.

Remember, even usually well-behaved children will misbehave at times and act in an unacceptable way.

It takes a long time for children to learn how to control their feelings and to 'behave', and sometimes it is impossible for them to do so.

Often, sudden changes in children's lives can affect their behaviour – sometimes it may be something as simple as tiredness. How much their behaviour is affected will depend on their age, their level of understanding and the attitudes and support of their parents.

Behaviour can be affected by a variety of factors, as outlined in the table below.

Boredom and frustration, especially if parents give the child little love and attention.	Jealousy, especially if there is a new baby in the family.
Moving house may make a child feel very insecure.	Tiredness can easily result in a child being uncooperative and badly behaved.
Starting playgroup or nursery can often make children feel afraid and insecure.	When parents return to work and/or children have a new carer and their routine is altered.
The death of someone close, or a pet, can cause a lot of emotional upset.	Parents separating or getting divorced.

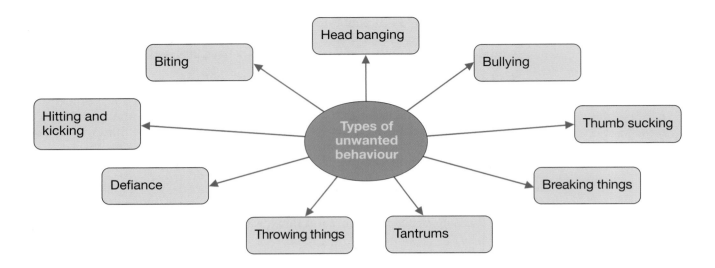

Sometimes behaviour is **regressive** – children begin to behave in a way that is much more like that of a younger child:

- bed-wetting
- clinging to parents
- refusing to communicate
- using 'baby talk'
- wanting to be fed.

Sometimes behaviour is **aggressive** – children may try to hurt themselves or others:

- head banging
- kicking
- biting.

Although Behaviourist Theory suggests that unwanted behaviour should be ignored, sometimes this isn't possible, especially when there is a danger that the child may harm themselves and/or others. Parents need to know how to cope, and may feel that they want to use some sort of sanction or punishment.

How they cope will depend on many factors and may vary according to the type of behaviour being shown, the age of the child, the place where the behaviour occurs, their own values and beliefs, and even their own mood and feelings.

Handling bad behaviour

Say no!	If said firmly this will often stop unwanted behaviour, especially if eye contact is made.
Distract the child	Younger children will not always be able to understand that what they are doing is unacceptable, or why. Offering a different activity will take their attention and defuse the situation.
Set clear rules and boundaries	Making children aware of what is acceptable and not acceptable behaviour, and sticking to it.
Explain to the child	If the child is old enough, unwanted behaviour can be stopped by explaining why it is wrong or what harm they might do by continuing.
Use sanctions	Sometimes parents may feel that taking away a favourite toy or not having a story before bedtime is a fitting punishment. Sanctions are always negative and parents should use these only in extreme cases. However, if a sanction is threatened and then not used, children learn that they can get away with certain things and will repeat them again and again. Any sanction chosen should be in proportion to the behaviour.
Use eye contact and facial expressions	Sometimes a 'look' is enough to tell children that what they are doing is not acceptable – and once the unwanted behaviour has stopped this can be reinforced by praise.

Comfort habits

Under no circumstances should any sort of physical punishment be given. Smacking, no matter how 'gentle', is not an option and, under the Children Act 1989, is illegal.

Comfort habits

Comforters, soothers and dummies are often used by children to help them settle at night. Many children, instead of behaving in an aggressive or regressive way, often use these to help them cope with difficult situations. Some may have imaginary friends and will talk to them or blame them for something they themselves have done wrong. Others may suck their thumb or use comforters, dummies, blankets or favourite toys, which they will take with them all the time but mainly when they go to bed, into an unknown situation or into a situation where they may be separated from their parents.

As long as children are still getting a lot of love and attention from parents and other carers a comforter can be a good thing. However, it should not be used as a substitute for love and attention.

Advantages and disadvantages of comforters

Advantages	Disadvantages
Dummies ✓ Use can be limited. ✓ Can soothe and comfort a child instantly. ✓ It is an easier habit to break than thumb sucking. ✓ Can be cleaned and sterilised. ✓ If lost can easily be replaced.	**Dummies** ✗ Need frequent sterilising. ✗ Need to be replaced regularly. ✗ Unhygienic if dropped on the floor or if parents 'lick' them to clean. ✗ May be dipped in honey and used as a soother, which could damage growing teeth. ✗ Child may constantly ask for dummy. ✗ Long-term use can affect speech and damage teeth.
Thumb ✓ Always available. ✓ No cost involved. ✓ In charge of own comfort.	**Thumb** ✗ Can cause sore thumb. ✗ Can be a hard habit to break. ✗ If it continues into childhood can cause problems with teeth.
Toy or blanket ✓ Can be taken anywhere. ✓ Especially useful at bedtimes. ✓ Doesn't cause any physical damage.	**Toy or Blanket** ✗ Can cause problems if lost – it's often a good idea to have a duplicate! ✗ Can get dirty and be unhygienic. ✗ Child may be reluctant to allow it to be washed.

Separation anxiety

This is the term given to the feelings children have, especially very young children, when they are separated from their parents and/or close family. This usually begins at five to six months – at this stage children do not yet fully understand that even if they cannot see their parents, they still exist. So if the parent goes out of sight they think they have lost them and will become upset. At the same age children also become fearful of strangers.

Can toys and games help?

As with all other forms of development toys, games and other activities are important in helping children to cope with and express their feelings, and to get rid of negative emotion (see pages 341–346).

Toy/game/activity	How it helps
Hammer toys 	Children love to hammer and bang; it helps them to get rid of tension and destructive feelings.

Toy/game/activity	How it helps
Drawing and painting 	Children often don't have enough language or know enough words to say how they feel and to get rid of anger. Painting and drawing are ways in which they can show their feelings, through what they paint, how they paint and the colours they use.
Play-Doh 	This can be squeezed, squashed, battered and flattened. Handling it can be a way of soothing or of getting rid of tensions.
Role play 	Children love to take on roles and play pretend games with others. They can act out their fears, feelings and emotions.

Toy/game/activity	How it helps
Chasing 	Running around allows children to 'let off steam'.
Soft toys such as teddy bears 	Playing with soft toys can give comfort and allow children to learn to care and show their feelings.

RESEARCH ACTIVITY

1. Work in a small group to plan and carry out a survey to find out the most common behaviour problems among children under the age of five, and how these are usually dealt with. Present the results as a report.

2. Design and make an information sheet giving simple guidelines about managing difficult children.

QUESTIONS

Question 1

a List four factors that might influence how children are expected to behave.

b According to Behaviourist Theory, how do children learn to behave?

c Suggest eight ways parents can encourage 'wanted' or 'desirable' behaviour.

Question 2

a Suggest six factors that might affect behaviour.

b List six different types of unwanted behaviour.

c List six ways a parent could handle unwanted behaviour.

Question 3

a Why might children develop comfort habits?

b Compare the advantages and disadvantages of using two different comforters.

c What is 'separation anxiety'?

d Suggest, with reasons, three toys or activities that might help children to get rid of negative emotions.

Question 4

What might be the most appropriate way to handle the behaviour of a child who:

a hits other siblings?

b has a temper tantrum in a supermarket?

c refuses to do as they are told?

56 An Overview of Physical, Intellectual, Emotional and Social Development

Newborn

Even in the first few weeks newborn babies are beginning to learn about and understand their world. They do this through their senses – by looking, listening, touching, tasting and smelling. They soon begin to make noises other than crying and will soon enjoy kicking their legs and waving their hands, as well as communicating with people.

Physical

Gross motor skills

- When held standing will make walking or stepping movements.
- When lying on back (**supine**) head is turned to one side.
- When lying on tummy the knees are tucked up, bottoms are in the air and head is to one side.
- Limbs are curled up to body.
- Head is floppy.
- If held in a sitting position head will 'lag' behind body.
- When held in a sitting position back is rounded.

Fine motor skills

- If a finger or object is placed in their hand they will grasp it tightly.
- Hands are usually closed.
- Thumb is often tucked under fingers.

Sensory

- Startled by sudden noises and bright lights.
- Turns towards sound.
- Begins to recognise main carer's voice.
- Cannot focus on objects more than 25 cm from eyes.
- Blinks at sudden bright lights.

Intellectual: concepts

- Soon begins to recognise primary carer.
- When seeing primary carer will make excited movements with arms and legs, coo and smile.
- Will react to tone of voice of carer.

Intellectual: language

- Begins to cry in different ways depending on need, e.g. if hungry, tired, lonely.
- Begins to make different vocal noises, e.g. coos, gurgles, grunts.
- Begins to listen and tries to imitate sounds.
- Will watch lip movement if held face to face.
- Will start to respond with noises when spoken to.

Emotional and social

- Begins to smile at carers.
- Will maintain eye contact when feeding.
- Turns towards carer's voice.

Toys and play

Newborn babies need to be held close and talked or sung to often. Eye contact is very important and holding babies face to face will help them to watch expressions and mouth movements. They need mobiles with bright colours and patterns, baby gyms and rattles.

Three months

Babies are still completely dependent on other people. They are beginning to show more interest in their surroundings. Reflex actions are disappearing, and fine and gross motor skills are beginning to develop. They may begin to play with simple toys, such as a rattle, and communicate with smiles and gurgles.

Physical

Gross motor skills

- When lying on front can lift head and turn from side to side.
- When lying on front, can push up on arms and raise shoulders.
- Can kick legs strongly.
- If held in a sitting position, head will lag a little.
- When held can sit with a straight back.

Fine motor skills

- Can hold a small toy for a short time before dropping.
- Looks at their hands, and plays with hands and fingers.
- Grasp reflex may have disappeared.

Sensory

- Finds hands and brings them to mouth.
- Begins to move head to look at things when hearing a voice.
- Will turn towards a sound.
- Fascinated by faces.

Intellectual: concepts

- Becoming more aware of surroundings.
- Begins to use mouth to explore objects.
- May smile when spoken to by carer.
- Looks intently at things that move.

Intellectual: language

- Coos and gurgles to show contentment.
- May smile when spoken to by carer.
- May begin to babble.
- Beginning to control muscles of lips, tongue, voice box.

Social

- Smiles both at family and strangers.
- Enjoys time with carers, e.g. bathtime and feeding.

Emotional

- Becomes very attached to mother or main carer.
- Shows feelings and emotions.
- Shows pleasure when held.

Toys and activities

Mobiles above or attached to cot. Soft toys and balls. Rattles, teething rings and other hand-held toys that are safe to put into mouth. Young babies should be held close and talked or sung to often.

Six months

By six months babies can usually sit on their own for some time without support. They are becoming more interested and curious, and will explore everything they pick up by 'mouthing'. They enjoy being with people and being played with but are becoming unsure of strangers.

Physical

Gross motor skills

- Can lift head and chest clear of floor using arms for support.
- Can sit for long periods if supported by cushions.
- Can sit for short periods without support but will topple over.
- May try to roll over from back to front.
- May try to crawl.
- When lying on back, grasps legs and feet and puts feet into the mouth.
- Kicks strongly when lying on back.
- May hold out hands to be picked up.

Fine motor skills

- Puts all objects to mouth (mouthing).
- Grabs toys using whole hand (palmar grasp).
- Begins to reach out for small toys.
- Can pass toys from one hand to the other.
- Has learnt to drop things.

Sensory

- Still 'mouths' toys and objects.
- Looks around curiously.
- If a toy falls out of sight will not look for it.
- Watches what people are doing.

Intellectual: concepts

- Knows to hold out arms to be picked up.
- Can recognise mother's or main carer's voice and will turn towards them.
- Spatial awareness is improving, so may notice toys that are half hidden.

Intellectual: language

- Cooing may cease.
- Babbling is more repetitive (e.g. 'da da da') and more tuneful (echolalia).
- Laughs, chuckles and squeals.
- Screams with annoyance.
- May understand simple words, e.g. 'bye-bye', 'mama'.
- Begins to imitate/repeat sounds.

Social

- Enjoys being played with.
- May display separation anxiety.
- May be afraid of strangers.
- May feed using fingers.
- May begin to play with family members in a simple way, e.g. stroking face.
- May play alone (solitary play) with a simple toy, e.g. rattle.

Emotional

- Will enjoy being played with.
- Laughs with pleasure.
- May 'cling' to mother or main carer for security.

Toys and play

As for three months (see above), plus activity centres, non-breakable mirrors, activity mats with textures and hidden noises, bath toys, cardboard boxes to put toys in, simple picture books, things to bang, playing 'peek-a-boo' and 'this little piggy'.

Nine months

Baby is now becoming more mobile and will be beginning to crawl or 'cruise'. Can now sit for long periods of time and reach for things without toppling over. Language skills are beginning to develop. Usually shy with strangers.

Physical

Gross motor skills

- Tries to crawl by rocking backwards and forwards.
- Can pull into a standing position by going on to knees first.
- May begin to sidestep (**cruise**) around furniture.
- Can stand when holding on to furniture.
- May begin to crawl upstairs.
- Can sit unsupported for longer periods of time.
- When sitting, can turn to look sideways and stretch to reach toys.
- May take some steps if held.

Fine motor skills

- Uses **primitive pincer grasp** (thumb and first finger) to pick up small objects.
- Can release a toy by dropping it but cannot put it down voluntarily.
- Will begin to look for dropped or fallen objects that are out of sight.
- Uses index finger to point.
- Pokes objects with index finger

Sensory

- Looks in correct place for fallen or falling toys.
- Begins to recognise familiar pictures.
- Enjoys joining in games such as 'peek-a-boo'.

Intellectual: concepts

- Can tell the difference between family and strangers.
- Recognises familiar games and rhymes.
- Recognises own name and will turn head when spoken to.
- Has no concept of danger.
- May look for a toy they see being hidden (**object permanence**).

Intellectual: language

- Repeats syllables, e.g. 'dad dad', 'mum mum', 'ba ba'.
- Uses sound deliberately to express emotions.
- Imitates sounds, e.g. blows raspberries, smacks lips.
- May understand simple words, e.g. 'no', 'bye-bye'.

Social

- May drink from a cup without help.
- Will still need to be close to a familiar adult.
- Will be happy to play alone.
- May hold out hands to be washed.

Emotional

- May need a comfort object or toy to take to bed, e.g. teddy.
- May still show fear of strangers.

Toys and play

As for six months, plus rattles and toys which will stick to surfaces, balls of different sizes and textures, stacking toys, fabric, card or plastic books, large soft bricks, feely bags or boxes. Will enjoy songs and rhymes with actions, e.g. 'Pat-a-cake'.

12 months

By 12 months the world is becoming a bigger and more interesting place because children are now becoming more mobile as they learn to crawl and walk. Also at around this age language development starts to 'take off'. Socially and emotionally, children will still be shy with others and need to be close to parents/carers.

Physical

Gross motor skills

- Becoming very mobile – either by crawling, shuffling, 'bear walking' or bottom shuffling.
- Can cruise along furniture.
- Can walk a few steps if held.
- May start to walk but will tend to fall or sit suddenly.
- Can sit unsupported for long periods of time.
- Tries to crawl upstairs forwards and downstairs backwards.
- Can stand alone.

Fine motor skills

- Uses a neat pincer grasp (thumb and first finger) to pick up small objects.
- Points at objects of interest with index finger.
- Uses both hands, but may begin to show preference for one.
- Puts small objects into a container, e.g. bricks into a beaker.
- Drops and throws toys deliberately.
- Uses tripod grasp to hold bricks and bang them together.
- May hold a crayon in a palmar grasp.
- May try to turn pages in a book but usually several at once.

Sensory

- Watches people, animals and moving objects for long periods.
- Drops and throws toys deliberately, and watches them fall.
- Looks for lost or hidden toys.
- Recognises familiar people and sounds.
- Turns to sound.

Intellectual: concepts

- Is learning through trial and error.
- Will pick up toys and hand them to others, when asked.
- Can understand and act on simple instructions, e.g. 'wave bye-bye'.

Intellectual: language

- Imitates simple words.
- Recognises simple words and points, showing understanding.
- Babbling becomes more tuneful and similar to speech.
- Learns first words (active vocabulary).
- Understands more words than they can vocalise (passive vocabulary).
- Talks incessantly in their own language (jargon).

Social

- Will still want to be close to familiar people.
- Enjoys others' company, especially at mealtimes.
- Uses fingers to feed themselves.
- May drink from a feeding cup by themselves.
- May help dressing by holding out leg/arm.

Emotional

- Shows affection for parents and family.
- Needs to hold hands to feel secure.

Toys and play

As for nine months (see above), plus musical toys and boxes, simple jigsaws, bricks and containers, push and pull toys, picture books with simple rhymes, 'hide and seek' games. Will also enjoy sand and water play, Play-Doh and copying adult activities, e.g. dusting.

15 months

By 15 months children are much more mobile and can walk along unaided, although they may bump into furniture. Fine motor skills are developing well and they may enjoy simple drawing activities. They are still very egocentric, and learn through trial and error.

Physical

Gross motor skills

- Walks independently, using arms to balance.
- Can crawl upstairs safely and downstairs feet first.
- Throws a large ball but may fall over.
- Can kneel without support.
- Can get up to a standing position without using the help of people or furniture.

Fine motor skills

- Claps hands together.
- May build a tower of two blocks if shown how.
- Can pick up and drink from a cup using two hands to hold it.
- Can make a mark with a crayon using a palmar grasp.
- Turns pages in a book but will turn several at once.
- Tries to eat with a spoon but will turn it upside down.

Sensory

- Looks with interest at pictures in a book and pats them.
- Stands at a window and watches what is happening for long periods of time.

Intellectual: concepts

- Understands object permanence – that things exist even if they cannot be seen.
- Still very egocentric.
- More adventurous and wants to explore.
- Grasps crayon halfway up with palmar grasp with either hand.
- Scribbles to and fro.

Intellectual: language

- Uses several words that parents can understand.
- Points and uses single words to indicate an item.
- Beginning to use words to communicate.

Emotional

- Shows love and affection to family members.

Social

- Becoming more helpful – will try to dress themselves but will need help.
- Can hold a cup and drink from it without help.
- May begin to understand when they want to go to the toilet but cannot control muscles.
- Still shy with strangers.

Toys and play

As for 12 months (see above), plus soft balls to throw, building bricks, cause-and-effect toys, e.g. jack-in-the-box, drawing and simple gluing activities, listening to nursery rhymes and stories, dancing to music.

18 months

By this age children can walk well, are becoming more adventurous and want to explore but have little understanding of danger. Fine motor skills are much improved and language skills are beginning to develop fast. They are becoming more sociable.

Physical

Gross motor skills

- Can walk confidently and steadily without using arms to balance.
- Can pick up toys by bending from waist.
- Can 'squat' to look for things without losing balance.
- May be able to walk upstairs and downstairs without adult help.
- Runs, but sometimes bumps into obstacles.
- Can push and pull toys when walking.
- Can crawl backwards downstairs.

Fine motor skills

- Can turn knobs and handles on doors.
- Can build a tower of three bricks.
- Can string together large beads.
- Uses mature pincer grasp to pick up objects.
- Beginning to use the tripod grasp when using pencils and crayons.
- Can pull off shoes.
- Fascinated by buttons, zips and other fastenings.

Sensory

Hand–eye coordination is good:
- can pick up small objects such as beads on sight with delicate pincer grasp
- enjoys simple picture books
- recognises and points to brightly coloured items on a page
- recognises familiar people at a distance.

Intellectual: concepts

- Can recognise and point to pictures in a book if asked.
- Memory is developing.
- When drawing uses scribbles and dots.
- Tries to imitate adult actions.
- Starts to match shapes to holes in a shape sorter.
- Knows and can point to parts of the body.
- Recognises objects from books and pictures.
- May start to do simple jigsaws.

Intellectual: language

- Active vocabulary increases.
- Words are used to mean more than one thing, e.g. 'cup' may mean 'Where is my cup?', 'I want my cup', 'I've dropped my cup'.
- Echoes and repeats words (echolalia).
- Enjoys trying to copy rhymes and simple songs.
- Words are symbolic, e.g. 'dog' is used for any four-legged animal (holophrases).

Emotional

- Will show different and strong emotions, e.g. fear, anger, happiness.
- May change from negative to positive emotions quickly.
- Becoming more independent.

Social

- Becoming more sociable.
- May refuse to obey instructions.
- Still egocentric and shy of strangers, needing a familiar adult close to them.
- Play happily alone (solitary play).
- May enjoy playing alongside others (parallel play).
- Can use a cup and spoon well.
- Can take off clothing quite easily and help to dress themselves.
- Can give warning that they need the toilet by words and actions.

Toys and play

As for 15 months (see above), plus shape sorters, hammering toys, toy telephones, Play-Doh, musical toys, books with joining-in activities, simple storybooks. Will enjoy simple sticking and gluing, modelling and finger painting, circle games, e.g. 'ring-a-ring-a-roses', and songs and rhymes with actions.

Two years

At this age children can run, walk and talk and are becoming more independent. They are curious and want to explore but still have only limited understanding of danger. When frustrated or stopped from doing something they throw temper tantrums. Pretend play is important at this stage.

Physical

Gross motor skills

- Can walk upstairs and downstairs confidently, two feet to a step.
- Enjoys climbing on furniture.
- Can kick a large ball that is not moving.
- Enjoys toys that are put together and pulled apart.
- Walks and runs more safely and steadily.
- Pushes and pulls large wheeled toys.
- Can sit on a tricycle and use feet to move it.

Fine motor skills

- Can turn pages of a book one by one.
- Has good hand–eye coordination.
- Can build a tower of five or six bricks.
- Uses mature pincer grasp to pick up and position small objects.
- Holds a pencil firmly and can form circles, lines and dots.
- Can zip and unzip large zippers.
- Uses preferred hand.

Sensory

- Enjoys looking at picture books.
- Recognises fine detail in favourite pictures.
- Recognises familiar adults in photographs.

Intellectual: concepts

- May make a letter V when drawing.
- Vertical lines and circular scribble forming.
- May begin to sort and match.
- Uses symbolic play, e.g. a twig from a tree will become a sword.
- Still very egocentric.
- Enjoys books.
- Learns by copying and imitating adults.

Intellectual: language

- Is learning new words quickly.
- Has a larger vocabulary.
- May use telegraphic sentences, e.g. 'Me want ball'.
- Beginning to use pronouns, e.g. 'me', 'I', 'you'.
- Beginning to ask questions.
- Talks non-stop.
- Begins to use negatives, e.g. 'no teddy'.

Emotional

- Will act out feelings and ideas through pretend play.
- Will have tantrums and show strong emotions when frustrated.
- Becoming more independent but will still often cling to an adult.
- May still display separation anxiety.

Social

- Will play near other children (parallel play).
- Still finds it hard to share.
- Can feed without too much mess and uses a spoon well.
- Can lift a cup and put it down without spilling.
- By two and a half, may be able to pour a drink for themselves.
- Can put on some clothing themselves.
- By two and a half, can unfasten buttons, zips and buckles.
- Can say when they need the toilet.
- By two and a half, should be dry during the day – may be dry at night.

Toys and play

As for 18 months (see above), plus dressing-up clothes, construction toys, dolls and teddies for pretend play, musical toys, e.g. xylophone. Outdoor toys could include simple climbing frame, small slides and swings, sit-and-ride toys, paddling pools. May enjoy painting and colouring in, and simple printing.

Three years

By this age children are much more independent and confident. They become less frustrated when trying to do things because they are becoming more skilful, so temper tantrums are less frequent. They are trusting and more sociable, so will play with others and enjoy creative and pretend play.

Physical

Gross motor skills

- Can walk and run forwards with precision.
- Can walk on tiptoe.
- Can kick a ball forwards.
- Can throw overhand.
- Can catch a large ball with extended arms.
- Pedals and steers a tricycle.
- Walks upstairs with one foot on each step.
- Can hop on one foot.
- Can manoeuvre around objects showing spatial awareness.

Fine motor skills

- Holds a crayon with more control and can draw a face.
- Can eat with a spoon or fork without spilling food.
- Can colour in more neatly and more within the lines.
- Can put on and take off coat.
- Can build a tower of nine or ten bricks.
- Cuts with toy scissors.
- Uses improved tripod grasp.

Sensory

- Knows names of some colours.
- Can match two or three main colours, usually red and yellow.
- Listens eagerly to favourite stories and wants to hear them over and over again.
- Can thread large beads.

Intellectual: concepts

- Beginning to understand concept of time – especially past and future.
- Beginning to understand number concept of 1 and lots.
- Beginning to use language to describe thoughts and ideas.
- Can count up to ten by rote.
- Enjoys music, both making it and listening to it.
- Concentrates for longer periods of time.
- Understands concepts of cause and effect.
- Enjoys pretend play.
- Can copy a circle but does not always join it up.
- May write letters V, H and T.
- Draws a head with one or two features.

Intellectual: language

- Vocabulary is large.
- Sentences are longer and close to adult speech.
- Often holds long, imaginary conversations when playing.
- Incessantly asks questions: why, when, where, what.
- May use incorrect word endings, e.g. 'drawed', 'sheeps'.

Emotional

- Shows feelings and concern for others.
- Sometimes develops fears, e.g. of the dark.
- Temper tantrums are not as frequent.
- May have outgrown separation anxiety.

Social

- Can use a fork and spoon to eat.
- Will go the toilet on their own during day.
- Should be dry at night.
- Can wash their hands but not dry them properly.
- Becoming independent – wanting to dress themselves.
- Will begin to show interest in other children and to play with them (joining-in play).
- More trusting.

Toys and play

As for two years (see above), plus small-world toys, pop-up books or books with lift-up flaps. Simple cooking, drawing and painting, building things. Will enjoy making 'dens', helping in the house, matching and sorting games, riding tricycle.

Four years

By this age gross and fine motor skills are quite well developed. Children are creative and imaginative, and enjoy making things. Language skills are good – they enjoy playing with other children, can usually take turns and may begin to understand rules. They are curious and love to explore and investigate.

Physical

Gross motor skills

- Can walk or run alone, and walk upstairs and downstairs, in adult fashion.
- Can walk along a straight line showing good balance.
- Can climb ladders and trees.
- Pedals and controls a tricycle confidently.
- Is becoming more skilled at ball games – can throw, catch, bounce and kick a ball and use a bat.

Fine motor skills

- Can build a tower of ten or more blocks.
- Can build three steps with six bricks, if shown how.
- Uses a mature pincer grasp.
- Can fasten and unfasten buttons.
- Can put together large-piece jigsaws.
- Can colour in pictures, but not always within the lines.

Sensory

- Can match and names four main colours.
- Follows storybooks with eyes and identifies words and pictures.

Intellectual: concepts

- Can count up to ten by rote.
- Beginning to understand number concept 1–3.
- Understands concept of past and future.
- Still muddles fact with fiction.
- Enjoys jokes.
- Can repeat songs and rhymes without mistakes.
- May know letters of the alphabet.
- Beginning to understand concept of right and wrong.
- Can concentrate for longer periods.
- May be able to copy letters V, H, T and O.
- Begins to trace shapes, letters and numbers formed by dots.
- Draws a 'potato person' with head, legs and trunk.
- Figures drawn may not have fingers or toes on arms or legs.

Intellectual: language

- May use about 1500 words.
- Talks about past and future.
- Sentences are more grammatically correct but may still get endings wrong.
- Uses a variety of questions.
- Uses positional words e.g. in, over, under.
- May mispronounce words.
- May mix up sounds like 'th' and 'f'.

Emotional

- Will be very affectionate towards family friends and people they see often.
- More trusting.
- Will tell their thoughts and feelings to people.
- Shows love for younger brothers or sisters.

Social

- Will begin to play with others (cooperative play).
- Will play alone for long periods without adult attention.
- Will share and take turns.
- Can feed themselves skilfully.
- Can dress and undress.
- Can wash and dry hands and face, and clean teeth.

Toys and play

As for three years (see above), plus counting and alphabet games, making collages, junk modelling, messy and creative play, simple board games, card games (e.g. snap), dressing-up and imaginative play. Outdoor toys could include skipping ropes, footballs, obstacle courses, toy gardening tools.

Five years

By this age most children's physical skills are well developed and they are becoming more agile and skilful. Language and communication skills are also well developed. They enjoy imaginary games and team games, understanding the need for rules, and can cooperate with others.

Physical

Gross motor skills

- Can skip with a rope.
- Very skilful at climbing, sliding, swinging, jumping, etc.
- Can use a wide variety of large equipment confidently.
- Can throw a ball to a partner, catch and hit a ball with a bat with some accuracy.
- Can balance on one foot for several seconds.
- Can hop on each foot.
- Can dance rhythmically to music.

Fine motor skills

- Dresses and undresses with little help.
- Can complete more complex jigsaws with interlocking pieces.
- Can cut out shapes using scissors more accurately.
- Can use a knife and fork when eating.
- Has good pencil control.
- Can colour in pictures neatly, staying within outlines.
- Can construct complex models using kits.
- Can copy several letters, e.g. V, T, H, O, X, L, A, C, O and Y.

Sensory

- Matches 10–12 colours.
- Vision and hearing developing to adult level.

Intellectual: concepts

- Can distinguish between fact and fiction.
- Begins to understand the concept of measurement.
- Can count up to 20 by rote.
- Uses reasoning based on experience.
- Can understand right and wrong.
- Can understand simple rules and the need for them.
- Talks about past, present and future.
- May begin to read.
- Recognises name when written and tries to write it.
- Can copy squares, triangles and letters V, T, H, O, X, G, A, U and Y.
- May write own name and simple words.
- Can draw a house with windows, door, chimney and roof.
- Pictures now have a background, e.g. sky.
- Draws a person and head with one or two features.
- Can copy a circle but might not join it up.

Intellectual: language

- Speech is grammatically correct and more fluent.
- Enjoys jokes and riddles.

Social

- May start to play more with own sex.
- Beginning to choose own friends.
- Will play happily with other children.
- Can pick up and replace very small objects.

Emotional

- Helps and comforts other children who are unhappy or hurt.
- Will respond to reasoning.
- Can still be selfish.

Toys and play

As for four years (see above), plus more complex painting and drawing activities and jigsaws. Games with rules, books with more characters and detailed stories and pictures. Outdoors will enjoy team games, large climbing frames, mini-trampolines, hopscotch, catch and chase.

57 Play

Play is something that children do instinctively – it is something they spend most of their time doing and it takes up a large part of their lives. While playing they will move from activity to activity and show different levels of concentration, enthusiasm and determination.

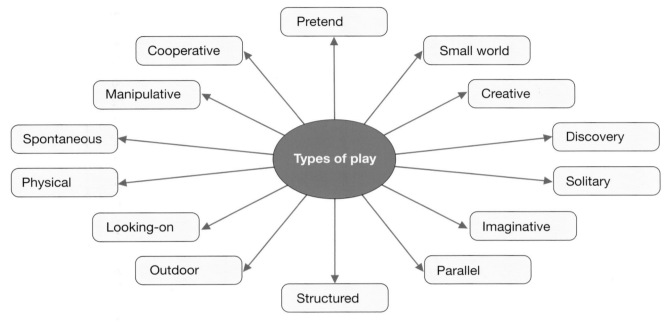

Play is something that children tend to choose for themselves. Parents may try to suggest ideas, but if children don't want to play at a particular activity, they won't. However, parents do have a role:

- they need to make sure that children have lots of opportunities and time to play at different activities, with different toys and in different situations
- they should be ready to give help and guidance when needed
- they may need to act as a referee.

Why do children play?

Children play because it is exciting and enjoyable. While playing they can also:

- learn and practise the different skills that they will need later in life
- learn to understand concepts such as time, space, number and shape
- have fun
- have the freedom to explore, to experiment, to try and to fail – but in a non-threatening way.

Spontaneous play

For most of their time, and certainly at home, children play in their own way and at their own pace – they use the toys and materials around them in lots of different and imaginative ways. So, a large cardboard box can become a car, a spaceship or a cooker – depending on the game. This is often called spontaneous play.

Structured play

In nurseries and playgroups play may be more structured. Here, it is planned by adults to help children develop certain skills or knowledge.

Whatever the way in which children play, and no matter what type of play children are involved in, they will be having fun and learning.

How play can help children's development

PHYSICAL
- develops fine motor skills
- develops balance and coordination
- develops senses – sight, sound, hearing, touch, taste
- exercises body and limbs

INTELLECTUAL
- develops language skills
- learns about the world
- develops memory and concentration
- learns to experiment and test
- learns concepts
- discovers new things
- develops imagination and creativity

SOCIAL
- learns to share
- learns to cooperate and take turns
- learns rules
- develops social skills

EMOTIONAL
- gives pleasure
- prevents boredom
- gets rid of tension
- lets off steam
- develops confidence and independence
- acts out feelings
- acts out roles

Different types of play

Just as children can learn to play together in different ways socially, they will also, at different times, be involved in different *types* of play.

There are four main types of play:

1. creative play
2. imaginative or pretend play
3. physical play
4. manipulative play.

These different types of play are often associated with particular activities and particular skills. However, it must be remembered that all the different types of play will allow children to use and develop a wide range and variety of skills, covering all aspects of development.

Dressing up, for instance, is a form of imaginative play that allows children to take on different roles and act out their ideas and feelings. But it will also help social and emotional development, language development, and often physical, fine motor and gross motor skills and sensory development.

Creative play

What is it?

Creative play takes place when children use different materials to make something from their own ideas and imagination.

It allows them to explore and experiment, and to use their senses to find out what can and cannot be done.

The end result may not be recognisable and they may not want to keep it. It is important that what they make is praised and not made fun of.

PHYSICAL

- Using crayons, pens, brushes, scissors and so on can help develop fine motor skills, hand–eye coordination and handling and control.
- Painting at an easel or doing foot/hand prints can help gross motor skills.
- Creative activities help to develop sensory skills, especially sight and touch.

INTELLECTUAL: CONCEPTS

- Using colours, textures, shapes and space will help to develop creativity.
- Creative activities such as painting, making collages and modelling will help develop the imagination.
- All of these activities can help to develop concentration and memory.
- Painting and making models will help to develop problem-solving skills.
- Helps children learn about different materials and properties.
- Helps to develop an understanding of different concepts.

INTELLECTUAL: LANGUAGE

- Children will enjoy talking about what they have made.
- They will learn new words.
- They will be encouraged to ask questions, listen and follow instructions.

EMOTIONAL

- All these activities allow children to experience both positive and negative emotions, e.g. pride, excitement, frustration, happiness.
- They can increase children's confidence and self-esteem.
- They encourage independence.
- They allow children to make choices.
- Children can express feelings without using words.
- Prevents boredom.
- Gets rid of tension – helps children 'let off steam'.

SOCIAL

Children will learn to:
- share
- cooperate and take turns.
- accept and follow rules and instructions.

TYPES OF ACTIVITIES

- Painting, drawing and printing.
- Collage.
- Making 'junk' toys.
- Sand and water play.
- Play-Doh and plasticine.

Imaginative (pretend) play

> ### What is it?
>
> Imaginative play takes place when children act out being somebody or something else, or invent make-believe worlds and people. It is sometimes called **pretend** play, **make-believe** play or role play.
>
> Children will often use toys and objects as 'props' and will enjoy dressing up for their part.

PHYSICAL

- Develops fine and gross motor skills when dressing up or making props for role play.
- Small-world play will develop fine motor skills and hand–eye coordination.
- Imaginative play outdoors can develop gross motor skills, balance and coordination.
- Develops spatial awareness.

INTELLECTUAL: CONCEPTS

- Helps to develop imagination and creativity when planning and making up stories and plays.
- Small-world play helps to develop understanding of the world and how things work.
- Helps children to understand the concept of past, present and future.
- May help to develop maths and numeracy skills.
- Problem solving.

INTELLECTUAL: LANGUAGE

Children will:
- learn new words
- talk to themselves as they make up and act out stories
- listen to and talk to other people as they play together
- instruct others how to act out a certain role
- re-tell known stories with small-world play
- retell their own stories with small-world play.

EMOTIONAL

Helps children to:
- experience and act out feelings, e.g. sadness, enjoyment, frustration, anger, happiness
- share and act out feelings that may be difficult to express
- release tension and stress
- build confidence and self-esteem
- understand how other people feel
- work through new or problem situations, e.g. moving house, going to the doctor/dentist, the arrival of a new baby.

SOCIAL

Playing with other children encourages:
- taking turns
- sharing
- cooperation
- negotiating about roles, space, equipment
- caring for others
- respect for other people's ideas and feelings
- solving problems together
- making friends.

TYPES OF ACTIVITIES

- Dressing up to be a nurse, pop star or footballer.
- Playing 'mums and dads', 'shops'.
- Making dens.
- Making cars, trains, rockets out of cardboard boxes and going on exciting adventures.
- Puppet shows.

Physical play

> **What is it?**
>
> Although most play is physical in some way, physical play takes place where children are using their whole bodies and their large muscles to move around. It is usually very active and involves lots of running around, allowing children to use up all their energy. It usually takes place out of doors as lots of space is needed.

PHYSICAL

Helps to develop:
- fine and gross motor skills
- hand–eye coordination
- balance and coordination
- strong bones and muscles
- the senses, especially vision, hearing, touch and smell.

INTELLECTUAL: CONCEPTS

Helps to develop concepts such as:
- size
- speed
- spatial awareness
- understanding cause and effect.

INTELLECTUAL: LANGUAGE

Children will:
- learn new words
- increase their vocabulary.

EMOTIONAL

Helps children to:
- 'let off steam'
- release tension and stress
- build confidence and self-esteem
- become adventurous.

SOCIAL

Playing with other children encourages:
- taking turns
- sharing and cooperation
- negotiating about roles, space, equipment
- respect for other people's ideas and feelings
- solving problems together
- making friends.

TYPES OF ACTIVITIES
- Playing team games, such as football.
- Hopscotch, skipping.
- Playing on slides, swings, climbing frames.
- Riding bicycles, tricycles.
- Rollerblading.
- Trampolining.
- Swimming.

Manipulative play

> **What is it?**
>
> Manipulative play usually involves children building or fitting things together.
>
> It is important because it helps them to begin to be more confident and competent in using all the different tools and equipment needed in life.
>
> Manipulative play involves children developing their fine motor skills and hand–eye coordination.

PHYSICAL

Helps to develop:
- different grasps and grips
- hand muscles
- skilful use of fingers
- hand–eye coordination.

INTELLECTUAL: CONCEPTS

- Helps to develop problem-solving skills if making models or building
- Encourages logical thinking.
- Encourages decision-making.

Helps to develop concepts such as:
- shape
- size
- volume
- spatial awareness.

INTELLECTUAL: LANGUAGE

- Encourages language development.
- Increases vocabulary.

EMOTIONAL

Helps children to:
- succeed and cope with failure in a fun way
- build confidence and self-esteem.

SOCIAL

If playing with other children, encourages:
- taking turns
- sharing
- cooperation.

TYPES OF ACTIVITIES

- Jigsaws.
- Using Duplo, LEGO or Sticklebricks.
- Playing with shape sorters.
- Play-Doh.
- Cutting and sticking.

Play and socialisation

Children use play as a way of learning how to get along (socialise) with other children. Most children will go through the following stages as they learn to play together.

Solitary play
This is playing alone and, from the age of birth to two, is often the only type of play observed.
However, older children will continue to have times when they will enjoy playing alone.
Parallel play
By the time children are two years old, they will begin to enjoy parallel play. This is where they play alongside other children but not with them.
Looking-on play
Looking-on play occurs from about three years old. It is when children will be happy to watch other children as they play and may copy them. At this stage they are often ready for nursery/playgroup.
Cooperative play
This also happens at about three years old; children will be happy to play together, share activities and take on roles, but arguments will occur.

KEY WORDS

Creative play where children make something original from their own ideas

Imaginative play where children make up games and act out ideas from their imagination

Make-believe play another name for imaginative play

Manipulative play where children are involved in using hands, fingers and hand–eye coordination

Physical play where children use their whole body, large muscles

Pretend play another name for imaginative play

Role play another form of imaginative play

REMEMBER!

Play is the way children learn – it is something they do naturally and it needs very little adult help. What adults must do, however, is make sure children have the time, the opportunity, and a range of toys, materials, equipment and space to do it.

QUESTIONS

Question 1

a Give three ways that parents can help encourage children to play.

b Give four reasons why children need to play.

c What is the difference between spontaneous play and structured play?

Question 2

Give two ways in which children can play that might help the following areas of development:

a physical

b intellectual

c emotional

d social.

Question 3

a Name the four stages of social play.

b Name and describe the four main types of play. For each of the main types of play, suggest two different suitable activities.

RESEARCH ACTIVITY

Try to organise a visit to a nursery or playgroup. Draw a detailed plan of the area, showing the different activities provided.

From your plan and observations, identify the different types of play being encouraged. You could also interview the teacher or playgroup leader about how and why the area is set up as it is.

58 The Importance of Play, and Play Malnourishment

Why is play important?

All child development experts agree that play is crucial to development. Play isn't just fun – although it is fun! Through play children can develop a huge range of different skills, as well as learning about the world they live in, and playing together as a family helps to create a secure, loving and happy environment for children to grow up in.

Play helps children to develop physically, intellectually, emotionally and socially. This is mainly done through spontaneous pretend play, where they can act out different roles, make up scenarios, share ideas, make up and follow rules, run around, learn to respect the ideas and opinions of others, and become more confident … the list is endless.

Spontaneous play

Through play, and especially social play, children can develop their language skills: as they talk about ideas and make up their stories they are increasing their vocabulary and improving sentence structure.

Play is important for good health – physical play helps to develop fine and gross motor skills, as well as muscle strength and stamina, but it is also important in preventing health problems. Children who are not encouraged to enjoy physical play (especially if they do not have a healthy diet) are more likely to become overweight and suffer health problems later in life, including chronic fatigue syndrome.

Play helps children to learn about trying and failing, and about taking risks – it allows them to practise skills, but also to attempt new things. This helps to build up their confidence.

Children need play to help them to learn, to be curious, to problem-solve and to concentrate. Creative, discovery and imaginative play all enable this to occur. Too much structured play with rules does not encourage children to think for themselves.

Play is very important in a multicultural society. Most children nowadays will grow up alongside children from different ethnic groups – so giving children the chance to play with a mixed-race group is important in preventing prejudice. Three-year-old children rarely show any signs of racial prejudice, but it can often be seen in children of four to five years of age.

The right kind of play is also very important for children with disabilities and behaviour problems (see pages 350–355). Above all, play can help all children to be happy.

Play malnourishment

One of the biggest changes to family life over the past 30 years has been the increase in the number of working mothers. In 1980, less than a third of mothers with young children worked, but by 2004 this had increased to 55 per cent. Over 90 per cent of men who work have children and, in general, people in Britain have a longer working day than in other countries – this means that parents have less time to play with their children.

Because play is so important to children's learning and development in so many ways, when children are not given opportunities to play or to experience different types of play their development will suffer.

Recent research suggests that children may be at risk of play malnourishment, or play deprivation, and that this problem affects children across all social groups. This is a serious problem, especially for children between the ages of seven and twelve years, but it can also affect children under the age of five.

Possible causes of play malnourishment

There are many possible reasons why this might be happening.

Working parents have less time to play with their children. They are often tired after work, and having to organise meals and shopping sometimes means that children are left to entertain themselves.
If parents are working, this often means that babies and young children are looked after at nursery or by a childminder. Although these are well organised, have to deliver the Early Years Foundation Curriculum (EYFC) and are Ofsted inspected, which ensures that children are offered play, this has to be organised and structured. Safety rules mean that they may not offer a lot of adventurous, physical outdoor play opportunities.
Many parents feel that if they don't supervise children all the time, and children get dirty, or get bumps or bruises, they are bad parents.
Lack of safe play space for children: there is less space available for parks and play areas, and those that are available are often unsafe and/or vandalised, or not easy to get to.
People who live in towns or cities may not have houses with gardens or secure yards for children to play in.
There are pressures put on children from a very early age to 'pass exams'. The new EYFC means that this is now starting at an even earlier age. Ambitious parents sometimes think – wrongly – that play is a waste of time.
We live in a consumer society: parents will now buy 'play experiences' for their children rather than let them play games with other children (e.g. at birthday parties).
Single parents often find it difficult to make time for play because they have more responsibilities.
'Stranger danger' means that parents have a real fear of possible abductions.
Even very young children are spending more and more time watching television – as a result they have fewer opportunities for enjoying physical play and developing social skills.
Many toys are now high-tech, pre-programmed electronic toys. Although these can encourage fine motor skills and memory, because they do what someone else has planned, children are not being encouraged to think for themselves or to be creative or imaginative.

In a report called 'Dirt is Good' (May 2005), Doug Cole, Chairman of the International Play Association, suggests that it is important for children to have the freedom 'to determine and control the content and intent of their play, by following their own instincts, ideas and interests, in their own way for their own reasons'. When they don't have this freedom, their learning, behaviour and development can suffer.

He goes on to suggest that, just as parents are encouraged to give children five portions of fruit and vegetables a day, 'children should be given the opportunity to engage in a minimum of three portions of play a day': creative, physical and imaginative.

Getting dirty is great fun!

Results of play malnourishment

Although research is still in the early stages, there is evidence to suggest that children suffering from play malnourishment are more likely to:

- have behavioural problems
- become more violent and aggressive
- be more likely to be obese and unfit
- have poor neurological development
- be unhappy and find it difficult to make friends.

 KEY WORDS

Creative play where children make something original from their own ideas

Imaginative play where children make up games and act out ideas from their imagination

Physical play where children use their whole body, large muscles

Play malnourishment when children do not

have the chance to play by themselves spontaneously and freely

Spontaneous play play that is unplanned

Structured play play that is planned to develop contact skills

---

 QUESTIONS

Question 1

a Why is playing together as a family important?

b How can pretend play help different areas of development?

c Why is play important in a multicultural society?

d Why is play important for good health?

e Give two other reasons why play is important.

Question 2

a What is the difference between spontaneous and structured play?

b How might too much structured play affect children?

Question 3

a Why do parents in Britain have less time to spend with their children?

b What is meant by play malnourishment?

c Describe six possible causes of play malnourishment.

d How much play does the report 'Dirt is Good' recommend for children each day?

e Give three possible results of play malnourishment.

 RESEARCH ACTIVITY

1. Interview your parents and, if possible, your grandparents about how they played when they were children. Analyse and evaluate how play has changed over the years.

2. Carry out further research into play malnourishment. Use your research to produce a booklet of play ideas for parents with young children that would allow them to have their 'three portions of play' per day.

CHILD STUDY ACTIVITY

1. Plan, organise, and carry out a play activity for the child you are studying that would encourage one of the following:

   a creative play

   b imaginative play

   c physical play.

   In your planning, indicate what materials and equipment you might need, where the activity would take place, any preparation needed, and safety factors. Identify what sort of areas of development this activity might provide for the child.

2. During your visits try to identify when the child you are studying has the chance to play.

59 Toys and Other Playthings

What is a toy?

Chambers Dictionary defines a toy as 'a plaything, especially for a child'. We have already looked at how children learn through different types of play. When playing, they will use different objects in different ways to help them to investigate and learn about the world around them. Some of these will be bought toys, such as dolls, LEGO sets or paints; some will be household objects, such as empty packets, pans or wooden spoons.

Strictly speaking, children don't need 'toys' as we understand them – they will use their imagination to make even the simplest of items into the most exciting of objects. A twig from a tree will become a sword, a laser gun, a magic wand; an empty cardboard box becomes a spaceship, a train or a boat.

Purpose-built toys, although not really essential for play, can have an important role both in helping children to explore, investigate and experiment, and in encouraging imaginative and creative skills.

The Trading Standards Toy Safety Regulations 1995 define toys as 'any product or material which is clearly intended for play by a child under the age of 14 years', so for this purpose, a toy is something that has been specifically designed and made for a child to play with.

Choosing toys

Choosing toys

Parents often spend hours trying to choose a toy for their child – they will think about what their child enjoys, how safe it is, if it's colourful and fun, how it works, what it will help the child learn, and, of course, how much it costs. Then they buy it and the child ignores it, uses it in a way that was not intended or gets more fun out of the box and packaging!

The fact is that it is almost impossible to buy the perfect toy for your child – and price is certainly no guarantee of success. Sometimes the best toys are the cheapest, and they are often the ones a child will want to use over and over again, but that will depend on the individual child.

There is no doubt, however, that well-designed and well-chosen toys can give hours of pleasure. The following points can help when choosing and buying toys.

1. The toy should be appropriate for the child's age and stage of development.
2. Children grow and develop very quickly, especially during the first three years. If a toy is too simple, the child will become bored very quickly. If it is too complicated, the child may not know how to play with it and may become frustrated.
3. The toy should be safe to use (see pages 49–50).
4. The toy should be stimulating and interesting for the child. The child should want to play with it – it should be exciting, colourful and fun, and what the child likes, not bought because the parent thinks the child should like it or because it is 'educational'.

5. The toy should have good play value. In other words, it should be simple enough and versatile enough to be used in different types of play for different purposes.
6. The toy should be colourful, both to attract and hold attention and, especially for babies, should be in primary colours (red, yellow and/or blue).
7. All new toys and equipment should have safety marks on them (see page 50). If they do not, they might be dangerous, have small parts or sharp corners, or may fall apart.
8. The manufacturer's age recommendations and instructions for use must be read. This will help adults to avoid buying a toy that might be dangerous for a child of a certain age.

Linking toys with ages and stages of development

Age	Development	Toys for indoors	Toys for outdoors
0–1 year	Development at this age tends to be mainly physical – children move from involuntary to voluntary control. They use hands and mouths to explore, and are becoming more mobile. They need to have toys that are easy to handle, safe to go in the mouth, washable, sensory and unbreakable.	• Rattles • Activity centre • Soft, fluffy toys • Card or fabric books • Bricks • Teething rings	
1–2 years	Children's physical skills are developing very quickly – both fine motor and gross motor skills. They need toys that will help them to develop and strengthen muscles, and help balance and coordination. Play is solitary.	• Push and pull toys • Shape sorters • Building bricks • Simple books • Simple jigsaws • Cause-and-effect toys	• Small swings and slides • Paddling pools
2–3 years	At this age children's physical skills are quite well developed and they can move and handle things confidently. This is a stage where intellectual development is speeding up – children's language skills are growing fast and they are very curious and adventurous. However, they cannot concentrate for long periods and are easily frustrated. Moving towards parallel play.	• Cuddly toys and dolls • Play-Doh • Books • Jigsaws • Paints and crayons • Pretend toys • Dressing-up toys	• Paddling pools • Slides and swings • Simple climbing frames • Sit-and-ride toys • Tricycle
3–4 years	Children's physical skills are now well advanced and controlled, and language skills are good. They particularly enjoy creative and imaginative play as they are moving quickly from parallel play to cooperative play. They need larger toys to encourage gross motor skills, and toys and games to stimulate imagination and understanding of concepts.	• Construction toys • Toys to develop imagination such as Playworld and Fisher Price • Water and sand • Play-Doh • Paints and crayons • Dressing up • Activity books	As above, plus: • Climbing frame • Bicycle with stabilisers • Balls of different sizes
4–5 years	By this stage children are confident at all sorts of gross motor skills – climbing, running, using large equipment and so on – and they do so with great coordination and balance. Intellectual skills are developing quickly – they are imaginative, love to discover and explore, and are curious about everything. They can usually take turns and follow rules.	• Paints and crayons • Paper • More complex jigsaws • Construction toys • Simple board games • Material for modelling and making • Storybooks	As above plus: • Skipping ropes • Rollerblades • Bats • Balls • Gardening tools • Obstacle courses

No single toy will ever help only one type of development, and as children grow and develop more skills, many toys are not used and need to be replaced. However, some toys will be used over and over again and give children hours of pleasure – although even they may need to be replaced when worn out or the child grows too big to play with them or on them.

Intellectual development
Helps to develop creative and imaginative skills as children use them for building and construction. Can help colour recognition, size, shape and number

Language skills can also be developed

Fine motor skills
Children learn to grasp, hold, fit together and build with them

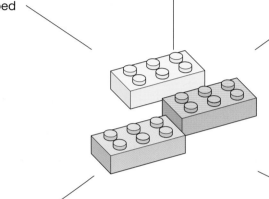

Social development
As children get older they may play cooperatively at construction and building activities

Emotional development
Children will experience pride and pleasure in what they have made, especially if praised

Intellectual development
Helps children to recognise shapes and colour – can also help object/number/letter recognition, depending on age of child

Fine motor skills
As children get older they develop more refined grasps, moving from palmar to tripod to pincer. Help hand–eye coordination

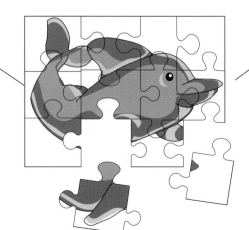

Language skills
Will help to increase vocabulary

Emotional development
Children get pleasure from complex puzzles

Intellectual development
Helps children to develop an understanding of size, speed and spatial awareness

Gross motor skills
Children build up and strengthen legs and muscles – develop coordination and balance

Social development
Children usually play with friends

Emotional development
Children can experience a lot of different emotions – pleasure, excitement, happiness. Can help children overcome fear and gain confidence

Intellectual development
Helps to encourage imagination and creativity

Emotional development
Children can cuddle them, get comfort from them. Can help children learn to be caring, think of others. Children can act out fears and feelings

Physical development
Playing with dolls and teddies can help fine motor skills and hand–eye coordination, especially when toys include dressing and undressing. Helps sensory development

Social development
If used in imaginative play can help children to learn how to look after others. Helps to encourage cooperative play. Can help children learn skills of fastening, dressing and washing, etc.

Language skills
Children often talk to themselves as they play with these toys – even young babies

Things other than toys

Children can be given the chance to play in exciting and imaginative ways without having to buy lots of expensive toys. All it takes is a little planning and imagination! Some ideas are presented in the table below.

Collect empty cartons and yoghurt pots, food boxes, biscuit tins, plastic bottles	→ These can be used to make junk toys, cars, musical instruments, or to play 'shops'	Have a box in which you can keep old (but clean) clothes, hats, shoes and jewellery	→ Children will become pop stars, pirates, spacemen and so on
Keep some large cardboard boxes close by	→ These can be made into ships or cars or aeroplanes	Let children have access to sheets and blankets, and boxes	→ They will quickly create 'dens' and 'houses' from them
Buy rolls of old wallpaper or lining paper	→ These can be used for painting and printing	A washing-up bowl filled with water and bubbles, and plastic cups	→ Children will play for hours, learning concepts such as empty, full, floating, sinking

Toy libraries

Many areas have centres where families can borrow toys, rather like borrowing books from libraries. They are often found in health centres, day nurseries and playschools. Sometimes play buses offer similar opportunities.

These centres:

- let children play with a greater variety and range of toys than might otherwise be possible
- let parents see what sort of toys their child likes to play with
- allow families to borrow toys
- save families money.

? QUESTIONS

Question 1

a Give a simple definition of a toy.

b Suggest eight points to remember when choosing and buying toys for children.

Question 2

Suggest, with reasons, suitable toys for the following:

a a six-month-old baby

b a two-and-a-half-year-old toddler

c a four-and-a-half-year-old child.

Question 3

a Suggest four safe household items a child could play with.

b Describe how each could be used for play.

c Why might a parent find it useful to visit a toy library?

RESEARCH ACTIVITY

1. Toys can be very expensive to buy. Research the ways in which parents could provide opportunities for play, both indoors and outdoors, without having to buy lots of expensive toys.

   Produce an information sheet of ideas for parents, detailing how this could be done.

2. Investigate how the types of toys children play with have changed over the years. As well as researching from books and the internet, interview your parents, grandparents and great-grandparents (if possible) about the toys they played with when they were children. Compare how their toys, and the toys children have today, encourage different areas of development.

   Comment on what you have found out, and produce a report or make a PowerPoint presentation of your results.

 CHILD STUDY ACTIVITY

Spend some time playing with the child being studied and her/his toys. As well as looking at how the toys help different areas of development, talk to the child about the toys and why they like them.

60 Toys and Play for Special Children

Children with special needs are no different to other children when it comes to toys and play – they need lots of both. What they often need more of is quality time with parents and other carers, as they tend to need more help and involvement from other people.

It is sometimes a mistake to think that they need 'special' toys. They need a variety of toys, games and activities and lots of opportunities to play, just like all children. They will still go through the same stages but they may do so more slowly (or in the case of gifted children, more quickly) or they may get stuck at one stage.

However, care in the choice of toys for some conditions can help children develop more quickly.

Autism and Asperger's syndrome

When choosing toys and activities for children with autism or Asperger's syndrome, it is important to remember that complex toys will be confusing for them and will make them withdraw even more. Basic, simple toys are best, such as those based on reality and everyday life, e.g. train sets, farms, cars and garages, etc. It is also helpful if these can be linked to visits, books, videos and so on, so that children can relate the toys to their lives.

Autistic and Asperger's syndrome children may become 'fixated' by one particular toy, so they need to be encouraged to handle and play with others. It is important to introduce them to other toys, but slowly and in a structured way – perhaps setting aside a time in the day when a box of special toys is brought out and played with.

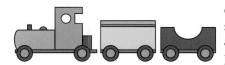

Care also needs to be taken when decorating children's bedrooms – they should be quite simply decorated. There need to be toys and posters around, but wallpaper and curtains that are too 'busy' and with lots of posters pinned on top of them can cause confusion.

Cerebral palsy

Children with cerebral palsy find it difficult to play naturally, because they may have little movement or control.

A child enjoying play in a multisensory area

From birth, it is important to give these children lots of sensory stimulation – especially sight, sound and touch. A mobile over the cot and musical mobiles are especially good for these children. Pictures stuck to the ceiling where they can be looked at, beds close to bright curtains and toys on shelves at eye level will all help to stimulate the senses. As children get older, any musical toys will help, as will textured objects, such as books, soft squeezy toys and 'feely' bags. Textured balls, which can be stroked, will encourage children to use their hands and extend their fingers as they tend to normally have clenched fists. A towelling facecloth in the cot will introduce a new texture to a young baby.

Down's syndrome

Children with Down's syndrome need similar toys and stimulation to those with cerebral palsy. They tend to learn by accident – to roll over, hand–eye coordination, head control. Until they are three or four years old, joints tend to be lax, and they will need physiotherapy. However, it is important to know that baby walkers are not a good idea as they damage ligaments.

Down's syndrome children learn by 'mouthing' – they use their mouths and tongues to explore toys, so it's important to make sure that toys are made of materials suitable to put into the mouth and that can easily be kept clean. Also, because some Down's syndrome children may have a heart condition, big physical activities are not always possible. As they get older, they tend not to play imaginatively a lot.

Cystic fibrosis

Children with cystic fibrosis are often very intelligent and usually very artistic – they often love reading and excel at music and art, so any toys or activities related to this are important.

Because children with cystic fibrosis have problems with their breathing, active physical games are not always suitable but should be encouraged where possible.

Sensory impairment: visual and hearing

In general, if a baby or young child cannot use one of its senses to find people or objects, then such things as colour, sound and movement need to be exaggerated.

Children with visual impairment tend to develop more slowly – because they have limited vision there is not as great a need for head control, so control of arms, body and legs will also be slowed down.

Choosing suitable toys and activities will very much depend on the level of impairment – that is, how much vision the child has. However, toys that make sounds and have flashing lights, glitter sticks, mirrored toys and brightly coloured toys will all help. Holographic paper can be used to make lots of things for children and will stimulate vision. Using holographic tape on the edges of tables and chairs can also help their spatial awareness.

If children have very little vision, black and white images are often easier for them to follow. Colour tracking is needed to identify colours that children can see, and then toys, books and decorations in a room can be chosen to encourage this.

From an early age children with visual impairment often need to be encouraged to use their hands – because they cannot see, the touch of new and unknown textures and objects can be frightening.

Children with hearing impairment need lots of different toys to keep them interested and alert. Toys need to be colourful and bright, and toys that move, light up or make a noise when the child makes a sound can help them to realise when the toys are making sounds. Musical toys and instruments are of great value as they help to develop motor skills and a sense of rhythm, and can help children identify certain sounds through vibrations.

Children confined to a wheelchair can still enjoy outdoor play

Muscular dystrophy and spina bifida

Children with spina bifida will have little or no use of their lower limbs and as they grow older may need to use a wheelchair. Muscular dystrophy may also result in children being confined to a wheelchair in later life. As a result activities using gross motor skills may be restricted or increasingly difficult. Other than this toys and games bought for these children will be no different from those for other children – except that they will have to be brought to the child's level.

 QUESTIONS

Question 1

Choose any three disabilities. Suggest suitable toys for each disability, giving reasons for your choices.

Present the information as a chart (you may wish to copy out and fill in the table below).

Disability	Suitable toys	Reasons

61 Books

The importance of books

A child is never too young for books and one of the most important things that parents can do for their children is to encourage an interest in, and a love of and respect for, books.

Books can, and should, be a source of great enjoyment and pleasure. They are crucial in helping to develop children's language skills, by increasing their vocabulary and giving them a good start with learning to read.

But listening to stories, reading and sharing books with parents does much more than this.

PHYSICAL

- Turning pages, following the words with fingers and pointing to pictures all help fine motor skills and hand–eye coordination.
- Looking at books and handling them helps sensory development (touch and sight).
- Sense of touch is developed when using books with different textures.
- Sitting still requires physical control.

INTELLECTUAL: CONCEPTS

- Encourages imagination and creativity.
- Helps to develop memory skills.
- Helps children learn to concentrate.
- Will help to develop an understanding of different concepts, e.g. numbers, letters, colours, size, shape, time.
- Increases knowledge and understanding of their own world and the wider world.

INTELLECTUAL: LANGUAGE

- Learn new words.
- Encourage children to ask questions.
- Improve listening skills.

EMOTIONAL

- Provides enjoyment and pleasure.
- Being able to read gives children confidence.
- Being able to read makes children more independent.
- Reading with parents makes children feel loved and secure.
- Children can begin to understand their own feelings through characters in stories.

SOCIAL

- Helps children to bond with parents.
- Children get to spend quality time with other children.
- Books can help children to know what is right and wrong.
- Reading can encourage sharing and taking turns.

OTHER AREAS

- Books can help children to learn about and understand a huge range of subjects.
- Develop an awareness of being able to use books as reference and research material.

Different types of books

Books come in all shapes, sizes and styles. Children need to be given the chance to handle, look at and read as many different types and styles of books as possible so that they can begin to decide for themselves what they prefer. They also need to be given books from a very early age – even as young as eight to nine months, when they become fascinated by pictures and images.

Although some books are more appropriate for different ages and stages of development than others, a good range and variety should be available for children to use as and when they want. These can be:

- picture books
- factual books
- storybooks
- feely books
- pop-up books
- activity books
- joke books
- poetry/rhyme books
- counting books
- bath books.

Choosing books for children

There are no hard-and-fast rules on choosing books for children as the choice may depend on:

- the age of the child
- the stage of development
- the interests of the child
- the purpose of the book
- the amount of money available.

However, there are one or two general rules that can help and these are noted in the table below.

Books for young children should:	Books for older children should:
<ul><li>be colourful</li><li>have large, clear pictures</li><li>have large, clear print</li><li>be about everyday objects</li><li>use lower-case letters</li><li>have an uncluttered background</li><li>have just a few words on each page</li><li>be easy to hold</li><li>be strongly made.</li></ul>	<ul><li>be colourful</li><li>match the child's interest</li><li>be suitable for the age of the child</li><li>be suitable for the child's stage of development</li><li>be of a suitable length.</li></ul>

A book should be chosen for the child, not because the adult thinks the child should like it.

Above all, books should show positive images of people, and avoid stereotyping (see pages 307–308).

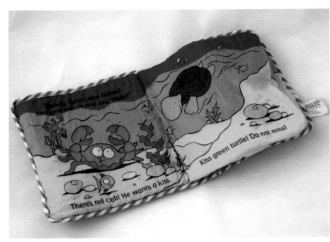

Age 0–12 months

Very young babies cannot focus well. At this stage children can hold and handle things although their fine motor skills are still developing.

Books should have only a small number of pages and be made from thick card. This will make it easier to turn the pages. Fabric and bath books are good because they can be washed easily.

Young children like to point to objects and will recognise objects in their own life. Pictures should be clear and simple, bright and colourful. These books don't need to have words as children like people to point to the pictures and talk about them.

If books do have words these should be in a simple clear font and lower case.

Age 12–18 months

Children can now recognise familiar objects, and memory skills are developing. They can turn the pages in a book more easily, although sometimes several at a time.

At this stage books will still be similar to those for 6–12 months but children will need more variety. Books that show everyday activities such as going to bed and getting dressed are useful as they show their daily routine.

At this age children love books they can touch and play with, so they will enjoy books with added interest such as flaps, peepholes and funny shapes.

Age 18 months to three years

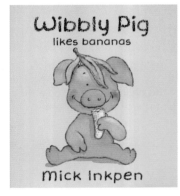

By now children's vocabularies are growing and their language skills improving. They will now need slightly longer books with a simple story, although there should be only a small number of characters in the story. They will enjoy books that involve joining in activities – especially clapping and nursery rhymes – and they need stories to encourage their imagination.

Pictures can be more detailed but still need to be bright and colourful. As children get older, books can have simple text but print should be large and clear.

By the age of two children will be able to sit for longer periods and listen to quite long stories.

Age three to five years

Children will now have a much wider vocabulary and will begin to read whole words. They often use pictures to help them understand what is written. They like pictures that have more detail so that they can talk about them.

Stories can gradually become longer with more characters, and the amount of text on a page can increase, although the print still needs to be clear and quite large.

At this age children will love to listen to stories, will want the same ones repeated over and over again and will often know stories off by heart. They will like stories about imaginary characters, such as monsters and fairies, but should also have some non-fiction books.

They will want to choose books for themselves, so parents should begin to take them to buy their own books and join a library.

Stories at this stage can be used to help children deal with everyday problems, such as starting school or going to the dentist.

Providing a range of books

Buying books can be expensive, especially when they are part of a large series and children want to collect them all. However, they do give good value for money.

To build up a good collection of books:

- make books with children
- go to book sales or car boot sales
- join book clubs
- ask relatives to buy books for birthdays.

How to encourage an interest in books

Always have books and comics within reach of children, i.e. on low shelves, in a bottom drawer or even in a cardboard box.
Let children see that you read.
Make reading fun – use different voices for different characters.
Plan regular times to read books with children – especially, but not only, at bedtime.
Allow plenty of time to 'read' with the child – cuddle up and make it a happy time.
Always follow the text with your finger as you read.
Encourage the child to join in and ask questions.
Answer questions.
Take children on regular visits to a library to borrow books and to join in story time-sessions with other children.
Switch off the television or radio when reading, so there are no distractions.

Talking books

These are books that have a CD to accompany them. They are useful if a child is ill in bed or likes to listen to stories on their own, but they should not be used too frequently. They cannot take the place of a parent or adult.

Story sacks

A story sack is a large cloth bag that contains a good-quality storybook and other materials, such as puppets, soft toys and a game to stimulate reading/language activities. They often also contain a non-fiction book related to the theme of the storybook.

There is usually a cassette tape or CD with the story recorded on to it so the children can follow along and act out.

They are designed to help adults share books with children in a special, fun way and to encourage children to become readers and enjoy books.

Bookstart

Bookstart is a national programme that began in Birmingham in 1992. It was developed by the Booktrust charity and its aim is to promote a lifelong love of books.

Through local organisations, parents and carers are given free packs of books for babies, as well as guidance materials on how to use them.

There are three different types of Bookstart packs available, for different age ranges.

Bookstart

Bookstart pack 0–12 months	Bookstart+ pack 18–30 months	Bookstart Treasure Chest Three-to four-year-olds
The pack contains: • a canvas bag • two board books • a list of great books for babies • a laminated rhyme placemat • guidance leaflets for carers on sharing books and how to develop a baby's language skills.	The pack contains: • a brightly coloured nylon satchel • two books • a colouring pad and crayons • a 'numbers' bedroom frieze • a set of bookplates • a book list • a 'More things to do with books' leaflet.	The pack contains: • a treasure chest • a colourful plastic carrier • two picture books • a set of book plates • a colouring book, pack of pencils and pencil sharpener • a fiction and non-fiction book list for children and their parents.

Booktouch

Booktouch is a programme for blind and partially sighted children from birth to four years. It was launched in 2003 by Booktrust and the Royal National Institute for the Blind (RNIB).

The pack consists of a cotton shoulder bag, two touch-and-feel and Braille books, a book list of great books for partially sighted children, as well as guidance for parents and carers about enjoying reading with blind and partially sighted children. There is also a Bookstart 'Rhymetime' CD and book.

Bookshine

Bookshine is for children up to the age of four who are deaf. The pack contains a cotton bag with two board books, as well as a nursery rhyme placemat. There is also a booklet of advice about sharing books with deaf children.

QUESTIONS

Question 1

a Give three reasons why books are important for a child's development.

b Give two ways books might encourage:

   (i)   fine motor skills

   (ii) concept development

   (iii) emotional development

   (iv) social development.

Question 2

a Give five points to consider when choosing books for children.

b Using a chart, describe the type of books that would be suitable for the following ages, giving reasons for your choices:

   (i)   nine-month-old baby

   (ii) two- to three-year-old

   (iii) four- to five-year-old.

c Describe how parents and carers could encourage children to have an interest in books.

Question 3

a Describe how Bookstart, Booktouch and Bookshine are working to encourage parents and children to have an interest in books.

b What is a story sack?

RESEARCH ACTIVITY

1. Work in a small group to plan and carry out a questionnaire to find out how parents encourage children to be interested in reading, and the sort of books and activities they use with their children.

   Present the results as a report, and use the information collected to design and make a colourful poster or help sheet about how to encourage reading.

2. Choose two favourite books of the child you are studying.

   Write a review about why you think they appeal to the child – you could look at the illustrations, size, type of font, number of words and characters, as well as the content.

   Talk to the child about why they like them, and compare what they say with your own ideas.

CHILD STUDY ACTIVITY

1. Depending on the age of the child, choose a popular or favourite story (e.g. 'Red Riding Hood') and make up a simple story sack to use with the child. Use this activity to look at different aspects of development.

2. Ask the child's parents to go to the local library with you and the child you are studying. Try to plan and organise this so that you go when there is a story-time session.

   While you are there, look at how the child reacts and behaves, the sort of books that attract them, the range of books available and how the children's area is organised.

62 Technology and Play

We live in a technological society, where computers, the internet, television, high-tech toys and video games are all an accepted part of family life. Children are growing up with technology and are often more confident using it than their parents. These skills are being developed from birth by toys and games that are more and more sophisticated – and expensive – than those that their parents played with.

Children still play with rattles, have mobiles over their cots, use baby walkers, are given books and play with toy telephones, but the rattles now have flashing lights and play tunes, the mobiles project pictures on to walls and ceilings, the baby walkers also play tunes, teach numbers, shapes and alphabet, the books are musical talking books, and phones are now of the mobile variety!

Television, DVDs and video games

Recent research suggests that toddlers spend up to five hours a day watching TV or playing on computers, and that the majority of children under five have a TV in their bedroom.

There are a large number of digital television channels, which means that children's TV programmes are available most of the day. Television and computers are now a very big part of everyday life and hard for us to ignore. All can be educational and all can be enjoyable – *if used sensibly*.

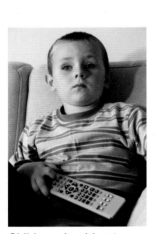

Children should not watch too much TV

The benefit children will get from watching television or DVDs and playing video games very much depends on what they watch and how. There are many well-planned interactive TV programmes and DVDs designed specifically for young children that are educational, help children to learn, are enjoyable and often teach children how to respect and be kind to others. Television doesn't, however, always have to be about learning something. It's not wrong for a busy parent to let their child watch TV while they get on with something else, and, like adults, sometimes even young children just want to relax and watch something that they enjoy. However, constantly letting young children watch TV on their own can harm development.

Television can widen children's knowledge of the world, and let them see and hear things they may never be able to see for themselves. However, television pictures are too complicated for a baby to understand. They cannot be touched and held in the same way as a book; they move and change very quickly, and if a child misses something the programme cannot be stopped (although with older children this can be done with DVDs).

When children are allowed to watch television and DVDs on their own and for a long period of time, their physical and social skills may be affected, and they may grow up not knowing how to play or how to mix with others. If, however, parents spend *time* with their children, watching *age-suitable* programmes for a *limited* time, and if they *talk about* what they have seen, or follow it up with *activities* such as painting, making models, playing games, reading books and pretend play, the programmes can be good educational tools.

> **Sensible use of TV, DVDs and video games may help children to:**
> ✓ develop language skills as they can become familiar with and copy new words
> ✓ learn about number, colour, shape, size, animals, etc.
> ✓ learn to count
> ✓ learn about different places in the world
> ✓ learn to read – buying books about favourite characters will encourage them to try to read, while some programmes have subtitles so they can see the words they hear
> ✓ develop fine motor skills and ICT skills
> ✓ improve observation skills
> ✓ learn to understand concepts such as time and space
> ✓ understand and use technology
> ✓ develop creative skills, by encouraging them to make things
> ✓ concentrate more and improve memory
> ✓ dance and sing along.

If children are allowed to watch too much TV or play video games for excessive amounts of time, this can get in the way of their development. If allowed to watch unsupervised, they may see unsuitable programmes. Because children copy what they see and hear, this may also encourage them to use bad language and learn antisocial behaviour.

> **Excessive use of TV, DVDs and video games may prevent children from:**
> ✗ developing social skills, as it tends to be a solitary activity
> ✗ developing language skills
> ✗ developing physical skills, especially gross motor skills as they will be sitting in front of a screen for long periods of time
> ✗ having opportunities to enjoy discovery and physical play
> ✗ developing their own creative writing and reading
> ✗ asking questions
> ✗ developing problem-solving skills
> ✗ being able to concentrate on other tasks for any length of time.

TV viewing: some guidelines for parents

- Good habits start young!
- Keep TVs and DVDs out of children's bedrooms.
- Read bedtime stories to children instead of letting them watch TV.
- Turn TVs off at mealtimes.
- Don't have a TV on just as background noise.
- Make sure TV programmes, DVDs and video games are age-appropriate.
- Set a good example – don't spend hours watching TV.
- Offer children alternatives (e.g. going to the park, playing games).
- Limit children's viewing.
- Watch programmes with children, and talk about what they have seen.
- Buy books involving their favourite programmes and characters.
- Don't constantly use the TV as a childminder – if this becomes a habit it's

difficult to break and parents may not realise just how much TV children are watching.

- Don't allow children to watch adult programmes in the belief that they are 'too young to understand'.

> ## ! REMEMBER!
>
> Many programmes, even during daytime viewing, deal with issues that are not suitable for young children. Programmes and adverts on television can reinforce gender stereotyping; bad language is often the norm and violence considered acceptable.

Computers

Computers and computer games are enjoyed by many children. Like television and DVDs they can be entertaining, they can be educational, and they can help children to know and experience the wider world.

While ICT (information and communication technology) is an accepted part of primary and secondary education, the new Early Years Foundation Stage (see pages 286–392) now makes this statutory in all nurseries and childcare settings.

Children under five years old are expected to find out about and identify the uses of everyday technology, and use information and communication technology and programmable toys.

Computers are part of everyone's life

The government has set ICT goals for children from birth to 60 months. In the 'birth to 11 months' age band, the goal is 'shows interest in toys that include the use of technology' and, from 8 to 11 months, the goals are to 'explore, press parts and lift flaps to cause sounds, movements and images'. Examples of goals in some of the other age bands are given in the table below.

Examples of ICT goals

16–26 months	22–36 months	30–50 months	40–60 months
Shows an interest in toys with buttons and flaps, and simple mechanisms	Acquire basic skills in turning on and operating some ICT equipment	Know how to operate simple equipment	Complete a simple computer program, and use a mouse and keyboard to interact with age-appropriate computer software

However, there is another view of this, and many educationalists believe that too much technology and being encouraged to spend more time in front of a screen is not good for very young children and can in fact get in the way of development.

All of this creates a dilemma for parents. They have to balance how to provide the opportunities for their children to experience and practise these skills (especially if they are 'stay at home' parents), what toys and games are best to buy and how much it will all cost, with the possibility that this may cause long-term harm to other aspects of development, such as language and social skills.

Computer learning is interactive and therefore ideal for children, and there are some excellent games, CD-ROMs and websites such as that of CBeebies (www.bbc.co.uk/cbeebies/) that help develop language and number skills, but it is important for parents to try these out themselves first. This is also a child's first experience with the internet!

Playing on a computer should be just one of a range of different play activities young children have. Too long spent in front of a computer screen can, as with television and videos, limit social, physical (gross motor skills) and language development – and children can become addicted. As a guide, short periods two or three times a week are enough for a young child.

Using a keyboard will help develop fine motor skills and recognition of numbers and letters. Computers with touch screens or concept keypads are also of great value to children with disabilities.

High-tech electronic toys

Toys and games for babies and young children are more sophisticated and expensive than ever before, and high-tech toys are becoming more and more popular. They are exciting and colourful, with lots of movement, sounds and

flashing lights, and they are interactive, When a child presses a button, a particular sound is made, a shape lights up or a tune is played. The child learns by both repetition and cause and effect, but because the responses are programmed, play is limited and repetitive. This sort of play does not encourage children to be creative or imaginative. Eventually the child gets bored with doing the same thing over and over again, or the batteries run out!

When buying toys, most parents believe that educational value is very important, and usually the packaging on these kinds of toys suggests that educational experts have been involved in their design, while the labelling (similar to labelling on food) claims that they can encourage a whole range of different skills and development, such as creativity,

An interactive toy

imagination, literacy and number skills, fine motor skills and problem solving. This all helps to persuade the parent that the toy must be good because it will help development, and they don't feel as guilty about spending so much because they are educational. Some parents may even think that the toy will help their child achieve all this without them having to do anything.

While there is no harm in buying such toys, research has shown that they are not really any more effective than more traditional toys and games.

QUESTIONS

Question 1

a What sort of technology is now an acceptable part of family life?

b How are the toys that children play with today different from the more traditional toys and games?

c How many hours a day do children spend watching TV and playing on computers?

Question 2

a Suggest five ways in which sensible use of TV or DVDs and video games might help children to learn and develop new skills.

b Suggest five ways that excessive use of TV or DVDs and video games might prevent children from learning and developing new skills.

c Why is it important for parents to supervise the TV programmes and DVDs that young children watch?

Question 3

a At what age are children expected to start to learn basic computer skills?

b Suggest four ways that computers can help learning and development.

c Approximately how much time a week should young children be allowed to spend playing on a computer? Give reasons.

d How can children benefit from playing with high-tech toys?

RESEARCH ACTIVITY

1. Use a TV guide and identify the programmes offered for the under-fives during one day/week.

   Produce a chart of your results, showing such things as:
   a title
   b type of programme (cartoon, puppet, activity, etc.)
   c time of programme
   d length of programme
   e content.

   Evaluate your findings.

2. Try to arrange to watch two TV programmes or DVDs for children under the age of five.

   Carry out a programme review. Give details of the programme/video (title, time on, length, etc.) and an outline of the content and how it was presented.

   Evaluate its suitability for the age range, both as entertainment and as learning.

3. Produce a leaflet entitled 'Guidelines for parents: TV viewing for the under-fives'.

Web Links

www.babycentre.co.uk	Wide range of articles and information on all aspects of pregnancy, birth, and care of babies and toddlers. Some good information on developmental milestones.
www.babyworld.co.uk	General information on aspects of childcare and development. Interesting section on testing and evaluation of toys and other equipment.
www.bbc.co.uk/parenting/childcare www.bbc.co.uk/cbeebies	A huge range of articles and information on all aspects of child development and caring for children, including having a baby. Ideas and activities on learning and development.
www.childdevelopmentinfo.com	Lots of information on development and learning, parenting, and health and safety issues.
www.fisher-price.com	Information on toys by age and type, and learning through play.
www.nurseryworld.co.uk	Some good ideas on activities for young children to help various areas of development, e.g. creative and physical development, communication and language.
www.parentscentre.gov.uk www.direct.gov.uk	Department for Education and Skills. Support, information and advice about learning, education and safety.
www.natll.org.uk	National Association of Toy and Leisure Libraries. Information on toy libraries, leaflets and training.
www.pre-school.org.uk	Pre-School Learning Alliance. Supports the work of community pre-schools.
www.raisingkids.co.uk	Lots of information on development and learning, from birth to teenage. Also covers related issues such as safety, temper tantrums and making friends.
www.under5s.co.uk	Fantastic website full of ideas on a wide range of topics.

PART 5

SUPPORT FOR THE PARENT AND CHILD

This part of the book looks at how different services and organisations can help families, carers and children to achieve a safe and stable environment to live in.

It includes information on:

- support services such as Social Services and Children's Centres
- childcare provision
- education up to the age of five
- the Early Years Foundation Stage.

 REMEMBER!

Every child deserves to:

- **be healthy**
- **stay safe**
- **enjoy and achieve**
- **make a positive contribution**
- **achieve economic wellbeing.**

Source: 'Every Child Matters'

63 Special Children and their Families

The term 'special needs' covers a wide range of conditions. Not all children with special needs have a recognised disability. Any child may be said to have special needs when they need help to satisfy one or more of the most basic human needs. There are many different conditions or impairments that special needs children may have and when these are known the correct term should be used rather than labelling a child as 'disabled' or 'handicapped'.

Why are some children disabled?

There are three main reasons why a child may be disabled.

1. Genetic (inherited) causes: this may be because the sperm or the egg may have contained genetic material that was imperfect. If there is a serious imperfection, then usually the mother has a miscarriage. Some genetic conditions may not always be obvious at birth; however, some, like Down's syndrome, will be. Other conditions may show up only when the child is a few months old.
2. Congenital disorders: this means that the child has been born with the condition. It may have been inherited. However, not all congenital disorders are inherited. If the child has been damaged in the womb or at the time of birth, then the problem may be congenital but not inherited.
3. Other causes: some chronic problems or disorders are caused by events after birth. Injuries due to infections or accidents, particularly those that affect the brain, are the most common.

Different disabilities

Autism

Autism is a rare developmental disorder that occurs in children before the age of three. An autistic child has difficulty in relating to other people. Autism is a lifelong disability. It is believed that the child is born with the condition but symptoms do not show until later.

An autistic child may:

- pay more attention to objects than people
- have problems with speech and language
- lack awareness of other people
- have learning difficulties
- lack the ability to play
- repeat activities
- become upset when unfamiliar things occur.

Autistic children can be helped by highly structured education, which involves skills training in situations that are highly organised and distraction free.

Some children are diagnosed as suffering from Asperger's syndrome. This condition is considered as a sub-group within the autistic spectrum.

Children suffering from Asperger's syndrome may:

- lack empathy
- find difficulty in making friends

- have poor non-verbal communication
- be clumsy and ill coordinated
- be naïve
- become intensely absorbed in certain subjects or activities.

Cerebral palsy

Cerebral palsy (CP) is a disorder resulting from damage to a child's developing brain before, during or after birth. It affects around one in 500 babies with some children being more severely affected than others.

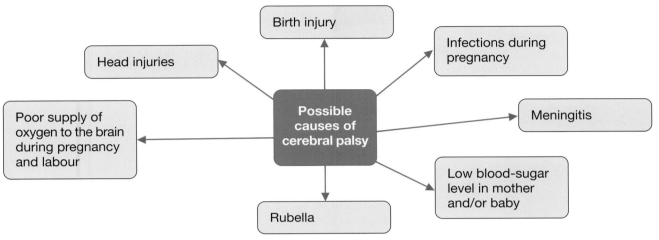

Cerebral palsy jumbles messages between the brain and the muscles. In some people, cerebral palsy is barely noticeable, but others will be severely affected. No two people will be affected in quite the same way.

The damage to the brain may cause:

- speech and hearing difficulties
- problems with coordination and balance (ataxia)
- sight problems
- floppy limbs (athetosis)
- jerky movements (spasticity)
- possible epilepsy
- possible learning difficulties.

This is Katy, aged four, who has cerebral palsy; she is sitting in her specially adapted chair, which enables her to sit and holds her head upright

Physiotherapy is a branch of medicine that uses physical methods including manipulation, exercise and massage to help manage cerebral palsy. Occupational therapists work with CP children and advise on specialist equipment that will help.

Cystic fibrosis

Cystic fibrosis (CF) is a hereditary condition that affects the lungs and digestive system. In this condition all the glands that discharge their secretions directly into the body are affected. The secretions are thick and sticky instead of being runny, so they block up some of the connecting tubes in the body's system.

One in 20 people carries the CF gene but it is only when both parents are carriers that there is a one in four chance that the child will have CF.

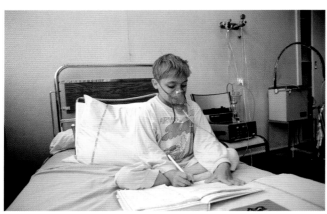

Children with cystic fibrosis need daily treatment

The effects of CF include:

- breathing difficulties
- chest infections
- food is not digested and absorbed properly
- the child fails to gain weight.

Children who suffer from CF need daily physiotherapy to help their breathing.

Down's syndrome

Down's syndrome is a genetic condition that causes a number of distinctive characteristics and some learning difficulties, which vary from child to child. This condition is caused by the presence of an extra chromosome, making 47 chromosomes in total. The possibility of having a baby with Down's syndrome increases as the mother gets older.

Signs of Down's syndrome include:

- eyes that slant upwards and outwards
- eyelids with an extra fold
- the back of the head may seem to be flatter than usual
- the tongue may seem to be too large, causing feeding problems
- a single crease running across the palm of the hand
- lower birth weight and slower growth rate.

Baby with Down's syndrome

There are a number of health problems associated with Down's syndrome, such as heart, chest and sinus conditions, but with advances in medicine today children with Down's can and do grow up to live long and happy lives. Babies with Down's syndrome need extra love and attention since they take longer to reach their developmental milestones. They may need extra support when they go to school. If they are given the correct help and opportunities they can go to school and some can go on to employment.

Haemophilia

This an inherited disorder that causes problems with the clotting of the blood, and spontaneous bleeding occurs. Children with haemophilia vary a good deal in how many times they bleed spontaneously – in some it occurs several times a week and in others only two or three times a year. The bleeding often occurs into the joints, which may become painful and stiff and then red, swollen and tender. The disease is passed on through the mother but affects only her sons.

A man with haemophilia will pass on the gene only to his daughters who will in turn become carriers. It is important that parents are more watchful especially with toddlers but there is no reason why children should not go to playgroup or nursery, and the vast majority go to ordinary schools.

Muscular dystrophy

This is a condition that causes muscle tissue to weaken. It becomes noticeable between the ages of two and five years. The child will usually not learn to run and will have difficulties in climbing. The muscles become steadily weaker and the child's walking is affected so that s/he may begin to stumble, fall or have difficulty with stairs. The most common type, Duchenne muscular dystrophy, affects only boys and, as with haemophilia, it can be passed by a mother to her son if he inherits the faulty gene.

Spina bifida

This a condition in which the spine fails to develop properly before birth (see page 82). Children with spina bifida will nearly always need special help – for example, from physiotherapists, paediatricians, orthopaedic surgeons or urologists – to make them as mobile as possible. Depending on where the defect is, some will need wheelchairs; others will be able to get around with callipers or even without any special aids.

 REMEMBER!

Each of the disorders discussed above can cause problems that mean the children will need special help, hence the term 'special needs'.

Children with specific educational needs

Specific learning difficulties

The term 'specific learning difficulties' is used to describe children who have difficulty in learning to read, write, spell or do mathematics. They do not have difficulty learning other skills.

Dyslexia

The term 'dyslexia' covers a wide range of difficulties, ranging from mild problems with spelling to a total inability to read and write. Early identification of the problem can reduce the problems, and strategies can be used to help children within school.

Attention deficit hyperactivity disorder

Attention deficit hyperactivity disorder (ADHD) is a specific learning difficulty since children with this disorder show behaviour traits that prevent them from learning. They may have difficulty sharing and taking turns; they often talk excessively; they are easily distracted and appear restless.

Gifted children

Gifted children may not have a physical disability but they can have problems with socialisation – that is, making friends with others. They may be academically more advanced than other children but it is still important for them to have friends of their own age. Wherever possible, parents of gifted children are advised that they should have opportunities to extend their ability by means of a specially adapted curriculum without being separated from their friends since this can cause social and emotional problems.

Special children and their families

Every child is a 'special child' but those with special needs require a good deal of understanding. It is important to remember that all children may reach stages or milestones of development at different ages. Children who have a disability are often made to feel that they are younger than they are because they have not reached 'normal' milestones. The basic needs of all children are stability, security and protection. Sometimes special children, especially those with obvious disabilities, find that their special needs override their ordinary needs. It is important to see the individual child first and then the special need or disability second, if the child is to develop to her/his full potential. Like all children, special children need to be helped to become as independent as possible. This can be achieved by carers and friends by:

- having patience, especially if the child has problems with communication
- using praise and rewards for effort rather than achievement
- showing respect for the child's personal dignity and privacy
- making sure that, whenever possible, the child is involved with other children (integration)
- showing empathy rather than sympathy
- responding positively to things over which the child has control
- allowing the child to make decisions.

The needs of parents and carers

Children with special needs can bring much love and happiness to a family but there can be difficulties, depending upon the nature of the impairment suffered by the child. All parents of young children need help and support because of the extra work needed to care for young children but families with special needs children require even more support.

- **Status:** the number of professionals involved in caring for a special child can be so large that parents need to be given recognition that usually they are the ones who know the child best, and that they have the most important role to play in the care of their child and should not be undermined or overwhelmed by the professionals.
- **Services:** everyone has the right to receive help and parents should be made aware of the opportunities and services open to them.
- **Leisure time:** looking after special children takes up a good deal of time and parents should not feel guilty about making time for their own needs and the needs of the rest of their family.
- **Practical help:** this could be help in the home, respite care, or help with transport and mobility.

- **Information:** parents have the right to be given full information about their child's condition.
- **Planning:** parents should be involved in all aspects of planning for their child's future education or care.
- **Consultation:** parents' opinions should always be taken into consideration.
- **Emotional support:** some parents may need help in adjusting to the change in their own lives and help in finding pleasure in their child.
- **Finance:** help may be needed to cover the costs of special equipment, aids and adaptations to the home, or frequent trips to hospitals.

The needs of siblings

It is often difficult for brothers and sisters of children with special needs because, however much they love their sibling, they will see that the child needs, and gets, much more attention than usual. Hospital appointments, special equipment and professional helpers can disrupt the usual routine of any home. Parents and carers need to make sure that brothers and sisters do not feel left out. Sometimes other children can be cruel about children who are different and this can hurt siblings.

Case study: Jemma, Jade and Jack

Jack is a very handsome boy who lives with his parents and his sisters, Jemma and Jade. When Jack was a baby all was well but as he grew older the family became aware that he was not progressing as he should. He was often ill and his speech did not continue to develop as it had.

Eventually Jack was diagnosed as having autism, and while the family were shocked, they loved him very much and did all they could to make him happy. This was not easy because, in common with most children with autism, Jack found it difficult to show any feelings and seemed indifferent to everyone, even his own family.

The parents felt that the girls were coping well with Jack's problems until Jemma explained that her friends at school did not understand about Jack and that she too wanted to know why Jack was different. In the following passage Jack's mum explains how she came to write a book for Jemma and Jade to help them understand. When the book was complete they took it to Jemma's school so that her friends could understand too. The book was so successful that it has been published by the Autistic Society and has been translated into many different languages to help brothers and sisters like Jemma and Jade.

> The reason I wrote 'My Brother is Different' was because my daughter Jemma wanted to know why it was that whenever she got any games out he ruined the game by sweeping the lot onto the floor in a satisfying heap, or why it was that when she did something wrong herself, a 'telling off' followed or an even worse punishment or banishment to the bedroom was dealt out, *but* if Jack did anything wrong the same did not apply. He was told gently but firmly which was the right way to behave. Things like this must have seemed so unfair in Jemma and Jade's eyes. Why did they have to go to bed at 7.30 pm when Jack was younger and allowed to stay up until past

midnight? Very unfair! Why did Jack, in Waitrose, wait until he was positioned behind a frail old lady leaning over the freezer counter, give a high-pitched squeal at the top of his voice and not get told off when she fell in, like they would have done? It was very hard for them to see that he got a very satisfying reaction from everybody in the shop from that one squeal, while the managers were pulling her out of the frozen sausages. In their eyes he was just being naughty and embarrassing.

I asked Jemma about all the things that Jack did that upset her and we wrote them down and I wrote down next to them why he did those particular things, to help her understand a little of what was going on in Jack's head. But a lot of it is still guesswork!

Louise Gorrod

QUESTIONS

Question 1

a What are the three main causes of disability in children?

b What are the main differences between congenital and genetic disability?

Question 2

Copy out the chart below.

Choose any three disabilities discussed in this chapter. Describe:

a what the disability is

b how it will affect the child.

Question 3

a What is dyslexia?

b Describe how children with ADHD might behave.

c What is a 'gifted' child?

Question 4

a Suggest six ways parents and carers can help special children to become more independent.

b Describe four ways that families with special children might need support.

c How might having a special child affect other children in the family?

Disability	Description	How it affects children
1.		
2.		
3.		

RESEARCH ACTIVITY

Try to visit a nursery or playgroup, or simply look around your own home.

Think about what problems there might be for a five-year-old in a wheelchair who wishes to play and join in different activities.

Suggest ways in which parents/staff can make this possible.

64 Support for Families

Being a parent is harder than a full-time job, and it is expensive! Parents are legally responsible for the care of their children – and for their actions – until they are 16 years old. They are expected to love them, make sure they are educated, and keep them safe and healthy.

Parents have to learn a whole new range of skills very quickly; however, there is a wide range of different types of services and support available to help parents and families.

The government introduced Every Child Matters: Change for Children to make sure that all children get the best possible start in life, by bringing together all the various services that support children and families. These are:

- education
- family support, including Social Services
- childcare
- health.

Some of these services have to be provided by law – these are known as statutory services.

Some are voluntary services – these are usually provided by charities, and some of the money will come from donations; others are provided to make money for someone else – these are private businesses. Often what is provided may vary from area to area, but the following are generally available in some form nationwide.

Statutory services

Health services

The National Health Service (NHS) provides a number of services to make sure children and their families are fit and healthy. These include:

- GPs
- health visitors
- dentists
- family planning clinics
- genetic counselling
- antenatal classes and clinics
- maternity hospitals
- hospitals
- school health service.

Health visitors

Health visitors can be qualified registered nurses, midwives, sick children's nurses or psychiatric nurses with special qualifications in community care – this includes child health, health promotion and education.

Most are attached to a GP practice, and every family with a child under the age of five has a named health visitor.

The role of the health visitor

The role of the health visitor is to support families from pregnancy and birth to primary school. They offer advice and help on the following matters.

Health visitors offer advice and help on:

- children's growth and development
- common illnesses and infections in childhood
- common skin problems
- behaviour problems (e.g. tantrums)
- breast-feeding, weaning and healthy eating
- post-natal depression.

They also:

- organise and run baby clinics
- carry out the immunisation programme
- help promote support groups (e.g. breast-feeding, baby massage).

Social Services

Under the terms of 'Every Child Matters', children's Social Services aim to promote the wellbeing of children in need and looked-after children.

They provide a range of support for children and families, including:

- children who are being assessed (including disabled children)
- children who may be being neglected or abused
- children who need to be looked after by the local authority (foster and residential care
- children who are placed for adoption.

Social workers

Each child needing support has a social worker. Social workers work closely with GPs and health visitors, who will refer the child to Social Services if they think they are being neglected or abused. The social worker has to assess the child and family and, if necessary, they can apply to the court for a care order or an emergency protection order so that the child can be taken into the care of the local authority.

Education and childcare

The government is committed to providing education opportunities from birth onwards through the Early Years Foundation Stage (see Chapter 66).

Because many parents need to work to support and provide for their families they often need to use childcare, and an extensive range of childcare has developed (see Chapter 65). In addition to nursery schools, all this is now included in the Early Years Foundation Stage (see Chapter 66).

Most childcare has to be paid for and it is often expensive, although financial help can be provided through tax credits and vouchers.

Financial support

Bringing up a family is a long-term expense from birth. There are a number of ways in which parents can get support, as outlined in the following table.

What's available	Details
Statutory Maternity Pay (SMP)	To help take time off before and after the birth of the baby. Amount depends on how long worked and how much earned before tax.
Statutory Paternity Pay (SPP)	Paid to fathers by employers to help them take time off work. Payment depends on how long they have worked and how much they earn.
Maternity allowance	Paid to those who do not qualify for SMP, are self-employed or have recently changed jobs.
Sure Start Maternity Grant	This is a lump sum to buy things for the baby – it comes from the Social Fund and does not have to be repaid. It is for people on low incomes.
Child benefit	Paid for every child until they are 16, or 18 if they stay in full-time education or training.
Child Trust Fund	A long-term tax-free savings and investment account for children born on or after 1 September 2002. The government gives eligible children a voucher worth at least £250 to start the account.
Tax credits	These are payments from the government. Those who are responsible for at least one child or young person who normally lives with them may qualify for Child Tax Credit. If you work but earn low wages, you may qualify for Working Tax Credit.
Help with childcare costs	Those who work and pay for childcare may be able to get tax credits to help with the costs. You have to work for at least 16 hours a week to qualify. You may still qualify if you worked 16 hours or more before going on maternity, paternity, adoption or sick leave.
Healthy Start vouchers	These may be available to those who are on a low income, are pregnant and/or have at least one child under four years, or are pregnant and under 18 years old. They can be used to buy milk, fresh fruit and vegetables, infant formula and vitamins.

A Children's Centre

Sure Start Children's Centres

Sure Start is a government programme that aims to improve the health and wellbeing of families and children under the age of five years, especially in deprived areas. It does this by providing an integrated service that includes health, education services, and family support and care.

Sure Start Children's Centres provide support for families from before birth until the children start reception or Year 1 at primary school.

The centres are sometimes based in local nurseries or primary schools, or health centres.

By 2010 every community will have a Sure Start Children's Centre.

Although the centres can vary from area to area, their aim is to offer:

- good-quality early education combined with full-day childcare provision from 8 am to 6 pm
- experienced teachers to help to plan and deliver the development of learning in the centre
- support and advice on parenting issues, local childcare options

and specialist services for all families with young children, including those with disabilities

- child and family health services, including antenatal services, health visitors, health screening and support groups (e.g. on breast-feeding)
- links with Jobcentre Plus, local training organisations, and further and higher education to help parents find work and/or training.

Sure Start is an important part of the government's new Children's Plan. This is a ten-year plan to make sure that all children have the chance to fulfil their potential, and 'aims to make England the best place in the world for our children and young people to grow up'.

Voluntary services

There are a large number of voluntary agencies that support children and families. These organisations are funded by donations and sometimes help from the government in the form of a grant.

Parentline Plus (www.parentlineplus.org.uk)

Parentline Plus is a national charity that works for and with parents.

It offers help, information and support for parents and families through:

- a free confidential 24-hour helpline, offering parenting advice and guidance on a wide range of parenting issues
- a free text service for people with speech or hearing impairment
- parenting courses
- information leaflets
- a website.

Contact a Family (www.cafamily.org.uk)

Contact a Family provides support, advice and information for families with disabled children, no matter what their condition or disability.

It provides:

- a freephone helpline to give advice on a range of issues (e.g. respite care, Social Services, education and local support)
- newsletters, reports and parent guides
- up-to-date medical information on disabilities and available support
- one-to-one support through family support groups, volunteer parents and local offices.

It also campaigns to improve the rights of families with disabled children.

Other voluntary agencies

These include:

- British Agencies for Adoption and Fostering (BAAF) www.baaf.org.uk
- Child Poverty Action Group (CPAG) www.cpag.org.uk
- ChildLine UK www.childline.org.uk
- Kidscape www.kidscape.org.uk
- National Autistic Society www.nas.org.uk
- National Childminding Association (NCMA) www.ncma.org.uk
- National Council for One-Parent Families www.oneparentfamilies.org.uk
- National Deaf Children's Society(NDCS) www.ndcs.org.uk

- National Society for the Prevention of Cruelty to Children (NSPCC) www.nspcc.org.uk
- Pre-school Learning Alliance www.pre-school.org.uk
- Royal Society for the Blind (RNIB) www.rnib.org.uk
- Royal Society For the Prevention of Accidents (RoSPA) www.rospa.org.uk
- Whizz-Kidz www.whizz-kidz.org.uk

QUESTIONS

Question 1

a Up to what age are parents legally responsible for the care of their children?

b Why did the government introduce Every Child Matters: Change for Children?

c Name four different services that support children and families.

Question 2

a Explain the difference between voluntary and statutory services.

b Give three examples of statutory services.

c Name five different services the National Health Service provides for children and their families.

d Describe the role of the health visitor.

Question 3

a What is the purpose of Social Services?

b Describe the type of support that Social Services provide for children and their families.

c What is the role of a social worker?

Question 4

a Name and describe four different types of financial support available for families with babies or young children.

b What is the main aim of the Sure Start government programme?

c What is the purpose of a Sure Start Children's Centre?

d Where are Children's Centres usually based?

e What are the main aims of a typical Children's Centre?

Question 5

a What is Parentline Plus and what help does this service provide?

b Describe four of the services that Contact a Family provides.

RESEARCH ACTIVITY

Find out about the range and type of services that are provided in your local area for children and their families.

Use your research to produce a leaflet for parents.

65 Childcare Provision

Most children under five years of age are, at some time, looked after by someone other than their parents before they are old enough to go to school. This could be grandparents, other relatives, friends or babysitters who are giving parents a break for a few hours. Increasingly, however, more parents are looking for someone to care for their children for longer periods because they both go out to work, or are ill or studying.

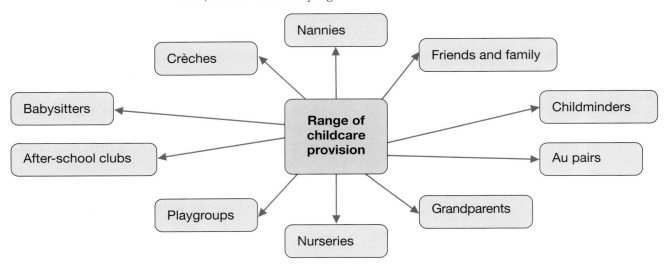

The range of childcare provision is very varied and parents need to take into consideration many factors before deciding upon the right type of provision that will suit them and their child. These could include:

- the length of time the child will need to be cared for
- the cost
- the closeness to home or work
- whether it is easy to get to if having to use public transport
- the quality and range of the care provided
- whether care in a home environment or within a group is preferred.

Some of the options are outlined in the diagram below.

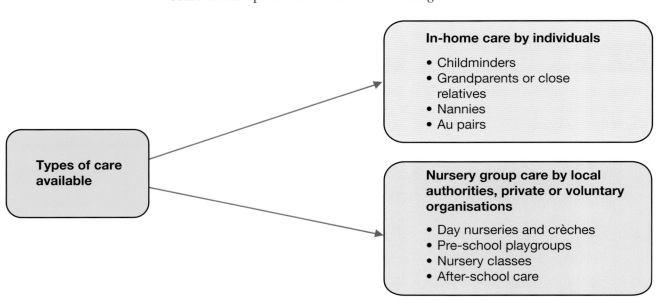

In-home care

This is where a child is looked after in a home environment. A nanny, au pair, grandparent or other close family member might come to the family home and care for the child full- or part-time or on a flexible schedule. Alternatively, the child might go to the home of a childminder or relative.

Childminders

Childminders work in their own homes providing day care for families. The Local Authority Children's Information Services are responsible for childminding provision within each local area. The Children Act 1989 states that those caring for children under the age of eight must be registered by Ofsted.

Ofsted will also carry out regular inspections to ensure that the care offered by the childminder meets national standards, such as:

- ensuring they're suitable to work with children
- checking that they provide a safe, stimulating and caring environment
- giving opportunities for children to play and learn
- making sure that they work together with parents.

The registration process is wide-ranging and thorough, involving references, a health check, and a police check on the childminder and all other adults in the family. The childminder's home is inspected to ensure that it provides a safe and suitable environment for young children.

Childminders are usually registered to care for up to three children under five and three five- to eight-year-olds, including their own children. These regulations are strictly enforced to allow children to have individual attention. Since childminders look after small groups of children, their daily routine can be very adaptable and they can cater for individual dietary requirements and sleep patterns.

Childminders are flexible in the hours they work, which can help parents who work shifts. Being cared for by a childminder gives children the opportunity to learn from real-life experiences. Everyday activities such as shopping trips, school runs, family mealtimes and visits to the park teach children life skills they might not acquire so easily in nurseries.

These days, many childminders make this their career and are undertaking training specific to the work they do, gaining qualifications such as those provided by the National Childminding Association (NCMA), which represents childminders in England and Wales, in association with the Council for Awards in Children's Care and Education (CACHE) – for example, Basic Food Hygiene and First Aid Certificate.

The advantages and disadvantages of using a childminder

Advantages	Disadvantages
For the child ✓ A cosy home-like atmosphere. ✓ Less exposure to infection than in a large centre. ✓ Only a small group of children, therefore more individualised care. ✓ The opportunity to be with other children. **For the parent** ✓ Relatively low cost. ✓ May live locally. ✓ There may be more flexibility regarding hours. ✓ May be prepared to drop off/pick up from nursery or school. ✓ Registered and monitored regularly by Ofsted. ✓ Can become close to family.	**For the child** ✗ More possibility of illness and infection than in own home. ✗ Health and safety problems may arise, although these should have been picked up during Social Services and police checks. ✗ High turnover of children. ✗ May have to compete for attention if there are children of different ages. **For the parent** ✗ May want to organise the day to suit herself or other children rather than your child. ✗ Lack of back-up if the childminder is ill. ✗ Worries about the competence of the childminder. ✗ Worries about health and safety issues.

Grandparents or close family

If there is a family member who is willing to look after your child this could be an ideal situation. Grandparents have brought up children themselves and will have lots of experience, so parents will feel happier about leaving their child with them. It will mean that the child can be looked after in a home environment, will have one-to-one attention and will receive lots of love. It may also be cheaper as grandparents may not wish to receive payment. With other family members this will need to be discussed carefully.

Grandparents often act as carers

It is important to remember that grandparents may have different ideas about bringing up children and discipline, therefore this should be discussed and agreed from the start. Also it may be advisable to agree to review the situation after a time. Grandparents may not have realised that looking after a child full-time is tiring and limits what they can do. Parents may feel their child needs to mix more with other young children.

The advantages and disadvantages of using family members

Advantages	Disadvantages
For the child	**For the child**
✓ A family member, particularly a grandparent, is likely to love your child almost as much as you do.	✗ Grandparents in particular may spoil the child.
✓ They will probably develop a close bond with the relative.	✗ Looking after young children may be too physically demanding for older grandparents.
✓ They may be able to have friends round to play.	✗ May have fewer opportunities to mix with other children.
✓ They will be cared for in a familiar environment.	
✓ They will have continuity of care.	**For the parent**
✓ Less possibility of contact with childhood illnesses.	✗ It may be difficult to ask them to do things your way.
	✗ They may have different ideas about discipline, potty training, etc.
For the parent	✗ If they're looking after a baby or toddler in their own home you may have to buy two sets of equipment.
✓ A grandparent, or relative who is already a parent, will be experienced with children.	
✓ A family member may live locally.	✗ Their home may not be as child-safe as yours.
✓ They'll probably be flexible about hours.	✗ If things go wrong it can cause long-term family problems.
✓ They'll probably be prepared to drop off/collect from nursery/school.	
✓ They may be able to look after your child if she/he is sick.	

Nannies

The term 'nanny' may be loosely applied to anyone who makes a career out of caring for a child in the child's family home.

Unlike childminders, nannies do not need to be registered and are not monitored by any outside regulatory body, therefore it is the parent's responsibility to check out their suitability. There are no national requirements for nannies to have professional qualifications; some employers are interested in the experience and personality of the person, while others will only employ those with recognised childcare qualifications. Some nannies are particularly well qualified, having undergone long periods of college training in how to care for children.

Some attend colleges such as the long-established private organisations that train Norland or Princess Beatrice Nannies. Other students attend courses in further education colleges to gain relevant qualifications such as the CACHE Certificate in Childcare and Education or the CACHE Diploma in Nursery Nursing (formerly NNEB).

Most nannies live with the family and care for the children when the parents are not there, while others come to the family each day and parents care for the children in the evenings and during the night.

The advantages and disadvantages of using a nanny

Advantages	Disadvantages
For the child ✓ The comfort of familiar surroundings. ✓ One-to-one care from the same person each day. ✓ More personal attention. ✓ Less time commuting (travelling to another place). ✓ Less possibility of contact with childhood illnesses. **For the parent** ✓ Fewer problems about getting to work on time or working late. ✓ No worries about picking up the child if delayed. ✓ No need to take time away from work if the child is unwell	**For the child** ✗ Fewer opportunities to socialise. ✗ Risk of confusion – if the parents work long hours the child may come to see the nanny as the parent figure. ✗ Possibility of a sense of loss if the nanny leaves suddenly. **For the parent** ✗ Problems of sharing the home with another person. ✗ Higher cost compared to au pairs and nurseries. ✗ Competition for the child's affection. ✗ Do not need to be registered with Social Services so may be concerns about safety issues. ✗ Are not monitored or checked. ✗ May not have qualifications. ✗ Lack of back-up if nanny is ill.

Au pairs

An au pair is a girl or boy aged between 17 and 27 who comes to the UK primarily to learn to speak English and live for a time as a member of an English-speaking family. They will be expected to help with the housework and care of the children and, in return, will receive their keep and pocket money. The great advantage is that they are often flexible and prepared to work for less money than would be expected by professional domestic help.

The reasonable maximum time during which an au pair may be expected to perform light domestic tasks (including looking after children) and some babysitting is five hours daily on 'working days' (i.e. 25 hours per week). They should have at least one and preferably two free days. They can be expected to help with such jobs as bed-making, washing-up, tidying, dusting, babysitting, taking children to and from school, and looking after them in the house, but they should not be asked to do heavy housework.

They rarely have any qualifications or experience with young children and should not be expected to have sole charge of a very young baby. They are more suited to caring for older children.

The advantages and disadvantages of using an au pair

Advantages	Disadvantages
These are similar to those of nannies but, in addition:	These are similar to those of nannies but, in addition:
For the child ✓ They can introduce children to different cultures. ✓ Because of their age they may bond with children more easily. **For the parent** ✓ They are often a cheaper alternative to nannies or nurseries.	**For the child** ✗ They often stay for a relatively short time, so children do not have continuity of care. **For the parent** ✗ Lack of qualifications may be a worry. ✗ Language difficulties could lead to misunderstandings.

Nurseries/group day care

This is where groups of young children spend all or part of the day together in formal care, looked after by teachers or nursery nurses.

Day nurseries

A typical nursery

Day nurseries will care for a child all day, either full-time or part-time. They are usually open from around 8 am to about 7 pm, and provide both care and education in suitable surroundings.

Day nurseries have to be registered with the Ofsted and inspected every two years. At least half the staff must be qualified in an early years discipline, and some must be qualified teachers. They vary in size, but most take between 25 and 40 children, and the ratio of staff to children will vary. Children are usually grouped together according to age and will almost certainly follow a government-approved Foundation Stage Curriculum (see below).

There are different types of day nursery, including the following.

- Private – independent profit-making businesses providing full-day care. Although private they must still be registered by the Registration and Inspection Unit of their local authority.
- Community – these are often run by voluntary organisations on a non-profit-making basis, so fees are generally lower than for private nurseries. They usually provide full-day care. Some may operate a sliding-scale fee scheme, so that parents pay different rates according to their circumstances.
- Workplace nurseries/crèches – these are run by employers who offer places to the children of their staff. They can also be found in shopping and sports centres where children can be looked after for a short time.
- Sure Start Children's Centres – these cater mainly for children under five and their families. Services within the centres are free, but childcare usually has to be paid for, although low-income families can get extra help through the childcare element of the Working Tax Credit. Centres usually operate from 8 am to 6 pm, and some are open at weekends (see Chapter 64).

The advantages and disadvantages of using nurseries/group day care

Advantages	Disadvantages
For the child ✓ Quality care from trained and experienced staff. ✓ A programme of activities for the correct age and level of development. ✓ Opportunities to play with other children of the same age. ✓ A wide variety of toys and equipment. ✓ Usually some government regulation of health and safety. **For the parent** ✓ Sufficient staff. ✓ Qualified staff. ✓ More likely to fit in with work hours. ✓ Usually open all year. ✓ All aspects of the nursery are regulated and inspected regularly.	**For the child** ✗ More exposure to illness. ✗ Possibly less individual care, although some have a 'key worker' system so that each child is assigned to a particular member of staff. ✗ Possibility of high ratio of children to teachers. **For the parent** ✗ May be less flexibility over hours for those who work late or work shifts. ✗ May not be one close by, so may involve travelling. ✗ Can be expensive. ✗ Waiting lists can be long for popular nurseries. ✗ Problems if the child becomes ill.

Most nurseries produce a leaflet or brochure for parents outlining the aims and objectives of the school, as well as detailing the school routine. It is important that parents examine the brochures carefully and visit the nursery before they enrol their child to ensure that they agree with its aims and are happy with the care provided.

The education of under-fives is taken very seriously these days and nurseries are independently inspected by Ofsted (the Office for Standards in Education) to ensure that high-quality educational nursery care is being provided.

From birth to five, children are legally required to follow the Early Years Foundation Stage if being looked after in a childcare setting. This sets goals to be reached by the time children enter Key Stage 1 of the National Curriculum.

The Early Years Foundation Stage covers six areas of learning that are designed to prepare children with key learning skills in these areas before they start school:

1. personal, social and emotional development
2. communication, language and literacy
3. problem solving, reasoning and numeracy
4. knowledge and understanding of the world
5. physical development
6. creative development.

Points to consider when choosing a nursery

Before choosing a nursery for a child there are certain points that parents should consider. As well as visiting the nursery, preferably at different times, it is also a good idea to talk to parents who are using the nursery or have used it.

When visiting it is important to consider the following questions.

- Is there a secure entry system to the premises?
- Do the members of staff know the children's names?
- Do they seem to make the children welcome when they arrive?
- Are the children playing happily?

- Is there a wide variety of toys and equipment?
- Is the equipment in good condition?
- Do staff notice if children need help?
- Are children praised and encouraged?
- Is there anywhere for the children to play outdoors?
- Is the atmosphere calm?
- What happens if parents are late?

A playgroup

Pre-school playgroups

Pre-school playgroups are non-profit-making groups, usually run by parent management committees. They must be registered with Ofsted. They are usually held in village or church halls, and children between the ages of two and four attend two or three half-day sessions per week, therefore they are not necessarily a good option for working parents as alternative care may be needed.

Parents usually pay a small fee.

Pre-school classes

These are attached to a primary school. Children spend half or full days under the care of teachers in a formal situation to enable them to be ready for school.

The advantages and disadvantages of using a pre-school playgroup

Advantages	Disadvantages
For the child ✓ Care given by experienced staff. ✓ A wide range of experiences available. ✓ A formal programme geared to the child's age and maturity. ✓ Children can be challenged academically. ✓ Opportunities to socialise with a group of children of the same age. ✓ Children can be schooled in essential skills. ✓ A varied range of play equipment. ✓ Health and safety standards monitored. **For the parent** ✓ Staff with recognised qualifications. ✓ Reliability – substitute found if teacher is ill.	**For the child** ✗ The programme may be too demanding for the child. ✗ More exposure to infection from other children. **For the parent** ✗ Less flexibility over hours. ✗ Can be expensive if privately run. ✗ Available only in term time.

Before- and after-school care

After-school care

There is a growing need for after-school care, which has led to a number of homework clubs being organised, usually on a local basis. These usually cater for children of school age.

Breakfast clubs

Breakfast clubs, usually run by schools, offer children a place to go before school and may include provision of a healthy breakfast as well as other activities.

Babysitters

Babysitters usually care for children in their own homes for *short periods* so that parents can have a break – they are not used for long-term care.

Many babysitters are young people who know the children and provide a service in exchange for pocket money, but the term can be used for people of all ages.

It is important that the parents make sure that the babysitter is someone who is responsible and is able to act sensibly in a crisis. Sensible parents take time to go over important points, which will help the babysitter if things go wrong or if the child is upset. Babysitters should always have details of the parents' proposed whereabouts and emergency telephone numbers in case they are needed. Since most babysitting is done in the evenings it is important that the babysitter understands the child's routine.

Bedtime routine	Babysitter's checklist
1. Does the child have a drink or snack before bed? 2. Does the child have a bath? 3. Is there any particular story or book they prefer? 4. Do they have a night light? 5. Do they have any other special routine at bedtime?	1. Where will the parents be? 2. Phone number where they can be contacted. 3. When are the parents expected home? 4. Name and number of someone else who may be contacted in an emergency, e.g. neighbours, grandparents. 5. Name and number of GP (family doctor). 6. Details of any allergies suffered by the child.

? QUESTIONS

Question 1

a Give five reasons why parents may sometimes need someone to look after their children.

b List the range of childcare provision available both inside and outside the home.

c What factors should be taken into consideration when choosing the right type of childcare?

Question 2

Draw a summary table to show two advantages and two disadvantages for both the child and the parent of the following types of childcare:

a childminder

b grandparent or close relative

c nursery/group day care.

You may wish to set your table out like this:

Question 3

a Which organisation is responsible for the registration and inspection of childminders?

b How many children can childminders care for? Why is this important?

c What checks are carried out when someone registers as a childminder?

Question 4

a List eight points to consider when choosing a nursery for a young child.

b What is a babysitter?

c Give six pieces of information that a babysitter might need to know.

Type of childcare	Advantages		Disadvantages	
	Child	Parent	Child	Parent
e.g. childminder				

RESEARCH ACTIVITY

Find out about the different types of day care provision available in your area.

Use your information and ICT to produce a leaflet for parents.

CHILD STUDY ACTIVITY

Interview the child's parents about any childcare provision they use or might use. Find out how they think it helps the development of their child.

66 The Early Years Foundation Stage

The Early Years Foundation Stage (EYFS) is an education programme for all young children from birth to five years. It is compulsory for all schools and childcare providers, such as childminders and nurseries, who are Ofsted-registered.

It is based on the belief that it is important for all children of this age range to be able to play in order to learn and develop, and that this provision should be consistent.

The EYFS has combined three previous initiatives: Birth to Three Matters, the Foundation Stage Curriculum for children aged three to five years, and the National Standards for Under 8s Daycare and Childminding.

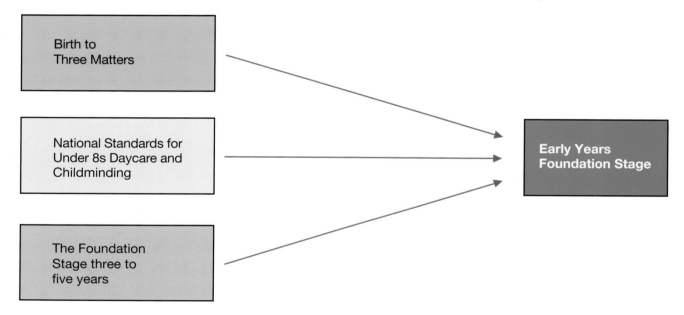

The EYFS aims to put into practice the government's commitment to improving family life, education, health and safe active play for children, as well as the crucial Every Child Matters: Change for Children agenda, which states that every child needs to:

- be safe
- be healthy
- enjoy and achieve
- make a positive contribution
- achieve economic wellbeing.

It is based on four 'themes' and principles:

Theme	Principle
1. A unique child	All children are individuals but all have the ability to learn and to be resilient and confident.
2. Positive relationships	Children need positive relationships with parents/carers. They will learn to be strong and independent if they are safe, secure and loved. Parents are important!
3. Enabling environment	The environment of the child is very important in supporting and encouraging learning and development.
4. Learning and development	Children develop and learn at different rates and in different ways – and all areas of learning and development are linked.

Learning and development

There are six areas of learning and development within the EYFS – all are connected and all are equally important:

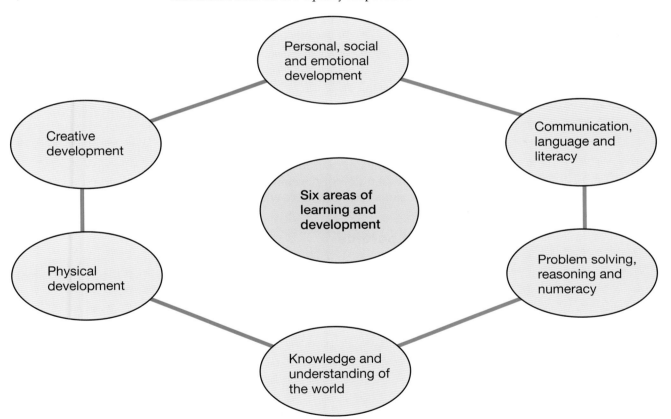

The six areas of learning

The six areas of learning and development are outlined in the chart below.

Six areas of learning and development	What will children learn?
1. Personal, social and emotional development	• Self-confidence • To be interested • To understand right and wrong • To be able to dress and undress
2. Communication, language and literacy	• The enjoyment of poetry, songs, rhymes, stories • Talking, singing and linking to the alphabet • To use a pencil, read and write
3. Problem solving, reasoning and numeracy	• To develop an understanding of numbers through game • Imaginative play • To understand concepts such as 'heavier than' or 'bigger than'
4. The development of knowledge and understanding of the world	• To question the world around them • To learn about everyday technology • To learn about different cultures and beliefs, and different family lifestyles
5. Physical development	• To be confident • To use equipment and control their bodies
6. Creative development	• To make music, dance, sing • To tell stories • To experiment with colour and shape

These six areas will be introduced gradually from the child's birth until the age of five years.

Children will continue to learn these skills after the age of five as the EYFS recognises that some children may not have met all of them by that age. It accepts that children do not develop physically, intellectually, emotionally or socially at the same rate, and there will be some overlap with the Key Stage 1 curriculum.

People and parents

Within the EYFS the people who work with children should be able to plan suitable activities (both indoor and outdoor) that are essential for the individual child to develop. These people include:

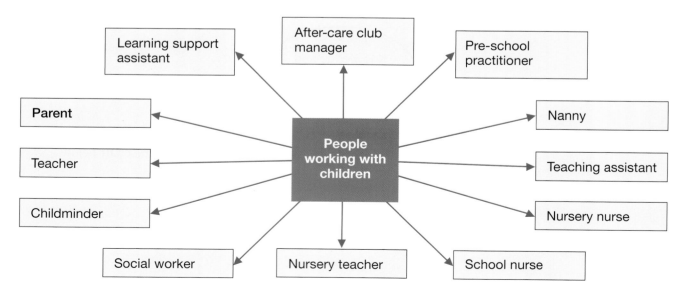

The importance of parents/carers

Parents play an important role in supporting the EYFS, to make sure that this works effectively for their children. Almost 70 per cent of children's lives is spent with family or in their own community.

The EYFS recognises that parents have a right to play a central role in making decisions about their children's education, and that children will do better when parents and professionals work together to get the best from the child.

The parent usually knows the child better than anyone else, and practitioners (e.g. teachers and childminders) are encouraged to ask parents about their child's progress, and use this information to support the individual child's needs.

It is important to know how well the child is doing, and parents are encouraged to have an active involvement to make sure that the child develops their full potential.

Six broad development phases of the EYFS

The EYFS has broken down the ages of development into six broad phases.

The EYFS recognises that children develop at different rates and, as a result, has provided six broad developmental progress phases to overlap the age ranges.

The reasons for this are:

- all children are different and individual
- a child's progress is unique to them
- a child will not suddenly move from one stage to the next
- some children may progress quickly in one area of development (e.g. physical development) but not as quickly in another (e.g. social development).

The chart below briefly summarises these and shows the aspects of the child's development that are important, and how teachers, parents and carers can support each phase.

Age	Area of development the child is learning	How to encourage the child's development
Birth to 11 months	**Physical** – control of muscles, hands, feet, limbs, head. Child becomes more mobile and is able to manipulate objects.	• by introducing a safe, stimulating, interesting environment with sensory toys
	Intellectual – language develops, the child's first spoken words	• hearing and responding to people talking
	Emotional/social – feelings of security	• sensitive caring and giving from special people (e.g. parent, family member carer) • routines to help the child understand the order of the day
8 to 20 months	**Physical** – walking, exploring, developing coordination and physical abilities	• safe and interesting environment, with toys from a suitable age range
	Intellectual – verbal/non-verbal communication skills, vocabulary increases rapidly	• people communicating about everyday things
	Emotional – learning about themselves and their feelings	• positive praise • allow child to express her/his needs and feelings
	Social – how to relate to others and control themselves	• lots of interaction and play with adults/children
16 to 26 months	**Physical** – muscular strength develops and skills increase; child has a lot of energy at this stage	• a mixture of lively action and quiet activities
	Intellectual – simple problem solving and planning	• problem solving through pretend play • playing with other children
	Emotional/social – understanding other people's thoughts and feelings, and cooperating with others. Self-confidence, learning boundaries and how to cope with frustration	• exploratory play • adult supervision and support
22 to 36 months	**Physical** – fine motor skills, mark-making using a variety of materials – gross motor skills	• creative play • adult to provide safe environment • walking, climbing, running, joining in active play
	Intellectual – listening skills, language skills, putting sentences together, able to join in conversations, learns past, present and future	• picture books, ICT, stories, games/play
	Emotional – self-confidence/self-esteem	• praise for new achievements
	Social – independence	• eat, dress and toilet themselves
30 to 50 months	**Physical** – to make healthy choices about food and exercise	• taught the importance of 'five a day', healthy foods, outdoor play and exercise
	Intellectual – literacy, numeracy, language becomes more complex with longer sentences	• games, activities, pretend play (e.g. shops)
		• adult conversations and guidance
	Emotional – developing close relationships	• comfort and care for parents, family carers
	Social – sharing and cooperation with other children, independence and doing what other people ask of them	• play and games that include make-believe and construction • help adults with everyday activities

Age	Area of development the child is learning	How to encourage the child's development
40 to 60 months	**Physical** – more challenging/skilful physical activities	• more skilful, make-and-do activities • adults to encourage play with balance in a safe, danger-free environment
	Intellectual – increased literacy skills, problem solving, reasoning and numeracy skills develop. Understanding of cause and effect	• books, reading, practise maths games, ICT, media, technology and writing
	Emotional – more controlled behaviour, strong sense of their own identity	• adult guidance • tolerance of others when playing games
	Social – understanding of the importance of social rules and customs, tolerance and sharing with peers, more able peers and adults	• challenging activities and social situations • playing in small groups to learn negotiation skills

Registration and inspection

All childcare providers (e.g. childminders and nurseries) have to be registered by Ofsted. They have to evaluate themselves using a self-assessment form and will be regularly inspected against the EYFS requirements

RESEARCH ACTIVITY

Investigate the EYFS curriculum. Look at the age range/phase that is closest to that of the child you are studying. Observe and identify to what extent your child matches the stages of development within that phase.

QUESTIONS

Question 1

a What is the Early Years Foundation Stage (EYFS)?

b What does the EYFS believe is important for all children?

c According to Every Child Matters: Change For Children, what are the five basic needs of children?

d The EYFS is based on four themes. List these and explain the principles related to them.

Question 2

The EYFS is made up of the following six areas of learning:

(i) personal, social and emotional development

(ii) communication, language and literacy

(iii) problem solving, reasoning and numeracy

(iv) the development of knowledge and understanding of the world

(v) physical development

(vi) creative development.

Describe two things that children will learn from each of these six areas.

Question 3

a What percentage of a child's life is spent with their family?

b Other than parents, name six other adults who could work with children.

c Why is it important for parents and these adults to work together?

Question 4

The EYFS has broken down the stages of development into six broad phases.

a What are the six different age ranges?

b Why do the ages within each phase overlap?

c Give four reasons why children develop at different rates.

Web Links	
www.ace-ed.org.uk	Advisory Centre for Education. Advice for parents on state education, special education and school admissions.
www.cry-sis.org.uk	Information and support for families with excessively crying, sleepless, demanding children.
www.disabledparentsnetwork.org.uk	A national organisation of and for disabled parents or parents-to-be.
www.everychildmatters.gov.uk	Information about the Every Child Matters framework.
www.gingerbread.org.uk	Self-help association for one-parent families. Support, friendship, information and advice.
www.mencap.org.uk	Royal Society for Mentally Handicapped Children and Adults. Works with people with a learning disability, their families and carers.
www.meningitis-trust.org	Informative and supportive website.
www.ncma.org.uk	National Childminding Association. Training, information and support.
www.nspcc.org.uk	National Society for the Prevention of Cruelty to Children. Aims to prevent all forms of child abuse. Helpful information on behaviour management and positive reinforcement.
www.oneparentfamilies.org.uk	Lots of information on issues affecting one-parent families and where help is available.
www.rnib.org.uk	Royal National Institute for the Blind. Information, advice and services.
www.signcommunity.org.uk	British Deaf Association. Advocacy and services for deaf people who use British sign language.
www.standards.dfes.gov.uk/eyfs/	Lots of information about the Early Years Foundation Stage.
www.surestart.gov.uk	Information about Sure Start initiatives, including support for children, families and communities, and details of local childcare and early years education.
www.qca.org.uk	Information on the Foundation Curriculum and Early Learning Goals.

67 Exam Preparation

No one really enjoys exams! Unfortunately, to get qualifications, they usually need to be done.

> **! REMEMBER!**
>
> No one is trying to trick you or deliberately make you fail. The exam is your chance to show what you *know and understand* about child development.

Success in exams needs to begin with **revision**.

Top revision tips

Tip 1	**PLAN** – both your time and what you need to do. You will have lots of subjects to revise for, so you need to work out how to fit everything in. A bit like doing a jigsaw.
Tip 2	Choose a revision style that suits you. This could include things such as: • revising with someone else • writing key words, notes and phrases on postcards • taping notes and playing them back on a personal stereo • highlighting important points in notes • writing notes out over and over again.
Tip 3	Have regular breaks and give yourself a treat to aim for as a target when you have finished one section. You will learn more in several short periods than you will in one long one.
Tip 4	Do lots of practice questions – your teacher will give you these from old exam papers. *BUT*, when you get your work back, don't just look at your mark – read the comments made. This will show you how to improve.
Tip 5	Don't miss out huge chunks of revision. The exam paper has to include questions to cover most of the specification in some way.
Tip 6	Don't leave it all to the night before the exam – or on your way to the exam!

So, you have done your revision – now, on to the exam.

Don't worry. When you first open an exam paper it's not unusual to think you don't know anything and can't answer any of the questions.

You need to learn how to make the exam paper work for you.

Look for the clues

Clue 1	Spend a few minutes reading through the whole paper – sometimes words and phrases used in one question might give you ideas for others.
Clue 2	Try to answer all parts of the same question at the same time – they are often about similar or related topics.
Clue 3	Look for any words in **bold** type or *italic* – underline these. These will give you an idea of what is needed in your answer
Clue 4	Underline any key words and/or phrases. As the words suggest, key words can help you to 'unlock' and understand the question. There may be two types of key words: 1 those used by the examiner to tell you what sort of answer is expected (see the Key Words below) 2 those that tell you what your answer has to be about – the topic.
Clue 5	Look at the number of lines given for each part of the question. This will give you some idea about how much detail or information you need to give. But remember, if your writing is big, you may need to continue on extra paper!
Clue 6	Look at the number of marks awarded for each question. Generally, the more marks, the more detail is needed – this might mean giving reasons, explanations or personal opinions, which you should support with facts.
Clue 7	Are there any illustrations, charts, graphs etc.? These might give you clues about the question.

🔑 KEY WORDS

Describe to give information in an accurate and detailed way

Discuss to describe and give an opinion about something, usually looking at different points of view; you will need to use facts and knowledge to back up your ideas and opinions

Explain to make something very clear, usually by giving facts and reasons

Identify to give factual information about something

Illustrate to give examples to explain something more clearly

List/Name to give facts in a simple, clear way

Suggest to put forward an idea – often you will be asked to *give* reasons

What kind of questions might you be asked?

Type 1

Some questions are **short, factual questions** and are worth a small number of marks. These often ask you to 'list' or 'name' or 'give', and may give you a set number of points.

Type 2

Some questions are more **structured** and give you more guidance.

They may be split into different parts. Each part will have a set number of marks.

Type 3

Towards the end of the exam paper, questions may be more general, and have a much higher mark allocation. These are usually called **free response questions**. They want you to show not only factual information, but also your knowledge and understanding of the subject, probably across a number of different areas of the specification.

These sorts of question will often give you a lot of space for your answers, so you need to think about them carefully.

Make sure you:

- read the questions carefully
- underline key words and phrases
- plan your answer – examiners like to see this, so use some of the space available to jot down your ideas.

In your answers try to have:

- a brief introduction to show you understand what the question means
- sound, factual, well-reasoned and explained information related to the topic of the question
- a conclusion.

In writing up your answer, the following words might be useful. They either **connect** or **start** sentences.

First(ly), . . .	Equally . . .	In particular . . .
Second(ly), . . .	Similarly . . .	Above all . . .
Then . . .	Likewise . . .	Notably . . .
. . . and then . . .	In the same way . . .	Specifically . . .
. . . after(wards) . . .	As with . . .	. . . especially . . .
Meanwhile . . .		
During . . .	However . . .	For example . . .
Whenever . . .	. . . but . . .	. . . such as . . .
Eventually . . .	Nevertheless . . .	Clearly . . .
Finally . . .	Alternatively . . .	. . . of course . . .
	Despite this . . .	. . . the following . . .
In addition . . .	. . . instead . . .	
Furthermore . . .	Whereas . . .	In brief . . .
Therefore . . .	Although . . .	On the whole . . .
Consequently . . .		To sum up . . .
. . . because/as . . .		In conclusion . . .
Accordingly . . .		
. . . as long as . . .		
Also . . .		
Moreover . . .		
As a result . . .		

Running out of time?

Use bullet points. They can:

- give information in a clear and quick way
- help you pick up marks.

Finally . . .

In answering many questions, it's not enough just to know lots of facts. The examiner is looking for your '**knowledge** and **understanding**'. This means that you have to show that you can use lots of facts and information to support and explain different ideas. Much of this information will come from the textbooks you have used – this one, for example. It will also come from discussion in your lessons when you have listened to the ideas and views of others.

But it could also come from your own experiences of being part of a family, from babysitting, reading magazines, talking to family and friends, watching TV and videos, and even watching soaps!

So use all of this background information to give you ideas.

What about your other subjects?

Child development is probably one of many subjects you are studying – don't ignore the others. Something you may have studied in Science, RS, Social Studies, etc. might be useful and relevant, so use that information as well!

 REMEMBER!

Revise thoroughly.

Read questions carefully.

Underline key words and phrases.

Look at the space available for answers.

Look at the marks available.

Use illustrations and other information given to help.

GOOD LUCK!

GLOSSARY

Active vocabulary The words a child is able to use when first learning to talk.

Additives Substances (often chemicals) added to foods by manufacturers to make them taste or look better, or last longer.

Adoption A legal process that transfers responsibilities for bringing up a child from the birth parents to another family

Amniocentesis A diagnostic test usually carried out between the 15th and 17th week of pregnancy to check for possible chromosomal abnormalities such as Down's syndrome.

Amniotic sac The sac inside the uterus where the developing embryo and foetus grows.

Antenatal care The care of the pregnant woman and her unborn baby during pregnancy.

Antibodies substances that the body produces to try to control/destroy a disease.

Apgar score A test given to newborn babies one minute after being born, and again five minutes later.

Assisted delivery When the baby needs help to be born. This is usually needed when the mother is very tired or the baby is becoming distressed.

Au pair Someone between the ages of 17 and 27 who is studying and learns English for up to two years by living with a family and looking after their young children.

Autism A development disorder that makes it difficult for children to communicate with other people.

Babbling An early stage of language development when a baby starts to make sounds and then repeat them over and over (e.g. da da da da). See also *echolalia* and *monosyllabic babbling*.

Baby blues This usually occurs in the first few days after the birth when the new mother feels sad and down. It is caused by tiredness and hormones.

Babysitter Usually a young person who looks after children for short periods so that they can earn some money and the parents can have a break.

Balanced diet A diet that provides all the nutrients needed in the correct amounts for the body to grow and work properly.

Binovular twins Non-identical twins formed when two eggs are released from the ovaries and fertilised by two separate sperm.

Birth canal Formed when the vagina, cervix and uterus become one channel during labour.

Birth plan An agreement made by the pregnant woman with the midwife about what choices she would like to make about the labour and birth.

Bonding The close feeling that develops between a baby and an adult.

Breech birth When a baby is born bottom first or feet first.

Caesarean section An operation where a cut is made into the mother's abdomen and uterus, and the baby is lifted out.

Centile charts Charts used by health professionals to check and compare the height and weight of children with average expected growth for their age.

Cerebral palsy (CP) A physical disability that affects movement.

Cervix The neck of the uterus (womb).

Childminder Someone who is paid to look after young children in their own home. They must be registered by Ofsted and are inspected regularly.

Chromosome A thread-like structure that carries genetic information.

Coeliac disease A food-related disorder where the body cannot digest the gluten found in wheat and other cereals.

Cognitive To do with thinking and understanding

Cognitive development See *Intellectual development.*

Colostrum The first milk the breast produces, usually for a few days before and after the birth. It is rich in fats, protein and especially antibodies, which protect the new baby from infection.

Concentration The ability to focus on one thing.

Concept A way of organising knowledge and information so it can be understood.

Conception The start of pregnancy. The moment when a male sperm and a female egg join together to form a new cell, and the start of a new baby.

Congenital disability A disability that is present at birth.

Contagious disease A disease that spreads from one person to another by contact.

Contraction The shortening and tightening of the muscles of the uterus during labour.

Cooing The earliest sounds a baby uses to show contentment.

Cooperative play When children play together and are able to share, take turns and follow rules.

Creative play Where children make something original from their own ideas.

Crowning During labour, the stage when the baby's head can be seen at the entrance to the vagina.

Culture The way of life, traditions, language, beliefs and behaviour of a society.

CVS A diagnostic test that can be given between 10 and 11 weeks of pregnancy if other tests have shown there is a high risk of abnormality.

Cystic fibrosis A genetic disability that affects the lungs and digestive system.

Development The ability to use more complex skills.

Developmental milestones The age and stage of development where an average child should have mastered a skill.

Developmental screening tests Regular testing of young children carried out by health professionals.

Diagnostic test A test that is carried out after a screening test has indicated a possible risk of abnormality of the foetus (e.g. amniocentesis test).

Dilation The gradual opening of the cervix by contractions of the uterus during the first stage of labour. At about 10 cm the cervix is 'fully dilated'.

Disability A physical, learning, emotional or behavioural problem that affects everyday life.

Doppler ultrasound A hand-held machine used to listen to the baby's heartbeat during pregnancy.

Down's syndrome A genetic condition caused by an extra chromosome 21, making 47 chromosomes instead of 46.

Echolalia Another name for *monosyllabic babbling*, which is the constant repetition of single syllables with no meaning (e.g. ba ba ba ba).

Eclampsia A serious medical condition that can affect a pregnant woman towards the end of pregnancy, which can cause convulsions and a coma.

Ectopic pregnancy This happens when the fertilised egg implants into the Fallopian tube (or sometimes the abdomen) instead of the uterus and begins to grow.

EDD Estimated date of delivery/estimated due date – the date when the baby's birth is expected.

Egocentric Self-centred – this means seeing things only from your own point of view.

Elective Caesarean A Caesarean that has been planned, and is usually carried out for medical reasons (e.g. multiple birth).

Embryo The term given to a developing baby less than eight weeks old.

Emotional development Learning how to express, handle and control feelings.

Endometrium The lining of the womb.

Epidural A type of pain relief used during labour and birth, where an anaesthetic is injected into the epidural space in the spinal cord.

Episiotomy A small operation where a cut is made in the perineum to enlarge the opening so that the baby can be born quickly, and to prevent tearing.

Extended family A family group that includes grandparents and other relatives living together or close to each other.

Fallopian tube Part of the female reproductive system, which links the ovary to the uterus. This is where fertilisation takes place.

Fertilisation The joining together of the egg and sperm.

Fine motor skills The ability to use and control hands and fingers to make delicate movements (e.g. fastening buttons).

Foetal alcohol syndrome A condition that affects the babies of women who drink a lot of alcohol during pregnancy.

Foetus The term given to the embryo from eight weeks of development until birth.

Folic acid A vitamin B complex that can help reduce the risk of spina bifida and other neural tube defects.

Fontanelle Soft spot on the baby's head where the bones of the skull have not yet joined together.

Food allergy This occurs when the body's immune system thinks a food is harmful and creates antibodies to deal with it. These can cause different symptoms such as rashes and breathing problems, some of which can be fatal. Allergies are often inherited.

Food intolerance This is a condition where someone has a physical reaction to a certain food, which does not involve the immune system (e.g. lactose intolerance occurs when someone cannot digest milk).

Forceps These are hinged metal instruments that look like spoons.

Formula milk A manufactured alternative to breast milk, usually based on cows' milk.

Foster care A type of care for the children of parents who cannot look after them for some reason. It gives them the chance to live in a family home, but the birth parents are still the legal carers.

Genes Part of the DNA. They are carried on thread-like structures called *chromosomes* and contain information that determines our inherited characteristics (e.g. blue eyes).

Genetic disability A disability caused by a faulty gene.

Gluten A protein found in wheat, barley, rye and oats.

GP General practitioner – a qualified doctor working in a surgery practice.

Gross motor skills The ability to move by using and controlling the whole body and larger muscles (e.g. running, hopping, walking).

Growth A change in size – usually height and weight.

Gynaecologist A doctor who specialises in women's reproductive problems.

Hand–eye coordination The ability to use the hands and eyes together to make precise movements.

hCG Human chorionic gonadotrophin – the 'pregnancy' hormone.

Health visitor A qualified nurse or midwife who has done extra training and works in the community looking after the health of children and families.

Heredity The passing of characteristics, such as the colour of eyes and hair, from parents to their children.

Holophrase Where one word may be used for more than one thing (e.g. 'dog' may mean any four-legged animal).

Hormones Chemical messengers produced by the endocrine glands. They are carried in the bloodstream to different parts of the body to stimulate them to work properly (e.g. oestrogen, prolactin).

Imaginative play This occurs where children make up games and act out ideas from their imagination.

Immunisation A way of trying to help prevent infection or disease, through the use of vaccines.

Immunity A person's ability to resist infection.

Infertility Unable to conceive or carry a baby. The term can refer to both men and women.

Implantation This is when the fertilised egg attaches itself to the lining of the uterus.

Infectious stage The stage of an illness when germs can spread from one person to another.

Intellectual development The development of the parts of the brain that control thinking, reasoning, remembering, problem solving, knowledge and understanding.

Involuntary movements An automatic movement that cannot be controlled (e.g. reflex actions of a young baby).

IVF In vitro fertilisation – a treatment for infertility.

Jargon The child's 'own' language, which may be understood only by those close to them.

Labour The process of giving birth.

Lanugo Fine, downy hair that covers the foetus from the fifth month of pregnancy.

Linguistic The stage in language development when children begin to use recognisable words to communicate. Often called verbal communication.

Looking-on play When a child watches other children playing and copies them.

Make-believe play Another name for imaginative play.

Manipulative play Any type of play where children are involved in using hands, fingers and hand–eye coordination.

Memory The ability to store and recall ideas and information.

Menstrual cycle The monthly cycle when the lining of the womb thickens so that a fertilised egg can implant.

Midwife A specially qualified nurse who cares for pregnant woman before, during and after birth.

Milia These are 'milk spots', which are small white spots on the nose of a newborn baby.

Miscarriage The loss of the baby (foetus) before the 24th week of pregnancy. Also called a spontaneous abortion.

Monosyllabic babbling The repetition of single syllables with no meaning (e.g. ba ba ba ba). This is sometimes called *echolalia*.

Moro reflex Sometimes called the falling reflex. Any sudden movement that affects the neck makes the baby think it is going to be dropped. It makes the baby throw out its arms then bring them back together as if trying to catch something.

Motherese The name given to the way in which adults speak to a baby in a simple, slow, clear, rhythmic manner.

Multicultural society A society made up of many different cultural and ethnic groups. Britain is a multicultural society.

Muscular dystrophy A genetic condition that affects the muscles and nerves to the muscles. It makes the muscles get weaker and weaker, and results in problems with walking and using the arms and legs.

Nanny Someone who is paid to look after a child or children in the family home.

Natural childbirth A labour and birth where the pregnant woman chooses not to use any medical assistance (e.g. pain relief).

Nature The talent and abilities we might inherit. See *Nurture*.

Neonatal The period up to four weeks after the birth.

Neonatal intensive care unit A specialist hospital unit that cares for premature, low birth weight and seriously ill babies.

Non-verbal communication See *Pre-linguistic*.

Nuclear family A family made up of parents (mother and father) and their children, living together.

Nurture Outside factors that can influence development. See *Nature*.

Nutrients Substances in foods that are needed to help the body grow, to keep the body healthy and provide energy.

Obesity This is the term used for people are seriously overweight. Obesity can cause serious health problems such as diabetes, heart disease, cancer and arthritis.

Object permanence Understanding that objects and people still exist even when they cannot be seen.

Obstetrician A doctor who specialises in pregnancy, labour and birth.

Oestrogen A female hormone that works with progesterone to control the female reproductive cycle.

Ova Female eggs produced from the ovary.

Ovaries The female sex gland that produces eggs (ova).

Ovulation The release of a mature egg from the ovary.

Oxytocin A hormone that stimulates the contractions of the uterus during labour, and the production of breast milk.

Paediatrician A specialist doctor who cares for babies, young children and teenagers.

Palmar grasp Using the whole hand to pick up and hold objects.

Parallel play When children will play happily alongside other children but not with them.

Passive vocabulary The words a child may be able to understand but cannot yet use.

Percentile charts Charts used to compare the growth of individual children with expected average growth – also known as *centile charts*.

Perineum The area between the vagina and anus, which may be cut when an episiotomy is needed during the birth of a baby.

Period The name usually used to describe the days of the menstrual cycle when the lining of the womb breaks down and leaves the body through the vagina.

Pethidine A type of pain relief that may be given during the first stage of labour. It is a drug, usually given as an injection that relaxes the pregnant woman and makes her feel sleepy.

Physical development Where children use their whole body, large muscles.

Physical play A type of play that helps to develop gross motor skills, balance and coordination.

Pincer grasp Using thumb and first finger to pick up and hold objects.

Placenta The organ that develops from the fertilised egg in the uterus with the foetus. It provides nutrients to the baby and takes away waste products. It is also called the afterbirth.

Play malnourishment When children do not have the chance to enjoy different kinds of play and to make up their own games.

Polysyllabic babbling An early stage of language development when children repeat the same syllables over and over (e.g. ma ma ma ma). It usually starts at around five to six months.

Post-natal After the birth.

Post-natal care The care of the mother and her baby during the first six weeks after the birth.

Post-natal depression (PND) A condition that can occur after the birth of the baby when the mother feels very sad, depressed and unable to cope with the baby. It is a serious condition, which needs medical help and support.

Pre-conceptual care The change in lifestyle that both the man and woman should consider when planning to have a baby. It can help to improve fertility, increase the chances of becoming pregnant, and of having a safe and healthy pregnancy.

Pre-eclampsia A medical condition that can occur late in pregnancy, which can lead to eclampsia.

Pre-linguistic The stage of language development when a baby cannot use words but uses cries, smiles and facial expressions to communicate.

Premature baby A baby born before 37 weeks of pregnancy.

Pretend play Another name for imaginative play.

Primary socialisation Social behaviour and relationships learnt from close family and carers.

Problem solving The ability to use and organise knowledge and understanding to solve both simple and more complex tasks.

Progesterone A female hormone that works with oestrogen to control the reproductive cycle.

Prolactin A hormone that is produced immediately after the birth. It makes the milk glands produce breast milk.

Puerperium The name given to the six-week period after the birth of the baby.

Reconstituted family Another name for a step-family.

Reflex actions The automatic movements made by a newborn baby during the first few months after birth.

Regression Going back to behaviour typical of a younger age (e.g. bed-wetting). It is often caused by emotional upset.

Role play Another name for imaginative play.

Rooting reflex When a baby's cheek is gently stroked it will automatically turn towards the touch as if looking for the nipple.

Rubella German measles.

SCBU Special care baby unit, also known as a neonatal intensive care unit.

Screening tests Tests carried out during pregnancy to see if there is a risk of having a baby with an abnormality.

Secondary socialisation Social behaviour and relationships learnt from people such as teachers, peers and friends.

Self-esteem How we feel about ourselves; sometimes called self-confidence.

Self-image What we think of ourselves; sometimes called self-concept.

Sensory development The development of the five senses – sight, hearing, touch, taste and smell.

Separation anxiety When young children become very upset and distressed when away from parent/primary carer.

SIDS see Sudden infant death syndrome.

Single-parent family A family where there is only one parent living with the child or children.

Small-for-dates baby A baby born full term (around 40 weeks) but weighing less than 2.5 kg.

Social development Learning to live with others, and to respect and value their ideas, beliefs and opinions.

Solitary play The first stage of social play when children play alone. It is the usual sort of play from birth to two years.

Spina bifida This is a congenital disability where the bones do not close round the spinal cord, allowing the nerves to bulge out on the unborn baby's back and become damaged.

Spontaneous abortion The medical term for a miscarriage.

Spontaneous play Play that is not planned and is usually made up by the child her/himself.

Startle reflex If babies are disturbed by a sudden noise or bright light they will clench their fists and throw their arms outwards. They may also cry.

Step-family A family formed when two parents who have been married or in a previous relationship, and who may both have children, get together to form a new family unit.

Stereotyping Expecting people to behave and act in a certain way – usually because of their gender, race or disability.

STI Sexually transmitted infection. These are passed from one person to another through sexual contact.

Stillbirth When a foetus dies inside the uterus, usually after 24 weeks.

Structured play Play that is planned and organised, usually by an adult, so that children will learn something.

Sucking reflex If a finger is placed in the baby's mouth it will begin to suck and swallow.

Sudden infant death syndrome The sudden and unexpected death of a young baby, for no apparent reason. Also known as cot death.

Symptom These act like signposts because they signal that something is wrong.

Synotocin An artificial version of *oxytocin* given to speed up the delivery of the *placenta*.

Telegraphic speech Simple sentences, usually of two words, that don't use linking words (e.g. 'want ball').

TENS A type of pain relief that uses small electrical impulses to block pain.

Topping and tailing Cleaning a baby's face and nappy area thoroughly.

Trial and error A type of problem solving where children will try lots of different ways of doing something, often making mistakes, until they find the right or best solution.

Triple test A blood test used to identify possible risk of Down's syndrome and spina bifida.

Tripod grasp Using the thumb and two fingers to pick up and hold objects.

Ultrasound scan A routine screening test given at different stages during pregnancy. It is mainly used to determine the age, growth and development of the baby, as well as possible risk of Down's syndrome.

Umbilical cord The baby's lifeline in the womb, which connects it to the placenta, and carries blood and nutrients to the foetus and removes waste products.

Uniovular twins Identical twins formed when one egg is fertilised and splits to form two babies.

Uterus The pear-shaped, hollow organ where an embryo will develop throughout pregnancy – also called the *womb*.

Vaccine A very weak amount of a bacteria or virus that causes disease. It is usually given by an injection. Vaccines work by making the body produce the antibodies to fight and control the disease.

Vagina The opening of the female reproductive system, where sexual intercourse takes place.

Ventouse extraction A type of assisted birth.

Verbal communication See *Linguistic*.

Vernix A white, greasy substance that covers the baby. Its purpose is to protect the baby's skin while in the uterus.

Viable The term used to describe a baby born early who is capable of surviving outside the uterus without medical help.

Virus A contagious infection that cannot be cured by using antibiotics.

Voluntary movement A movement that can be controlled.

Walking reflex When babies are held upright, with their feet touching a hard surface, and make stepping movements as if they are trying to walk.

Weaning The stage between a diet completely made up of milk and a diet composed of milk and solid foods.

Womb See *Uterus*.

Zygote Another name for the fertilised egg cell before it implants in the uterus.

INDEX